Inter-American Politics Series

SPONSORED BY THE

Center for Inter-American Relations / New York

THE NEWER CARIBBEAN
Decolonization, Democracy, and Development

editors:
Paget Henry & Carl Stone

ISHI A Publication of the
Institute for the Study of Human Issues
Philadelphia

Manufactured in the United States of America

2 3 4 5 6 7 8 9 90 89 88 87 86 85

Library of Congress Cataloging in Publication Data

Main entry under title:

The Newer Caribbean.

(Inter-American politics series; v. 4)
Bibliography: p.
Includes index.
1. Decolonization—Caribbean area—Addresses, essays,
lectures. 2. Representative government and representation
—Caribbean area—Addresses, essays, lectures. 3. Caribbean
area—Economic conditions—1945—Addresses, essays, lectures.
4. Caribbean area—Foreign relations—Addresses, essays, lectures.
I. Henry, Paget,   II. Stone, Carl.

JL599.5.A91N48   1982   972.9'052   82-11817
ISBN 0-89727-039-8
ISBN 0-89727-049-5 (pbk.)

For information, write:

Director of Publications
ISHI
3401 Science Center
Philadelphia, Pennsylvania 19104
U.S.A.

Preface

As was true of its three predecessors, this latest volume in the Inter-American Politics Series grew out of a group of seminars that explored in depth and from all angles those themes and issues having a direct political impact on the lands and peoples of the Americas. The objective of these seminars has always been to establish a sense of real communication and exchange of ideas among diverse but highly knowledgeable groups of participants. The books later emerging from these discussions have been designed to reflect the collective thinking of many of the most outstanding authorities in the field of inter-American affairs. The seminars brought together social scientists as well as policymakers representing a wide range of intellectual and professional backgrounds, encouraging the broadest dialogue on those subjects deemed critical to an understanding of hemispheric politics.

The aim of each volume in the Inter-American Politics Series is to reach beyond the seminar participants and the specialists to a wider public concerned about contemporary affairs in Latin America and the Caribbean. It is my hope that this book, along with previous and forthcoming volumes in the Series, will contribute significantly to ongoing research, practical problem-solving, and a climate of better understanding throughout the hemisphere.

RONALD G. HELLMAN
General Editor

Introduction

Examining the process of national development in any group of countries is always a difficult task. This difficulty arises from the many levels on which changes are occurring. Under these circumstances, it is often difficult to attach the appropriate or correct significance to a given set of events. Events that at one moment may seem to be of the greatest significance sometimes turn out to be of little or no consequence. The observer of Caribbean affairs is presently faced with this type of mesmerizing complexity that is the result of rapid changes on several levels. Consequently, the task of the observer must be a discerning one as it requires the separating of significant from insignficant changes.

The various territories of the Caribbean are currently at widely differing stages of national development. But they all have a long way to go in terms of the internal transformation of inherited social structures. In spite of this, the birth pangs of nationhood, experiments with the new freedom, and participation in the international arena have all combined to give the region a high visibility and to create an image of rapid change.

One of the most visible characteristics of the Caribbean in the postcolonial period has been its changing pattern of ties with the major world blocs. In 1971, Guyana declared itself a cooperative republic and began pursuing a policy that increased its ties with the socialist bloc. Between 1976 and 1979, five left-oriented regimes came to power in the region, specifically in St. Lucia, Dominica, Grenada, Nicaragua, and Jamaica. At present only two of these are still in power: the Bishop regime in Grenada and the Sandanistas in Nicaragua. The others, especially in Dominica and Jamaica, have been replaced by right-oriented regimes with strong ties with the capitalist world and with the United States in particular. In Guyana there has been no change of government, but a policy reversal has taken place on the part of the Burnham regime. It is these shifting alignments with the major blocs that have been largely responsible for the high visibility of the region and for the image of change that marks it.

Although not completely false, this shifting pattern of alliances hides a basic institutional inertia that if overlooked would lead to the view that significant institutional changes are taking place. Hence it is important that long- and medium-term analysis be focused on some of the more permanent institutional features of Caribbean societies. This book examines the process of national development in the light of the more permanent structures that characterize the societies forming the Caribbean community.

Nation-building as a form of political activity in the Caribbean is almost two hundred years old. Like other countries in the hemisphere, these nations emerged from former imperial domains as European colonialism slowly relaxed its grip on the northern, southern, and central portions of the Americas. Caribbean nation-building began with the revolution in Haiti in 1804 and has continued to the present, with long periods of stagnation in between. Following the Haitian revolution and its subsequent collapse from isolation, the momentum shifted to the Dominican Republic, Cuba, and Puerto Rico as Spanish colonialists began their retreat from the area. Finally, in the second half of the twentieth century, the spirit of nationalist revolt has taken hold of the British, French, and Dutch portions of the region and has helped to accelerate the retreat of these powers. The cumulative effect of this slow exit has been a proliferation of the number of independent nations in the region striving to make it on their own.

The chapters in this book examine in detail these ongoing processes of national development, as well as some of the major problems that Caribbean nations have been facing in their postindependence periods. They all have been revised and updated since their presentation at the "Decolonization, Democracy and Development in the Caribbean" seminars held in New York and Jamaica between 1978 and 1980.

The problem of national development is examined in three different but interrelated parts. The object of Part 1 is an evaluation of the process of decolonization by which the territories of the region have become or will become nations. In Part 2 the constraints and possibilities that the current international order imposes and opens up for national development in the area are examined. In Part 3 the emerging postcolonial structures of Caribbean societies are described, and their implications for democracy and national development are carefully assessed.

The selection of these major themes was based on the assumption that a thorough consideration of such interrelated processes would provide an excellent framework for analyzing the factors affecting national development in the region. The examination of processes of decolonization enables us to assess a very important set of new possibilities and constraints that condition the exercise of power by the new political regimes. For example, to what extent are these countries still dominated by the foreign policies of other countries? To what extent are they able to transform their economies with the new powers they now possess? In short, we were interested in the real increase in autonomy that decolonization gave to the leaders and citizens of the new Caribbean nations. By examining the contemporary international order, another set of possibilities and constraints facing the new governments in the area can be scrutinized. For example, the patterns of industrialization that this order encourages and the structures of dependence that it generates are important for an understanding of the direction in which these countries are going. By examining the postcolonial structures of Caribbean societies, a third set of important constraints and possibilities can be assessed. In this case it is the new patterns of class formation and of economic and political organization that are the critical determinants of how far the process of national development will go and what bottlenecks it is likely to incur. It is through the examination of these interrelated factors that this book can make a real contribution to the study of the Caribbean world.

The chapters in Part 1 focus exclusively on processes of decolonization in the English-speaking Caribbean. As with most former British colonies, these territories have become nations through processes of constitutional decolonization. This path to nationhood differs from both the revolutionary and the departmentalized routes taken by some of the French and Dutch territories. As such it has definite consequences for the kinds of changes and options that have accompanied the birth of these nations. Thus in each of the chapters that constitute Part 1, the impact of this process of decolonization on particular institutional areas of the Caribbean is carefully examined. Each chapter addresses such problems as decolonization and the state, decolonization and the economy, and decolonization and culture.

The results of these analyses reflect the diversity that characterizes the national situations of Caribbean territories. They indicate that some territories are further along the path to nationhood than others. In the political arena great variation can be observed in the extent to which colonial ties have been broken. Some territories are still colonies, some are associated states, and some are politically independent. Significant variation is also observable in the new relations that these territories have with the international community. Some have retained close ties with their former colonial caretakers, while others have gone in search of new ties. In the economic arena, the increase in autonomy was used in similar ways by the various elites to initiate processes of transformation and diversification. The results of these initiatives vary from country to country. While they have brought about changes, this section suggests that these changes have not been the desired ones. For example, there have been shifts in the major exports of most of the new Caribbean economies, but the basic institutional framework of production has remained in place—hence the assessment that things have changed but at the same time have remained the same. In the cultural sphere a similar pattern is revealed. Here also the process of decolonization has initiated changes but has not been able to maintain the momentum necessary for their institutionalization. These initiatives toward change concerned the social status of the various racial and ethnic groups in these societies and the normative evaluation of their cultural traditions. Decolonization held out the possibility of a significant increase in the societal demand for and use of the products of these long-suppressed local cultural traditions. Although small increases have occurred, the results suggest that the postcolonial societies of the region have not yet found the appropriate institutional space for their suppressed cultural traditions.

In short, the conclusions reached in Part 1 point to a variety of changes that have turned out to consist of little more than appearances of change. Beneath these deceptive appearances there runs a common thread: the severe limitations on the power that regimes are able to exercise, even though decolonization has taken place.

The chapters that make up Part 2 are focused on Caribbean relations with the international community. In particular, they are concerned with the consequences of these relations for the national development not only of the English-speaking Caribbean, but of the region as a whole. The conceptual context in which these discussions are set is the transition from the European-dominated political order of the years preceding the Second World War to the mixed order of the present day. It permits the examination of the new constraints and possibilities that Caribbean nations are facing as they move from the position of colonies and quasi-colonies to that of peripheral nations in an international system that has come to be dominated by the interests of the United States and the Soviet Union. The rivalry between these two superpowers places great pressure on new nations to ally themselves explicitly with one or the other. This pressure has become another major factor making for diversity and division in the relations of the Caribbean with the international community. In a category by itself is Cuba, which has become the only Caribbean nation to ally itself openly with the Soviets. In a second category, trying to steer a path of nonalignment and independent socialism, are the present regimes in Grenada and Nicaragua. The other nations of the Caribbean fall into a third distinct category. This group has remained within the capitalist orbit, but has shifted its external orientation away from Europe and toward the United States.

This ideological categorization cannot provide a full conceptual framework for an understanding of the relations that modern Caribbean nations have with the international community. This framework becomes more complex with recognition of the fact that the nonaligned countries are still to a large extent tied economically to the international capitalist system. Further complications are introduced by the fact that individual relations with this system are not all the same. Throughout its history, the capitalist world has employed three basic strategies in the incorporation of peripheral societies: (1) through relations that encourage the export of primary products; (2) through relations that encourage import substitution; and (3) through relations that encourage export-oriented industrialization. It is the simultaneous existence of these three modes of incorporation that is responsible for a number of important differences in the relations that Caribbean nations have with the capitalist powers.

Each of these modes of incorporation gives rise to economies with their own special problems. For example, stagnation due to declining demand for major regional exports is a chronic problem associated with the first mode of incorporation. In the second, chronic balance of payments problems seem to be a new source of crisis, while in the third there is a deepening of a dependence that had earlier been on the decline. Consequently, the specific needs and the nature of dependence on international capital vary with the mode of incorporation. Trinidad represents the case of a Caribbean nation that has made ample use of import substitution and is about to start making use of the possibilities for further industrialization inherent in the third mode of incorporation. Antigua, on the other hand, represents the case of an island that has been unsuccessful in making use of available opportunities for import substitution, and, in spite of the switch from sugar to tourism, remains primarily the exporter of one dominant commodity. As a result, its relations with the international capitalist system are very different from those of Trinidad. When these economic differences are combined with the political and ideological differences mentioned earlier, we begin to get some idea of the kind of conceptual framework that is necessary for an understanding of the relations that Caribbean nations have with the current international order.

It is within such a framework that the chapters in Part 2 are set and the constraints and possibilities of the contemporary world order analyzed. The conclusions reached in this section are difficult to summarize without tampering with the positions of the individual authors. These positions vary a great deal, as some authors stress the possibilities inherent in the contemporary world order more than the constraints, others stress the opposite. However, in spite of diverging positions, the general trend is toward the view that severe constraints flow from the imperatives of the current world order, even though in some cases available possibilities have not been exhausted.

The chapters that comprise Part 3 have as their focus the changes in the social structure of Caribbean societies in the postcolonial period. In particular they focus on the democratic institutions of these societies and how the structural changes are affecting their growth and functioning. In the postcolonial period, whether Caribbean societies are experiencing processes of democratization or de-democratization has become an increasingly controversial issue. The emergence of this problem is largely the result of the fact that these societies are being forced to make a number of difficult adaptations to the demands of both the local and international environments. In spite of the changing relations with the current world order, the economies of these societies are still subject to persistent crises that affect productivity and growth. The managing of these crises is, of course, the responsibility of the new governments and has become their major challenge. How these crises are managed affects not only the fate of a particular government, but also the institutional form of the state as it adapts itself to the challenges and difficulties these crises generate. In the effort to find solutions, the state may involve itself more explicitly in the economy, the political elite may change its ideological outlook, or it may become more repressive in an effort to reduce the level of participation of a segment of the population. Whatever the adaptation, these crises force the state to make changes in its organization, in its functions, and in its understanding of itself—changes that lead to a questioning of the inherited system of parliamentary democracy.

Another related set of factors that is helping to change the nature of the Caribbean state is the manner in which the new political elites have been adjusting to the exercise of power and to sharing power with older foreign and local economic elites. The patters of adjustment vary widely throughout the region, but there are a number of important common factors of which we will mention two. The first is the tendency toward very intense, almost life-and-death patterns of party competition. So intense have these contests become that party discrimination and conflict have eclipsed class and racial tensions in these societies. Whether it is in Antigua, Guyana, or Jamaica, the absence of a relatively peaceful mode of party competition is one of the most striking features of Caribbean political systems in the postcolonial period. The violence and the repressive legislation to which it has led have become another important factor challenging the democratic self-image of the Caribbean state.

The second common factor is the tendency for a system of interests between the economic and the political elites to develop and grow over time. This system of interests is rooted in the needs of the economic elites for the cooperation and protection of the state, and in the needs of the political elites for the investments and the personal contributions of the economic elites. The claims of this system of interests have led the political elites to reverse or discard many of the promises of the period of nationalist struggle and have resulted in a corresponding decrease in the capacity of the masses to influence decision-making. This decrease is often compensated for by an increased reliance on patronage and the cultivation of clientelistic ties that developed earlier but were eclipsed by the more ideologically oriented politics of the decolonization period. As a result, the tendency toward machine-type politics and corruption has increased in the postcolonial period, posing yet another challenge to the democratic self-image of the Caribbean state.

It is within the framework of these and other related factors which are forcing Caribbean states to make questionable adaptations that the chapters of Part 3 have examined the prospects for democracy in the region. The conclusions drawn in this section are more varied and difficult to summarize than those of the previous two. This is so for two reasons: first, the authors differ significantly in their conceptualizations and evaluations of the role of democracy in third-world societies, and second, the problems of democracy are analyzed in relation to a different set of institutional processes in each of the chapters. While these factors make a brief summary extremely difficult, the chapters raise at least two important questions: Is the Caribbean an exception to the pattern of one-party or military rule that has come to characterize much of the third world in the postcolonial period? And is it just a matter of time before these countries begin the characteristic slide into authoritarian forms of rule? While no agreement has been reached on this issue, a deep concern remains about the implications of present trends.

These, in brief, are the themes and ideas around which the chapters of this book are organized. These are the features that give this collection its unity. Each chapter, although complete in itself, contributes to the unifying themes of the three parts. In each of these the first chapter, in addition to raising concerns of its own, establishes the basic framework and some of the major concerns of the section to follow. Hence, it also serves as a needed introduction to that section.

Throughout the course of this opening discussion references have been made to the divergent nature of the findings and their resistance to brief summations. This divergent character is in part the result of a paradigmatic crisis that the study of development in the Caribbean is currently experiencing. In the early fifties a consensus had formed around the work of Arthur Lewis as to how problems should be conceptualized and resolved. By the mid-sixties, however, this consensus had been shattered by the course of economic and political events in the region. Its place was taken by a number of approaches that were influenced by Latin American dependency theory and Marxist political economy. These approaches have done much to reorient Caribbean thinking, and have shed new light on many of the economic and political problems facing the area. In spite of these very real achievements, the new paradigms have not been adquately reworked so that they are able to capture and reflect accurately the specifics of the Caribbean situation. As a result, no consensus has emerged over a basic set of theoretical orientations and approaches. This lack of a theoretical consensus has in turn, generated widely varying policy recommendations, the appropriateness of which is constantly debated.

It would have been a great thing indeed if, in addition to providing these regional and specific analyses, this book had made a contribution to the resolution of this crisis. But the truth is that it is caught in the middle of the crisis. The new competing paradigms are reflected and used in most of the discussions presented here. Hence it bears all the marks of the current period. However, in this state the book dramatized very clearly the need for theoretical approaches that reflect more closely the actualities of the Caribbean world. This closer mirroring of the regional situation at the theoretical level will improve the chances of generating policy recommendations about which there will be wider agreement. It is only through such a reworking of the newer paradigms and their recommendations that usable alternatives to the older models will emerge. It is to this task of fashioning new alternatives that the limitations of this study are directed. We hope to make a contribution toward meeting this challenge in a subsequent work.

We would like to thank Ronald G. Hellman and Vaughn Lewis for their assistance in organizing the seminars out of which this book developed. We would also like to thank the Ford Foundation and the Inter-American Foundation, whose grants provided the funding for these undertakings.

PAGET HENRY
CARL STONE

Contributors

Paul Ashley is Lecturer in Government at the University of the West Indies, Mona, Jamaica.

Rubén Berríos Martínez is an attorney and leader of the Puerto Rican Independence Party.

George Danns is Lecturer in Sociology at the University of Guyana.

Trevor Farrell is Lecturer in Economics at the University of the West Indies, St. Augustine, Trinidad.

J. E. Green is Director of the Institute of Social and Economic Research at the University of the West Indies, Mona, Jamaica.

Paget Henry is Assistant Professor of Sociology at the State University of New York at Stony Brook.

Irving Louis Horowitz is Hannah Arendt Professor of Sociology and Political Science at Rutgers University.

Vaughan Lewis is General Secretary of the Organization of Eastern Caribbean States (OECS).

Luis Maira is Senior Researcher at the Centro de Investigacionas y docencias Economicas (CIDE) in Mexico City.

Nita Rous Manitzas is a specialist in Cuban affairs, who formerly served as Program Advisor on Latin America and the Caribbean for the Ford Foundation.

Carl Parris is Lecturer in Government at the University of the West Indies, St. Augustine, Trinidad.

Vincent Richards is Executive Director of the Association for Caribbean Transformation (ACT), Antigua.

Carl Stone is Senior Lecturer and Head of the Department of Government at the University of the West Indies, Mona, Jamaica.

Francisco Thoumi is an economist at the Inter-American Development Bank in Washington.

Contents

PART 3 / DEMOCRACY AND NATIONAL DEVELOPMENT

PART 1

Decolonization and National Development

1

Decolonization in the English-Speaking Caribbean: Myth or Reality?

TREVOR M. A. FARRELL

In 1962, Jamaica and Trinidad and Tobago became politically independent. This event ushered in a period of formal decolonization of the English-speaking Caribbean. Since 1962, Jamaica and Trinidad and Tobago have been joined by Guyana, Barbados, Grenada, the Bahamas, Dominica, St. Lucia, St. Vincent, Belize, and Antigua, while the other smaller islands of the Caribbean have obtained virtual political independence through "associated statehood" with Britain. This status meant full internal self-government with Britain, the colonial power, retaining responsibility for external affairs and defense. Even British responsibility for external affairs was readily and willingly abdicated several times, on request, for example, to permit the islands to engage independently in international negotiations such as those leading to the regional integration movement.

Britain has also stood ready to grant these islands full political independence any time they wish it, since these former jewels of the British Crown are now no more than so many albatrosses around the collective British neck, breaking the fundamental law of colonialism that the net benefit from a colony be positive to the dominant elites in the colonizing country. Britain would gladly approve their flags, national anthems, and disposable constitutions, give them a few pounds as a going away gift, a visit from some lesser lights in the Royal Family, and send them packing, to sink or swim as best they can. Their purpose, as far as the British are concerned, has been served.

Political independence then, *de jure* or *de facto*, has either been attained in the English-speaking Caribbean or is just around the corner.

3

These islands also seem to suggest decolonization to the casual observer, simply through their participation as independent actors on the international stage. They belong to the United Nations and its tributary organizations, participate in and host international conferences, sign international treaties, and take positions on matters ranging from the Law of the Sea to the need for nonproliferation of nuclear weapons.

Decolonization appears to be manifesting itself not only politically but also economically. One of the most striking features of Caribbean economic life over the last decade or so has been the rapid growth of state and local intervention into the economy and the apparently systematic encroachment on what were formally the exclusive preserves of the metropole. In Guyana, the state owns some 80 percent of the domestic economy. Bauxite, rice, sugar, the control of trade, and even the vast holdings of Bookers have fallen under the flag.

The other Caribbean territories have not gone as far; but in Trinidad and Tobago and Jamaica, what superficially seems to be extensive economic decolonization has taken place. Oil, bauxite, sugar, communications, hotels, meat processing, public utilities, banking and finance, international air transport, flour milling and cement, to name a few, have come under state ownership. Local capitalism has also grown significantly, in these two countries, especially in the manufacturing sector. In the Windwards and the Leewards, sugar, tourism, and the utilities have apparently been extensively localized.

But the most salient indicator of formal decolonization would seem to the casual observer to be the sociological changes of the last two decades. Around the region, black faces adorn boards of directors, inhabit ministerial offices, and man all reaches of the civil service. The administrative and political structures of the region have become almost completely Africanized and Indianized. New elites have burgeoned. In Jamaica and Trinidad and Tobago particularly, the rise to power and privilege of the local elites has been the most visible and most flaunted. Huge, garish new houses have gone up in exclusive neighbourhoods, testifying cogently to their owners' affluence, if not to their taste.

Mercedes sports and touring cars bump and jounce their way through the potholes. The materialistic wives and children of the new elite, to whom social concern is as foreign as their color TV sets, shop in Miami, finger their way through boutiques, and display a disdain for their less fortunate fellow citizens of which any nineteenth-century British aristocrat would have been proud.

Almost as significant as the changed sociology of Caribbean administrative and political life, and much more alarming to certain metropolitan observers, is the enunciation by certain Caribbean states of independent political philosophies sharply at variance with the philosophies and perceived interests of the dominant hegemonic power—the United States. Guyana, Jamaica, and Dominica had regimes that affirmed a faith in socialism as their preferred political and economic path into the future. And while these expressions may in some cases be less than serious and in others abortive, these faint stirrings of independent decisionmaking suggest to some that the Caribbean may in fact be already decolonized, or at least decolonizing.

The blunt truth, however, is that all this is largely epiphenomenal. The reality is that the English-speaking Caribbean remains essentially colonized. What has changed is the form of the colonization, the mechanisms through which it operates, and the colonizing agents. This is not to say that no change has taken place. Change has, in fact, taken place, and more change will follow. The dynamic of events in the Caribbean, as in other areas of the Third World, thrusts toward ultimate and real decolonization. But that time has not yet arrived.

Events in the Caribbean are affecting, and are being profoundly affected by, what is taking place on the international scene. This is nothing new. From its inception the Caribbean has always been profoundly affected by, and in turn has affected, international events. Thus decolonization as a dynamic is integrally bound up with events in the outside world, with what is happening to the exercise of American power globally, with the increasing clash of rival, metropolitan capitalisms, and with other international political and economic developments.

At the present time, however, decolonization is more apparent than real. In examining this contention, it is necessary to elucidate the essence of the colonial condition, and then seek to measure contemporary Caribbean reality with this yardstick.

In the nineteenth century, John Stuart Mill enunciated what is still one of the best, frankest, and most succinct descriptions of what a colonial relationship is about, a definition which permits one to see the essence of the colonial condition. In his *Principles of Political Economy,* Mill declared: "If Manchester, instead of being where it is, were on a rock in the North Sea . . . it would still be but a town of England, not a country trading with England: it would be merely, as now, the place where England finds it convenient to carry on her cotton manufactures. The West Indies, in like manner, are the place where England finds it convenient to carry on the production of sugar, coffee, and a few other tropical commodities. All the capital employed is English capital; almost all the industry is carried on for English uses; there is little production of anything except the staple commodities, and these are sent to England, not to be exchanged for things exported to the colony and consumed by its inhabitants, but to be sold in England for the benefit of the proprietors there."[1]

The essence of the colonial condition is twofold. First, the organization of the resources of the colonized is effected in the interests of the alien, colonizing power, rather than in the interests of the colonized. While this is not necessarily a zero-sum game, the colonial condition implies that the net benefits are skewed toward the colonizer. There is then the enforced subordination of the victim's interests to those of the controlling power.

Second, colonialism fundamentally implies the lack of control over the dynamic of one's own movement or development (whether political, economic, or cultural). Herein lies an essential difference between dependence and interdependence or even ordinary, relative weakness vis-à-vis another country. The classic colony is unable to make its own decisions, to choose how to adjust to a given configuration on the international scene. Its response is dictated or tightly circumscribed by the dominating power.

At a technical minimum in assessing decolonization one has therefore to focus on two fundamental issues: in whose interests, preponderantly, are a country's resources organized, and to what extent is a country in control of its own dynamic. Decolonization can also be dealt with at a second level which extends above this technical minimum.

For people brutalized by centuries of exploitation, contempt, indifference, slavery, and metropolitan racism, decolonization should also mean the building of a new society as advocated by Franz Fanon—one dedicated to humanity and to the eradication of injustice and exploitation nationally as well as internationally. It should mean the restructuring of social relationships, the abrogation of the grosser forms of class differentiation, and the opening up of the economic and political system to genuine popular participation and shared control by all the people.

At this level, decolonization cannot simply mean the exchange of white overseers for black ones. It cannot mean the exchange of white overlords for black ones, or of white brutality, repression, insensitivity and arrogance for black brutality, repression, insensitivity, and arrogance. Decolonization for the Caribbean and other Third World countries should mean more than this.

Let us look more closely now at the contemporary Caribbean, beginning with the first and basic level of the "technical minimum" for identifying real decolonization. It is necessary at the outset to be quite clear that flags, national anthems, local legislatures, black cabinets, and boards of directors do not by themselves say anything about whether real decolonization has been effected. What is perhaps less widely recognized is that the apparent capture of local ownership and control of significant areas of economic life does not necessarily mean substantive change in the colonial nexus. Ever since the publication of Kwame Nkrumah's book *Neo-Colonialism: The Last Stage of Imperialism*, the Third World has been well aware that the retreat of direct colonialism did not in fact mean the end of colonialism.[2]

The granting of political and administrative apparatus did not signify any fundamental change in the colonial relationship as long as ownership and control of the commanding heights of the local economy remained firmly in the hands of metropolitan investors and their home governments. The organization of local resources in foreign interests continued unabated in many cases and startlingly enough, was even intensified in certain cases. It was quickly discovered that control over the dynamic and path of development had been retained abroad.

One can mark this dawning recognition in several ways. Intellectually there was the rise of the "dependency school" in Latin America and the Caribbean, launched by academics who focused attention on the phenomenon of the continuation of effective colonialism through indirect, economic means. The cry against neocolonialism went up and demands grew for nationalization. "Localization," 51 percent control, and the perpetuation of the colonial situation were felt to be bound up with continued foreign ownership of key areas of economic life. The capturing of equity ownership, it was felt, would mean the effective ending of colonial control—direct and indirect, political and economic.

This belief has turned out to be erroneous, which is essentially why the widespread nationalizations and state interventions into economic life in the Caribbean do not by themselves mean that decolonization has really been achieved. As it turns out, the metropolitan stranglehold has once again simply shifted its grip.

When the assault on direct (political) colonialism was launched, the white West retreated, after the French adventures in Vietnam and Algeria and the British adventures in Kenya and Malaysia, into the hasty granting of political independence. Direct colonialism, which was manifested most clearly in political control, gave way to indirect, neocolonial control exercised through the economy and through direct foreign investment and the concomitant ownership and control of the commanding heights of Third World economies.

The assault on neocolonialism, manifested this time through nationalization, through repeated complaints in international forums such as UNCTAD and, most dramatically, through OPEC, has resulted in yet another maneuver. Once again the form was conceded, but the substance was retained. In its search for liberation and development, the Third World is like a man groping in the dark for a door he cannot see, moving by successive approximations. Often the wrong protuberance is grasped; then the error is discovered and another attempt is made.

The belief that colonialism would be eradicated simply by achieving political independence has turned out to be mistaken. With hindsight it is clear that Nkrumah's dictum, "seek ye first the political kingdom, and all other things shall be added unto you," is not true. Similarly, it is now being recognized that the measure believed to be the corrective for the original error (i.e., effecting state or local ownership of key economic sectors) is also ineffective, and may indeed be irrelevant.

Ownership, it turns out, does not necessarily mean control. The multinational corporations have learned to make nationalizations work for them. Through the media of marketing agreements, management contracts, service agreements, and licensing agreements, effective control over industries or entire economic sectors can be maintained while equity ownership is happily conceded.

A shrewd company now finds that there are positive advantages to be reaped from a retreat from a relationship too easily stigmatized as neocolonial. The surrender of equity ownership can lead to an improved cash flow and enhanced profitability, or to getting an ignorant Third World government to prune local operations of unwanted or obsolete properties at a high price to the state. It also has the attraction that it reduces a company's visibility and defuses local criticism while essential interests are maintained intact. Moreover, because a nationalization may now be effected on attractive terms, the risk of a worse deal from a tougher, more competent host government sometime in the future may be obviated.

It is necessary not only to look at what kind of nationalizations or localizations have been effected, but also to investigate exactly what has been acquired. This may amount to meaningless, economically insubstantive assets, even though such assets are nominally located in the key sectors of the economy.

Close observation of economic decolonization in the Caribbean demonstrates that this decolonization is more apparent than real. Only in Guyana can meaningful control over the commanding heights of the economy be said to have been effectively transferred to local hands. In Trinidad and Tobago, for example, two oil "nationalizations" have taken place which permit the government to pretend that it has gotten into the producing and refining business. One of these turns out not to have been a genuine nationalization at all. The state's acquisition of a 50.1 percent (majority) equity in Trinidad-Tesoro masks the effective locating of real control in its foreign, joint-venture partner's hands.[23]

Furthermore, both this and the 1974 nationalization of Shell-Trinidad turn out to involve economically insubstantive areas of the local oil industry. The key areas in producing and refining remain firmly under foreign control. Trinidad's oil resources continue to be organized in the service of foreign metropolitan interests, not in local interests. Large quantities of crude are brought in by one company for refining (Trinidad having served as its Caribbean refining center), while another carries away large quantities of crude to be refined elsewhere.

A study of the output mix of the Trinidad refineries shows a composition heavily weighted toward residual fuel oil, the cheapest of the major products, because this fits in with metropolitan requirements, whereas Caribbean needs are quite different. Even the use of Trinidad's natural gas resources, the fertilizer plants in operation and planned, can all be seen, on close investigation, to represent the systematic organization of the country's resources in line with metropolitan rather than local needs.

Petroleum nationalization in Trinidad and Tobago is largely farce and fantasy. So, too, is bauxite nationalization in Jamaica. Despite government control of 51 percent of the operations of key companies in the bauxite industry, the agreements guaranteeing decades of bauxite reserves and the arrangements made with respect to price and taxation mean that Jamaica has still not achieved effective control over her key mineral resource.

Two significant features of the manufacturing sector in the contemporary Caribbean must be noted. Manufacturing is largely based in Jamaica and in Trinidad and Tobago. It turns out, on closer examination, that local ownership and control of this sector is effectively vitiated in salient areas by means of the licensing agreements entered into for accessing foreign technology. In the Trinidad-Tobago vehicle assembly industry, for example, the local industry might as well be foreign-owned, since all the key economic and technological variables are under the control of foreign licensors.[4] Decisions on model changes, plant layout, pricing, and the use of purchased technology are as subject to foreign decisionmaking as they would be if the plants were wholly owned subsidiaries of a foreign corporation.

The second interesting feature of this sector in the Caribbean is its control by the old, white plantocracy, who took advantage of incentive legislation, state-provided resources, and the 1960s' faith in import-substitution to move from their estates into the new "screwdriver" assembly plants.

In agriculture, it is true that local ownership and effective local control of export staples such as sugar and bananas have been successfully achieved in many cases. But this sector still remains subject to metropolitan dictates and the metropolitan dynamic. Here, however, the foreigner can hardly be blamed. The annual beggar's pilgrimage to Europe capitals to beg for better sugar prices under the Lomé agreement, for example, is something that Caribbean governments have the power to stop. They lack the courage and the perspicacity, however, to radically restructure the region's agriculture, thus demonstrating that one of the most powerful and tenacious effects of colonialism is in the minds of the colonized.

The economy of the Caribbean thus can hardly be said to have been effectively decolonized. Caribbean resources continue to be organized in accordance with metropolitan interests. This is true for oil and gas, for Jamaica's bauxite, and, to a large extent, for the region's agricultural export sector. Manufacturing remains technologically dependent and effectively foreign-dominated. And while a few indigenous banks have appeared in the larger territories, banking remains effectively under domination despite the so-called localization in Trinidad and Tobago.

The continued subjection of the Caribbean economy to metropolitan dictates is exemplified most starkly by the Jamaican experience in 1977 and 1978. Jamaica's balance of payments crisis, manipulated to some extent by the metropole and rooted at base in the effects of the 1974 rise in oil and other import prices, has resulted in humiliation at the hands of the U.S.-controlled International Monetary Fund. Beginning in 1977, Jamaica had been reduced to a virtual colony of the IMF. By 1978, the island was being effectively, if unobtrusively, ruled by the IMF, acting as proxy for the U.S. aluminum industry. Guyana also fell into similar toils.

The Caribbean has been unable to effect the reorganization and restructuring of its economy that would have been the hallmark of real decolonization. The kinds of linkages that could be created, and which were so brilliantly outlined by Havelock Brewster and Clive Thomas more than a decade ago have not been made.[5] In fact, the one really dramatic attempt at forging such linkages was speedily aborted. This was the proposed aluminum smelter to be located in Trinidad and to combine Jamaican and Guyanese bauxite with Trinidad natural gas. The partners rapidly fell out with each other, but it is now an open secret that the Trinidad government was told in no uncertain terms by a very senior person in the World Bank that such a project was not at all acceptable to metropolitan interests.[6] What is not known is whether the disagreement between the partners had any relation to the foreign intervention.

It must also be noted that the domination of the Caribbean by metropolitan interests is not simply economic. It is political as well, and this influence and control operate at several different levels, from the openly diplomatic to the clandestine, and through a variety of international organizations and foundations. In fact, there can be little doubt that the Caribbean is one of the most thoroughly penetrated regions in the hemisphere today.

Of additional significance is the extensive cultural and psychological colonization which still marks the contemporary Caribbean. The cultural absorption of the Caribbean into the "one-world" of the giant American multinationals is obviously not unique to the region. But the ease of communication, the nearness to the North American centers, the lack of language barriers, and the absence of any rooted, resistant traditional culture all mean that the cultural penetration of the Caribbean can proceed even faster and more thoroughly than in most other underdeveloped regions. Especially in those people over forty, the psychology of the colonized is very apparent.

At the level of the technical minimum, therefore, it is clear that decolonization in the English-speaking Caribbean is more apparent than real. But at the second, higher, level at which decolonization can be approached, the picture is even more grim. This is because the mass of people continue everywhere to be firmly shut out from real participation in their country's political and economic life. Moreover, the old white plantocracy, after a decline in the early and mid-1960s (the period of political independence) are now experiencing a rapid resurgence more economic than political.

The local capitalist class in Trinidad and Tobago, for example, is once again dominated by whites, several of whom were formerly old estate families. Riding on the crest of incentives and import substitution, they have captured control of key areas of the local economy not in foreign hands and have begun to take over the communications media using profits given to them by the state. Furthermore, these white families have begun to exercise open influence on state policy and on the political process. The wheel thus threatens to come full circle.

Far from experiencing a diminution in stratification, and with it the growth of egalitarianism and reduction in racial tensions that might have been expected, the Caribbean has experienced the converse. Racial feeling is on the rise in Guyana and in Trinidad and Tobago. Class distinctions have grown tremendously, especially in Trinidad and Tobago and in Jamaica, and there is increasing polarization and repression. The media have fallen under the control of either the state or the capitalist classes, and these groups have not hesitated to impose severe censorship. Antilabor legislation has engendered considerable bitterness and political unrest, and dissidence and political opposition have been increasingly met by the denial of work permits, deportation, denial of the right to demonstrate, march, or meet, and even by death at the hands of American-trained police forces. The Caribbean is not yet Idi Amin's Uganda, but there is a serious threat of fascism, as more and more development programs prove unworkable and as the insecure governing elites lash out in their attempt to maintain dominance.

The Caribbean is in fundamental crisis. The crisis is stark in the cases of Jamaica and Guyana. Trinidad's large foreign reserves due to the OPEC initiative mask the bankruptcy of its domestic policies and, for the time being, have kept the wolf from the door—the wolf which was so clearly lurking between 1970 and 1973. The blunting, blocking, and possible eventual destruction of OPEC will put Trinidad and Tobago back into eyeball-to-eyeball confrontation with the desperate reality now faced by its sister territories.

The smaller islands—so neglected, so unnoticed, so ignored—are in a state of endemic crisis. They are locked into the vicious circle of the lack of resources (except for sun, sand, sea, and the sexual prowess of the beach boys), continued lack of even basic infrastructure, flight of their young, skilled people, and the depressing effects of poverty and malnutrition. These islands are of little interest to the metropole, to, foreign capital, and to the international aid agencies, for they offer so little to exploit. Their allure seems directed to the odd tourist, the fly-by-night entrepreneur skirting the borders of illegality and, of course, the denizens of the new demimonde—the Mafia. One after another, these beautiful islands with their poor, beautiful, historically battered people are succumbing in desperation to the tourist complexes and their uncertainties, to freeports, offshore banking, casinos, and organized crime.

The Caribbean may not be decolonized, but it is in serious crisis and it is fundamentally unstable. Like in other areas of the Third World, however, there is a basic dynamic at work leading inexorably to conflict, with the ruling elites currently overseeing the region in the interests of their metropolitan overlords and with those metropolitan overlords themselves. For the urge to freedom is one of the strongest impulses known to man. The history of the twentieth century is really the history of the struggle of the colonial world for freedom from its bonds. Metropolitan maneuvers may hinder or sidetrack this struggle, but no serious analyst would dare to claim that decolonization can be reversed or ultimately prevented from running its course.

Notes

1. John Stuart Mill, *Principles of Political Economy* (London: Routledge & Sons, 1900), p. 454.

2. Kwame Nkrumah, *Neo-Colonialism: The Last Stage of Imperialism* (London: Nelson, 1965).

3. Trevor M. A. Farrell, "In Whose Interest? Nationalization and Bargaining with the Petroleum Multinationals: The Trinidad and Tobago Experience." Paper presented to the Institute of International Relations Conference on Contemporary Trends and Issues in the Commonwealth Caribbean, St. Augustine, Trinidad, 1982.

4. M. A. Farrell and A. M. Gajraj, *Technology and the Manufacturing Sector in Trinidad and Tobago: The Vehicle Assembly Industry* (in press).

5. Havelock Brewster and Clive Thomas, *The Dynamic of West Indian Economic Integration* (Institute of Social and Economic Research, University of the West Indies, 1967).

6. House of Representatives, Trinidad and Tobago, *Budget Speeches of the Prime Minister and Minister of Finance, 1977 and 1978* (Port-of-Spain: Government Printery, 1979).

2

Decolonization in Antigua: Its Impact on Agriculture and Tourism

VINCENT A. RICHARDS

The global process of decolonization has led since World War II to substantial constitutional advancement in the Third World. In the Commonwealth Caribbean, Guyana, Trinidad and Tobago, Bahamas, Barbados, Grenada, Dominica, St. Lucia, St. Vincent, Belize, Antigua, and Jamaica have achieved constitutional independence, the first two proceeding to republican status. St. Kitts-Nevis-Anguilla is preparing to move to full independence from its present status of associated statehood with the United Kingdom. The latter arrangement gives the island governments full control over internal matters and some international economic affairs, while Britain assumes responsibility for external affairs and defense. The remaining countries—Montserrat, the Cayman Islands, the Turks and Caicos Islands, and the British Virgin Islands—retain colonial political relationships. In all these countries there is substantial local political decisionmaking and control in all matters, although the United Kingdom assumes some role in foreign affairs and defense. It is generally admitted that the countries may proceed to full independence if there is a popular determination to that effect.

One result of the decolonization process is that the state apparatus is now under the control, nominally at least, of nationals, so that decisions relating to the polity are informed primarily by indigenous analyses. Given that the working class movement played a pivotal role in the struggle to eliminate colonialism, one might expect that governmental policy in the postcolonial era would have a working-class bias and that economic policy would consciously attempt to structurally transform the economy along lines that reflect the concerns of the masses. Put another way, has the process of decolonization weakened the metropolitan stranglehold of the island economies characteristic of the colonial era? Have any fundamental changes in economic and social relations resulted from or accompanied the constitutional advances?

In this chapter we attempt to consider these questions as they relate to Antigua, concentrating on the agricultural and tourism sectors. The choice of economic sectors is deliberate. For more than two centuries the material fortunes of Antigua and Barbuda were inextricably linked to agriculture, more specifically, cane sugar. The country was, and to some extent still is, a plantation economy of the first order. Since the collapse of the sugar industry in 1971, international tourism, which grew rapidly in the 1960s from modest beginnings in the 1950s, assumed the key position in the economy of the twin-island state. We are therefore concerned with industries which have held the leading position in the country's economic history and development.

The remainder of the chapter is organized as follows. In the section below, we present a review of the decolonization process in Antigua. Next we discuss some aspects of the plantation system—the organizational structure that has dominated the economy of Antigua and Barbuda, and indeed the entire Caribbean. The two following sections take up agriculture and tourism development, respectively. An effort is made to determine the extent and nature of the neocolonial production relations that still remain.

The Process of Decolonization

The present political status of constitutional independence, should be seen in the historical context of the struggle of the Antiguan working class to gain control over its destiny. We will now attempt a brief outline of that historical context.

EARLY POSTEMANCIPATION DECOLONIZATION ACTIVITIES

The emancipation of the black masses from chattel slavery in 1834 improved only marginally their position in the sociopolitical-economic system. While Antiguan and Barbudan planters were compensated with £425,500, the newly won freedom of the blacks was severely circumscribed by a set of economic and political forces. First, the relative land scarcity that prevailed meant that a substantial proportion of the ex-slaves would have to continue working on the plantations. Planters readily admitted that blacks "were *entirely* dependent on the estate owners for the means of procuring food because the climate was precarious and because there was little unoccupied land."[1] Second, the enactment and enforcement of a contract act which, in effect, tied blacks to the estates on which they worked meant that their material conditions as well as their human dignity were not much better than during slavery. Third, it was widely accepted by the dominant classes in Antigua and England that remuneration of the laboring classes should be as close as possible to subsistence level. The daily wage paid in 1842 under the terms of the contract act was less than the cost of slave labor and only labor supply difficulties brought them into approximate equality.[2]

Further, in their efforts to assert their freedom and end the human destitution that they encountered, blacks resorted to two methods, moving off the estates to establish comparatively independent social arrangements and emigration. Planters strongly opposed these methods and sabotaged such efforts when economic circumstances permitted. A fifth point may also be noted. It is to be recognized that the Antiguan masses had no say in determining political leaders and played no role in national affairs. The Antigua representative assembly, like other colonial legislatures, was most unrepresentative. With a population of some 36,000 in 1838, only a mere 323 votes were cast in the election.[3]

It is to the tribute of the Antiguan masses that despite severe obstacles, they very quickly set in motion the decolonization process. While they used the traditional social institutions, such as the established churches, to build coherent communities, they also organized benevolent societies which acted as collective buffers against the degrading features of the colonial plantation system.[4] These societies were to play a major part in the continuing decolonization struggle. For example, the Antigua Trade and Labor Union, which played the key role from 1939 to 1967, "was born during the influential period of the lodges and in looking for leadership for the trade union, it was to the lodges that all eyes were turned; for it realized from early that the trade union had to be a people's organization and therefore could only draw its membership from the working class people who comprised the membership of the several lodges."[5]

A friendly society of some historical significance was the Ulotrichian Universal Union established in 1915. It arose out of the continuing efforts of the working class to link decolonization at an island level to a Caribbean struggle. The lodge movement in St. Croix was instrumental in its founding. The Ulotrichian Universal Union, besides providing benevolent and welfare services, engaged in underground and revolutionary education for working class people "as to their rights and downtrodden condition." The speeches of members contributed to the resentment of the white ruling planter class by the black masses.[6]

Of equal importance were the founding of the Antigua Progressive Union in 1918 and its efforts to make fundamental changes in the island's socioeconomic order by demanding revisions in the Masters' and Servants' Acts which, in effect, legitimized plantation society. With a series of fires that occurred on sugar estates and land adjacent to the governor's residence, together with attacks on the colonial security forces, it is clear that "workers were out for complete liberation from the colonial order."[7]

On the economic front, early decolonization activity hit very quickly at the stranglehold of the planter class over the country's productive forces. It was the establishment of "independent" villages, the first in 1835, which allowed the blacks to negotiate better employment conditions on the plantations and to enjoy a measure of economic security through the cultivation of their small plots. Despite the low wages they received, workers were able to accumulate funds so that by 1842 there were 27 independent villages of some 3,600 people. Among the short-run consequences of this relative escape from economic dependence and domination were an increase in wage rates by 50 percent and a shift to task rates from daily rates, which permitted doubling of daily wages in some cases. By 1846, the population of the independent villages had increased to 9,273.[8]

THE MODERN PHASE OF DECOLONIZATION PROCESS

The founding of the Antigua Trades and Labor Union (ATLU) in 1939 opened the modern phase of the decolonization struggle. Within a year, organized working class confrontation with the plantocracy had begun. A union official recounts it as follows:

> In January 1940 even before the Union was registered about ninety percent of the workers at the Antigua Sugar Factory had become members of the Union. Enthusiasm was high among these workers and they felt that at long last they would be able to make demands on management. The sugar crop was scheduled to start early but the factory workers decided among themselves they would not start the crop until agreement was reached to pay increased wages. Management took no notice of them for up to then the Union had only been in the process of formation and was not sufficiently strong to make firm demands as it was yet to be recognised by Management. With their effort spurned by management the factory workers decided to call a strike at the factory. The strike last for seven weeks.

The crop was delayed and the strike was spread to the waterfront where waterfront workers refused to work unless claims for increased wages by them were recognized by management. These strikes were unauthorised by the Union but was a struggle by workers to force the hands of management until the Union was strong enough to fight their cause. The factory and waterfront workers had island wide sympathy during the strike and many people joined the Union as a result.[9]

Several points relating to the above quotation should be noted. First is the serious commitment displayed by Antiguan workers to the decolonization struggle. Even without a strong organization, with the continuing pressure of extreme economic hardships which triggered a series of riots across the Caribbean two years earlier, and with every effort being made by the colonial authorities to convince the working class that its energies should be engaged in supporting to the fullest the mother country's war effort and not its own liberation, it is remarkable that the strike was so prolonged.

The second point is the widespread impact of the strike. With the sugar factory inoperative, harvesting operations at the farm level could not occur. Plantation agriculture was at a standstill. With dockworkers participating, import-export activities, the lifeline of plantation economies, were disrupted. Indeed, the head of the colonial administration was forced to convene conciliatory talks between the ATLU, the factory management and planters. The third point is the solidarity of the working class that is evident. The direct struggle of two key groups of workers received support from other groups.

The short-run results of the strike included 50 percent increases on all normal daily wages for the factory workers, but even a second strike did not help the waterfront workers make income gains. Labor market conditions in this sector were highly favorable to the shipping companies, and they made full use of them. Although the union leadership agreed to suspend further strike action during the course of the World War, several strikes did occur when negotiations between the Union and the sugar interests were not making satisfactory progress. Such was the case in 1943.

Besides being active on the industrial front, the ATLU spearheaded the struggle for political advancement. Prior to constitutional changes in 1937, when five elected seats were allowed in the Legislative Council, the members of this body formed a virtual who's who of the local white planter class and its supportive colonial officials. In the 1937 elections that were held under a very limited franchise, Reginald Stevens, who was to become the first President of the ATLU, won one of the elected seats. He was subsequently disqualified by the property ownership requirement. While he successfully contested the by-election on the taxable income qualification, it was evident that the ruling class was reluctantly conceding constitutional gains. Nevertheless, by 1945, two of the five elected seats were held by senior officers of the ATLU.

A major achievement was made in the 1946 election when the Union contested and won all five of the elected seats; and in 1951, when universal adult suffrage was introduced with the majority of the legislative seats becoming elective, the ATLU again made a clean sweep. At this time a committee system of government was initiated, with three of the committees headed by elected members. Further constitutional progress was made in 1956 with the introduction of a ministerial system of government in which working class leaders took all three ministerial positions.[10]

In 1961 the elected membership of the legislative assembly, which numbered only eight since the introduction of universal adult suffrage, was increased to ten, while the nominated component was decreased from three to two. The position of Chief Minister was introduced with provisions made for two additional ministers. All of these positions were held by officers of the ATLU.

The constitutional status of associated state was achieved in 1967 and, as noted earlier, allows for complete local control over internal matters and some international economic affairs, while Great Britain retains responsibility for defense and external affairs.[11] Finally, after much indecision, full political independence was attained in 1981.

It is significant to observe that since 1946, when the working class movement made its entry into the parliamentary arena, no candidate has been elected without the support of the trade union movement. Political parties established on bases other than labor unions have performed miserably at the polls and have disappeared from the scene either through death or absorption by the union-based parties.

The Plantation and Development Obstacles

The decolonization process should mean not only the removal of the colonizer but the incorporation of at least the initial stages of nation-building, involving, among other things, the establishment of national institutions conducive to individual and collective human progress. It should mean the elimination or major transformation of those colonial institutions which historically accounted for the subjugation of colonial peoples and whose continued existence, after the transfer of political power to nationals, is likely to be inimical to the development of a national consciousness and to the construction of and indigenous control over a national economy.

The plantation has played a pivotal role in the history of Antigua's economy and society. It has been the dominant form of agricultural organization for centuries. Its all-pervasiveness has been highlighted by Beckford:

> The plantation is a total economic institution. It binds everyone in its embrace to the one task of executing the will of its owner or owners. And because it is omnipotent and omnipresent in the lives of those living within its confines, it is also a total social institution. Social relations within the plantation community are determined by the economic organization that governs production.[13]

Given the all-embracing character of the plantation system, several questions come to mind for countries that experienced it and are now asserting national independence. Does the plantation system pose problems for national development? Can meaningful economic advancement occur within plantation economies? In his major study, Beckford concludes that the plantation system generates and sustains persistent underdevelopment and that the system itself is the major obstacle to meaningful human and material progress in countries with a plantation history.

Among the economic limitations of the system noted by Beckford which are important in the experience of Antigua and Barbuda are the following:

1. The perpetuation of an extreme divergence between national resource supply and the production structure on the one hand and national demand on the other.
2. Inequality in the distribution of income and wealth.
3. Expatriate ownership and control of enterprises and the consequent loss of funds for investment from the national income flow.
4. Export bias of the production structure and cumulative adverse movements in the terms of international trade.
5. The low skill content of plantation activity which limits skills diffusion and qualitative improvements in labor inputs.
6. Distortions in resource use that limit reallocation to relatively productive areas of the economy.
7. Canalization of production linkages by metropolitan production enterprise, which severely restricts intersectoral linkages within plantation economy.
8. The international nature of investment allocation by the multinational plantation corporations, which reduces the funds available to be invested in national development.

9. Extreme concentration of technological research on a narrow range of plantation crops, which results in limited technical information on production possibilities and which thwarts the development of a broad-based system of agriculture.[14]

10. Uneven distribution of labor demand over the production cycle, which leads to high seasonality of employment and a reserve army of under- and unemployed people surviving on the fringes of the plantation.

11. The existence of a supporting services structure (extension and education services, availability of farm inputs, marketing arrangements, technical supports, etc.), which can handle plantation produce but is incapable of promoting and servicing non-plantation agricultural production.

12. The presence of a banking and financial system, owned and controlled by foreigners, with features similar to the supporting services structure, resulting in inadequate financing for growing crops not of the plantation specialty.

Beckford also identifies several important social and political obstacles to development attributable to the plantation legacy. Of relevance to the Antigua and Barbuda situation are:

1. The lack of local development initiatives because of the absence of viable local and regional administrative units, the latter due to weak family organization and community structure.

2. Low factor mobility because of a rigid social structure.

3. A strong state apparatus which discourages effective popular participation in community and national affairs and in the process of development.

4. Badly developed educational systems as a result of very little social responsibility.

5. The excessive power and prestige of the planter and associated classes and the use of power primarily in the interest of a small elite class.

6. The relative absence of progress-oriented values among all the people of plantation society due to the persistence of strong traditionalist elements among the planter class and hostile attitudes toward intellectual pursuits which are vital for innovation and progress.

7. A strong individualism which retards cooperative and collective responses to problems affecting the community.

8. A tradition of exploitive and authoritarian decisionmaking, which prevents emergence of participatory forms of problem-solving.

9. The widespread presence of values which attach high importance to the consumption of imported luxuries and investment in nonproductive assets, and low esteem for production activities and productive investment.

What have been the consequences of the changes in the economy, more specifically agriculture and tourism, as regards the above developmental obstacles which resulted from the plantation experience? Have the changes been of a fundamental nature, so that at least some of the obstacles are eliminated? If the decolonization process in Antigua is to be ascribed some measure of success, some of the above limitations of the plantation system should have been eliminated. The dominance of the plantation organizational structure should have significantly decreased, and development-oriented approaches and business structures should be emerging. Determining whether this has occurred is the task of the following two sections.

Decolonization and the Transformation of Agriculture

Because of the pervasiveness of the plantation system, and the set of obstacles to socioeconomic transformation it generates, it is to be expected that the decolonization process and attempts at significant restructuring of agriculture would come into conflict with this form of socioeconomic organization. The establishment of independent villages in the nineteenth century constituted the first postemancipation confrontation. The development of an Antiguan peasantry and class of small farmers through the setting up of land settlement schemes was the first program in the present century which seemingly challenged the hegemony of the plantation in the agricultural sector.

PLANTATION AND PEASANTRY IN ANTIGUAN AGRICULTURE

The Royal Commission of 1897 had noted:

> The existence of a class of small proprietors among the population is a source of both economic and political strength. No reform affords so good a prospect for the permanent welfare in the future of the West Indies as the settlement of the labouring population on the land as small peasant proprietors.[16]

Forty years later, the West India Royal Commission was emphasizing the same point, even though in 1929 a sugar commission had made it for a second time. The reasons for the reminders no doubt relate to the fact that the implementation of the idea was generally disregarded.[17]

The reality of, course, is that the land settlement schemes were not intended to radically change the structure of Caribbean agriculture. In fact, their first official proponent made it clear that:

> We see no objection to the system of large estates when they can be maintained under natural economic conditions. On the contrary, we are convinced that in many places they afford the best, and sometimes the only, profitable means of cultivating certain products, and that it is not impossible for the two systems of large estates and peasant holdings to exist side by side with mutual advantage.[18]

The compulsory acquisition of land by government to facilitate the land settlement program was tolerated by the Royal Commission only when cultivation of the lands had ceased—a sure signal that agronomic and economic configurations were not favorable to profitable operations.

The peaceful coexistence of the plantation and the peasantry echoed by the above quotation meant, in fact, the continued dependence of the Caribbean working class on the plantation and not the establishment of an independent peasantry. In Antigua, land settlement schemes began comparatively early, in 1916. Within twelve years, there were five settlements. Some basic information on these pioneer cases is revealing. They comprised a total area of 3,989 acres, with 1,822 acres occupied, but only 226 acres were classified as arable. Only one of the five areas, which constituted 5.7 percent of the total acreage, had what were termed "conditions [which] favour [sugar] cane growing." While the soil classification may have sugar cane bias, the fact remains that by 1928 only 5.7 percent of the lands available for the settlement schemes were classified as arable, and of the occupied land only 12.4 percent was in the classification, even though all of this class had been taken.[19]

Additional information on the first land settlement is equally revealing about metropolitan scholarly assessment of colonialist programs. In 1939, Professor C. Y. Shephard carried out "a very thorough investigation into peasant agriculture" in Antigua and the other Leeward Islands. Among his findings we have the following:

> Sawcolts settlement was commenced in 1916 when the shortage of shipping had made it desirable to encourage local food production. The lots were to be of not less than one, and not more than three acres in size, and half the original lots were, in fact, on one acre. *The lots were not intended to provide full-time occupation for the allottees.* Sweet potatoes were to

be the principal crop grown both for family consumption and family sale: but these small food plots soon lost their popularity and sugar cane crept in even before the end of the war and soon became a major crop. The experiment at Sawcolts was regarded as a great success.[20]

It is clear that the establishment of the first land settlement had nothing to do with the promotion of an independent peasantry. That the above experience could be seen as a "great success" is most incredible, unless success in maintaining the stranglehold of the plantation system is meant. Later settlements in Antigua followed a similar pattern.

By 1954, when the newly established Peasant Development Organization took over the responsibilities of the Land Settlement and Development Board, there were nine freehold settlements and 24 leasehold settlements. The former had 1,147 allotments totalling 2,515 acres, implying an average size of 2.2 acres; while the latter had 3,310 allotments with an average size of 1.7 acres and a total of 5,512 acres.[21] Significantly, the leasehold plots which were developed later are of smaller average size than the freehold units, which certainly suggests no commitment to establish economic peasant farms. The continuation of this trend is confirmed by the data for 1962. At this time, the extent of the freehold settlements remained basically unchanged, but the leaseholds had increased to 52 settlements, with 5,650 allotments with an occupied area of 7,422 arable acres, giving an average size of 1.3 acres.[22] Thus, while allotments increased by 71 percent, occupied acreage expanded by only 35 percent, reflecting a further reduction in average unit size.

Despite the growth of the peasant sector, it was never intended to challenge the plantation system. The extremely small units which made independent economic activity untenable have just been noted. Add to this the fact that Antiguan peasants, like their counterparts elsewhere in the Caribbean, received the poorest quality land. Add also the existence of a rudimentary supporting services structure for agricultural production other than the plantation export crops of sugar and cotton and we see that peasants were locked into the production pattern as well as the marketing, credit, and services arrangements of the plantation. Note the quick shift to plantation crops by the Sawcolts peasants. Most important, however, was a development in the plantation sector itself; namely, its consolidation coupled with the earlier centralization of factory operations.

This consolidation, which began in earnest in 1943 with the establishment of Antigua Syndicate Estates Ltd., was virtually complete by 1950. It brought under one ownership and management more than 30 of the roughly 50 estates which were previously independently owned and managed. It is important to note that this "monopoly controlling the best lands in the island," as working-class leaders accurately characterized it, was closely interlocked through ownership and management with the Antigua Sugar Factory Ltd., which controlled the milling operations.[23] It should not be surprising, then, that in 1961 land distribution was as follows. Of a total of 5,747 farms 91.1 percent were under 5 acres and accounted for a mere 26.9 percent of the 34,089 acres of farmland. This implies an average farm size of 1.7 acres. Farms of size 5 to 50 acres accounted for 8.1 percent of the total and 11.8 percent of the acreage, while farms 50 acres and over (49 in number) represented a negligible 0.8 percent of the total number but controlled a massive 61.3 percent of total farmlands. This land distribution was among the worst in the Eastern Caribbean.[24]

Toward the end of the 1950s signs were emerging that the sugar industry and the plantation system within which it existed were in serious trouble. The effects of the working class struggle, the emergence of tourism, and emigration to Great Britain and elsewhere were among the factors which lessened the plantation stranglehold. Its supply of manual labor was not forthcoming, and from 1958 cane cutters had to be recruited from the Windward Islands.[25] While a serious program of mechanization was undertaken, it was not enough to reestablish the economic viability of the sugar industry under plantation arrangements. by 1965 the companies controlling the factory and the syndicate estates were in a state of insolvency for several years and were kept afloat only with substantial financial support from the sugar cess funds and the Antigua government. In 1966, to keep the industry going, the government took a major shareholding position in the companies. Within a year the planter class had given over full ownership and control to the government, no doubt realizing that, in the words of a British economist, "it is clear that in its present form sugar cannot easily survive modern conditions."[26]

For the next five years the government made valiant efforts to keep the plantation system of sugar production intact, but it finally collapsed in 1971. The Antigua Caribbean Liberation Movement saw the final death throes:

> When in 1967 the British planters saw declining profits or no profits at all facing them squarely in the face, all the Bird Regime could conceive of was to save the planters by buying them out at a 'fair' price and then continue the same old plantation system of labour and of production. The exploiting planter had been saved and knighted. The exploited peasant and agricultural labourer had been ruined and set adrift.[27]

Buying out the planters meant that the government now had control over all of the country's prime agricultural land, some 14,000 acres by a 1964 estimate.[28] With 8,000 acres of government lands controlled by peasants under year-to-year leasehold conditions, the government had 65 percent of all farmland with which to effect fundamental changes in agricultural organization, management and production.[29]

Since this period coincided with the attainment of associated statehood, the government possessed the constitutional powers to initiate such restructuring. What has occurred? As noted above, up until 1971, strenuous efforts were made by successive regimes to continue the plantation setup. Since then there has been no clear statement or action which suggests a commitment to transform plantation agriculture. The three major activities to have taken place on the initiative of the state represent no more than the continuation of the plantation economy with all its economic, social and political obstacles to meaningful development and transformation.

The first and most important activity includes the "realienation" of the prime agricultural land that was liberated from British planters in 1967. This realienation began in 1976, when the government leased to an American company, for 15 years, approximately 10,000 acres, some 71 percent of the 14,000 acres acquired from the Antigua Syndicate Estates Ltd. The lessee retained the option to renew for an additional 15 years. The company had privileged access to the island's scarce water resources but paid rental rates that were ridiculously low.[30] The result was that where we once had the sugar monoculture, we had for a short time the corn monoculture together with the reintroduction of domination by metropolitan plantation enterprise. If the agreement had run its course, alienation of the country's choice agricultural resources would have continued until the year 2005. However, this project collapsed late in 1978 with a debt of $15 million.

The second activity is the establishment of a state capitalist farm on parts of the former sugar lands. The social relations of production are no different than under the plantation structure, except in regard to who appropriates the surplus. That this is so is evidenced by the several strikes that have occurred on the farm since its inception. Like the "corn people," the farm has privileged access to the country's water. With the whole state apparatus to support it, and with no pressing compulsion to be concerned with economic calculations, it is directly competing with and threatening the financial viability of peasants and small farmers. This is particularly disturbing from a development standpoint, since the latter, having been released from the grasp of the sugar plantation, have now embarked on an independent existence and are concentrating on vegetable and root crop production—a cropping pattern that is more directly related to the consumption and national needs of the society. If, as Clive Thomas argues, "one of the most fundamental laws governing the transformation process is the planned implementation of a structure of domestic output consistent with domestic demand patterns,"[31] the Antiguan peasants and small farmers are pioneers, albeit in a somewhat unplanned fashion, in the transformation of Antiguan agriculture.

The third activity worth mentioning is the establishment by government of two schemes for small farmers. One aims at exposing a few small farmers to vegetable production that uses irrigation. The project covers 50 acres of land comprised of 12 farms of sizes ranging from 1.4 to 4.5 acres and a state-run demonstration farm. A number of setbacks have been experienced, including the breakdown of farm equipment and marketing difficulties, despite the existence of a state marketing agency for agricultural produce. The other scheme takes up 300 acres with farms of 3 to 8 acres. The cropping pattern concentrates on vegetables, root, and fruit crops, and irrigation facilities are not available. The scheme has had its ample share of problems.[32] What is important to note is that they seem not to be significantly different from earlier land settlement schemes. Their lack of success to date may not be unrelated to their conception.

DECOLONIZATION AND AGRICULTURAL TRANSFORMATION

We have just seen that with a substantial amount of choice agricultural lands in state hands, there has been no attempt to encourage or introduce new organizational structures in agriculture or to make lands available to the peasant sector in economically viable sizes. Further, local self-initiated efforts which involve new and progressive approaches to agricultural organization and management have failed to receive state support. Therefore, even though an advanced stage of the decolonization process has been reached in constitutional terms, the achievements are not reflected in developments in the agricultural sector, save for national ownership, not control, of lands. The old plantation system has died, but it is being replaced by a new one that brings with it additional developmental obstacles.

What progress has been made is due almost single-handedly to the peasant and small farmer class which, having been released from the direct influence of the sugar plantocracy has shifted its production emphasis from traditional export crops (sugar and cotton) to crops with substantial local demand (vegetables and root crops). However, with the extreme land fragmentation characteristic of this sector, there are limits to which it can go with the existing configuration resources available to it. If it is not given access to the 14,000 acres of prime arable farmland acquired a decade ago by the state, and if some consolidation of the roughly 6,000 farms on government leasehold property with average size of 1.3 acres does not occur, the peasant sector will remain on the fringes with a new metropolitan plantation enterprise at the center of agricultural activity. This, however, had not yet occurred. To avoid these possibilities, it will also be necessary to build upon the rudimentary cooperative and collective experiences of the peasant sector so that humanist and participatory organizational and management processes emerge.

Decolonization and Tourism Development

The tourist industry, which has now assumed the leading position in the economy of Antigua and Barbuda, had its modest beginnings in the early 1950s but experienced massive growth during the late 1950s. Among the factors that account for the sizable expansion are:

1. The considerable international publicity the island received with the establishment of the Mill Reef resort by a group of American millionaires.
2. Antigua's excellent beaches and historical sites.
3. The country's status as a land-lease area, which led to the erection of American bases and subsequent development of an international airport.
4. "The quite unreserved attitude of the Antigua government in its wholehearted pursuit of capital from overseas for investment in tourism and allied industries."[33]

Several indicators show the growth of the industry.[34] Between 1957 and 1960 the number of hotels went from three to eight, with several others under construction and projected. By 1970 there were 33 hotels—a quadrupling within a decade. Tourist arrivals were roughly 4,300 in 1953, and increased to 8,300 in 1956, to 25,000 in 1962, and to 55,800 in 1968. Between 1961 and 1967 the annual growth rate in tourist arrivals was 24.4 percent. Statistics on hotels and tourist arrivals for the 1970s are shown in Table 1. Expenditures by tourists were estimated at $1.8 million in 1953, $4.6 million in 1957, $21.2 million in 1968 and $44.8 million in 1973. Finally we note the growth of hotel beds. These increased from 560 in 1961 to 1,689 in 1967, reflecting an annual growth rate of 20.1 percent. As can be seen in Table 1, by 1975 the number of beds had increased to 2,496.

The substantial growth in tourism reflected in the above figures, combined with the collapse of the sugar plantation system, led to a structural change in the Antiguan and Barbudan economy. In 1953 agriculture accounted for 35.2 percent of gross domestic product, while tourism accounted for 7.7 percent. By 1968 agriculture's share had fallen to 4.8 percent, while that of the tourist industry had increased to 14.1 percent. With respect to the industrial distribution of the work force, agriculture's share fell from 33 percent in 1960 to approximately 14 percent in 1970, while tourism's share increased from 2 percent to 5 percent over the same period. Tourism employment trebled while agricultural employment declined in absolute terms by more than 50 percent.

TABLE 1 / Selected Tourism Statistics (1970–1975)

				Tourist Arrivals	
Year	*Hotels*	*Hotel Rooms*	*Hotel Beds*	*By Sea*	*By Air*
1970	33	1,051	2,102	18,705	63,595
1971	34	1,031	2,062	37,658	66,067
1972	32	1,124	2,248	63,784	70,140
1973	31	1,109	2,218	52,174	71,065
1974	32	1,194	2,388	27,062	68,897
1975	34	1,248	2,496	32,385	56,398

Source: Department of Tourism, Antigua.

In short, the decline and ultimate collapse of the sugar plantocracy was coupled with the emergence of an industry of modern vintage which displaced agriculture from its primary position. Consequently, even though the development obstacles attributable to the plantation system still impede agricultural development, the possibility exists that the new sector can escape such limitations and constitute the basis for meaningful economic development in Antigua. We need to look at tourism in this context.

During the early rapid growth of the industry, doubts were expressed about its structural features. In 1961 Carleen O'Loughlin wrote:[35]

The next basic economic problem, which has become marked in the last few years, is the fact that the growth of tourism, now the island's second industry, has been of a rather unbalanced nature, emphasizing mainly the high-rate or highest-rate branches of the trade. At the present time, to criticize high-rate tourism may appear rather like looking a gift-horse in the mouth, but it is highly important that the future utilization of Antigua's natural tourist facilities be considered carefully. Otherwise, it may well happen that the physical limits of expansion are reached at an unnecessarily low rate of return in terms of income to the community. Even in Antigua, white sand beach, for instance, is a scarce resource in the long run. Therefore, one has to consider returns in the form of income per acre of farmland from different crops. As regards tourism, however, it is likely that a diversity of high and medium-rate would make for the most stability of the industry; with certain areas specializing in one type and other areas in the other.

High-income tourists were characterized as "notoriously fickle" in terms of destination, and it was cautioned that an economy based upon such a market would be extremely vulnerable to external economic developments.

It will be useful to look at other structural features of Antiguan tourism, especially in relation to the development obstacles of plantation economy noted earlier. First is the aspect of ownership. The distinguishing feature here is that the majority of hotels are foreign owned. In 1968, out of a total of 1,780 hotel and guest house beds, only 200 were locally owned and of these 135 were guest house, and hence poorer quality, beds.[36] In other words, 90 percent of tourist beds were owned by expatriates. Since then the ownership pattern has moved somewhat in favor of national ownership, due to the real or fabricated insolvency of several large foreign-owned hotels and the subsequent government takeover. It is important to note, however, that these state-owned hotels are still under expatriate control. In addition, the present government policy is to encourage as much as possible new foreign investment in the hotel sector, and at least two large projects are contemplated.

Factors which explain the high foreign ownership include the reluctance of indigenous owners of capital to enter the industry, the attractive incentives offered foreign investors by government, and the former's somewhat easy access to local funds through the local branches of metropolitan banks.

One of the main benefits of the industry is the generation of employment. Direct employment in the hotel industry in 1975 was estimated at 1,785 in the high (winter) season and 1,173 in the low (summer) season. This, however, was a mere 5 percent. In 1968 a sample survey, with a coverage of 29 percent of available hotel and guest house beds, showed that 62 percent of the employees were women during the high season, the percentage being 57 percent for low season.[37]

Distinguishing features of tourist sector employment include:

1. The relatively high proportion of employees who are semiskilled or unskilled.

2. The comparatively high proportion of women in the semiskilled and unskilled categories.
3. The high proportion of non-nationals who occupy top and middle management as well as technical and skilled positions.
4. The high seasonality of employment.

These features are not dissimilar from those of plantation agriculture.

As a major earner of foreign exchange, tourism is normally seen as important to countries like Antigua and Barbuda, which need to earn hard currency to promote economic development. While *gross* foreign exchange earnings are substantial, *net* earnings are less impressive because of income leakages. A breakdown of tourist expenditures in 1963 indicated that 49 percent accrued as local incomes, 10 percent as government revenue, and 41 percent was spent on imports.[38] When it is appreciated that because of the structure of employment in the industry, a good part of local incomes accrue to non-nationals who repatriate some of it, it should be clear that the first round foreign exchange leakage is greater than 41 percent.

The extent of linkages with other sectors of the economy can be gauged by the size of the tourist multiplier, which gives the direct and indirect impact on domestic income of a unit of tourist expenditure. Estimates for Antigua, based upon plausible assumptions, range from 0.71 to 0.88, reflecting the very small income-generating impact of tourist expenditures.[39] In other words, tourism has not been able to generate substantial linkages with other productive sectors.

Another feature of the tourist industry is the high underutilization reflected in the low occupancy rates in hotels and guest houses. In 1967 the high season occupancy rate was 58 percent; for the low season it was a dismal 18 percent. There was very little change from the occupancy rates of 1963.[40] In fact, the structure of the industry is such that even today it is not unusual for hotels to close for four to six months each year. While data for more recent years is unavailable, it is doubtful that the picture has improved significantly. The result is that with the industry based primarily on foreign demand, national human and physical resources are idle for a good part of each year.

It is necessary to comment on the foreign demand feature referred to in the previous paragraph. The industry exists by providing services to nonresidents. This reinforces the openness of the economy that characterizes the plantation structure. Further, during the early period of the growth of tourism, tourists came mainly from North America, implying an extreme geographical concentration of demand. While some progress has been made in widening the demand structure, tourism has not reached a stage where it can comfortably weather a major downturn in North American business activity.

In short, the structural features of the tourist industry in Antigua and Barbuda mirror those of the agricultural sector due to the plantation legacy. The conclusion made in a recent study is that Caribbean "tourism does not now serve to strengthen linkages between the sectors of the economy, to place greater control of the economy into national hands and to reduce dependence on and vulnerability to changes in external situations."[41] This statement applies equally to Antiguan tourism.

There are, in addition, the social aspects of tourism with which to contend. A regional consultation on the role of tourism in Caribbean development admitted several economic benefits, but sounded a caution on the basis of social disadvantages. It reasoned that:

> . . . centuries of colonial domination have prevented the emergence of a positive affirmation of the unique potentials of this pluralistic Caribbean society. Different cultural backgrounds are now being welded into an integrated culture which incorporates, but also transcends each of the individual contributing streams. At this crucial stage large scale tourism might prove to be a serious hazard to the process of cultural metamorphosis which the Caribbean countries are going through . . . Moreover, in countries which have inherited a history of slavery and the historic experience of being identified as black servants of white masters, a large influx of predominantly white tourists might help to perpetuate a slave/master relational pattern and a kind of cultural neo-colonialism could easily emerge.[42]

Additional social disadvantages have been raised by others.[43] These include the perpetuation, through the demonstration effect of tourist consumption styles, of values which give high importance to the consumption of imported luxuries and little prestige to the utilization of locally produced goods. It will be recalled that this was one of the social obstacles to development created by the plantation system.

Considerable foreign management and decisionmaking govern all major aspects of the industry except the budgets of tourist boards. This limits indigenous determination of the product and does not promote the acquisition of managerial skills and experience on the part of the nationals. Naturally, authoritarian styles of decisionmaking persist, and participatory management approaches do not develop. The consequence has been that "the image of Caribbean tourism has been shaped by foreigners."[44] The particular picture portrayed is such that the tourist visits the Caribbean not because he respects the culture, the people, or the level of development of the society, or because he anticipates a learning experience, but rather because the Caribbean is a convenient destination.[45] Bastardization of the national culture to satisfy foreign pleasure-seekers and racist behavior are not uncommon.[46] The inference here is that whatever the potential of tourism to transform the economy and society of Antigua and Barbuda so that they more closely reflect the concerns of the broad mass of the population, its present economic structure does not provide such a basis. With the present structure it is unlikely that the social disadvantages can be removed.

Notes

1. Douglas Hall, *Five of the Leewards, 1834–1870* (St. Laurence, Barbados: Caribbean Universities Press, 1971), p. 33.
2. Ibid., pp. 28–39.
3. Ibid., pp. 35–50, 150.
4. For an excellent extensive discussion on plantation society, see George Beckford, *Persistent Poverty* (New York: Oxford University Press, 1972), especially Chapter 3.
5. Novelle H. Richards, *The Struggle and the Conquest* (St. John's, Antigua: Workers Voice Printery 1964), p. 3.
6. Tim Hector, "Workers Move for Liberation, 1915–1968," *Outlet Fortnightly,* May 21, 1975.
7. Ibid.
8. Hall, pp. 43–50.
9. Novelle H. Richards, pp. 15–16.
10. Ibid., p. 24.
11. For a detailed discussion on this constitution arrangement, see Urias Forbes, "The West Indies Associated States: Constitutional Arrangements," *Social and Economic Studies* 19 (March 1970), pp. 57–88.
12. Antigua Caribbean Liberation Movement, "Basic Programme for Peoples Power," *Outlet Fortnightly,* 29 (March 1978).
13. Beckford, p. 55.
14. Ibid., p. 216.
15. Ibid., pp. 216–217.
16. *Report of the Royal Commission of 1897,* as quoted in *Report of the Commission Appointed to Enquire into the Organization of the Sugar Industry of Antigua, 1949,* (London: Crown Agents, 1949), p. 26 (Soulbury Commission Report).
17. Bill Riviere, "Exploitation and Dependency in the Caribbean with Special Emphasis on the Period Since 1938: An Overview," Africana Studies and Research Center (Ithaca, N.Y.: Cornell University, April 1973), p. 5.
18. *Report of the Royal Commission of 1897,* as quoted in Soulbury Commission Report, p. 26.
19. Computed from data in *Soulbury Commission Report,* Appendix K.
20. C. Y. Shephard. *Report on Peasant Agriculture in the Leeward and Windward Islands, 1939,* as quoted in Soulbury Commission Report, p. 27 (emphasis added).
21. Antigua Department of Agriculture, *Annual Report, 1954,* pp. 20–30.
22. Antigua Department of Agriculture, *Annual Report, 1962,* pp. 10–17.
23. *Soulbury Commission Report,* Minority Report by V. C. Bird, pp. 110–111.

24. Carleen O'Loughlin, *Economic and Political Change in the Leeward and Windward Islands* (New Haven: Yale University Press, 1968), p. 103.

25. D. T. Edwards and L. G. Campbell, *Agriculture in Antigua's Economy: Possibilities and Problems of Adjustment* (Barbados: Institute for Social and Economic Research, University of the West Indies, 1965), p. 4.

26. O'Loughlin, p. 107.

27. Afro-Caribbean Liberation Movement, *Liberation: From the Old Wreckage to the New Society* (St. John's, Antigua, 1947), p. 5.

28. Edwards and Campbell, p. 34.

29. The remaining farmland was comprised of owner-occupied farms of at least 50 acres in size (7,000 acres), peasant freehold units acquired from government (2,500 acres), and peasant leaseholds and freeholds from private owners (2,600 acres).

30. Information derived from personal communication of writer with government officials.

31. Clive Y. Thomas, *Dependence and Transformation* (New York: Monthly Review Press, 1974), p. 141.

32. Michael G. White, et al. *Case Study Report on an Integrated Production and Marketing System for the Antiguan Agricultural Sector* (Barbados: Caribbean Agro-Economics Society, April 1977), pp. 24–25.

33. O'Loughlin, p. 27.

34. Statistical sources are: John M. Bryden, *Tourism and Development* (Cambridge: Cambridge University Press, 1973); Carleen O'Loughlin, "The Economy of Antigua", *Social and Economic Studies*, 8 (September 1959), pp. 229–264; Carleen O'Loughlin, "Problems in the Economic Development of Antigua," *Social and Economic Studies*, 10 (September 1961), pp. 237–277; Carleen O'Loughlin, *Financial and Economic Survey of the Hotel Industry in Antigua* (Barbados: Institute for Social and Economic Research, University of the West Indies, 1964); Antigua Department of Tourism, tourism statistics for various years.

35. Carleen O'Loughlin, "Problems in the Economic Development of Antigua," *Social and Economic Studies* 10 (September 1961), p. 237.

36. John M. Bryden, *Tourism and Development* (Cambridge, Cambridge University Press, 1973), p. 121.

37. White, et al., p. 13; Bryden, p. 127.

38. Carleen O'Loughlin, *Financial and Economic Survey of the Hotel Industry in Antigua* (Institute for Social and Economic Research, University of the West Indies, 1964).

39. Bryden, pp. 151–161.

40. Ibid., p. 119; O'Loughlin, *Financial and Economic Survey*, pp. 4–5.

41. Edwin Carrington and Byron Blake, "Tourism as a Vehicle for Caribbean Economic Development," in Caribbean Tourism Research Centre, *Economic Impact of Tourism* (Barbados, 1976), p. 8.

42. Caribbean Ecumenical Consultation for Development, *The Role of Tourism in Caribbean Development* (Barbados, 1971), p. 8.

43. O'Loughlin, *Economic and Political Change*, pp. 148–154; Bryden, pp. 35–36, 89–96; Antigua Caribbean Liberation Movement, *Liberation: From the Old Wreckage to the New Society*, pp. 5–6.

44. Neville Linton. "Tourism in the Commonwealth Caribbean: An Overview," *Caribbean Issues*, II (April 1976), pp. 36–47.

45. Ibid., p. 40.

46. O'Loughlin, *Economic and Political Change*, pp. 148–154.

3

Decolonization and the Caribbean State System: The Case of Jamaica

CARL STONE

For small Third World states recently emerging from European colonialism and caught in the constraints and pressures of dependent incorporation into world capitalism, the analysis of decolonization as a process provides an important perspective from which to assess their political development. This is especially so of the English-speaking Caribbean, and the island of Jamaica with its small two million population is no exception. This chapter will attempt to examine the process of decolonization in the Caribbean by drawing on the experience of Jamaica.

Decolonization in the English-speaking Caribbean is not a single revolutionary event transferring authority, power, or even economic control from foreign imperial centers to local ones. It is a complex process which evolves from stage to stage as it moves closer to achieving local decisional autonomy in the economic and political spheres. For small territories such as Jamaica or the other islands of the Caribbean, its attainment will always be partial, and the decolonization issue will therefore always be on the agenda of political action and debate (Lewis 1976).

Essentially, its transition over time can be divided into two main stages separated into the period prior to formal independence from colonial rule and the period thereafter. Central to both phases of the process is the development of qualitative changes in relations between the main social classes and the state (Munroe 1972). In attempting to understand the decolonization process, it is necessary to focus on the complex and often elusive area of class-state relations.

37

The two stages of decolonization can be grouped into the following main phases:

1. *Preindependence (stage one)*

   a. Emergence of mass parties as "opposition alternatives" to colonial rule.
   b. Apprenticeship of mass party leaders into Westminster parliamentary politics (Munroe 1972).
   c. Elimination of the limiting legacies of the colonial state by broadening the legitimacy of the state through party politics and broadening the class-clientele of interests served by state institutions beyond the elite.
   d. Transfer of state control to local politicians (or anti-colonial opposition).

2. *Postindependence (stage two)*

   a. Development of functional and effective state institutions capable of undertaking expanded and more complex policy and administrative functions.
   b. The growth of local territorial nationalism built around indigenous cultural symbols and identity and the replacing of Anglophile and colonial empire loyalties with attendant Eurocentric values.
   c. International realignment from the status of satellite state to Western metropolitan powers to a self-conscious Third World identity.
   d. Economic nationalism (Beckford 1972; Girvan 1971) or the drive to increase decisional autonomy over the local economy and to increase local benefits from foreign investments and external economic transactions (by nationalization, joint ventures, tax levies on multinational corporations, trade diversification, international supplier cartels).
   e. Joining with the global struggle by small and poor nations to wrest a larger share of the world's wealth in the context of widening rich-poor international gaps and declining living standards in some Third World states (Meier 1974).

The first stage of the process evolves from oppositionist party movements to legitimizing the state and institutionalizing the governmental process along British parliamentary lines under British colonial tutelage and supervision. The four phases of stage one of the decolonization process have been initiated in all Commonwealth Caribbean states, including those not yet fully independent. The level of success attained in the legitimation and localization of state control is, however, unevenly advanced in these Commonwealth states. Where these processes of decolonization are incomplete, the effect is to limit considerably the capability of the state in stage two of the decolonization process. The sequence in which these four phases of the first stage of decolonization are attempted is as set forth above.

The transition from stage one to stage two of the decolonization process implies and involves an increase in domestic class pressures and demands on the state, with a consequent expansion of the economic, regulatory, management and social development roles of the state. Stage two centers first on development administration and nationalism. At a later and more advanced stage of development, the focus is on international realignment, economic nationalism, and aggressive involvement in the north-south struggle for wealth and control of global resources.

Implicit in the processes identified is the notion that some states, after independence, will evolve further along the various phases of the decolonization tasks than others, and that some states may bypass some phases entirely or develop to a very incomplete stage of development. The small size and limited resource endowment of Caribbean states means that the decolonization process in the region is likely to be partial and incomplete in most states.

The only escape route from this incomplete and partial decolonization path is by way of social revolution or militarization leading toward a Cuban-type incorporation into the Soviet-dominated socialist system. Setting aside the uncertain case of Grenada, none of the Commonwealth Caribbean states as yet possesses the necessary disciplined leftist cadres or organized forces, or a sufficiently politicized military which is capable of becoming the catalyst for such a development. Nor is the Soviet Union likely to sponsor any such development in the region after the high costs of Cuban incorporation into the international socialist system.

Some independent Caribbean states (e.g., Antigua and the Bahamas) are still in the early phase of stage two of the decolonization process, development administration and territorial nationalism. Trinidad has gone beyond this stage, but only partially into the second phase of stage two of the decolonization process, economic nationalism. Jamaica and Guyana, however, have fully entered this second phase of stage two of the decolonization process. They have consequently experienced all the local class pressures and external stresses that accompany efforts by small Third World states to redefine some of the external economic and power parameters that stifle development.

Their balance sheet of gains and losses represents a mixed picture of failures and successes that underlie the continued hegemony of international capitalism in the face of these minor anti-imperialist assaults from the periphery.

One major question demanding a clear answer concerns the forces that propel some states (Jamaica and Guyana) to the more advanced phases of stage two of the decolonization process involving international and nationalist militancy over economic benefits from transnational transactions and control of national resources. While the shifting parameters of world economic power facilitate such developments, as does the weakening coercive capability of the imperialist state apparatus, these do not explain why some states move in this direction while others do not. The impetus toward these militant strategies of bargaining has come from a combination of ideological tendencies among the preeminent political leaders (in the recent past, Manley and Burnham); mounting domestic social pressures which demand increased state revenue to pacify militant support; the appeasing of radical leftist demands from the left intelligentsia for anti-imperialist measures; and international commodity price escalation demanding defensive aggression.

Full development of the militant bargaining by Caribbean states with external metropolitan interests and radical assertions of economic nationalist policies invariably falls short of the millenarian expectations often attached to these developments. Poverty, social backwardness, and arrested development persist, while the hegemony of metropolitan economic power adjusts to the new bargaining situation with unanticipated levers of power. Decolonization efforts turn out to be survival strategies rather than earth-shaking developments likely to redefine the power equation between the metropole and the hinterland in the international capitalist system. Anti-imperialist militancy in the Caribbean, while preserving the rhetoric of Third World militancy, has given way to accommodationist clientelism vis-à-vis metropolitan power centers in search of new aid. Decolonization has therefore failed to resolve the internal contradictions and internal class pressures on the Caribbean state.

All states perform certain basic roles. These include the following:

1. Definition of goals and the means of their attainment (policy).
2. Regulation of behavior (laws, security forces, legal system).
3. Management and deployment of resources in programmatic action (administration).
4. Rationalizing, justifying or legitimizing the role of the state by various means (nationalism, party politics, ideology, etc.)

The decolonization process outlined above defines a set of tasks to be performed in the liberation of social and economic forces from the inhibiting and limiting constraints of colonialism (stage one) and dependent incorporation in the international capitalist system. Not all the tasks are essential to this objective, as some merely describe the decolonization path followed in the Commonwealth Caribbean. In particular, Westminster parliamentary institutionalization is not essential to decolonization but has evolved as the institutional framework into which the process has become embedded, with obvious consequences. All other tasks identified are, however, essential features of the process of decolonization.

The state, of course, is more than simply a cluster of governmental institutions performing certain roles and functions for the society. It is also a system of power enmeshed in domestic class relations, pressures, and conflicts and in relations with external actors and political centers of power. Comprehending the character of the state in any society or political culture requires a theoretical framework that illuminates and specifies these interrelationships and identifies the precise social and political forces which determine the content and character of the state. In the final analysis, the class character of the state determines how far the decolonization process can go in liberating creative forces for development.

Toward a Theory of the Caribbean State

The first major issue in understanding the Caribbean state is its imperialist class origins and over-development relative to the domestic or local class forces. The Caribbean state apparatus emerged as an integral part of the British colonial empire. It was set up to protect British imperial interests and was structured according to the political culture of the British ruling class (Munroe 1972). More importantly, its power and hegemony over the colonized society derived from the hegemony of the imperial power and the related economic and military strength on which this colonial superstructure rested. These interrelated features raise a problem for the Caribbean state in stage two of the decolonization process.

With the transfer of state control from imperial to local interests in the period following World War II, the power of the state diminished in both the domestic and international domains which lacked connection with metropolitan economic and military strength. Secondly, whereas in the colonial period state power was integrally connected with the hegemony or effective control of locally relevant economic forces by the imperial power, in the postcolonial or neocolonial (stage two) period, the state no longer exercises hegemony in this sense. Incorporation into international capitalism means that hegemony, or determining and effective control of economic forces operative in the domestic system, resides overseas. The tendency, therefore, is for the state to become a client of externally located hegemonic interests, while attempting to respond to local class demands, expectations, and pressures. The state therefore functions in the context of cross-pressures from the domestic class structure and external centers of power, but with the latter exercising the determining critical influence over outcomes. This applies even at the highest stages of decolonization, when efforts are made to modify these power parameters.

A second and related proposition is that the domestic class formations remain underdeveloped because of small size and the economic backwardness inherent in the process of dependent incorporation into the international capitalist system. The ascendant or strongest class in the colonial period, the planter-merchant class, evolved and developed into a local urban bourgeoisie as the economy modernized and expanded in manufacturing, processing, industrial production, and extracti e and service industries. This bourgeois class tends to remain either a dependent appendage of foreign interests, a basically small business formation lacking effective control of local economic forces, or grows as a client of state promotion through import substitution policies. The bourgeoisie lacks class hegemony because of its basic weakness. Although it invariably exerts influence on the policies projected by the state, the Caribbean bourgeoisie lacks the power to convert the state into an executive committee administering on behalf of its interests (Stone 1973). Whichever class or faction controls the state is in a position to control and dictate to the local bourgeoisie, provided external pressures can be managed effectively. The local bourgeoisie is simply one class within a wider group of elite interests competing to influence the state, but has no hegemonic control over it in the sense in which the metropolitan bourgeoisie as a class has control over the state systems of advanced capitalist countries.

The political power of the Caribbean bourgeoisie is further weakened by the ethnic minority character (Stone 1973; Munroe 1972) that sets it apart from the main ethnic components of Caribbean society and by the illegitimacy of its wealth and privilege, deriving historically from its oppressive, slave-society origins which lacked normative legitimacy (Stone 1973). As a consequence, political attacks, ideological assaults, and harassment directed at sections of the bourgeoisie are condoned by the masses, although the latter believe in the private property and the free enterprise system and lack real socialist commitment to an alternate political economy.

Paralleling the relatively weak bourgeoisie is a weak and fragmented working class population. It consists of a more privileged
minority, represented by militant trade unions, and a majority made up
mainly of a service-labor subproletariat, petty traders, peasants, own
account workers, and the unemployed. While working-class militancy
among organized labor evidences the culture of alienation into which
Caribbean labor has been socialized by oppression and exploitation,
working class support for ideological radicalism is as yet underdeveloped. Moreover, multiple and incoherent ideological tendencies
(Stone 1976) are to be found among the fragmented working population
of the Caribbean. The Caribbean working class still follows flamboyant
demagogic and charismatic leaders "in the square" from whom it expects deliverance in accordance with millenarian political expectations
(Stone 1973, 1974). When these leaders fail to deliver, the organized
workers fall back on militant business unionism to defend their interests against the system. What is totally absent is any working-class or
peasant aspiration to or contention for state power, which is viewed by
them as a prerogative preserve of the educated middle class (Stone
1976). Working-class demands on the state are therefore limited to
pressure for employment, welfare benefits and community and individual patronage.

The Caribbean state is not ideologically neutral. It functions
within an inherited role to protect the market mechanisms and property
relations that form the core of the capitalist system governing these
economies. In spite of redistributive policies governing land acquisition from the rich and allocation to the poor, progressive income and
property taxation, welfare income, job creation and services for the
poor, and the financing of small business and peasant productive activities (all of which have attracted the "socialist" label in the region),
the Caribbean state fundamentally protects the central core areas of
the capitalist market economy as its first priority. What often confuses
the picture is the fact that the state increasingly owns and controls the
means of production. State protection of the sanctity of private property; regulation of wages and salaries, as well as prices, in the interests
of systemic market viability; regulation and management of external
financial transactions, credit, and trade; state investment promotion
and business acquisitions, and state facilitation and promotion of
foreign investment; and a positive external economic image are all
evident in the independent Caribbean states. They imply and involve
state management of the market economy and the increasing role of the
state in protecting and monitoring market forces.

In the mercantilist, slave-plantation, historical traditions of the
colonial Caribbean, the state was always at the center of the monitoring and management of economic forces. As these societies moved

from slavery to a free citizenry, the dominant planter-merchant class sought to limit the economic role of the state in the interests of expanding its independent class and economic power base free from imperial bureaucratic control. Following similar ideological currents in the early period of capitalist Britain, the planter-merchants, with the support of the free peasantry (where it existed), legitimized a notion of limited government and a laissez-faire economic system which guaranteed the independent and preeminent (local) power of those who owned property. The emergence of petty bourgeois and bureaucratic political ascendancy (in the second stage of decolonization) over property owners reversed these early laissez-faire trends by increasing state management of market forces. Some analysts mistakenly refer to this process either as socialism or as representing noncapitalist development because the capitalist class no longer gives the directions, and because the state is increasingly appropriating the commanding heights of the economy and regulating economic transactions. The reality, however, is that the state is assuming direction of the capitalist *market economy* in the Caribbean, thereby creating and evolving a *state capitalist* system.

In this process, the state assumes the burden of protecting the market system. It therefore polices both wage labor and the capitalists in the interests of maintaining these market mechanisms. The market system and the fiscal trade, incomes, prices, and other policies necessary to protect it are legitimized in terms of the national interest. In protecting the market system, however, it is sometimes necessary to restrict profits or wipe out sections of the capitalist class. In that sense, state capitalism means that the state does not necessarily see a coincidence of interests between the market system and sections of the capitalist class. Some state policies are often hostile to that class and pave the way to greater state control and ownership of wealth. Bureaucratic capitalism, led by the radical leftist petty bourgeoisie, fuels the acceleration toward state capitalism in the Caribbean. Moreover, the state acts invariably to protect those productive and service enterprises which it owns and in which it has a stake, using the full battery of its fiscal, financial, budgetary, and regulatory powers. As the state's ownership stake in the economy expands, the state's economic policies become instruments of advancing its corporate investment interests, disguised often as the national interests, in circumstances that often are prejudicial to the interests of major classes in the society. As this process evolves, the state bureaucracy becomes more and more the instrument of bureaucratic capitalism and corporate interests not owned by the domestic capitalist class.

The natural enemies of Caribbean forms of state capitalism are the domestic capitalist class, whose role in the economy is restricted, limited, and diminished by the expansion of the state's role and by the working class, who confront the state in the hostile domain of employer-employee antagonisms. The conflict with the capitalist class takes the form of an ideological and power confrontation where the political directorate (as in Jamaica) professes socialism and defends its increased economic power in socialist ideological terms. The conflict between the state capitalist regime and the workers takes the form of an economic wage struggle. The effect, however, is to alienate organized labor from socialist ideology by associating socialism with anti-worker tendencies. This development is accelerated where tight wage control policies and price-escalating devaluation policies are pursued to control inflation and meet the demands of international aid agencies and investors.

The Caribbean state in the postindependence era has also inherited a legacy of authority controlled by complex bureaucratic procedures that mystify and alienate the masses. The illegitimacy of that inherited authority is rooted in the popular mass notions of the distant and alien character of a government which has served privileged interests over the centuries of colonial rule. In the eyes of the masses, privileged class preferment, bias, and patronage have tarnished governmental institutions with an anti-people bias. To the masses, hope for justice rests with politicians and political parties who force the essentially unjust institutions to function in their favor. Noncomprehension of the operative bureaucratic rules, resentment at overt class discrimination and bureaucratic arrogance, added to a sense of powerlessness before the whims and seeming arbitrariness of the governmental process, preserve these negative orientations intact even in the "transitional" or immediate postindependence era.

The emergence of mass parties, popular leaders, and elected governments as the political directorate managing the state's institutions only partially reduced these negative orientations in the second stage of the decolonization process. Parties, dominant personalities, and elected governments are accredited with legitimacy, but the institutions of government still attract profound distrust. The problem is compounded by the fact that the vast knowledge gap between the middle-class technocracy and bureaucracy and their mass clientele generates suspicion and distrust, since the people (because of the backwardness of the education system) feel vulnerable to manipulation and lack the knowledge base to confidently verify or assess "authoritative" information received from the bureaucracy. The end result is a "game" of mutual suspicion, distrust, manipulation, noncommunication and the cunning disguise of real intentions and goals. The effort is to limit the mobilization capability of the state's institutions.

Finally, the state falls victim to a crisis of credibility in all Caribbean societies because of the "excess social demand" built into the political system (Stone 1973). Social and material expectations, as well as social problems, grow at a rate beyond the resource capability of these societies as presently organized. Located on the periphery of North America, with strong mass media links and social immigrant ties to the latter (strengthened by common language), the Caribbean represents a virtual poor suburb on the fringes of North American affluence and high consumption. Consumption tastes in the urbanized centers are heavily influenced by those in North America and bear little relationship to economic and income opportunities in the Caribbean. More importantly, rapid urbanization combined with high birth rates, the decline of agriculture production, and the limited labor-absorptive capacity of the new service and manufacturing industries have meant upwardly spiraling unemployment levels, continued nutritional problems, poor housing, and overcrowded and overtaxed public and social services and amenities. The physical infrastructure of modernity has been erected in the Caribbean against a background of social demands and pressures for qualitative improvement in the level of living for an increasingly militant, expectant people. These pressures are generated in a context in which public and private resources of wealth, knowledge, and organization fall far short of minimal and acceptable levels of fulfillment of these demands. As a result, governments elected with massive mandates are predictably and frequently turned out of office by the electorate in competitive party systems. One-party-dominant systems based on racial polarization often generate mass withdrawal from electoral involvement by the alienated. Stable one-party dominance invariably rests on corrupt practices, electoral manipulation, and the intimidation of opposition forces by loyal security forces and armed political thugs.

Excess social demand from the social and economic problems and pressures fashions a style of politics which seeks to extend periods of high mass credibility and legitimacy by heavy reliance on symbolic assurances and manipulation of mass aspirations. Highly developed organs and channels of political propaganda financed by the state; promotional buildup of party leaders as messianic, biblical, or magical figures; identification with hostility toward well established symbolic "enemies" (such as the planter class, imperialism, capitalists, alien racial groups or minorities, privileged non-nationals, migrant labor) and identification with symbols of mass culture all form part of the armory of symbolic politics. The content of symbolic politics is therefore a diversion from the central policy dilemmas which arise from this pressure of excess social demands.

In the weaponry of symbolic politics, ideology and ideological concepts become transformed into slogans designed to generate supportive mass responses, rather than ideas intended to convey clearly articulated policy intentions and programmatic goals. Radical ideological pronouncements do not unusally accompany conservative-reformist policy intentions and initiatives. As a mobilization device, such ideological symbolism fails to develop as guides to action or effective instruments of mass education. Rather than advance mass political understanding, they merely titilate millenarian expectations. Political communication is heavily shrouded in coded symbolic messages replete with emotional appeals but with little informative content. Political debate therefore assumes the character of exchange in emotive sloganeering often disguised in some societies by ideological language. The masses play the game by learning to evoke ritual fervor indicating emotional support, but with an absence of real or even partial comprehension of the content and meaning of many of the symbolic political messages. Leaders and followers play the game with an intensely involved sense of drama and spontaneity that disguises its ritual and superficial character.

The Decolonization Process in Jamaica

Jamaica is clearly one of the Caribbean states that in the 1970s entered fully the second stage of the decolonization process. It therefore provides an interesting case study from which to examine the decolonization process as it reflects both the weaknesses and the strengths of the Caribbean state system.

Although currents of social and political protest can to traced back to much earlier periods, the decolonization movement in Jamaica began essentially with the formation of the People's National Party (PNP) in 1938. This party represented a coalition of members of the middle-class intelligentsia which put the issue of self-government on the agenda and attempted to politicize the masses around commitment to local management of the state and a nationalist political identity. The PNP emerged as one of two alternate oppositions to the colonial regime. The Jamaica Labour Party (JLP) emerged as the second alternative opposition, representing not a nationalist force but a trade union party working on behalf of the working class and the poor peasants.

The majority of the masses still remained wedded to empire loyalties. While bargaining militantly for better wages and social conditions and more say in the local political arena, the working class and the peasantry viewed the metropolitan power and its continued overlordship in Jamaica in terms of a benevolent paternalism supported because it brought material benefits.

Even the PNP, however, had a limited view of decolonization (Munroe 1972). The central focus was on the claim by the middle-class intelligentsia that it had mastered British culture and could therefore be entrusted with taking over from the colonial overlords the running of the institutions of state. The masses, they insisted, were "civilized enough" to participate more fully in the political process. No demands were made for immediate self-rule, nor were any attacks mounted on the economic aspects of British and other external control of the Jamaican economy. Indeed, the assumption was that the benevolent paternalism of the British imperial interest would continue to prevail indefinitely (Stone 1974), and that on top of it could be added a large inflow of North American investment, the security of which would be guaranteed by stable parliamentary rule.

The masses initially rejected the lukewarm decolonization position of the PNP, supporting instead the anti-decolonization and "bread and butter" union politics of the JLP. Between 1944 and independence in 1962, the JLP's nationalist position converged with that of the PNP. Two operative factors account for the change. First, the PNP rapidly grew into the larger of the two parties by capturing the loyalty of the youth, the younger workers and younger peasants and the more literate, upwardly mobile and urbanized sectors of the labor force. The PNP grew especially strong in those new areas of economic expansion that created more literate, urbanized and socially aware additions to the labor force in the expanding and growing areas of service and manufacturing production that accompanied the postwar diversification of the Jamaican economy. Both the PNP challenge and the intergenerational changes affecting the growth of more positive nationalist sentiments and consciousness in the labor force pushed the JLP to a more nationalist position.

Second, both sets of party leaders increasingly concentrated their energies on preparing the way for local management of the state, beginning with internal self-government in the 1950s. JLP leaders, like the PNP leaders, therefore, came to recognize that they had a vested interest in promoting some form of self-government since it implied an increased increment of power for those who managed the institutions of state (Munroe 1972).

In the gradual process by which the state's control was shifted from British colonial officials to local politicians, the relations between the state and the local class structure also changed. The planter-merchants continued to influence public policy, but they had to contend with two growing constraints on their manipulation of the state. These were the growing independent power of the middle-class petty bourgeois politicians who inherited a state system which still had for a short time the aura of legitimacy and authority left by the imperial power. Second, the state was now increasingly being used to promote and assist the weaker classes, such as the peasantry and the urban poor, with expanded bureaucratic and social services and technical and financial inputs. This latter initiative was encouraged by the Colonial Office and aggressively supported by the petty bourgeois party leadership to establish a basis for legitimizing their leadership and their competing party machines. Patron-clientelism and service institutions oriented toward meeting the needs of the poor and the oppressed thus became the central legitimizing bases for the state and replaced the imperial legitimacy of the colonial state.

This situation, however, created a problem. The process of mass legitimation was extended to the politicians and their party machines. The state's institutions were always seen as remote and alien, but under colonial rule they enjoyed an aura of authority based on the imperial legitimacy of the British Crown and the supporting "myths" of benevolent paternalism and British justice and fairplay. The withdrawal of imperial legitimacy left the state with only party legitimacy and the personal legitimacy of charismatic figures and political patrons and bosses as a protective umbrella, but also with the tradition of remoteness and alienation from the people. Between internal self-government in 1953 and independence in 1962, the legitimacy of the state's institutions suffered from the intra-elite contentions for ascendancy over institutional and bureaucratic power between the senior public servants (socialized in the colonial period) and the newly emergent and impatient political leadership urged on by popular pressures and the excess social demands built into the social system.

In the postindependence period the massive and growing state bureaucracy functions almost as a power base for the conservative middle class. The middle-class-controlled state bureaucracy contends with the lower-class-influenced party machines, continuing the contentions between "party politics" and "administrative politics." The effect is to erode the legitimacy of the state's institutions in the perceptions of the masses while enhancing the legitimacy of the competing party machines and the political leadership which controls them.

The result is weak government, as politics disrupts administration and hidden class contentions between the middle and lower classes foment antagonisms between service institutions and the clients they are designed to serve. The weak mass legitimacy of the institutions of the state means that the state performs the requisite management and regulatory functions very poorly while performing the rationalizing and goal definition roles adequately. As a consequence, leadership becomes consumed with the latter two functions at the expense of under-performance in the other two functions. This deficiency has fundamental implications for the decolonization process in Jamaica, particularly in light of its development along a state capitalist path. Added to the traditional service function of the state are the rapidly expanding production and economic management tasks inherent in state capitalism.

In addition, the colonial traditions of the civil service, with its emphasis on legalism, proper procedure, and time-wasting paper work, was never attuned to the overall development tasks to which the state had to respond in the immediate preindependence period and, even more so, in the postindependence period.

The main policy emphasis and directions pursued by the state have varied in the different stages of the decolonization process. Between the early stages of the decolonization movement and internal self-government in 1953, the colonial state responded to political and social protest by initiating welfare and social policies designed to palliate the militancy of the working class and peasantry. These included minimum wages, land settlement and redistribution, agricultural credit, agricultural co-op development promotion, and increased expenditure on public works and infrastructural development to facilitate more employment.

This attempt at a client relationship between the state and the more oppressed classes was designed to stabilize the society in the face of the social and political pressures created by excess social demands. The growth in social and economic expenditures over the period in the areas of agriculture, social welfare, and public works reflected the new emphases. The state had finally won the battle with the planter-merchant oligarchy, which had militantly sought to restrict tax revenue by limiting the expenditure burdens assumed by the state vis-à-vis the social and economic needs of the poor peasantry and the subproletariat.

Having established a client relationship with the more oppressed classes, the colonial state sought in the period after internal self-government to take on (in addition) the role of coordinating and orchestrating the path to modern capitalist development. This attempt to sponsor accelerated modern capitalist development took place against the background of a convergence of ideological tendencies between the two dominant political parties—the JLP and the PNP.

Initially, and between 1938 and 1952, the presence of an influential left-leaning faction of the middle-class intelligentsia in the PNP produced an espousal of socialist goals which complemented that party's nationalist objectives. These socialist policy objectives included advocacy of greater state ownership of the critical sectors of the economy, cooperative worker-peasant ownership in agriculture, and the development of enlarged worker-peasant influence in the polity through the creation of more democratic organizational forms and mass political education. The JLP, on the other hand, attacked state ownership and socialist ideas as disguised communism and anti-Christian political heresy designed to enslave the masses on behalf of the hegemony of the "brown middle class" PNP leaders. On this ideological cleavage, the JLP aligned its lower-middle-class-led and older generation worker-peasant mass support with the planter-merchant oligarchy in opposition to the PNP's socialist posturing. Neither party had the power to pursue any clear ideological direction over this period, since state power was still in the hands of the colonial officials (Munroe 1972). To this extent, the ideological differences were mainly symbolic rather than programmatic and represented opposition-party alternatives to the colonial regime.

The economy up to that point consisted of a dominant export sector in sugar and banana production supported by small peasant production of domestic food crops and a large commercial sector distributing imported consumer goods (Jefferson 1972). The export sector was controlled by large foreign-owned enterprises and the traditional big landowning families complemented by middle-sized peasant production.

The thrust toward more modern capitalist development attempted to harness foreign capital investment to stimulate growth and generate a more dynamic domestic capitalist class operating in the nontraditional areas of manufacturing production, tourism, food processing, real estate, and the revitalized financial and commercial sectors. Implicit in these efforts was the objective of discovering a path to growth and diversification beyond the increasingly apparent limits of monocrop plantation production and the vicious circles of fluctuating fortunes and foreign income tied to the traditional export staples.

The discovery of bauxite and the opening up of bauxite mining fueled by U.S. and Canadian corporate investments set the stage for a harnessing of local energies in this general direction. Complementing this new thrust toward capitalist modernization was the abandonment of its leftist goals by the PNP leadership hierarchy and the jettisoning of socialist goals and ideology in 1952.

The period between 1953 and independence, in 1962, saw an ideological convergence of the two parties around the common goal of modernizing capitalist development in partnership with North American investment. This development was reinforced by a promoted expansion of an urban-based national bourgeoisie around import substitution and manufacturing, tourism, corporate finance and banking, real estate, and construction (Jefferson 1972).

The inherent weaknesses of PNP socialism and its retreat in the face of countervailing ideological forces can be traced to several factors. The socialist ideas espoused by the PNP were an offshoot of colonial British influences rooted in an imitation of the British Labor Party. It represented a vague commitment to state ownership operating within a mixed economy which permitted and encouraged corporate capitalist expansion, but sought to tax profits in order to finance welfare or redistributive social policies for the poor. Welfare socialism and state ownership had no methodology or prescription for expanding the productive base of the economy to meet the needs of the growing surplus social demands in the society. The accepted view of the society as poor, small, and endowed with limited resources encouraged the broad consensus that foreign capital, entrepreneurial dynamism and technology were prerequisites for the level and scope of economic modernization required. The continued assumption of the benevolent paternalism of metropolitan power centers both in Europe and North America and the feeling of fatalistic dependence on trade and transactional links with these advanced economies suggested the desirability and inevitability of continued but diversified incorporation within the world system of international capitalism. PNP leftists had no answers to these pragmatic issues of survival, growth, and economic viability. Uneven development creates a basis for an ideology of dependence.

The Jamaican economy shifted from the domination of agricultural export staples to a more diversified dominant modern sector including bauxite and alumina, tourism, manufacturing production and food processing, construction and real estate, expanded service and utility sectors, and corporate finance and banking.

The rapid growth that took place expanded and increased the power domain of all elite interests that converged around a broad consensus about directions, priorities, goals, and the agenda of issues to guide political debate in the party arena and communication media. The old elite formation of white colonial officials, and white and brown planter-merchants accommodating the newly emergent mid-elite of brown and black party politicians and trade union leaders, gave way to a new elite formation. No clear pattern of ascendancy emerged, but there evolved instead a coordinate system of functionally interrelated elites with clearly defined domains of autonomy and a commitment to mutual support.

Party leaders and governmental officials had responsibility for maintaining a stable social order to facilitate an environment compatible with enhancing the security and confidence of foreign and local investment capital. The party leaders allocated patronage benefits to all classes and guaranteed mass legitimacy to the state through party support and welfare pork barrel politics. They mystified the masses with charismatic manipulation and outpourings of propaganda which played on their expectations while constantly promising to administer the system on their behalf. These symbolic assurances (millenarian and utopian in the case of the PNP and pragmatic in the case of the JLP), complemented by the use of revenue to allocate marginal benefits to the poor, incorporated the masses into the state system. Frustrations with utopian PNP promises that heightened mass expectations led to support for JLP pragmatism in the 10-year cycles of alternations in office between the two parties.

Divisive class and racial issues were excluded from the agenda of party debate and political discussion in the mass media. A convergence of conservative party elitism transformed the two parties into two committees or factions of the newly unfolding regime of modern capitalism.

Trade union leaders bargained militantly for more wages, but mainly on behalf of the better-off strata of the labor force located in the modern sector of the economy. They narrowed their role to plant-level collective bargaining while concentrating on intense intraunion rivalries for dues-paying membership. The earlier role, whereby the unions merged with the two main political parties as a class lobby advocating broad social and political changes on behalf of the majority of the poor, was abandoned in favor of a narrow collective bargaining function. In the process, a separation of functions and specialization of roles increasingly differentiated the unions from their affiliate political parties. Nonideological business unionism thus became institutionalized as a complement to the new modernization of the capitalist system and to the coordinating and overall public management functions of the party leaders.

The business class was accorded due respect and deference in economic matters, and its leading spokesmen played key advisory roles in all spheres of public policy. They occupied leading and directing roles in public corporations and statutory boards which emerged as part of the rapid growth segment of the public sector. The latter brought private sector influence, thinking, and expertise into the public sector to complement and often usurp the administrative and advisory role of the traditional civil service.

Emerging alongside the new political directorate, the union leaders and the urban bourgeoisie comprised a growing and increasingly influential professional middle class in the public and private sectors of the economy. As the economy expanded, and as the new coordinate power elite consolidated local control of the institutions of state, the professional middle class merged with the political and business elite into a tightly knit power elite. This power elite administered and managed all key domains of power on the basis of rules of the game that guaranteed the autonomy of each elite segment, ideological consensus and mutual intraelite support and solidarity. At the center of the emergent power elite was the lubricant of bauxite investments by North American corporations, which fueled the underlying growth.

The spectacular growth of the economy over the 1950 to 1962 period created a situation in which there was a nonzero sum increase in the power base and power domain of all four segments of the coordinate power elite. As corporate profits and private wealth accumulated, the new bourgeoisie's economic power and political influence grew. As the economy diversified and expanded, dues-paying union membership also expanded, as did the bureaucratic apparatus in the public and private sectors manned by the professional middle class. As the economy expanded, so did public sector revenue, jobs, and patronage resources to increase the patron-client support base of the party leaders. Also, as the economy modernized, the role of the public sector grew considerably beyond the traditional law and order, defense, and service functions and spilled over into the area of economic services and management.

The dilemmas between welfare expenditure and revenue-financed social benefits for the poor and the demands of the capitalist system for the maximum accumulation of capital and wealth to enhance investment growth and job creation did not appear on the agenda of policy discussion. Rapid growth sustained the illusion that both could be maximized at the same time. Ideological notions of class conflict were viewed as mischievously irrelevant attempts to create antagonism where harmony existed, in spite of militant class bargaining over income shares. Foreign investment interests were seen as perfectly compatible with local political and bourgeois interests, and intellectuals who challenged this orthodoxy were isolated as irresponsible troublemakers. No power contentions emerged between the public and private sectors as the former promoted the latter by appropriate fiscal and regulatory policies, and the latter was encouraged to believe that its interests were identical with the interests of the nation.

As Jamaica entered the postindependence period of the 1960s, the four-sectored power elite was safely entrenched in power in spite of muted sounds of discontent within the militant strata among the nonunionized subproletariat and the unemployed urban lumpenproletariat.

The full transfer of state power to local hands was preceded by the first major disagreement within the power elite over the political direction to be followed. Although they clung to the belief in metropolitan benevolent paternalism, the power elite as a whole favored continued membership in the British-promoted Federation of the West Indian Islands to overcome the disadvantages of small size and weak bargaining power vis-à-vis the metropolitan power centers. Sensing the growth of a reasonably strong Jamaican territorial nationalism in the 1938 to 1958 period, however, the JLP challenged this consensus and won a referendum (which pulled Jamaica out of the Federation) and the 1962 "independence" election. the contentions over federalism or unitary status for independent Jamaica pushed into the background the growing economic and social discontent among the nonunionized lumpen and subproletariat.

The spectacular economic growth experienced left behind the poorest 50 percent of the labor force, increased sharply the levels of income inequality, and projected into focus sharp contrasts in living standards between the newly affluent and those trapped in persistent rural and urban poverty.

During the economic growth period of the 1950s and early 1960s, the only voice of protest was that of the Rastafarian movement, a millenarian sect which rejected the Jamaican power elite and advocated migration to Africa and an Ethiopian national identity. Its focus was African cultural and religious consciousness, and it articulated the alienation of the lumpen and subproletariat. In its prophetic vision, the power elite was a latter-day Babylon set to rule over the black majority to punish them. True redemption and liberation were to be found in an escape into African identity and religiosity, not in political rebellion.

By implicitly challenging the hitherto unquestioned assumption about the desirability of full incorporation into a world system dominated by white metropolitan power centers, Rastafarianism created a revolution of popular consciousness on the racial and national questions. By legitimizing black and African identity symbols, by challenging the moral basis of a white world and local power domination, and by projecting a myth of black superiority, the Rastafarian movement generated a new level of national consciousness that influenced many among the younger generation of urban masses. Out of this emerged a challenging Black Power movement that in the late 1960s forged an alliance between the left university intelligentsia, students, and militant ghetto youth to demanding an end to local and foreign ownership of the means of production and black majority control of the economic system.

In the decade immediately following independence the growth process, fueled by foreign investment in bauxite and import substitution, came to an end. Unemployment increased, food production declined, inflation reached unprecedented levels, and private sources of investment capital dried up. This leveling off of the momentum of the domestic economy quickly developed into a prolonged period of negative growth in the 1970s, triggered off by worldwide inflationary trends, oil price increases, fluctuation in export income, and the recession in the dominant centers of world capitalism.

It is against this background that the PNP government led by Michael Manley came to power in 1972 and sought to define a renewed effort at decolonization. The economic decline shattered all the assumptions of metropolitan benevolent paternalism. The decline of foreign private investment removed the material basis for the hitherto unquestioned and slavish pro-U.S. foreign policy pursued by the JLP government between 1952 and 1972. The emergence of the powerful OPEC lobby of oil-producing countries set the stage for the establishment of a bauxite producers' lobby, the IBA, in which Jamaica played a leading role. The nationalization of U.S. MNC property in Guyana, Peru, and Bolivia suggested possibilities for militant positions vis-à-vis foreign capitalist interests that implied a weakening of U.S. hegemony in the region. All these international developments pointed to the need for greater Third World collaboration and alliance linkages at the expense of metropolitan ties.

On the domestic front, the new PNP government had coopted into its ranks most of the alienated and the militants who had opted out of the two-party system. It embraced into its fold communists, socialists, Rastafarian militants, Garveyites, and the Black Power radicals and alienated ghetto youth who joined forces with the traditional PNP working class, peasants, middle-class and capitalist support. The militants warmed to Manley's populist style, which grew progressively leftist as pressures mounted from within this coalition for a new order of social justice and majority control of the economic forces currently in the hands of the ethnic minorities that owned the leading sectors of the economy.

The convergent pressures and promptings on the international and domestic fronts generated a return to ideological politics in the reaffirmation of socialism by the PNP; the denunciation of imperialists, ethnic minorities, capitalists, and the U.S. by leading governing party spokesmen; and a counteroffensive of anticommunist and antisocialist attacks from the opposition JLP and the leading spokesmen in the capitalist class. It was a return to the war of ideological rhetoric of the 1940s, but with three critical differences. The new ideological politics now had a firm following of committed militants among cadres of urban youth and disaffected intellectuals. This new ideological polarization involved foreign actors both real and mythical. And the two party leaders, Manley and Seaga, were (unlike the party leaders during the first wave of ideological politics in the 1940s) the main driving forces propeling the war of ideological symbols on either side.

Socialist reaffirmation by the PNP was rapidly joined to rhetorical posturing of antagonism to imperialism and to the U.S., and was complemented by the posturing of Third World solidarity and fraternity with Communist Cuba 90 miles to the north. Out of this a new foreign policy was born between 1974 to 1976. A posturing of socialism on the domestic front was a prerequisite for Third World legitimacy and fraternity with its leading spokesmen and states, especially Cuba and Tanzania. The pressures for socialist development on the domestic scene in turn demanded new alliances and linkages outside of the traditional North Atlantic framework of metropolitan capitalist dominance.

In response to the increase in petroleum prices and the anticipated cost of imports, the Manley government in 1974 unilaterally increased its foreign exchange revenue intake from bauxite by imposing a levy on the bauxite companies. This levy was imposed after negotiations on a demand for more revenue were at a point of deadlock due to resistance by the U.S. and Canadian companies. The government asserted its sovereignty by imposing the levy by legislative fiat, with solid bipartisan and broad multi-class national support. The levy had the effect of raising the foreign exchange revenue earnings from approximately $25 million to approximately $180 million per year.

The impact of this decision was to enhance and strengthen nationalist sentiments and confidence that corporate foreign interests were not beyond the reach of the sovereignty of the state. The issue itself was amicably resolved in the long run when the leading companies entered into partnership arrangements with the government in ownership of the local bauxite plants and mining operations after withdrawing the international litigation initiated by them.

Relations between the Manley government and U.S. administration of President Ford cooled considerably between 1974 and 1976, as fraternal links between Jamaica and Cuba intensified over the period. As the Jamaica-Cuba links increased, the JLP, the local and the North American mass media, the local business class in both the merchant and manufacturing sectors, and a vocal minority among the professional middle class orchestrated a chorus of accusations about impending communist tendencies and directions within the governing PNP. Jamaica became another example of conservative local and foreign interests converging to create political hysteria to block a center-left regime from proceeding with what appeared to be a commitment to radical leftist changes.

To be sure, concrete evidence of far left policy developments were not much in evidence. The real basis for the accusations of communist drift was related to the close links developing between the PNP and the

Cuban Communist Party, the emergence of a coalition of influential leftist leaders in the PNP as key advisors to the Prime Minister and party leader Manley, and the growing radicalism and anticapitalism of the latter's public statements.

While the majority of the Jamaican electorate continued to be hostile to communism, the anticommunism campaign failed, as Manley's denial of communist intentions struck chords of mass support and credibility within the populist mass expectations for social and material betterment which his rhetoric evoked. The masses had long been accustomed, in the island's political traditions to hostility from elite interests toward ideas and proposals for change that would benefit the masses. The more the conservative coalition of interests attacked socialism and anti-imperialism, the more support for the Manley government consolidated. The PNP won the 1976 election with a 57 percent popular vote.

Where these conservative ideological tendencies failed to turn the tide of public opinion against the Manley government they succeeded in destroying private investors' (foreign and local) confidence in the economy. There was a massive outflow of capital and foreign exchange by business interests alarmed into a panic by the anticommunist propaganda. Both manufacturing and merchant activities were jolted by the drying up of hitherto reliable sources of foreign supplies, credit, and financing. Investment plans were hastily set aside, presumably until the political uncertainties cleared, and many business enterprises closed in quick succession as their owners and managers migrated in waves of panic to the U.S. and Canada. No private capital came into the country from North America as OPIC and other agencies cautioned against the dangers of expropriation while others, such as the U.S. Department of Commerce, warned U.S. suppliers against the impending collapse of the Jamaican economy.

This flight of capital had the effect of accelerating the process of state capitalism. As enterprises failed or faltered, government stepped in to keep employment going or to assume responsibility where it had guaranteed large loans to private interests. As the foreign exchange crisis intensified, the state was forced to set up elaborate machinery for the regulation and distribution of foreign exchange and import licenses. Moreover, the exigencies of the crisis forced the state to assume a larger and larger role in the management of the economy in such areas as banking, finance, credit, imports, and exports.

Immediately following the elections, the government announced that it had rejected proposals to seek foreign exchange assistance from the IMF on the grounds that the IMF was an imperialist institution. This followed a flood of allegations by government party spokesmen that the CIA had joined forces with the opposition party, the JLP, in sabotaging the national economy and in attempting to defeat the elected government of the people. The left in the PNP under the party's General Secretary D. K. Duncan, appeared to be taking over the direction of economic policy from the traditional party moderates with the full backing of the Prime Minister. Self-reliance and anti-imperialism were announced as the essence of the new direction. Marxist economic advisors and economists reputed for their militant nationalist and anti-imperialist positions were recruited by the left in the governing party to chart the new course forward.

While all this leftward drift was appearing to accelerate, the leading moderate in the government, P. J. Patterson, was given the Foreign Ministry portfolio, and lines of communication opened up with the new Carter government in the U.S. and its black congressional support. The advisors of the left were given a mandate to prepare an anti-imperialist economic plan as an alternative to the IMF austerity route. In the process, there was a build up of mass mobilization in meetings and teach-ins all over the country and in extensive leftist rhetoric on the government-owned mass media (television and radio).

These developments caused greater panic within the ranks of both the local capitalists and the middle class and triggered further waves of emigration and capital flight. Mobilization of leftist popular backing for these initiatives concentrated on the 30 percent of PNP voters and mass following who supported the Marxist-Leninist route and pulled into its embrace Marxist-Leninist fringe organizations and intellectuals who joined forces with the left in the party.

A supporting left political thrust also emerged around leftist demands for a new constitution modeled on the Cuban constitution. A program of constitutional reform directed by leftists was also initiated to politicize the masses and tie constitutional change to sweeping revisions of land tenure, government's powers to acquire property, the development of popular and community based organizations, revision of the structure of the legislature and the executive, and the establishment of a republic.

After this massive buildup of anti-imperialist leftism, the PNP govenment reversed itself by rejecting the left direction and falling back on IMF support. The economic advisors of the left failed to come up with proposals to keep employment levels from declining on a massive scale and to enable minimal shortrun access to foreign exchange without which the entire economy would collapse into chaos.

The inevitable followed. The left was publicly discredited as IMF negotiations resumed and pragmatism replaced anti-imperialism. Overtures were made directly to President Carter to reestablish friendly relations. The moderates took over the party machine as the leadership of the left rapidly fell from grace. In the immediate aftermath of this rightward reversal, Fidel Castro was brought in on a state visit to endorse the pragmatism of the new directions and repudiate what was now defined as "ultra-leftism." The radical constitutional reform program was scaled down in size and its radical content diluted to fit the new situation.

The Jamaican government then proceeded to set up a tight austerity program designed to restrict wage increases, reduce inflation, restrict imports, and reduce government spending. The short-run effect was an acceleration of the recessionary trends in the economy as employment levels dropped dramatically, commodity shortages escalated, and mass alienation from the regime quickly replaced the euphoric populism that surrounded the 1976 election victory. Mass expectations for change were lowered. Cynicism and hopelessness replaced vibrant populist optimism between 1976 and 1977.

To be sure, the mass basis for the leftist anti-imperialist initiatives was quite tenuous, as the majority mass tendency was toward populism and not anti-imperialism. A national poll carried out by the author in May 1977 showed that 76 percent of the population favored U.S. aid. Another poll, done in September 1977, revealed that 60 percent of the population actively desired to migrate to the U.S.A.

As the economy slowed down, the mass public's rating of government's economic performance declined. Although a 52 percent majority gave the government credit for effort in the September 1977 poll, only 8 percent rated the performance as good. Most importantly, by September 1977, 66 percent of the voters of the country expressed the conviction that the economy would not improve for the remainder of the PNP's term of office. Between October 1976 and November 1977, the PNP's standing in mass support fell drastically by 9 percent. The trend pointed ominously to an increased pattern of antigovernment alienation and a failure of the opposition party to grow in absolute strength of mass support.

The real issue, however, is that in political systems like Jamaica, in which broadly based support is a precondition for remaining in power, decolonization can never be an end in itself. It has to be viewed by the political directorate as a means to enhancing accelerated social and economic development. Where it appears to conflict with mass welfare levels even in the short run, it is likely to be abandoned and scaled down for more neocolonial initiatives such as those that emerged in Jamaica. The issue is larger than Jamaica, and it must ultimately be analyzed in the context of the options of small, formerly colonial territories in the Caribbean region and the precise objectives of decolonization that arise from the parameters of late twentieth-century international power and economic constraints.

Bibliography

Beckford, George. *Persistent Poverty: Underdevelopment in Plantation Economies of the Third World* (New York: Oxford University Press, 1972).

———— (ed.). *Caribbean Economy* (Kingston: Institute for Social and Economic Research, University of the West Indies [hereafter given as ISER] 1975).

Eaton, George, *Alexander Bustamante and Modern Jamaica* (Kingston: Kingston Publishers, 1975).

Girvan, Norman. *Foreign Capital and Economic Underdevelopment in Jamaica* (ISER, 1971).

Hawkins, Irene, *The Changing Face of the Caribbean* (Bridgetown, Barbados: Cedar Press, 1976).

Jefferson, Owen. *The Postwar Economic Development of Jamaica* (ISER, 1972).

Lewis, Vaughan (ed.). *Size, Self-Determination and International Relations: The Caribbean* (ISER, 1976).

Marx, Karl. *The Eighteenth Brumaire of Louis Bonaparte* (New York: International Publishers, 1963).

Meier, Gerald. *Problems of Cooperation for Development* (New York: Oxford University Press, 1974).

Munroe, Trevor. *The Politics of Constitutional Decolonization: Jamaica, 1944–1962* (ISER, 1972).

Nettleford, Rex. *Manley and the New Jamaica: Selected Speeches and Writings, 1938 1968* (London: Longmans, 1971).

Stone, Carl. *Class Race and Political Behaviour in Urban Jamaica* (ISER, 1973).

————. *Electoral Behaviour and Public Opinion in Jamaica* (ISER, 1974).

————. "Perspectives on Decolonization: A Comparative Analysis of Parliamentary Speeches in Trinidad and Jamaica." *Journal of Social and Behavioural Sciences,* Fall 1974.

————. "Class and the Institutionalisation of Two-Party Politics in Jamaica." *Journal of Commonwealth and Comparative Politics,* July 1976.

————. *Stratification and Political Change in Trinidad and Jamaica* (Beverly Hills, Cal.: Sage Professional Papers, Vol. 2, Nos. 1–26, 1972).

Thomas, Clive. *Dependence and Transformation* (New York: Monthly Review Press, 1974).

4

Decolonization and Militarization in the Caribbean: The Case of Guyana

GEORGE DANNS

On the Nature of Colonization and Decolonization

Colonization represents a system of localized rule or domination by an imperial power over the peoples of another country who, initially at least, may be ethnically and culturally distinct. This system of rule involves political domination, economic exploitation of the labor power of the colonized peoples and the natural resources of their country, and sociocultural subjugation. Sustaining these three facets of colonial rule are a variety of distinct but interrelated institutional forms. In the political sphere, rational-legal or bureaucratic institutions manned by officials from the imperial country govern the colony and are the localized representatives of the imperial power. These officials form part of a colonial civil service, and each colony is often headed by a governor or administrator who represents the titular presence of the imperial monarch. In the economic sphere, a plantocracy in the area of agriculture and the local arms of multinational corporations in the area of industry predominate. In the sociocultural spheres, the church, the mass media, the educational system, and the whole style of life represent wholesale transplants from the metropolitan empire. The nature of sociocultural domination is such that these institutional patterns are superimposed on those of the colonized peoples and are established as proper, progressive, superior, and ideal or prototypical. Reinforcing this sociocultural imposition is the perpetration of myths and symbolic imagery or racial, ethnic, and cultural superiority.

It is important to note that all three spheres of domination, the political, economic, and sociocultural, mutually reinforce each other in maintaining the overall colonial rule. This is not to say, however, that conflicts do not arise at the interinstitutional and intrainstitutional levels. At the intrainstitutional level, the plantocracy may view as a threat and oppose the establishment and growth of transnational corporations in industry, while at an interinstitutional level it poses a serious challenge to the colonial bureaucracy. Indeed, in the latter instance, the American struggle for independence can be seen as resulting, among other things, from interinstitutional conflicts. Generally, however, institutional conflicts in colonial societies criss-cross and function to sew the social system together (Coser 1956).

If colonization represents a system of domination or rule by an imperial power, then decolonization must be seen as the process of bringing such rule or domination to an end. But in order to understand this process it is necessary to conceptualize a system of domination as a unique phenomenon. Max Weber defined his ideal types of domination in terms of the nature of legitimacy accorded it by the dominated and came up with a typology of charismatic, traditional and rational-legal or bureaucratic domination. Elsewhere (Danns 1976) it was shown that defining types of domination in terms of the nature of legitimacy tends to obfuscate the meaningful adequacy of the typology, since no allowance is made for the logical and conceptual opposite of legitimate domination—illegitimate domination. The legitimacy or illegitimacy of a system of domination rests on the consensual support or lack of such support for it by the dominated. Systems of domination can and do exist despite resistance and opposition to them by the dominated. Colonial domination in the Caribbean was conceptualized as a system of illegitimate bureaucratic domination in so far as the great masses of people were concerned, but as a system of legitimate bureaucratic rule in so far as the various ruling elites and the administrative staffs were concerned.

It is important to note here that as much as decolonization involves the systematic destruction or replacement of an existing system of foreign domination, it also requires its systematic replacement by an indigenous system of rule. In as much as it demands the systematic breakdown or transformation of supporting institutional patterns of colonial rule, it also requires the systematic creation or reconstruction of new institutional patterns of rule. In short, decolonization represents the systematic destruction of the social reality of a foreign presence and the construction or reconstruction of an indigenous reality. More concretely, in the Caribbean in general and Guyana in particular the process of decolonization involves:

1. The granting of political independence—the replacement of foreign political rule by local political rule.
2. The attempt at introduction of "new" or changed systems of ideologies and values to legitimize the new system rule.
3. The creation or recreation of supportive social institutions.
4. The "promise"—the proposal and planned implementation of strategies of development and modernization.
5. The wresting of economic control or ownership from the metropolitan countries.

Governments in the region are concerned with the removal and delegitimization of European colonial domination and the legitimization of their own peculiar system of domination. However decolonization may be conceived, it represents in the final analysis the replacement of an expatriate system of rule with a local or indigenous one. Tremendous social, political, and economic problems are encountered in the region, however, in the transition from the colonial system of domination to the establishment of a "national" system of rule. Because of this, decolonization is seen as a process of undoing and doing over. Some of the problems encountered in the decolonization process will be discussed later.

On the Nature of Militarization

Militarization refers to a condition in which increasingly large sections of the population of a society become progressively influenced by, or inducted in one way or another into, military or paramilitary institutions. It is a condition in which miiltary-type institutions become viewed by the ruling elite as an organizational panacea for the "ills" of external defense, social instability, indiscipline, and problems of national mobilization, control, and development within a society. It is a social condition in which regimentation is seen as a way of life. Individuals are either involved in or perpetually controlled by military institutions.

A society can be said to be militarized or experiencing militarization when several distinct military, paramilitary, and quasimilitary institutions are set up by a ruling elite with the expressed aim of mobilizing the members of society for one purpose or another. A "military" way of life is set up as one of the key cultural ideals or values of such a society. As a premium way of life, military status becomes a key variable in determining the class of status rankings of the members of such a society. Militarization in an excolonial society represents a particularly effective method for displacing an "old" indigenous elite and replacing them with a "new" and different type of elite.

The Problem

The nature of governmental rule in colonial and postcolonial Caribbean society can be immediately seen as authoritarian. The authoritarian character of colonial domination is clearly manifest in its history of slavery, indentured labor, and other forms of plantation peonage that are so typical of the region. The inability of the colonies to determine their own policy, both domestic and foreign, and the dictating of such policy by the imperial government are further indicative of this authoritarian rule. Colonialism is synonymous with authoritarianism, if not outright totalitarianism. Colonial society is a captive society.

While it is patently obvious that colonial rule is authoritarian, how do we explain the continuity of authoritarian rule by the nationalist governments of the independent countries or self-governing territories? In offering an explanation we must look at the society the nationalist governments inherited and the transformation they are trying to achieve. West Indian society is largely the creation of an imperial power and mirrors colonial domination in its purest form. Archibald Singham (1968:13) notes:

> The general disruption caused by colonial conquest was greatly complicated in the West Indies where a completely new social structure came into being. Unlike the pattern in Africa or Asia, the conquering power in one way or another had virtually exterminated the indigenous population in the West Indies and the island societies became the artificial creation of the colonial power, which planned and executed the transfer of population from Africa and Asia.

Slaves were imported from different parts of Africa for plantation work. With the abolition of slavery, Chinese and Indians were brought from Asia and Portuguese from Europe to serve as indentured laborers to fill the vacuum created by the African slaves who fled the plantations and settled in villages and towns. This involuntary assembly of peoples of different ethnic and cultural backgrounds who mixed but never intermingled led anthropologists such as Leo Despres (1967) and M. G. Smith (1965) to revive J. S. Furnival's notion of cultural pluralism in analyzing the social structure of the Caribbean. This ethnic diversity and cultural pluralism, and the conflicts resulting from these cleavages, were deliberately exacerbated, if not also designed, by the colonial system of domination pursuing a strategy of divide and rule.

Conflicts among the ethnically plural groups sustained colonial domination. Even after colonies were given independence or self-governing status, structural conflicts persisted. National governments are therefore constrained to be authoritarian, not only because they merely moved into the established seats of political power vacated by the colonial rulers, but also in order to maintain their unaccustomed rule amidst the conflicting and not infrequently violent interests within their society.

Yet another important factor resulting in the persistence of authoritarian rule is that of the crises of legitimacy currently experienced by Caribbean governments. These governments took over the reins of power from the imperial rulers in an aura of popularity and of presumed legitimacy. The leaders or "heroes" of the governing parties were given the consensual support of the people to govern. The challenge to bureaucratic colonial rule eroded the people's respect for such rational-legal systems of authority in favor of more personalized relationships between leaders and followers. The dominated in the colonial Caribbean saw the bureaucratic institutions of the colonial government as being distant, somewhat mysterious, and unresponsive to their needs. This crisis of obedience to a government organized along bureaucratic or rational-legal lines was itself aided and abetted by West Indian leaders, who felt that much of their administrative staffs were still steeped in their colonial ways or for other reasons recalcitrant to their demands (Danns 1978: 52–54).

The change-over from colonial rule and the occupation of top bureaucratic positions by locals did not really remove this basic distrust and hostility, but only converted them into a disrespect for government based on attitudes of mass cynicism toward governmental bureaucracy and ridicule of the incumbents. The more ruling parties and their leaders entrench themselves in government institutions built and vacated by the colonial rulers, the more the peoples of the region distrust and withdraw their legitimacy from them.

Along with the crisis of legitimacy that governments in the region are experiencing is a not unrelated crisis of credibility. In Guyana, for example, the government promised to "feed, clothe and house the nation by 1976," and as well to "make the small man a real man." These promises resulted in floods of rising expectation. The failure to meet them has resulted in outbursts of rising frustration and a concomitant credibility crisis. These rising frustrations are being rapidly transformed by the region's peoples into outbursts of rising political violence and protests directed at their governments. The one-time "fathers of the nation" are now being viewed increasingly as betrayers of the cause of the people. Faced with this crisis of credibility, and denuded of the halo of popularity and legitimacy enjoyed in the prein-dependence phase and early stages of their rule, the governments now rely on and use the authoritarian bureaucratic institutions they have inherited or created in order to maintain themselves in power.

If the politics of protest and aggression was the style of the leaders of national governments when in opposition prior to political indepen-dence and self-government, then the politics of suppression and de-fense became a logical and factually necessary approach if government was to be at all possible. The inheritance of an authoritarian sociopolit-ical structure from the colonial era seems to be a legacy that the na-tional governments cannot get rid of and find functionally imperative in the volatile postcolonial milieu. Authoritarian rule, which began as a voluntary and tailored adaptation by the metropolitan rulers, now ends up as a Hobson's choice for ruling governments of the region.

The problem facing governments in the region is one of how to maintain law and order, and how to mobilize their people for the pur-pose of decolonication, development, and societal transformation. These ruling elites attained political power and the other organizational objectives of their political parties and allied labor unions through agi-tation and the exarcerbation of dormant conflict. They conditioned their supporters to strike, to struggle, to demonstrate, and to protest against colonial rule. They have now inherited the authoritarian struc-tures of their predecessors and, as stated above, have been unable to meet the promises of prosperity and plenty for all. The people of the region react to them in the exact way that they reacted to their colonial predecessor, with the result that national governments have now be-come the "new colonizers." This fact underlies our position that just as colonization refers to a system of imperial domination, the essence of decolonization can only be its replacement by national or localized rule. It was already shown that the structural parameters for the exer-cise of national rule are, initially at least, delimited by the colonial experience.

In any authoritarian system of rule reliance on the instruments of coercion is pronounced. The greater the degree to which military and paramilitary institutions, "managers of the instruments of violence," are involved in day-to-day activities, the greater the degree of authori-tarianism. In the colonial Caribbean the imperial rulers relied on de-tachments from the British West India Regiments, the planters' militia, and the paramilitary police forces to maintain order and to suppress rebellion. In the postslavery period, however, the police were charged with responsibility for day-to-day maintenance of order. It is of interest to note that these police forces were established immediately after slavery was abolished and the ex-slaves fled the plantations and settled in villages and towns. The ex-slaves were seen as a serious threat to the plantocracy in particular and to imperial rule in general.

The history of colonial rule in the Caribbean is checkered with the frequent interventions of the military in suppressing civil uprisings and other forms of protest and disturbance. Although large detachments of the military were never really continuously present in any one colony, the imperial rulers, with their vast military resources, readily summoned in the event of an emergency such military assistance as was necessary. The independent countries in the region, however, could no longer rely on external military intervention in times of domestic political crises. It seems logical to conclude that the greater the threat of internal crises, particularly crises resulting in political violence, the greater the need to establish strong local military and paramilitary institutions. We have already argued that the structural conflicts that plagued the ex-colonies continued even in this largely postcolonial period. The necessity for continued military intervention and/or a strong military presence is essential if social order is to be at all possible. The larger and stronger the military and paramilitary institutions, the greater the perceived threat by the national governments to their rule. The greater the degree of military intervention, the more authoritarian is the regime.

Having outlined, in part, the conceptual framework of this chapter, we will now move on to a concrete examination of the former British colony of Guyana.

Decolonization in Guyana

Guyana attained political independence in May 1966, after nearly two hundred years of British colonial rule. It became a republic in February 1970, thus finally severing the ties of imperial political rule. The country is located on the mainland of South America and is the only English-speaking country in that region. It is bordered on the north by the Atlantic Ocean, on the south by Brazil, on the east by Surinam, and on the west by Venezuela. It has an area of 83,000 square miles and a population of approximately three quarters of a million. The population consists of six different races of people—East Indians, Africans, Whites, Portuguese, Chinese, and Amerindians. Table 1 gives an ethnic breakdown of the Guyanese population.

Despite its geographical location, Guyana shares a common culture with the people of the West Indies, and Guyanese commonly regard themselves, and are commonly regarded, as West Indians. The government of the country is headed by Forbes Sampson Burnham,

TABLE 1 / The Population Groups
of Guyana

Group	1970	Percentage of Total
East Indians	337,256	51.4
Africans	227,091	30.6
Mixed	84,653	11.2
Chinese	4,678	0.6
Portuguese	9,668	1.3
Amerindians	32,794	4.4
Whites	4,056	0.5
Total	740,196	100.0

Source: Statistical Department, Ministry of
Economic Development, George-
town, Guyana.

the powerful black leader of one of the two major parties, the People's National Congress (PNC). The other party, the People's Progressive Party (PPP) is headed by an East Indian, Dr. Cheddi Jagan. The majority of the PNC supporters are the largely black, urban-based population, while the PPP is supported by the largely rural-based East Indian population. There is a third significant party, the United Force (UF), which is supported by the minority Portuguese, Chinese, Amerindians, and mixed members of the population.

In the 1964 election, the UF, which was then headed by Portuguese businessman Peter D'Aguiar, merged with the PNC under a system of proportional representation to prevent the continuation of the PPP in government. The PPP had ruled the self-governing colony from 1957 until losing to the coalition. The coalition government was headed by Burnham, whose party later ran the government alone after skillfully persuading some UF members of parliament to cross the aisle. The PNC then won the 1968 elections after introducing "overseas votes" and proxy voting through the post office. The party also won the 1973 elections by a two-thirds majority, which empowers it to make alterations to the constitution.

It is of interest to note that the history of political participation in Guyana is one distinguished by intense racial conflict. The plurality of ethnic groups has been always continuously engaged in some form of internal warfare. Within the last two decades the two major ethnic groups, the East Indians and the Africans, have had the most bitter and most violent conflicts. In the early 1960s severe racial strife between these two ethnic groups plagued the country. Many lives were lost and many more were injured. Indians burned down the houses of the blacks and chased them out of the villages in which the former were predominant. Blacks, in turn, committed similar acts against the Indians in the urban areas. Not unnaturally, voting and elections were always conducted along serious racial lines, and party politics in the society was synonymous with race politics. The election victories by the black PNC party in 1968 and the winning of a two-thirds majority in 1973 were extraordinary feats in light of the prevailing race differences.

The last decade of colonial rule, then, was rife with party struggle along purely racial lines. This interethnic conflict led Leo Despres to conclude, in his analysis of Guyana as a plural society, that after the British withdrew and independence was granted, there would be serious interethnic conflict for control of the government. For the past fourteen years, this battle has been won by Burnham's PNC. Not unnaturally, the pattern of rule of this regime has been authoritarian. The mass media, radio, and press are largely owned or controlled by the PNC government. The government is the largest single employer of labor, and the allocation of jobs is not entirely unrelated to ethnic origin and, more importantly, to political loyalties. In this chapter, however, we wish to concentrate on the role of the military in maintaining this authoritarian rule and in furthering the process of decolonization and development.

Militarization in Guyana

Perhaps the most conspicuous feature in Guyanese society over the last five years is the high visibility of uniformed military and paramilitary personnel. Indeed, these uniformed personnel appear omnipresent to the civilian population because they are encountered at every few corners, in offices, in factories, and generally in the interior of the society going about their routine business. The Guyana Defence Force (GDF), the police, the Guyana National Service (GNS), and the People's Militia have a total estimated strength of close to 22,000 (see Table 2) compared to their total strength of 2,135 in 1964, when the PNC government first took office. the GDF, the GNS, and the People's Militia are all creations of the government. The Defence Force was formed in 1965, the National Service in 1975, and the People's Militia in 1976.

Indeed, the creation of the National Service and the People's Militia was a first within the region. So far, only Jamaica and Dominica have attempted to introduce a National Service institution, and the equivalent of a People's Militia exists only in Grenada.

The estimated total numerical strength of the armed forces repre-

TABLE 2 / *Estimated Organizational Strength of the Armed Forces**

	1964	1966	1977
Guyana Defence Force	500	750	4,000
Police	1,635	1,881	3,751
Guyana National Service	–	–	4,000
People's Militia	–	–	10,000
Total			21,751

*Information on the numerical strength of the GDF, GNS, and People's Militia are classified and not easily obtainable. The figures given were supplied by officers in the respective institutions. Those on the police were obtained from the 1977 estimates of the government of Guyana.

sents a 1000 percent growth in size since 1964. The GDF increased by 700 percent, the police by 100 percent, and the GNS and People's Militia by approximately 1000 percent since their formation in 1975 and 1976, respectively. In 1964 there was approximately one military employee for every 300 citizens. So rapid has been the growth of the military that by 1977, one in every 35 Guyanese was a member of the armed forces.

The meteoric growth in the size of military institutions in the country is paralleled by the increased proportion of the national budget spent on these institutions (see Table 3).

The expenditure on military institutions rose from about 2 percent of the national budget to 7.7 percent in 1973. Between 1973 and 1976 the proportion of expenditure on the military increased steadily and doubled over this four-year period. This marked increase in spending and meteoric growth in size of the military can be attributed to several factors. In the first place, since its independence in 1966, Guyana has experienced incursions and threats of incursions on its territorial borders by its larger and more powerful neighbors, Venezuela and Brazil. Surinam has posed a similar challenge. These external threats resulted in increased attention given to the military preparedness of the society. In the second place, the coming of independence and the declaration of republic status necessitated the establishment and strengthening of indigenous armed forces, since the country could no longer rely on the former colonial rulers to solve problems of internal disorder (and external aggression). Third, increased spending on military institutions, particularly those newly created by the ruling regime, reflects the need to provide new infrastructures and weaponry in this formative period.

Though the above reasons may in part justify the increases in expenditure and size of the military, they certainly do not explain the

TABLE 3 / Comparison of National and Defense Budgets

Year	Size of National Budget	Total Defense Budget	Percentage of National Budget
1973	290,636,261	22,494,569	7.7
1974	358,543,194	38,064,342	10.6
1975	580,701,957	78,917,236	13.5
1976	795,148,167	113,136,610	14.2

Source: 1977 Joint Estimates of the Government of Guyana.

variety and overall functioning of such institutions. In short, they may be necessary but not sufficient causes of the increasing militarization of Guyanese society. It appears that insofar as the military can be viewed as an institution of coercion and control, the increases in the size, expenditure, and diversity of the military are indicative of the growing reliance of the authoritarian PNC government on armed force in order to sustain its rule in the face of growing crises of legitimacy and credibility.

This rapid growth in the size and the variety of military institutions, coupled with the increasing proportion of the national budget allocated to them, is further evidence of the great emphasis laid by the governing regime on the role of the military in transforming the society. Militarization in Guyana is seen by the government as an approach to modernization and development of the society just as much as it is viewed as a strategy for control, mobilization, and external defense. Militarization in the society is the ruling regime's way of coping with the volatile postcolonial environment. Mobilization and control are seen as prerequisites to development, and military institutions are expected to combine all these roles in their operation. Indeed, strikes for prolonged periods in the sugar industry (Guyana's mainstay) witnessed the army, the police, and members of the National Service providing manpower to cut the cane and thus rescue the sugar crop. With the government as employer in the nationalized sugar industry, strikes by sugar workers are regarded as politically motivated, since the opposition leader, Cheddi Jagan, is the driving force behind the recognized Guyana Agricultural Workers' Union (GAWU). Thus, not only did the armed forces maintain order in the restless sugar belt, but they were also seen as contributing to national development by cutting the cane and breaking the strike directed at the government. Military intervention thus functions to ensure not only that social order is maintained at all costs, but also that efforts at developing the society are not subverted, and that a reliable supply of manpower is available in the event of disaffection by regular workers. It seems that as long as military institutions are continuously relied upon by the ruling regime as a panacea for the problems faced by its rule, it would be natural to expect the continued expansion of the military and the concomitant process of militarization of the society.

The great importance attached to the military and the process of militarization is further demonstrated by the fact that the Prime Minister himself assumes the title of Minister of Defense, directly in charge of the GDF, the GNS, and the People's Militia. The police come under the Minister of Home Affairs. As if to dramatize the importance of the military institutions for whose formation his government is responsible, the Prime Minister, who is not known to have had military training of any sort, wears a general's uniform on ceremonial occasions for both the GDF and the GNS. In addition, the Prime Minister is the chairman of the Defense Board, which includes the heads of all four military institutions. Although the President of the Republic of Guyana is also Commander-in-Chief of the Armed Forces, the Prime Minister, who controls executive power, can be considered the real head of the country's armed forces. In the following section we will take a closer look at the role and function of each military institution before proceeding with more general arguments.

The Guyana Defence Force

The Guyana Defence Force (GDF) emerged out of the British Guiana Special Service Unit (SSU) which was set up on February 26, 1964. The SSU was formed by the governor after recognition of the limitations of the police force and the British Guiana Volunteer Force (BGVF) in coping with the upsurge of civil unrest and political violence brought about by racial struggles between the two major ethnic groups.

The SSU was mandated to "preserve law and order and peace, repress internal disturbances, protect property, prevent and detect crime, apprehend offenders and perform such military duties as may be authorised by the Governor" (Granger 1975: 20). This unit was equipped to assist the police, and the BGVF, and its hybrid character enabled it to perform military duties as well as exercise powers of search and arrest. The SSU was commanded by police officers and unlike the police force and the BGVF, which both contained over 80 percent blacks, this unit consisted of equal portions of blacks and East Indian personnel. It should be noted that the Jagan government in 1962 attempted to set up a national army in the light of racial violence, but this move was vetoed by the governor, who then opted two years later for the SSU. Jagan had complained about the "ethnic imbalance" in the security forces which he felt were partisan in favor of the PNC. Perhaps among the reasons for the governor's veto was the fact that Jagan had declared himself a Marxist-Leninist and was pursuing socialist policies.

After the coalition government took over and independence for Guyana was guaranteed for May 26, 1966, the colonial regime permitted Burnham, whose policies were much less resentful to the Western powers, to transform the SSU into a full-time military organization to be known as the Guyana Defense Force, on November 1, 1965. The British garrison, which settled in the country as a consequence of the disturbances in the early 1960s, returned home, and the GDF was trained to replace it in carrying out internal security operations. It should be noted that the GDF was initially set up, organized, and trained by British officers. These officers left in 1968, after two years, and were replaced by Guyanese officers who understudied them during this period. Nevertheless, Colonel Ronald Pope, the commander of the army and an Englishman, did not give up his charge until 1969. Meanwhile, in 1968, the Burnham government for the first time won a clear majority over the PPP and the UF and set itself up in office for another four years of rule. It was ironic, however, that the nation's army was being tutored by British officers when the country was at the same time trying to sever ties from Britain. Not unexpectedly, the officers of the army behaved and acted as the British officers did, and the army was for all intents and purposes "British" in its outlook. Officer cadets were trained in Britain at Mons and Sandhurst military colleges.

It seems that the first task of the governing regime in consolidating its power was the decolonization of the army. In the light of the wave of military coups in Africa, in Latin America, and among new nations in general, the reorientation of the army was seen as imperative. This decolonization of the armed forces was to take place immediately after the country became a republic in February 1970. Indeed, it can be said that the GDF was the first institution into which the Burnham government implanted its concept of societal transformation and from which it demanded unquestioning legitimacy and loyalty. To date, the army in particular and the armed forces in general represent the only institutions which have been purged of the colonial normative structure. This hallmarks arguments made by Morris Janowitz (1964), John J. Johnson (1962), and Lucian Pye (1964) that the armed forces in new nations are not only developmentally superior institutions but also congenial receptacles for introducing and bringing about social change.

It took the April 1970 mutiny by the neighboring Trinidad and Tobago Regiment, which was also trained by British officers, to hasten this process of decolonizing the army. Prior to that time the local army had merely done away with wearing ties and crown-shaped epaulets and had begun to spearhead the development thrust in the country's interior in the form of building roads and other projects. On October 20, 1970, Prime Minister Burnham addressed the officers of the army laying out his government's policies and what role he expected the armed forces to play. He warned that the GDF was not, and was never intended to be, an elite corps of gentlemen. The British army is a "spit and polish" army, but the GDF is supposed to be a people's army that is part of the people and part of the society.

The Prime Minister made the officers aware of his government's intention to nationalize the major industries not owned by Guyanese and cautioned officers who were in opposition to this policy to resign. He commissioned the army with the task of building all major interior roads and, with their knowledge and commitment to his government's philosophy, to turn out "leaders in the community, and leaders in the society." The army must display a high sense of discipline to the people in Guyana, who "are singularly indisciplined and mistake indiscipline for democracy" (1970: 12). With this authoritarian note the Prime Minister saw as part of the role of the army imposing "discipline" on the rest of the society. Yet he contended that *"We are not a militarist country even if we are so inclined.* The GDF, therefore, while standing ready to carry out the two primary tasks of assisting the civil authorities and defending our borders, must be an army, a body of men and women identified and identifiable with the rest of the community and with the aims and aspirations of the nation. They must be leaders in the new things that are happening in Guyana and contribute to our making of Guyana" (1970: 19).

In this statement the Prime Minister clearly sees the military as an organizational panacea for societal transformation. Clearly, too, he assigns the military the position of leadership in bringing about this transformation and expects the army at one and the same time to support the policies made by his party and his government, even though it has no meaningful say and there is no structural or constitutional provision for the military playing a part in the formation of such policies. Clearly, his styling the army as "leaders in the community and leaders in the society" amounts to littls more than an ideology of legitimacy and a rhetoric of compliance. This point will be further developed later.

What was stated in words soon became expressed in action when the Prime Minister launched the Education Corps, which was set up with the expressed purpose of politicizing the army. Courses were initiated for both officers and enlisted ranks, and the government ministers and other officials who delivered lectures on the philosophy of the government soldiers soon dropped the title "sir" in addressing their officers and instead addressed them by their rank. The political education of the army was further reinforced by the officer corps, whose members belonged to the Social, Political and Economic Council (SPEC) that was set up by Minister of Information Elvin McDavid as a body for doing "backroom research" for the PNC. By the same token, all GDF officers were at one and the same time members of the ruling People's National Congress. These actions on the part of the government and the PNC served to ensure the continued surveillance and loyalty of the officer corps. Indeed, allegations of officers being sacked for criticizing the prime minister and making antiparty or antigovernment statements were not uncommon.

Not only is the GDF characterized by a high level of party infiltration, but also a great deal of personalism. The Prime Minister takes a direct hand in the promotion and firing of officers. Noting this, Cynthia Enloe states: "The power that the Prime Minister exercises over the GDF is such that he takes a direct hand in promotions—a power important in a force that is too small to have a very elaborate assortment of senior rankings" (1976: 86).

In 1971, a major shakeup occurred in the army. According to an informed source, "the shakeup which involves either the honourable discharge, transfer or promotion of some nine officers has come in the midst of what informed sources described as a concentrated effort to politicise the army" (*Guyana Graphic*, Thursday, January 6, 1972). The shakeup involved, among other persons, the first Guyanese commander of the GDF, Col. Clarence Price, who was, in the opinion of some, "kicked upstairs" by being promoted to the rank of brigadier, and became chief-of-staff and military adviser to the Prime Minister. The other officers were senior army officials who were in their mid-forties and who came across from the Volunteer Force. These men were either retired, sent on overseas courses, or sent back to perform civilian duties in other sections of the Public Service. Writing on the history of the army, Lieutenant Colonel David Granger, Education Officer at the time, described the event as "far reaching structural changes which permitted greater flexibility and mobility" (1975: 42). Granger, then, saw the move as an attempt to create avenues of vertical mobility for the younger and more committed officers, as well as an attempt to facilitate the unquestioning obedience to the Prime Minister which the older officers, more steeped in the British tradition and at the same time contemporaries of Burnham, may not have given so easily. Cynthia Enloe (1976: 86–87) reasoned that these officers may have resented the personalism and party infiltration of the army. Opposition leader Cheddi Jagan viewed this event with deep suspicion and felt that it clearly indicated "the sinister intentions of the government to establish a police state" (*Sunday Graphic,* January 9, 1972, p. 5).

However, the entire sequence of events involving the politicization, party penetration, and infiltration of the GDF may have been viewed, it is our contention that these events can be analyzed as being part of the deliberate process of the decolonization of the army.

In trying to analyze the purpose of the regime in securing the army's loyalty to the Prime Minister, the PNC, and the government, it is necessary to understand the relationship among them. The regime's position is that the party would "assume unapologetically its paramountcy over the government" (*News Release,* Embassy of the Republic of Guyana, Newsletter No. 4, September–December 1974). Elvin McDavid, former Minister of Information of the PNC government during this period, throws further light on this point in stressing the role of the army in a developing society: "The philosophy of the Party must be embraced by all as the Party is the only institution that can educate, unite and develop the nation. It is the golden thread linking everything together and it should be accepted once and for all that the Party is the supreme national organisation; its supremacy extends over all executive and legislative institutions" (1971: 72–73).

Prime Minister Burnham is head of the party, head of the government, and Minister of Defense. The army is seen as an integral part of the government and as the institution most readily adaptable to the demands of the changing society. The army as a coercive institution was seen as a way to institutionalize and sustain the authoritarian rule of the PNC regime. The interweaving and integration of the army with the party and the government was ensured by the powerful figure of the Minister of Defense, Chairman of the Defense Board, Prime Minister, and party leader Forbes Burnham. The upshot of this is that the army automatically was seen as, and automatically became, first and foremost an arm of the PNC and secondly an arm of the government.

Some key functions of the army were thus defined:

1. Repudiate the doctrines of capitalism, elitism, self-indulgence, and economic oppression and proclaim cooperative socialism.
2. Unite the officers and men of the GDF with the broad masses of people of Guyana so that we become genuinely a *People's Army* and the masses become the *Army's People*.
3. Support the government to the end and implement its policies unhesitatingly (*The Scarlet Beret* 1971: 14).

The program of decolonizing the army and securing its legitimacy in the changed system of rule met with considerable success. In the

1973 elections, the ruling PNC won an astounding victory over all the other rival parties. The party polled two-thirds of the electorate, and the army was in the forefront, taking full control of the ballot boxes after ballots were cast, then taking the boxes away in an armed convoy to GDF headquarters. It was alleged that attempts to follow the army with the ballot boxes were futile as the convoy went on an elaborate detour, and representatives of the opposition parties were not allowed to accompany the ballot boxes in accordance with accepted practice. Moreover, three East Indian civilians were shot dead by the army and others injured in one PPP stronghold in clashes between the army and irate civilians who protested army intervention in the electoral process. One informed PNC source explained that "the use of the soldiers was necessary because of prior threats by the Opposition PPP to create chaos and to seize ballot boxes being conveyed to the official counting centres" (*Caribbean Contact*, November 1977, "New Nation Defends Army's Role in 1973 Elections," p. 18). The army was seen as "fulfilling a civic duty" in conveying the ballot boxes. It is of interest to note, however, that the chief-of-staff of the GDF and military adviser to the prime minister claimed in the Guyana High Court that "he was 'unaware' of the army's involvement in the July 1973 general elections, and that he knew of no authority for the GDF soldiers to take the ballot boxes to the army headquarters" (*Caribbean Contact*, November 1977, pp. 18).

From all appearances, the army's involvement in the elections can be seen as demonstrating its unquestioning loyalty and support for the ruling PNC regime. This raises the broader question of whether the army as presently organized would allow another party to use the democratic process to obtain control of the government, and, if so, whether they would be allowed to rule. It seems that the odds are presently heavily against any new government being supported by the army. Army personnel, in comparison with the rest of the public service, obtain high allowances and, in many instances, also duty-free privileges. It appears that officers who demonstrate greater loyalty are rewarded with rapid promotions, and the army as a whole is allowed to play the leading role in national ceremonial displays. Perhaps most importantly, the fact that army officers are at the same time members of the ruling PNC seems to militate against their standing by and allowing the PNC government to lose power. Instead, the strength of the PNC regime is in no small way attributed to the symbolic and actual might of the GDF, which they control so well.

Added to the partisan loyalty of the army is its ethnic composition and commitment. Despite the ethnic balance of the SSU, which had equal numbers of East Indians and blacks, the GDF that emerged from this body is presently estimated to contain approximately 85 percent blacks, compared to Indians and other ethnic groups. The officer corps of the army contains 90 percent black officers, with the remaining 10 percent consisting of East Indians and the other minority races. Since traditional PNC support stems from the black population, the army's commitment to the party is made easier and more readily understandable. The army also provides a valuable agency through which unemployed PNC party activists and supporters can find employment. In a country whose unemployment rate is in the vicinity of 30 percent, the offer of a job in the army in return for, or as a result of, partisan loyalty and support seems a convenient arrangement.

In sum, then, the varied roles and functions of the GDF are:

1. To assist in the maintenance of law and order in Guyana when required to do so.
2. To contribute to the life of the country by organizing voluntary service, engaging in engineering and other projects, and providing a labor/rescue organization in an emergency.
3. To maintain the integrity of the borders of Guyana and define aggression.

In relation to the first function, the army is ever present in times of industrial disputes, when striking plantation workers protest unfair wages or conditions of service in the recently nationalized sugar industry. Not only did the army disperse demonstrating workers, but, after the PPP-controlled trade union called a strike that lasted for one hundred days, armed soldiers were sent to cut the cane and consequently broke the strike. The army, then, performs the additional function of a fluid labor force for strike-breaking in industrial disputes. The army also frequently patrols East Indian villages, and army intelligence keeps a close watch on the activities of PPP activists. In a symbolic demonstration of its strength and powers of coercion, the army would engage in tactical maneuvers along with the police just prior to the passing of an unfavorable bill in parliament or the airing of another austere national budget. The sight of armed soldiers engaging in mock security displays in the streets dampens any thoughts in the minds of the populace about engaging in mass demonstrations against the government.

The army's role in national development, too, is not to be ignored or lightly treated. As a large reserve of disciplined manpower, the army has been engaged in building roads and airstrips in the most remote regions of the country's hinterland, performing mercy missions for the sick and the suffering, providing medical treatment for those away from medical facilities, farming, fishing, hunting, and in many other tasks which contribute in a more or less significant way to the country's development.

The GDF had to encounter actual combat related to border defense on three occasions. In January 1969, some ranchers in the Rupununi district who were known supporters of the United Force, the party representing the mixed, Portuguese, and Chinese minorities, launched an uprising with the aim of bringing about a secession of that district from the rest of the country. These ranchers, together with a gang of Amerindians, attacked the police station and other government offices, killing and injuring some officials in the process. The army moved into the area and put down the uprising, but not before the ranchers fled across the border to Venezuela. Again in 1969, the army captured some Surinamese in the New River area on the Corentyne coast. These Surinamese had invaded Guyana's territory and had plans for setting up a large-scale settlement. Third, soon after independence the mighty Venezuelan army invaded and occupied Ankoko island and defied the much smaller and lesser-equipped GDF. The matter was temporarily settled, however, through diplomatic channels. With the constant threat of Guyana's three neighbors Brazil, Venezuela, and Surinam all staking claim to the Guyana's territory, border defense has become one of the primary functions of the army.

The Guyana Police Force

The police force in Guyana is an institutional product of colonial rule. It was formed in 1839, after the freed slaves had fled the plantations for the villages and towns. One study noted that "the colonial masters established the local police force not so much to ensure that the laws of the land were maintained by all, but to ensure that the freed slaves and indentured servants did not violate their conception of public order. It is not by coincidence that the first Guyanese officer in the police force, S. W. Simon, was appointed as recently as 1943. It was not that the 'natives' could not have been trained to become officers earlier but rather that the maintenance of white non-Guyanese police officers served as a reminder or symbol of the political domination of British colonialism" (Danns 1974: 4).

The police have displayed a history of selective law enforcement. In colonial times they were not expected to arrest European residents but only persons of color. The police were never capable of dealing with any mass protest or demonstration. The British colonies summoned army detachments from abroad whenever the threat of disrupting the society was imminent. The history of strikes and labor unrest is replete with evidence of police inability to restore order in times of crisis. Despite the shooting of workers by the police during major labor uprisings such as the Ruimveldt and Enmore riots, the numerical strength of the force proved inadequate. Moreover, the police were ill-equipped with technological instruments of violence. Pairadeau Mars (1976: 316), in his study of political violence in Guyana, pointed to this numerical and technological inadequacy of the police in coping with crises. Mars also showed that as expenditure on military institutions and the size of the army and police increased the incidence of political violence in Guyana decreased. Perhaps the most blatant case of police inadequacy occurred during the riots and "extreme spate of violence" in Guyana in the early 1960s. The police were locked in a virtual civil war with the people, who attacked policemen and stoned their vehicles despite the commendable and stoical constraint displayed by some sections of the force in trying not to incite the masses.

Like the army, the police personnel also reflect a heavy black bias. Historically, this trend was encouraged by the British, and, despite protests to correct the imbalance in the force by the PPP, the institution still contains 90 percent blacks in both the officer corps and the rank and file. The protest from Jagan's PPP stemmed from the inability or hesitancy of the police in preventing audacious and violent attacks on East Indians by blacks in the bauxite mining town of Linden and also in the capital city of Georgetown. East Indians had executed similarly violent attacks on blacks in some rural areas, but never with such efficiency. Allegations were made that the police themselves were either directly involved in attacking the East Indians or stood by and allowed it to happen. At this point Janet Jagan, who as Minister of Home Affairs was in charge of the police, resigned in protest after the police refused to follow her instructions. Indeed, in an inquiry conducted by the International Commission of Jurists over the February 16, 1962 disturbances, the British Commissioner of Police stated that he swore allegiance to the governor and the Queen and thus owed no loyalty to the Minister of Home Affairs. In addition, Premier Cheddi Jagan and a number of his ministers were in one way or another abused and insulted in the presence of the police by demonstrating members of the public and supporters of the opposition parties. If all these events are to be accepted, it can be concluded that the largely black police force supported the PNC party even while it was in opposition. It was not that there were not some officers loyal to the Jagan government, but that the majority had their loyalties elsewhere.

The virtues of the police are best seen during times of noncrisis, when they maintain law and order and good relations with the public.

In recent times the police have not really been put to the test, since the function of maintaining order is also carried out by the army and, to a lesser extent, by the People's Militia and the National Service. Because it was not a personal creation by the PNC regime, the police have not been given the "pampered" treatment meted out by the regime to the army and other military institutions. The expenditure pattern of the military shows that the police receive smaller increases than other institutions. The placing of the police under the Minister of Home Affairs is perhaps further indicative of the level of importance attached to it by Prime Minister Burnham.

It was not because the police received none of the pampered treatment of the other coercive institutions that they were left to continue their old colonial ways. A somewhat similar strategy to that used on the army was carried out on the police. Top officers who served under the colonial rulers, or who displayed loyalty to the PPP or refused to acquiesce to party demands, were made to resign. Noting this development, Cheddi Jagan stated: "The Government hounded from the Police Force two senior officers, McGill Smith and Lambert, because they were instrumental in breaking up the PNC terrorist organization the previous year. Commissioner of the Police Felix Austin promoted above two more senior officers was soon relieved of his post being forced to retire at the age of 55 although only six months earlier he had been sent on a special training course in USA" (*Sunday Graphic,* January 9, 1972). As the top police officers who survived from colonial rule were removed, a new crop of officers was promoted to the top positions. These officers were, like the army officers, integrated with the party. They also became members of the party "backroom research" group SPEC. The commissioners who followed Felix Austin were Carl Austin, Henry Fraser, and Lloyd Barker. As is to be expected, these commissioners are all black and publicly echo the police commitment to the government and therefore the party, as well as to the "cooperative socialist" policies being advocated.

The police set up a credit union and cooperative supermarket, invested in government defense bonds, as did the army and the National Service, and even engaged in farming and setting up kitchen gardens in police compounds. These small but symbolic gestures were aimed at showing the force's commitment to the regime. Even more striking was the fact that the police joined with army officers in attending, in uniform, the biennial party congress of the ruling PNC. Police officers were similarly encouraged by the Prime Minister to demonstrate loyalty to his government and to adopt the correct attitudes if they wanted to advance in the service. The ideology of legitimacy and the rhetoric of compliance also became an integral part of the decolonization process of the police. However, since the structure and functioning of the force were established during the heyday of colonial rule, the process of decolonization is somewhat slower, and the police still refer to their 138 years of existence as a "glorious tradition." Consequently, the police are viewed with a measure of reserve by the party, although many police officers have been instrumental in carrying out party instructions in no uncertain terms. Indeed, unquestioning party loyalty is a precondition for any position of major importance in the organizational structure of the force.

Like the army, the police provide an avenue for absorbing jobless party supporters and party activists. Thus the process of integrating the police with the party is facilitated as new and young policemen are employed. The police protect civilians by breaking strikes in the nationalized industries and are alleged to have badly treated female Indian sugar workers who were squatting to prevent strikebreakers from going to work. Their commitment to the government and party is thus pronounced. Finally, the role of the police overlaps considerably with that of the army. The police, as a paramilitary force as well as a civilian institution, performs the unique task of border defense just as the army does. As defined in the laws of Guyana, the police can be called upon to carry out these military duties and, prior to the army, did carry out such duties along with the regular one of maintaining order. It is of interest to note that the oath of office of the policeman does not include the function of maintaining "law" but rather that of maintaining "order." Since law and order are not necessarily identical, it seems that the government can be seen as the sole determinant of public order.

The Guyana People's Militia

The Guyana People's Militia is a part-time military organization set up with the expressed aim of making "every citizen a soldier" and thus providing large numbers of people skilled in soldiering to engage in the task of national defense. More precisely, the role of the militia is to:

1. Provide a framework in which mass preparations for emergencies can be carried out during a period of rising tensions.
2. Support the People's Army in all of its functions when called upon to do so.
3. Assist the People's Police in the maintenance of law and order when called upon to do so.

4. Provide a reservoir of trained recruits for the army.
5. Contribute to the life of the community by engaging in productive work and providing a labor rescue organization in an emergency. (*Guyana People's Militia: What It Does* 1976:9)

Among the reasons given for the formation of the militia are the following:

1. Grave threats have been posed to the territorial integrity and national sovereignty of Guyana. These threats have been posed by foreign powers which are opposed to the government's thrust to abolish capitalism, eradicate foreign exploitation and make national independence meaningful.
2. The government has gradually and deliberately over the past ten years repossessed the natural resources of the country and taken control of the commanding heights of the economy through a process of nationalization of foreign enterprises.
3. In the political sphere it has unapologetically accepted socialism as an ideological program and position for total development.
4. The government has pursued a nonalignment foreign policy and has been a tireless fighter in the nonaligned movement, seeking to follow its own path of development without participating in the global power struggle. It has also resolutely opposed apartheid, zionism and neocolonialism and has upheld the right to self-determination of nations.
5. Because of the above, which the government sees as wholeheartedly embraced by the Guyanese people, foreign states have disapproved and sought to "destabilize" Guyana by spreading vicious lies about the country. The ultimate objective of this campaign is to demonstrate that Guyana, under its present government, is a threat to peace and thereby to create the conditions for intervention in order to preserve "peace" in the hemisphere.
6. In order to defend the country effectively against this threat, a large portion of the civilian population needs to be mobilized, trained, and equipped to carry out defensive duties while maintaining normal economic production. The establishment of the militia is further viewed as necessary because Guyana's borders are long and because the country is large in comparison to its small population and therefore vulnerable not only to direct foreign intervention but also *to domestic sabotage by bad elements* and infiltrated agents acting in the interest of hostile powers. The small size of the combined security forces and the large

area over which they are responsible make it difficult to move regular troops quickly from place to place whenever the need arises, either for internal or external security or defense against external aggression. It is therefore the people themselves who must provide the surest guarantee for maintaining peace and defending the country. The Guyana People's Militia is defined as "a military body of citizens, trained in military skills, imbued with a high sense of loyalty and dedicated to the nation and its program for socialist development." In sum, their duties include straightforward military operations for territorial defense against hostile invading forces, police duties in detecting antinational crimes such as sabotage (and apprehending such offenders), civil defense duties in the event of a natural catastrophe or a manmade disaster, and community development work of a productive economic nature. All citizens above the age of 14 years are eligible for membership (*The Guyana People's Militia* 1976:1–11).

With this outline of the role and functions of the militia, it is clear that, barring the fact that it is largely a part-time reserve military body, its defined duties are not dissimilar to those of the army or the police. Nor is its relationship with the ruling PNC any less intense and intertwined than that of the army and, to a lesser extent, the police. The ethnic composition of the militia again reveals 90 percent blacks and 10 percent people from all other ethnic groups. It appears that although membership in the countrywide militia is open to anyone, the chief source for recruiting its members is the organized PNC party groups. The People's Militia is a militia of the ruling PNC.

Militia members who are also PNC party members or supporters are expected to act as a sort of "spying agency" on opposition groups and to report any clandestine acts by groups opposed to the governing regime. Citizens who in any way oppose policies of the government are defined as "enemies from within" and those who criticize from outside the country, "enemies from without." Nonsupporters of the government and the party are also regarded, if not treated, as potential enemies of the regime. The degree of involvement of the militia in projects involving community development is minimal or relatively unknown. The militia is still in the process of crystalizing its organization and operations and, in general, cannot presently be seriously viewed either as an efficient or a reliable reserve army. Apart from ceremonial appearances and cutting cane during sugar strikes, the militia has not had occasion to be called upon to demonstrate what it can do. The large Indian population, however, views this body with great concern and suspicion and, in general, has nothing to do with it.

The Guyana National Service

The Guyana National Service (GNS) represents a large, multifaceted, multipurpose paramilitary organization. It was set up less than five years ago to accomplish the following objectives:

1. To provide training and skills which are consistent with national needs.
2. To increase national production.
3. To provide manpower for development.
4. To achieve self-reliance.
5. To develop and populate the hinterland.
6. To develop an understanding of national objectives.
7. To provide rescue and relief operations during national disaster, emergencies, or catastrophies.
8. To unite the various racial, social, and economic groups in Guyana for our survival and development.
9. To promote the national defense.

The National Service Board, which is chaired by the Prime Minister, formulates and directs policy to a National Service Secretariat, headed by a Director-General. The institution consists of six field corps:

1. The Young Brigade for children between the ages of eight and fourteen attending primary schools.
2. The National Cadet Corps for young people between the ages of twelve and eighteen attending secondary and technical schools.
3. The New Opportunity Corps for Guyanese up to the age of sixteen in approved schools such as the Belfield Girls' School and the Essequibo Boys' School. These two schools are correctional institutions for juvenile delinquents who were in trouble with the law.
4. The Pioneer Corps for unemployed Guyanese between the ages of fourteen and twenty-five and employed Guyanese between the ages of eighteen and twenty-five. This is the category for those who wish to enter the University of Guyana and the public service.
5. The Special Service Corps for persons who have qualified as professionals or possess special skills.
6. The National Reserve Corps for graduates of the Pioneer Corps. Members are on call for duty in any area vital to the stability, productivity, or security of the country (e.g., floods or military aggression).

In accordance with the statutes enacting the National Service, any citizen of Guyana can be called upon by law to perform national service if necessary. This, however, is not carried out in practice, and national service is largely voluntary, except for students who want to enter the University of Guyana. A perusal of the varied tasks of the National Service would indicate that it is set up by the government as an organizational panacea for the problems of decolonization, development, and social control. It is expected to socialize the members of the society from as young as eight years old into developing a sense of national consciousness, a socialist orientation, and a loyal commitment to the government. In doing this, the National Service is set up to invade the structure or permeate the framework of other established institutions such as the educational system, industry, the military, and correctional institutions. Whereas the task of engaging in development projects and hinterland settlement is somewhat peripheral to the army, police, and militia, these tasks are seen as central to the role of the GNS. Whereas these other institutions are concerned largely with decolonizing themselves, the GNS is concerned with the decolonization of the entire society. In principle at least, the GNS is seen as the nucleus institution, the prototype on which the "New Guyana" will be patterned. Out of this institution it is expected that the "New Guyana Man" conceived by the ruling PNC regime will emerge.

Despite the laudable objectives of the GNS, it presently resembles little more than an amorphous, ill-structured military institution that has accomplished very little more than teaching militants how to march and requiring them to compulsively obey the commands of their functional superiors. Not only does the National Service lack the learned traditions that characterize the other three military institutions, but it also lacks proper planning an the required personnel to carry out its highly varied and multifaceted program. National Service is a novel institution. It is a unique experiment in nation-building. Although National Services can be found in Tanzania, Uganda, and Ghana, the wide scale with which it is envisaged has been unparalleled elsewhere.

Because of the lack of proper planning resources and skilled personnel, many of the schemes the GNS has set up have failed. Cotton production has declined, and the scale of planning for other agricultural projects has not been realized. The GNS was expected from its inception to be a largely self-reliant institution which, after the initial investment, would generate self-growth and wealth for the country. However, the realities are that the GNS is not only not expanding as rapidly as was expected, but has begun to contract.

The PNC party penetration in the GNS is largely coercive. National Service militants are constrained to picket on behalf of the government. This applies in particular to university students, who are constrained to picket or sacrifice their scholarship or university career. In addition to this, certain National Service Centers are involved in serious military training which is in no way undervalued when compared to the training received by the Army. While coming under the GNS umbrella, the trained militants constitute a large and efficient military unit. It is of interest to note, however, that training is conducted by GDF personnel.

The National Service provides yet another avenue for employing party faithful. In addition, it absorbs retired police and civil service personnel with party connections into administrative positions. It is not that the GNS has not and cannot achieve some of what it has set out to do, but rather that so far it is ill equipped to so do. The GNS, then, is the final of the four major types of military institutions found in Guyana. In what follows we will attempt to draw general conclusions and analyze their implications for the society.

The "New Colonizers"

In our examination of the GDF, the GNS, the Police, and the People's Militia, we found certain common trends in all of them. These can be summarized as follows:

1. Defending the country's borders against territorial aggression.
2. Maintenance of internal order as defined by the government.
3. Being loyal in support of the PNC regime and carrying out its policies unconditionally.
4. Setting examples for the rest of the society by being leaders in the task of national development.
5. Propagating the cooperative socialist philosophy among their members and the society at large.
6. Spearheading the government's plans for developing the society by establishing hinterland settlements, engaging in agricultural pursuits, building roads, and bridges, and facilitating the spread and establishment of cooperatives.
7. Ensuring that organized opposition, detractors, and saboteurs of the PNC regime are either crushed or weakened.
8. Providing avenues of employment for the absorption of PNC party supporters.

In short, the military institutions form an authoritative and coercive buffer between the ruling PNC regime and the rest of the people.

The party penetration of these institutions is so effective that there is a very low probability of a military coup of any sort. Civilian control of the military seems guaranteed for some time. The military are the veritable pillars on which the dominance of PNC regime is sustained, if not also founded. The military defines the very character of the government as much as the ruling party defines the very character of the military. This heavy reliance of the government on the military to sustain its rule is a condition brought about by party penetration into these institutions. The authoritative and coercive buffer that the military forms between the government and the people also reflects the personal ambition and determination of the party leader, Prime Minister, and Minister of Defense to remain in power regardless of opposition to his rule and the rule of his government. This point underlies our argument that a system of domination can be viewed as a phenomenon *sui generis* that does not have to rely on the consensual support or legitimacy of the ruled to sustain itself. Once loyalty from the ruling elite and administrative staffs (especially the institutions of coercion) is obtained, such a system of domination can maintain its illegitimate rule.

In sum, then, the factors contributing to the increasing militarization of Guyanese society can be traced to the following:

1. The need to have armed forces as an independent republic.
2. The threat of territorial aggression and incursions by bordering countries.
3. The provision of institutions to absorb the growing masses of unemployed and underemployed.
4. The creation of new institutions to attain the goals of modernization and development in a volatile postcolonial milieu.
5. The mobilization and control of the population for achieving national objectives.
6. The decolonization of the society through institutionalizing and sustaining the rule of an indigenous regime.

Identification of the factors contributing to militarization in postcolonial Guyana provides us with analytic tools for assessing the changes that have occurred and are occurring in the society, enables us to ascertain the nature of governmental rule, and gives us a basis for comparing and contrasting colonial society with a more or less decolonized society.

The authoritarian rule that characterized colonial society has certain marked differences from that which obtains in postcolonial Guyana. Colonial authoritarianism was repressive and wholly exploitative.

The natural resources of the country and its labor power were utilized to fill the coffers of the metropolitan rulers. In contrast, the authoritarian rule of the postcolonial government reflects a genuine concern to find solutions to the problems of dependent underdevelopment. The military of the colonial era were almost exclusively instruments of repression and control. The military of the independent society are instruments for decolonization and development. It is not, symbolically at least, that they are not instruments of control, but rather that the purpose of such control is to provide an atmosphere for societal transformation. Any social or economic development of colonial society was brought about or encouraged only insofar as the interests of the metropolitan empire were served. Social or economic development in the postcolonial society is aimed purely at uplifting the lives of the people. Governments are reacted against for their inability to develop their countries in a hurry, not for exploiting their peoples. The cry is not "you rob and exploit us," but rather "we are hungry and jobless and you do not seem to know how to solve our problems, despite your promises."

The peoples of the colonial and postcolonial society were and are heavily inclined to be dependent on their system of rule. Under the colonial regime they were made dependent on the authoritarian system of rule. Individual initiative ws discouraged, and the colonial individual was induced to be passive to authoritarian dictates. Under the present system of rule this attitude of dependency very much persists. People are not self-reliant, and they expect and demand that their government provide answers and point out directions for their actions. That is, the peoples of Guyana and the rest of the Caribbean, particularly the large masses of the working class, do not mind an authoritarian rulership, and from their dependent dispositions actually encourage one. Nevertheless, they react strongly and withdraw their sanction from a system of rule that cannot administer to their needs.

The small-scale nature of Guyanese society, where the military can be seen as part of the people and the people are certainly part of the military, attenuates any perception of the military as an institution of repression. Many Guyanese have relatives, friends, and acquaintances who are members of one of the four military institutions. All of the military institutions continuously provide various community services. Many of the young people are attracted to the smart uniforms of military personnel. The military drives no fear into the hearts of the citizens of Guyana. Moreover, military personnel are themselves affected by the traumatic changes affecting the country's economy and society as a whole. They do not represent an elite group of any sort in the society, and they share the same joys and sorrows as of the regular citizens. They are, however, members of authoritarian institutions and supporters of an authoritarian government. They are symbolic rather than actual dissuaders of attempts at destabilizing the government or creating disorder. Since the present regime attained power, the military in Guyana were never really called upon to suppress any mass disturbance. They were never put to the test and thus have escaped the label of repressive.

Finally, in light of the nature of postcolonial society in the Caribbean in general and Guyana in particular, it is unrealistic to expect a democratic environment. It is also shortsighted for scholars in the region to think that the country has become authoritarian following independence. Colonial rule was authoritarian, though the coercive apparatus tended in the latter stages to be less obtrusive. Caribbean society, then, has never known any but authoritarian rule. It is not that there is less freedom, but rather that these countries are experiencing decolonization, a process of undoing and doing over—the changing of colonial rule for indigenous rule. In addition, indigenous rule can establish itself amidst ethnic and cultural conflicts only by being as authoritarian as the colonial rulers who engineered the society in the first place. In so establishing themselves, the indigenous rulers became the "new colonizers." Previously not exposed to the onerous task of running a government and having as their only model of government the colonial system, the indigenous rulers, barring structural constraints, are further induced to become authoritarian. The "old colonizers" became the mirror through which the "new colonizers" saw themselves. This syndrome of authoritarianism becomes all the more pronounced as the people of the region encounter the same incumbents of rule day after day, year after year. Governors no longer return home or are posted elsewhere because of their unpopularity. The "governors" now belong permanently to the people and the yoke of their rule is all the heavier. A probable solution to this syndrome of authoritarianism is time and enlightened governmental rule. After all, the legitimacy of any system of domination can only be "false consciousness over time." The realities are that governments in the region which attempt to democratize their societies before fully controlling them will be fragmented and destroyed by plural structural forces. It is from "unfreedom" that freedom can develop. In all of this, the military has a role to play.

Bibliography

Burnham, Forbes. *A People's Army.* Two addresses by the Hon. L. F. S. Burnham to members of the GDF at Thomas Lands (Georgetown: Government Printery, 1970).

Coser, Lewis. *Functions of Social Conflict* (New York: Free Press, 1956).
———————— (ed.). *Political Sociology* (New York: Harper & Row, 1966).
Danns, George K. "The Role and Function of the Police." Paper presented at the National Conference on Crime and the Penal System in Guyana, 1974.
————————. *Leadership, Legitimacy and the West Indian Experience: A Rethematization of Max Weber's Typology of Domination* (Georgetown: Institute of Development Studies, University of Guyana, 1978).
Despres, Leo. *Cultural Pluralism and Nationalist Politics in British Guiana* (Chicago: Rand McNally, 1967).
Enloe, Cynthia. "Civilian Control of the Military: Implications in the Plural Societies of Guyana and Malaysia." In Claude E. Welch, Jr. (ed.), *Civilian Control of the Military: Theory and Cases from Developing Countries* (Albany: State University of New York Press, 1976).
Edelman, Murray. *The Symbolic Uses of Politics* (Urbana: University of Illinois Press, 1970).
Granger, David A. *The New Road: A Short History of the Guyana Defence Force 1966–1976* (Georgetown: Guyana Defence Force, 1975).
Hintzen, Percy. *Civil-Military Relations in Guyana and Trinidad: A Comparative Study* (Unpublished manuscript, Yale University, 1976).
Jagan, Cheddi. *The West On Trial* (Berlin: Seven Seas, 1975).
Janowitz, Morris. *The Military in the Political Development of New Nations: An Essay in Comparative Analysis* (Chicago: University of Chicago Press, 1964).
Johnson, John J. *The Military and Society in Latin America* (Stanford, Cal.: Stanford University Press, 1964).
Mandle, Jay R. *The Post-Colonial Mode of Production in Guyana: A Framework of Analysis of Radical Decolonization* (Unpublished manuscript, University of Guyana, 1978).
Mars, Pairadeau. *Political Modernization and Stability in a Developing State: The Guyana Example* (Unpublished doctoral thesis, Carleton University, June 1975).
McDavid, Elvin. "The Army: Its Role in a Developing Society." In *The Scarlet Beret Journal of the Guyana Defence Force, 1971*.
Moskos, Charles C. *The Sociology of Political Independence* (Cambridge, Mass.: Schenkman, 1967).
Munroe, Trevor. *The Politics of Constitutional Decolonization: Jamaica, 1944–62* (Kingston: Institute for Social and Economic Research, University of the West Indies, 1963).

5

Decolonization and Cultural Underdevelopment in the Commonwealth Caribbean

PAGET HENRY

Colonization and Consciousness

To the extent that a people have been colonized, they will find themselves in possession of a "false" or distorted consciousness, just as they find themselves with distorted economic, cultural, and political institutions. In the same way that the process of colonization uproots and reorganizes the economic and political institutions of the native, it also uproots the cultural institutions, whose transformation uproots and reorganizes, in turn, the consciousness of the colonized. As a result, the native is less able to see himself accurately, and to explain his situation in history as it really is. Cultural decolonization is thus an important condition for the liberation of this distorted consciousness.

If, as Lukacs has argued, reification is the structural distortion imposed upon consciousness as a result of the commodification of the social relations of capitalist societies, then flight or movement away from oneself and one's situation and toward identification with the colonizer, is the distortion that colonization imposes. This distortion is rooted in two factors that are a part of the social condition of the colonized. The first is the image of the latter that colonial societies carry within them. As Fanon has so ably shown, the formation, elaboration, and institutionalization of an image of the colonized is an integral part of the process of cultural colonization.[1] This process requires and always produces its Calibans, whether they are "the Ne-

gro," "the Coolie," "the Fellah" or "the Injun." This image becomes
the social definition of the colonized—his new identity. Because it is a
negative identity, the colonized is forced to deal with it if he is to live
with himself. He can either assert himself as the cultural being that he
is, or he can deny the image by various avenues of flight, such as
religion, art, or identification with the colonizer. This is the dynamic
element in the structure of flight that burdens the consciousness of the
colonized.

The second factor responsible for the distortion in the consciousness of the colonized is his subjection to the colonizer's explanations of
his arrival, presence, and intentions. Thus the Europeans were to bring
civilization; now the Americans and the Russians are to bring freedom
and the liberation of the proletariat, respectively. To the extent that the
colonization process has taken root and identification with the colonizer has occurred, the colonized will be susceptible to such rationalizations and so find himself in possession of false explanations of his
situation. It is toward the uprooting of the set of social and psychological processes that generate these distortions that the decolonization of
consciousness must aim. This uprooting, guided by critical and aesthetic self-reflection, must involve the comprehensive decolonization
of the society, including its cultural institutions.

In this chapter our focus will be on the cultural institutions of
Commonwealth Caribbean societies. More specifically, it will be on the
colonization and relative decolonization of these institutions, and how
these processes have affected the growth of consciousness in the region.

In the literature on development, a sharp dichotomy has developed between theorists using cultural and structural explanations of
underdevelopment. The culturalists tend to emphasize the causal importance of value systems, ideas, attitudes, and personality, while the
structuralists tend to emphasize various aspects of the social, economic, or political structure of the society. This dichotomy is certainly
mirrored in Caribbean development literature, as the dialogue between
the cultural pluralists and the political economists indicates.[2] These
two positions, I think, are more sharply drawn than they need be. By
examining local cultural processes in terms of the same imperialist
project that established local economic and political processes, I hope
to make a contribution toward the closing of this schism.

Cultural Colonization in a Slave Society

The cultural colonization of the Commonwealth Caribbean is best conceptualized as a part of the process of subjugation that followed the

conquest of the region by one of the more developed of the European capitalist societies, Great Britain.

This conquest of the Caribbean region resulted in a case of what Lloyd Best has termed a "hinterland of exploitation," as opposed to a hinterland of conquest or settlement: "A hinterland of exploitation is a direct extension of the economy of the metropole. Its *raison d'être* is to produce a staple required for metropolitan consumption and for entrepot trade to third countries. It thus forms part of the overseas empire of the metropole."[3] The major staple that was required of the Caribbean was, of course, sugar. This crop was grown on large plantations with the aid of whatever labor the colonizer could command. At first, the dominated labor force was made up of indigenous Indians and European indentured servants. Both of these, however, were soon replaced by an African labor force. This labor force was now to make possible the manufacture of the staple.

However, people do not allow themselves to be transported and incorporated into another's economy without resistance. Given the freedoms of a normal working class, they were sure to run away. Hence it was that the African had to labor under the most oppressive of conditions, those of slavery. His natural inclination to resist had to be drummed into silence by superior force. This drumming into silence of the resistance of the colonized sets up the fundamental dialectic of colonial societies. It does this because the resistance is never really silenced. The latter will at times burst forth with all the violence that silenced it. This is the fundamental conflict at the heart of colonial societies.

We have just seen that the colonizer must break the resistance of the colonized. He must force him to accept his role as slave, as worker, as property of his master. In order to do this, the colonizer must dehumanize the colonized. He must whip him, intimidate him, imprison him, depoliticize him, and deculturalize him, all in an effort to wrest from him his freedom to act in accord with his will, particularly his will to resist.

During this early phase, colonization manifests itself on the cultural level primarily as the deculturalization of the colonized. To the extent that the oppressor finds the culture of the oppressed getting in the way of the colonial project, the latter will be forced to give up these cultural practices. If their use is to be continued, it must be done in secret: "a national culture under colonial domination is a contested culture whose destruction is sought in systematic fashion. It very quickly becomes a culture condemned to secrecy. This idea of a clandestine culture is immediately seen in the reactions of the occupying power which interprets attachments to traditions as faithfulness to the spirit of the nation and as a refusal to submit."[4] This statement by

Fanon not only points to the problem of secrecy, but also describes for us the nature of the bicultural situation that develops during this phase of colonization. It portrays the colonizer as being on the attack, as one relentlessly destroying the culture of the colonized in order to ensure his submission.

We have already seen that the aim of early colonization was to force the African to submit to his role as worker on the sugar planta-tions. As a result of his forced incorporation into the colonizer's econ-omy, the African was alienated from his own economic practices. Consequently, among the first elements of his cultural universe to fall into oblivion, uselessness, or secrecy, were those rites and rituals that were concerned with economic productivity. These were quickly re-placed by the skills and discipline necessary to work in the oppressor's economy. One should carefully note the kind of limbo in which this situation left the African. It separated him from old and familiar modes of economic productivity and exposed him to new ones that he was never to master to the point of making his own. Thus begins his eco-nomic dependence on his oppressor.

For the colonial project to realize itself, there must have been communication between colonizer and colonized. But as colonization is not about the learning of native languages, the African was forced to learn the language of the European. This forced learning was system-atically pursued by a variety of means, such as the separating of slaves who spoke the same languages and the rewarding of those who learned quickly to express themselves in the oppressor's tongue. This linguistic situation parallels the economic one described above. Here, too, the slave is forcibly estranged from a familiar cultural setting and exposed to one that he will not be able to master. He will not master the colonizer's language because his forced instruction does not have proficiency as its aim. Rather, its aim is the minimum of communica-tion necessary for the incorporation of the slave into the master's economy. Consequently, the process of reculturalization is limited and partial in nature. Under these conditions, the slave ends up speaking a dialect that further separates him from his past and stands between him and his present by not permitting full participation in the society.

It is worth commenting further on the linguistic situation of the colonized, for it is symbolic of his larger cultural situation. His whole culture, it may be said, tends to become a dialect, for he is in a situation that alienates him from his past but does not allow him to gain a strong foothold in the present. As a result, his cultural products are hybrids that make autonomous existence in the present impossible. Under more normal conditions, the exposure to another language makes one bilingual. Not so under colonialism. Here the colonized loses his language but never really gains another. This is true for his larger cultural situation as well. Instead of becoming bicultural, he loses his heritage and is left with a "dialect."

However, the extent to which the various institutions that make up the culture become "dialectized" varies with the nature and phase of the colonization process. During the early phase, the institutions that displayed the most resilience were, of course, the religious ones. But these religions were by no means the original African religions. Too much had been lost in the disruption of traditional societies and much mixing had occurred after relocation in the Caribbean. Consequently, there developed what could be called Afro-Caribbean religions such as Cumina, Cumfa, and Myalism. The major continuity between these religions and the African religions was the centrality of possession by a spirit or an ancestor as a basic mode of religiosity.

The major discontinuity was the loss of the mythologies and cosmologies that described the life of the gods and the origins of the world. From communicating with spirits and ancestors through possession the community derived much needed psychic support and a variety of helpful techniques (e.g., herbs for healing and magical rites) for intervening in the natural and social processes of life. The practice of intervening "negatively" in social processes is generally known as "working obeah" and has proved to be one of the most tenacious elements of this heritage. In addition, through communicating with spirits and ancestors the idea of Africa and the African past was kept alive. Hence it was around these religions that certain proto-nationalist sentiments could crystalize. The role of these religions in slave rebellions and the subsequent outlawing of practices such as drumming are well known and will not be further explored here. During this early phase, despite the loss of mythologies and cosmologies, the religious sphere remained largely uncolonized; that is, it had not yet been "hybridized" and "dialectized" as had other areas of the culture.

Finally, in this process of deculturalization, we must mention the forceful estrangement of the African from his traditional image of himself, and his gradual internalization of the colonizers' image of him. As a result of these two processes, earlier tribal or other identities were slowly replaced by the image of the negro, the colonizer's social definition of the African. The internalization of this image is probably the most fateful step in this process of deculturalization. Its importance lies in the fact that it separates the African from a positive and familiar sense of himself, and imposes one that he cannot really accept. Once this occurs, the structures of flight which generate the false consciousness of the colonized begin to take root. The imposition of this image parallels on the level of the self the processes of hybridization and dialectization of the various forms of cultural expression of the colonized. By making the African into a negro, the colonizer makes him inferior and lowers him in "the great chain of Being." Once he became objectified as a negro, it was easier to justify the subjugation and enslavement of the African.

We may sum up our analysis so far with the following remarks. In its early phase, cultural colonization was largely the deculturalization of the colonized. The native was forcibly removed from his cultural moorings as part of a larger effort to incorporate him as a worker in the colonizer's society. But to realize this incorporation the colonizer had to do more than just alienate the colonized from his past; he had also to impose on him certain elements of his own culture. Under these conditions, the culture of the colonized soon acquired the status of a dialect, with religion being the least transformed area of the heritage.

Cultural Colonization in Postemancipation Society

As pointed out earlier, "the culture of silence" that characterizes the colonial situation is a deceptive one. Every so often this silence was broken by a noise that revealed the violence and domination that are at the heart of colonial societies. The early phases of colonization in the Caribbean were no exception. They were punctuated by rebellions which, together with other factors, helped to bring an end to colonization in its "pure form" (slave society). However, the continuities between slave society and postemancipation society by far outweighed the discontinuities. That is, in spite of the legal abolition of slavery, the region remained a hinterland of exploitation whose primary collective project was still the production of the staple. The major difference was that now it would have to be done with a labor force slightly removed from the conditions of slavery. This change in the concrete situation had important repercussions on the cultural level: the colonizer, having physically subdued his victim, was forced to let go of him. To continue to appropriate his labor he had now to try to "win" his cooperation. In other words, he had now to make the colonized want to do what he had to do. To the extent that this had not already been achieved, it meant that he had to socialize the colonized more fully into his society. Consequently, there was in this period a shift in emphasis from deculturalization to reculturalization. This was done primarily through two instruments: Christianization and education. We will look at the first rather briefly and at the second in greater detail.

Even though the Christianization of the African began decades before, it was not until the emancipation of 1834 that Christianity received the full support of the colonial office and the local elites. By this time both had become convinced of the stabilizing influence of Christianity on the colonized. This was largely the result of the inactive asceticism that characterized its program of salvation. This program, in contrast to more active forms of asceticism, focused the attention of the colonized on efforts toward overcoming his own sinful nature. The rewards for these efforts were to be had not in this life but in the next one. Consequently, by so structuring the general outlook of the colonized, Christianization resulted in the withdrawing of worldly expectations, including expectations of the colonial situation and of an African redemption. This accounts for the depoliticizing effect of the process, which was very important for colonial development at this phase.

With the imposition of Christianity, the formerly uncolonized religious sphere was finally overtaken. The colonized was now under the influence of the colonizer's religion. Even though we cannot here go into the further details of this process, it could easily be shown that Christianization continued in less forceful ways the tendencies toward cultural alienation that followed incorporation into other areas of the colonizer's society, that the African would lose a familiar cultural item and never really master the new, and that to the extent that he would gain new religions they would be hybrid creations (Shango, Native Baptists, Zion, etc.)—creations that had lost their past and were without a real future in colonial society. With this arresting of native religiosity, the program of deculturalization begun in the first phase is now complete, in the sense that it has now invaded all areas of the culture of the colonized.

However, it is in the area of education that the new methods of cultural colonization are most apparent. The act of emancipation contained within it a grant from the imperial government for the education of the ex-slaves. Behind the provision of this grant were a number of concerns about the future of the colonial project. Those relating to the continued appropriation of the labor of the ex-slaves were summed up by the Rev. J. Sterling:

> About 770,000 persons have been released from slavery by the Emancipation Act and are now in a state of rapid transition to entire freedom. The peace and prosperity of the empire at large may be not remotely influenced by their moral condition. . . . It is plain therefore that something must be done. . . . For although the negroes are now under a system of limited control (apprenticeship), which secures to a certain extent their orderly and industrious conduct, in the short space of five years from the first of next August, their performance of the functions of a labouring class in a civilised community will depend entirely on the power over their

minds of the same prudential and moral motives which govern more or less the mass of the people here (England). If they are not so disposed as to fulfil these functions, property will perish in the colonies for lack of human impulsion; the whites will no longer reside there; and the liberated negroes themselves will cease to be progressive.[5]

In more succinct terms, Rev. Sterling gives us another perspective on the same problem; "the certain result of the new situation (emancipation), when the minds of the people are all in movement, will be a consciousness of their own independent value as rational beings without reference to the purposes for which they may be profitable to others."[6] We noted earlier that to be colonized was to be transformed into a living instrument of the colonizer. During this second phase, cultural colonization becomes the process of socializing the colonized in such a way that he realizes no other identity.

With concerns such as these in mind, the imperial government proceeded to administer the grant. Allocations were made to the various religious bodies that had already been engaged in educational work in the region. With this money primary and secondary schools were opened, and so began the effort at popular education. In addition to the money, the colonial office also dispatched some of its own ideas about the content of education in the colonies.

These included a knowledge of Christianity, the English language, skills that would help the small farmer, and a knowledge of the people's relationship to authority. About the latter the dispatch had this to say: "The lesson books of the colonial schools should also teach the mutual interest of the mother-country and her dependencies; the rational basis of their connection and the domestic and social responsibilities of the coloured races."[7] These, in brief, were the conditions under which the program of education aimed at control over the minds of the colonized. It was a program that would ensure that the colonized had the "correct" image of himself and of his colonizer.

However, with the termination of the grant in the 1840s, significant changes occurred. The responsibility for popular education now fell to the local assemblies. These assemblies consisted mainly of planters who were opposed to popular education that was not of an agricultural nature. Consequently, these bodies soon began allocating as much as a third of the educational budget to maintenance of the secondary schools attended primarily by their own sons. This system was justified by the two or three places that it would open for poorer students and the availability of an equally small number of university scholarships. With such a large commitment to secondary education, primary education could not but suffer. So as late as the 1890s, less than half the previous number of school age children were registered in primary school.

But if the system did not achieve this goal, it did achieve others. By opening up a few positions of secondary education to the colonized, the appearance was created that a fair competitive principle was at work which determined mobility and position in the society. This provided legitimacy not only for the educational system itself, but also for the hierarchical system of the society.

Finally, it must be pointed out how the positions opened up by this educational system continued the processes of cultural alienation that began with the colonized's force incorporation into the economy of the colonizer. While discussing that first phase we saw that the most that processes of resocialization would allow was cultural hybridization. But within the confines of the new cultural space opened up by secondary education and Christianization, the colonizer could go further: he could now attempt the impossible—he could attempt to assimilate. That is, he could mistakenly try to rid himself not only of his African past, but of his dialect culture and of his image as a negro as well, and become European. It is this built-in resocialization process that links this system of education to earlier forms of cultural colonization.

The option to assimilate was real only for the middle elements of the colonized. In the lives of those who were ensnared by it, all the problems of colonial biculturalism became manifest. In these individuals we see the most desperate efforts of the colonized to escape from himself, his situation, and his imposed image by making himself resemble his colonizer. They have all internalized and accepted the colonizer's judgement of them and their cultural heritage. Consequently, with unending resolve, all surviving manifestations of the cultural heritage are removed from public view. This of course exacerbates the bicultural division within their psyches. For as African or creole elements are removed, they are replaced by European ones. For example, speaking "good" English now becomes extremely important. So are things like being European in one's dress and in one's eating habits—in short, in one's whole lifestyle. When this occurs the process of reculturalization is complete, in the sense that the colonized has moved as far away as he can from his original cultural moorings. He is completely caught up in imitating and appropriating the lifestyle of the colonizer. Consequently, he is now completely dependent on him for all his cultural values and orientations—for his very identity.

In addition to the factors of Christianization and education, two others must be mentioned to complete the cultural picture of post-emancipation society. The first was the emergence of carnival and Christmas celebrations as predominantly black rituals. This was important because it provided another major occasion of cultural expression for a people still unable to read or write. The basic artistic form of these rituals was, of course, the *"mas"* band, and through the various *mases* played on these occasions, we are able to get major insights into the deeper psychic life of the West Indian masses. With Canboulay and Jon Canoe emancipation was celebrated. In the bands in which men dressed up as women and vice versa, sex-role conflict was enacted. In the Shango bands and with Moko Jumbee the African heritage reasserts itself. In the Jamet bands and the Devil bands a Satanic rejection of colonial society was expressed. In the drama of the John Bull, the colonized ritualistically expresses his hostility toward the colonizer. In many of the so-called "fancy bands," with their portrayal of kings and queens and other elaborate productions, we see the identification of the West Indian with his colonizer. All these contradictory strains within the West Indian psyche were expressed in the *mases* of carnival and Christmas. They were expressed with a comic irony that made resignation possible. This comic irony was most evident in the songs that accompanied the playing of these *mases,* the Cariso (Trinidad) or the Benah (Antigua) which preceeded the Calypso.

The other factor referred to above was the introduction of indentured Indian labor into a number of the territories of the region as a replacement for the lost African supply. This importation of Indian labor lasted from about 1845 to 1917 and brought both Hindus and Moslems to the region. As in the case of the African, these new arrivals meant new cultures for the colonial mill. However, coming under the social conditions of indenture as opposed to slavery, the Indian did not undergo as extreme a process of deculturalization as the African. The more totalitarian nature of slavery resulted in the more thorough subjugation of the African to the processes of deculturalization and reculturalization. But inspite of this difference in the degree of totalitarian control, the basic elements in the process of cultural colonization were the same in both cases. As in the case of the African, the Indian had to abandon traditional economic modes of production and to adjust to the role of plantation laborer. He was forced to leave behind his native tongues and to learn the language of the colonizer. Like the African, he internalized the colonizer's image of him—that of the coolie. Consequently, he too has come to know the phenomenon of flight that afflicts the consciousness of the colonized. Finally, the Indian has also been subjected to the processes of Christianization and colonial education, and has used them as means for assimilating.

If, in spite of these common factors in the process of cultural colonization, the Indian heritage has fared better than the African, it is probably for two reasons. The first is the already mentioned fact that under the social conditions of indenture, the impact of these processes was somewhat softened. The second is that the Indian tradition was a more developed one, having a long established written heritage, and was thus capable of greater resistance. But in spite of this slightly better fate, the Indian heritage shows all the marks of cultural colonization: hybridization, dialectization, and underdevelopment. As a result, the Indian in the Caribbean has experienced a marked degree of creolization; and it is the above processes of cultural colonization that have been largely responsible for this process of creolization.

In sum, we can say that postemancipation society saw the following important changes in its cultural situation. The first was the Christianization of the African. This process completed the first phase cultural colonization, which uproots the colonized and relocates him on the margins of the colonizers' culture. There the colonized is forced to inhabit a dependent, hybridized cultural universe which has been socially reduced to the status of a dialect. Precisely because of its arrested and dependent nature, this cultural universe may be described as underdeveloped, as opposed to undeveloped, culture.

Second, not only did Christianization complete the first phase of cultural colonization but, together with education, it constituted the primary instrument of the second phase. During this phase, "the mutual interest" of colonizer and colonized was to be taught; and through education and religion the latter were to be kept from a consciousness of their own independent value as rational beings. In addition to this, the educational system opened up possibilities of assimilation. These possibilities were significant for two reasons. First, they gave legitimacy to the educational system itself and to the class structure of the society; and second, they made it possible for the colonized to further alienate himself by attempting to conform to the image of the anglicized African that these institutions upheld. By doing all of this, Christianization and education only reinforced the tendencies toward cultural underdevelopment already begun in the first phase.

The third important change was the emergence of carnival and Christmas as occasions of cultural expression for the masses, through the use of the *mas* band. Fourth, and finally, there was the arrival of a new cultural group, the Indians, who, for reasons similar to those of the African was forced to make adaptations to a dominant British cultural presence. These, then, were the important cultural changes that took place in Caribbean society between the middle of the nineteenth century and the beginning of the twentieth.

Decolonization

While these efforts at Christianization and mass education were taking place, events in other areas of the society were not standing still. In the economic arena, the colonizer now had major problems to face. the "golden age of sugar" was soon to be over, and new staples would be introduced only to meet a similar fate a little later. These problems were brought on by a number of factors: Britain's conversion to free trade, competition from Cuba, and the appearance of sugar beet on the world market. It was not until the central factory system had been introduced, the protected market returned, and a rise in prices brought on by the First World War that profitability returned to agriculture. This, however, did not last too long, as the depression of the thirties was soon to follow.

In the political arena, despite the efforts at social control, the colonized refused to remain silent. The loudest of these refusals was, of course, the Morant Bay rebellion of 1865 in Jamaica. The worsening economic situation described above did not help political matters either. On the contrary, it produced serious discontent among the masses, which resulted in a large number of "blind protests." It was to address these circumstances that the commission of 1897 was appointed.

However, problems and resistance did not occur only in the economic and political arenas. They took the form of the resurgence of the Africanist presence in the cultural outlook of the colonized. In Jamaica, this presence can be dimly seen in the revival movement of the 1860s; it later becomes more visible in Bedwardism, and finally emerges full blown in the Garvey movement at the turn of the century. In the other islands, this presence was nurtured in the lodges and friendly societies that began appearing in the 1840s. In Antigua, for example, the St. Johnson's uprising of 1918 was lead by George Weston, John Furlonge, and Sunny Price, all members of the Ulotrician Universal Lodge. Immediately after the riot, Mr. Weston left for the U.S. to become one of Garvey's right-hand men.

In spite of this history of resistance to the second phase of colonization, it is not until the uprisings of the 1930s that the movement for decolonization really begins to show signs of success. Even though these were not the most violent uprisings in the history of the region, they are of extreme importance. As was the case with previous uprisings, they provided the occasion for an outpouring of Africanist, nationalist, anticolonial, and other sentiments. On all of these occasions one gets a glimpse of the world of the colonized that has been forced into silence: his desire for freedom, his vision of a life independent of the colonizer, and his feelings of pride in his African past. What made the thirties unique was the fact that these feelings that had surfaced so many times in the past were not allowed to submerge again. Rationalized and subsumed under the principle of nationalism, they were able to take root in the everyday consciousness of the masses. With this achievement, the long repressed political personality of the colonized finally found a voice and a small place in society.

Several factors contributed to this permanent crystalization of a national consciousness. First, there must have been the effect of the gradually increasing ability of the populace to read and write. This must have extended their social and intellectual horizons. Second, there was the availability of capable leaders eager to ensure the realization of these national strivings. Here is Normal Manley on his role as a leader: "There is a greater and bigger problem. . . . It is the problem of what to do with the new hope that has been found to exist in Jamaica, how to keep alive this new spirit, how to mold it and harness it to greater benefit."[8] Third, and finally, political consciousness gained further permanence through its institutionalization in unions and political parties. This liberation of the political personality and the organization of political consciousness around nationalism was the supreme achievement of the uprisings of the thirties.

Decolonization and Culture

With a political consciousness as part of the general outlook of the populace, the stage was now set for the building of the West Indian nation; it made possible the entertaining of nationalist possibilities that could replace colonial actualities. This urge to replace the colonizer is the driving force behind the movement for decolonization. It is a calling into question of the rule of the colonizer. The attempts that are then made to challenge this rule often lead to violence. As the clashes between colonizer and colonized increase, the urge grows stronger as does the movement for national liberation.

The impact of this nationalist movement was first apparent in the political arena. There it manifested itself in the demand for self-government and the rejection of colonial rule. In the economic arena, it manifested itself in the rejection of the imposed role of staple producer for the metropole. This resulted in attempts at breaking the monopolistic and monopsonic relations imposed by the colonizer, attempts at industrialization, and the opening up of the region to other (mainly U.S.) foreign investors. As a result, significant changes took place in the economic and political life of the region. Politically, the individual societies moved from crown colony government to formal independence or associated statehood, and economically, oil, bauxite, and tourism gradually took the place of agriculture.

Though less extensively examined, the impact of this new nationalism on culture was almost, if not equally, as dramatic. This should come as no surprise since a national culture is the embodiment of the national consciousness in painting, writing, ritual, and music. As in the economic and political arenas, in all these areas of cultural endeavor, the new nationalism manifested itself in the rejection of colonial realities. In this instance, however, it was the long process of cultural colonization that came under attack. One by one, all the legitimating rationales for the process—from racial superiority to the civilizing mission—were exposed and rejected. Having done this, the colonized then proceeds to turn upside down the world of the colonizer, all in an effort to reclaim himself. All that the colonizer deemed bad he now declares to be good. Whatever was at the bottom he puts on top. Attempts to reverse the long process of cultural alienation are made by celebrating things African and rejecting the European identity. African religions, clothes, and languages now become proud symbols of a new identity. Blackness is revalorized and whiteness correspondingly devalued. The more thoroughly an individual has been colonized the more extreme his rejection appears to be, once the process of decolonization has set in. But whatever form the rejections take, mild or extreme, they are all attempts to undo and reject the process of cultural colonization. To the extent that colonization has suppressed these nationalist feelings, the sense of peoplehood is also undermined. If there is not the sense of a people, then there is little reason to write or to articulate alternative visions of the future. The breaking through of this long-suppressed national consciousness provided much needed inspiration to Caribbean artists, whose work, in turn, helped to keep the nationalist flame alive

This reciprocal relationship between culture and the nationalist movement was true for both middle and working class cultural creativity. Among the middle classes cultural creativity most often took the form of writing. However, this should not be taken as being representative of the members of this class. For we have already seen that they were a highly assimilated group in whose view education was anything but creative. Rather, it was the exceptional, the dis*solution*ed, and the less assimilated among them who turned to writing.

Even before the events of the 1930s, there were indications of significant changes in the Caribbean novel. These could be discerned in the writings two white West Indians, Tom Redcam and H. G. de Lisser. Prior to these two writers, the literature of the region was the literature of the colonizer. It was highly imitative of British literature and was permeated by the racism and chauvinism that have characterized colonial writing, be it history, science, religion, or literature.[9] Redcam was the editor of the *Jamaica Times,* a poet, a playwright, and the author of two novels, *Becka's Buckra Baby* (1913) and *One Brown Girl and . . .* (1909). De Lisser was the author of several novels, including *Jane's Career* (1913). Kenneth Ramchand explains the significance of this novel: "Jane is the first full West Indian fictional heroine; and it is in *Jane's Career* that de Lister's attitude to his raw material and his characters comes closest to being like that of later West Indian writers."[10] However, it was ironic that this novel should have been written by a man who in later life was such an outspoken critic of West Indian nationalism.

The next important surfacing of full West Indian fictional heroes occurred with the formation of literary groups around the following periodicals: *The Beacon* (Trinidad, 1931) *Bim* (Barbados, 1942), *Focus* (Jamaica, 1943), and *Kyk-over-al* (Guyana, 1945). The short stories, poems, plays, and essays that filled these volumes revealed the new values that were emerging and the attempts at unravelling the snares of the colonization process. In their focus on the colonized African, his life and problems, these new writers were turning upside down the world of the colonizer in their literature.

While the issues of these periodicals were appearing, novels were also being written. Alfred Mendes published his first novel, *Pitch Lake,* in 1934 and his second, *Black Fauns,* in 1935, while C. L. R. James published *Minty Alley* in 1936. Both James and Mendes had been active in the group around *The Beacon.* These authors were soon followed by Mittelholzer, Mais, Ried, Lamming, Selvon, Naipual, Hearne, Carew, Salkey, Wynter, and others—a veritable outpouring of literature as never before seen in the region. Between 1950 and 1965, over 100 novels were written by West Indian authors.[11] In these novels the calling into question of the colonial situation and the celebration of the nationalist movement are taken even further. In them we can see the growing power and presence of the Caribbean masses. Lamming says that the Caribbean novel "is perhaps the only type or example of the novel, in which . . . the central character is really the mass. There is always a sense of mass whether it is The *Castle of my Skin* or Mais' *The Hills Were Joyful Together* or Reid's *New Day.* It is not so much the individual consciousness as central character, but mass."[12] This movement of the masses onto the center of the literary stage was in step with similar movements in the larger society.

In the theater, developments were equally dramatic. As in the case of the novel, these new currents signaled the end of the colonial theater. The latter was maintained primarily by travelling companies from England, whose productions, quite naturally, were predominantly English. Consequently, "the performed dramas were for the most part alien to the territories, alien in the sense that they said little or nothing about conditions of Caribbean life."[13]

The first movements away from this situation can be seen in the works of Tom Redcam and Mac Gregor James. However, credit for the appearance on stage of the first full blown West Indian fictional heroes and heroines, must go to the indefatigable Marcus Gravey. These characters appeared in three plays, *The Coronation of an African King*, *The Roaming Jamaicans* and *Slavery*, which were all staged in 1930. The performances took place at the open air theater established by Garvey at Edelweis Park in Jamaica.[14] These plays were soon followed by Cupidon's adaptation of H. G. de Lisser's, *Susan Proudleigh* (1930), *Jamaican Bandits* (1931) and *Jane's Career* (1933). In 1936, C. L. R. James' *Toussaint L'Ouverture* was performed in London, with Paul Robeson in the leading role. 1936 also saw the production of De Wilton Roger's *Blue Blood and Black*, which was followed by *Trinidad* in 1937. In 1938, there was the performance of Una Marson's *Pocomania*, and in 1939 Frank Hill's *Upheaval*. The former dealt with a Jamaican religious cult, while the latter focused on the labor riots of the previous year.[15] This ferment in the field of drama continued through the following decades so that by 1963 more than 160 plays had been published by West Indian playwrights. Even though we cannot examine any of these plays in detail, many of the titles are very revealing. They hint at a concern for the condition of the West Indian. Those by Garvey and James are perhaps the most obvious. In their works the problem of recovering and revalorizing the past of the colonized gains explicit treatment.

Not even the area of education was unaffected by the new burst of nationalism. To complete the system already described, the imperial government established a university in Jamaica as a "parting gift" to the region. Under the initiative of the new local governments, significant expansions took place in the fields of primary and secondary education. Large numbers of these schools supported by government funds, were opened throughout the region. As a result, a secondary education was more within the reach of the average West Indian.

The establishment of the university made possible other important developments, such as the institutionalization of science. As a result, the years that followed saw impressive developments take place in the social sciences. The numbers of volumes on West Indian history increased, complementing the pioneering efforts of scholars such as Ragatz, Pares, and Williams. However, the discipline that has shown the most vigor is economics. Drawing on the pioneering work of Arthur

Lewis, economic thinking has mushroomed to the point where it now pervades thinking in many other disciplines. For these developments in economics, in addition to Lewis, credit must go to men like George Huggins, Clive Thomas, Havelock Brewester, Norman Girvan, and George Beckford. Although coming a little later, important strides have also been made in the field of political science. These have largely been the result of the work of individuals such as Gordon Lewis, Archie Singham, Vaughan Lewis, Trevor Munroe, and Carl Stone. Developments in sociology have not been similarly impressive. In anthropology, things appear to have been on the decline since the departure of Raymond Smith and Michael Smith. Even though we cannot go into detail, it is worth pointing out that the ideas generated in these disciplines have contributed greatly to the further development of national consciousness and to the building of the West Indian nation.

In the religious sphere, the new nationalist spirit manifested itself in the formal decolonization of most of the established churches. Local ministers and priests in increasing numbers began replacing foreign ones. Formal ties of domination were broken with the various denominational heads in England, with the result that local churches were not formally independent representatives of the various Christian denominations. To further establish religious independence, a theological seminary was opened at the university which provided local training for future ministers. However, at the more substantive levels of beliefs, rituals, and programs for salvation, there has been little or no change. To the extent that change has occurred, it has been primarily among working class sects such as the Rastafarians. Consequently, in spite of formal decolonization, the Christian churches have continued to function primarily as reducing agents; that is, as social forces that reduce the worldly expectations of the masses which, in turn, reduces the pressure on the economic and political systems.

This may be as appropriate a moment as any to note the absence of a developed indigenous metaphysical tradition. The failure of this to emerge points to the loss of an indigenous religion, since most metaphysical systems are intellectual rationalizations of already existing religious beliefs. It also points to the uncreative nature of the relationship that West Indians have with Christianity. For in spite of the many calls for the decolonization of theology,[16] the decolonization of religion occurred only on the formal level. No secular philosophy among West Indian intellectuals has developed from this theology. Rather, if it has given rise to anything among this group, it is a general skepticism about religion.

To the extent that intellectual rationalism has given rise to philosophy, it is a social philosophy. It is the philosophy of developmentism which, although rooted in economics, underlies so much of West Indian thought. This philosophical orientation is operative not only among elements of the middle classes, but also among elements of the working classes, albeit in less carefully articulated forms. For without plans for development it is virtually impossible to gain the political support of the working class.

While the emergence of national literature, a national theater, and the institutionalization of science were largely middle-class phenomena, the emergence of national rhythms was largely a working-class phenomenon. It was in the 1930s that the steel band emerged in Trinidad, soon to be followed by the calypso—a continuation of the old cariso tradition. In Jamaica, the Rastafarian cult, from whose peculiar rhythms were to come the ska, the rock steady, and finally reggae, had already crystallized.

In the Eastern Caribbean, the growth of the steel band and calypso was accompanied by significant changes in the mass rituals, carnival, and Christmas celebrations. In some cases these changes involved changes in the organization of the rituals, while in others, changes in the music that was part of the rituals. An example of the former is the initiation of Trinidad-style carnivals to replace Christmas celebrations in a number of islands. While there were definite commercial reasons behind these moves, there are also strong indications that much of the psychic relevance of the Christmas celebrations had passed with the emergence of the new nationalism and the processes of decolonization that it set in motion.

In a similar vein it could be argued that many of the *mas* bands customarily played on both of these occasions also began to lose their relevance under the changed conditions. The disappearance of bands such as Perrot Grenade, the John Bull, and Pow are indications of important social and psychological changes that took place after the 1930s. On the other hand, the popularity of the U.S. sailor bands and bands that created a sense of exuberance and gaiety through color (e.g., Wild Indian bands) is among the factors that gave these rituals their new tone. Also, the sense of comic irony that characterized so much of the old music was now replaced by escapism and hedonism as responses to the new forms of working-class domination.

These, then, were the cultural forces that were released by the movement for decolonization. In literature, in drama, in social philosophy, and in music, the world of the colonizer could be seen on the retreat, while that of the West Indian moved to center stage. The real movements that this inversion reflected were creating new cultural space for the colonized. It made it possible for him to feel more at home with himself, his African past, and his dialect culture now that he had shattered the lies and the false values of the colonizer. In short, in this newly created space he could have his moment of "Negritude." It is this easing of the bicultural division within the colonized that gives the process of cultural decolonization its significance.

Cultural Decolonization and Neocolonialism

In spite of this impressive showing, it was clear that by the middle of the 1960s the societal space, cultural and otherwise, created by the movement for decolonization had been used up. As a result, people were once again feeling cramped and oppressed and found it necessary to resort to violent political activity. Between 1965 and 1974, there were few islands that had not experienced major disruptions of institutionalized political processes. These events signaled the collapse of the forces that had come together in the preindependence period. In addition to this, the decolonization process itself, with its reassertion of Africanness, brought out similar sentiments among the Indians. Consequently, a more tense relationship between both groups has become part of the contemporary social scene.

This breakdown presented itself as an appropriate moment for a new assessment of the changes taking place in the region. The analyses that were presented to explain this breakdown[17] revealed that there had been an overestimation of the significance of the changes that had come with decolonization and that we had failed to see both the many ways in which old colonial patterns were being reinforced and the new ones that were coming into being. As a result, new interpretations of Caribbean development appeared that were organized around concepts such as "plantation society," "plantation society further modified," and "neo-colonialism." These new theoretical orientations all sought to correct the overestimation of the extent to which Caribbean society had decolonized itself. They did this by revealing the extent to which the society was still dependent on the old colonizer and on new ones. In the economic arena, they showed Caribbean society to be dependent on foreign aid, foreign trade, and imported consumption and production patterns.[18] In the political arena, they showed Caribbean states to be falling more and more under the influence of the U.S. now that the European presence was on the decline.[19] In terms of class relations, analysis revealed widening gaps between the middle and working classes. This gap, it was suggested, resulted from the fact that decolonization, without altering certain basic aspects of the social structure, had succeeded in replacing the colonizer with the more educated and assimilated members of the middle classes.[20] As a result, we get a process of internal colonization which only increases the distance between the classes. Finally, in the cultural sphere, the demand for imported culture continued to grow. As we shall see, there was a demand not only for the products of British culture but also for those of American culture. These structures of domination that the new analysis revealed are, in my view, best summed up under the label of neocolonialism. In the most general terms, it describes a social situation in which a people is formally free of the colonizer, but remains under his domination through being tied to him in a number of substantive ways.

This substantive presence of the colonizer, in spite of his formal absence, was felt in all areas as a compromising of West Indian nationality. In the economic and political arenas, it produced demands for localization and nationalization. In the cultural sphere, the cry was for West Indianization and indigenization. The cry came with the realization that the tone of the society was still not West Indian, that the society was still producing culturally colonized individuals who were unsure of who they were. "I came from nowhere worth mentioning," the hero of Patterson's *An Absence of Ruins* replies to his English questioner, "I have no past except the haunting recollection of each passing moment which comes to me always as something having been lost . . . If I appear to be like you, please understand that it is out of no vain wish to be identified with you, but out of a simple desire not to draw attention to myself."[21] This is the cultural identity problem that the West Indian faces as a neocolonial. He is free, but is still unable to be himself without appearing to be like his colonizer.

Even though Patterson's hero might have been an extreme case, he provides valuable insight into the cultural identity problem that is still to be resolved. He helps us to understand the demands for West Indianization that shook the cultural institutions of the region,[22] the paradoxical situation of demands for black power in societies with black governments, and the resurfacing of anti-white and anti-imperialist sentiments. In order to understand the social roots of this continuing struggle for Caribbean culture to maintain itself, we must identify the social processes and arrangements that continue to undermine a strong sense of West Indianness. As the analyses mentioned earlier suggest, these are to be found in the structures of dependence and underdevelopment that emerged during the early phases of colonization. In the area of culture, we have already seen that these processes and arrangements began with the deculturalization of Africans and Indians, followed by processes of forced Anglicization. These cultural impositions were economically and politically motivated; that is, they had as their aim the reorienting of the cultural world of the colonized so that he could function in his assigned roles in the economic and political systems of Caribbean societies. Consequently, the degree of imposed Anglicization was largely determined by these factors. However, the process of cultural colonization was a dynamic one, with a momentum that was not completely under the control of either the colonized or colonizer. As a result, we saw that the above impositions were followed by a process of internalization which resulted in a tendency for the colonized to negate his traditional identity and to strive after an ever receding Anglicized self-image. This tendency was reinforced by the institutionalization of British norms and standards in most public places, such as schools and churches. In this way, the demand for foreign culture became rooted in the alienation of the colonized and ceased to be a direct result of the processes of economic and political domination referred to above.

As a result of this locally rooted demand for foreign culture, the cultural system of Commonwealth Caribbean societies may be conceptualized as having two sectors: a local or creole sector and a foreign or British-oriented sector. It is the relationship between these two sectors that explains the underdevelopment of the local sector and hence the crisis that continues to accompany the process of West Indianization. This relationship has been both a part and a reflection of a broader dualism that has characterized these colonial societies: a cleavage between the subjugated local sector and the dominant foreign-controlled sector. The English cultural tradition shared in the dominance of the latter sector; its local growth must therefore be understood within this hegemonic framework. Similarly, the negative growth of local cultural traditions must be understood within the framework of the process of domination imposed on the larger social worlds of which they were a part. These processes of colonial domination succeeded in severing a number of important relationships, two of which are important for an understanding of the underdevelopment of local cultures.

First, there was a change in the relationship that the colonized has with his own culture. As a result of colonial domination, he ceased to have an easy, creative, and self-reflexive relationship with his cultural environment. Elements of it had now been systematically imposed from without, thus giving it its hybrid quality. This replacement of a creative relationship to elements in the cultural environment by an authoritarian one must have stifled creativity, discouraged critical thinking, and so inhibited growth.

Second and more important, colonial domination succeeded in severing most of the systematic ties that the local cultural system had with processes of economic and political production. The important result of this severance was that the latter two processes now ceased to generate an increasing demand for the words, songs, ideas and other products of the local cultural system. Rather, to the extent that there was a growth dynamic, this growth generated a greater demand for foreign cultural products. It is this separation of the local cultural system from the stimuli of the demands of other sectors of the society, that has largely been responsible for its underdevelopment. This separation was effected through the institutionalization of ties between the cultural demands of the major centers of social reproduction and the British cultural tradition. These ties manifested themselves in the fact that the British cultural tradition came to be the accepted one in these more dynamic areas of the societies. Consequently, the expansion of these sectors meant the further Anglicization of more Africans and Indians. These additional recruitment needs were often complemented by the desire of the colonized to assimilate and make real his imaginary identification with the colonizer. These two tendencies have had the effect of reinforcing the separation of the local cultural system from the dynamic centers of social life. This reinforcement, in turn, deepened the process of cultural underdevelopment. This was essentially the situation until the period of decolonization.

What decolonization achieved was a slight but significant shift in the relationship between the two sectors of the cultural system—a shift that brought the local cultural system into a closer and more systematic relationship with the dominant centers of these societies. Through the institutionalization of West Indian norms, the greater acceptance of the African and Indian traditions, the greater participation of creolized individuals in the running of the society, and the new status it gave to local cultural creativity, the process of decolonization resulted in the establishing of more systematic relationships of use between the local cultural system and the dominant sectors of the society. But this whole process of change was limited, as were the links that were forged. They were both limited by two sets of factors. The first was that the process of decolonization only partially uprooted the set of social and psychological processes that generated the demand for imported culture. As a result, both the preference and the demand for British cultural products continued. The second factor was that the level of the internal development of the various media of expression that made up the local cultural system was not sufficient to meet immediately the demands of the more developed sectors. By level of internal development I mean the degree of differentiation, relative autonomy, technification, and commodification—in short, the degree of rationalization that characterized the social organization of the various media of expression. Thus, in addition to the continuing preference for imported culture, the demand for foreign cultural inputs was also a result of differences in the level of development of the local cultural system and the more foreign oriented sectors of the society.

Contrary to earlier impressions, this demand for imported culture shows no signs of abating. Rather, it is showing resilience and a new dynamism. The major new dynamic in the foreign sector of the cultural system is the institutionalization of a growing American presence. In contradistinction to the British presence, the American presence is set within the network of relations that have come to define imperialism in a period of U.S.-Soviet hegemony as opposed to European hegemony. The part of this process of penetration which concerns us most is the establishment of local outlets for the products of the American mass culture or entertainment industry. This industry is culturally important in that the consumption of its products affects the attitudes, outlooks, and values of the consumers. In other words, it affects the consciousness of the consumer, and consequently, the cultural world he inhabits. The major media of expression of this industry are the television, the movie, the novel, the record, the newspaper, and the magazine. Through these media, the industry makes available a steady flow of foreign (mainly U.S.) cultural products. The values, life styles, images, and sensibilities, that are coveyed through these media constitute a powerful challenge to indigenous ways, which are seldom so attractively packaged. The worlds disclosed by these media not only present tempting opportunities for the West Indian to try to be other than what he is, but they also encourage him to do so. This they do by presenting the American way of life as exemplary. Whether intentional or not, the effect is to invite the consumer to accept new values, new heroes, new models, and, in short, to participate in a new cultural orientation. Consequently, this industry, more than any other, is responsible for the many Americanisms, both black and white, to be found in the West Indian cultural milieu.

From this discussion of the importance and the role of imported culture I hope I have indicated some of the countervailing forces which succeeded in limiting the processes of cultural decolonization. These countervailing forces were rooted in a pattern of dependent growth which generated a greater demand for the products of foreign cultural systems than for those of the local cultural system. Consequently, the latter has remained underdeveloped and unable to provide guidance in the creation of modern institutions. It is this structural imbalance, together with active foreign penetration, that is the source of continuing cultural dependency and the accompanying crisis of West Indianization that has become characteristic of the neocolonial period.

Conclusion

In this chapter we have tried to present a sociohistorical analysis of cultural decolonization in the Commonwealth Caribbean. The analysis began with an examination of cultural colonization. This was divided into two phases both of which were united by the common aim of social control. In the first phase, control was achieved through the deculturalization of the colonized. In the second, it was achieved through a resocialization process that made use of the instruments of education and religion. The first phase left the colonized with a hybrid, dialect culture, while the second opened up possibilities of assimilation. Together, they resulted in the cultural estrangement of the colonized and in his dependence on his colonizer.

Cultural decolonization is the attempt to undo this process; the attempt to shake off the values of the colonizer and to reclaim and revalorize the native heritage. This process was always a tendency within the society, but really established itself only in the 1930s. However, once started, impressive strides were made toward the development of a national culture. But as this process proceeded (along with decolonization in other areas), hidden and deep-rooted countervailing forces began to make their appearance. These were the social processes and arrangements that stemmed from the dependent nature of Caribbean institutions and the ravaged state of Caribbean culture. It is against these countervailing forces (with the goal of a national culture in mind) that the achievements of decolonization must be measured and assessed.

When viewed in this perspective, the achievements of the movement seem less impressive. Our attention is captured by the long way that is still left to go with our local languages, religions, and arts. How are we to cover this ground? What can we do? We can write more books, more poems, more plays. We can proclaim more loudly our West Indianness, our Africanness, our Indianness. But all of these responses, while relevant, miss the deeper dimensions of the problem. They all forget to ask what it was that arrested the growth of national culture in the first place, and what it was that produced its current renaissance. The answers to these questions reveal "the reciprocal bases of national culture and the fight for freedom in colonial societies." It was colonial domination that called a halt to the growth of national culture; and it was the movement for decolonization that made possible the current flowering. But if this rebirth has not provided us with a vibrant national culture and a firm identity, it means that decolonization is not complete and that colonial domination is still at work. The extent to which we can enjoy such a national culture is in direct proportion to the extent to which the colonizer has been substantively removed, and in direct proportion to the extent to which the national culture has ceased to be a contested culture condemned to secrecy or to the periphery. Hence, the extent to which the society successfully decolonizes itself must become the broader framework for evaluating the strides made in the direction of a national culture. This process of decolonization must be complemented by a process of indigenization rooted in the internal development of the various media of expression of the local cultural system, and in the forging of systematic relationships of use between the latter system and the more dynamic centers of these societies. Without these structural changes, the process of indigenization will not take root and the demand for imported culture will continue.

If this is indeed the case, then we cannot evaluate the process of cultural decolonization by counting the number of novels written, poems composed, or cultural alternatives imaginatively elaborated. This is not to say that writers should cease writing and poets stop composing. On the contrary, critical and aesthetic self-reflection are important elements in the liberation of the colonized consciousness. So also is the elaboration of cultural alternatives. Rather, it is to say that the struggle for a deeper national reality, one that would permit these and other local cultural creations to take root, is an equally important cultural act. To turn away from this is to move against history, to rob culture of a more vibrant future, to condemn it to the past, and to abandon the liberation of the consciousness of the colonized.

Notes

1. Frantz Fanon, *Black Skins, White Masks* (New York, 1976).
2. See, for example, Rex Nettleford, *Caribbean Cultural Identity* (Kingston, 1978), p. 31.
3. Kari Levitt and Lloyd Best, "The Character of Caribbean Economy," in G. Beckford (ed.), *Caribbean Economy* (Kingston, 1975), p. 39.
4. Frantz Fanon, *The Wretched of the Earth* (New York, 1963), p. 237.
5. Quoted in Shirley Gordon, *A Century of West Indian Education* (London, 1963), p. 20.
6. Ibid., p. 21.
7. Ibid., p. 58.
8. Rex Nettleford, *Manley and the New Jamaica: Selected Speeches* (Kingston, 1971), p. 103.
9. For a good discussion of this literature, see, E. Brathwaite, "Creative Literature of the British West Indies During the Period of Slavery," *Savacou*, Vol. 1, No. 1, June 1970, pp. 46–71.
10. Kenneth Ramchand, *The West Indian Novel and its Background* (London, 1974), p. 57.
11. E. Brathwaite, "The Love Axis (1); Developing a Caribbean Aesthetic, 1962–1974," in Houston Baker, Jr. (ed.), *Reading Black* (Cornell University, 1976), pp. 20–36.
12. George Lamming, *Caribbean Contact,* Vol. 5, No. 11, (March 1978), p. 10.

13. Errol Hill, "The Emergence of a National Drama in the West Indies," *Caribbean Quarterly*, Vol. 18, No. 4, December 1972, p. 15.

14. Ibid., pp. 39–40.

15. Ibid., p. 21.

16. Idris Hamid, (ed.), *Troubling of the Waters* (Port-of-Spain, 1974).

17. These analyses were done primarily by a group of scholars known as the New World Group.

18. W. Demas, "Situation and Change," in G. Beckford (ed.), *Caribbean Economy*, p. 64.

19. Vaughan Lewis and A. Singham, "Integration, Domination and the Small-State System: the Caribbean," in T. Munroe and R. Lewis, *Readings in Government and Politics of the West Indies* (Mona, 1971), pp. 171–178.

20. Lloyd Best, "Independent Thought and Caribbean Freedom," in N. Girvan and O. Jefferson, (eds.), *Readings in the Political Economy of the Caribbean* (Kingston, 1971), pp. 7–28.

21. O. Patterson, *An Absence of Ruins* (London, 1966), p. 70.

22. In particular, the events surrounding the occupation of the Creative Arts Center at the University of the West Indies.

PART 2

The Contemporary
World Order and
National Development

6

Caribbean State Systems and the Contemporary World Order

VAUGHAN A. LEWIS

The end of the 1960s and certainly the first years of the decade of the 1970s witnessed a generalization to various countries of the South American continent and of the Caribbean of the trends already prevalent in the Third World of assertive political and, more importantly, economic nationalism. The nationalization of American multinational holdings in Peru and Chile was paralleled by the nationalization of Canadian-American bauxite holdings in the recently independent state of Guyana. The explosion of petroleum prices in and after 1973 was followed by the nationalization of American petroleum holdings in Venezuela and the imposition of extensive taxation on the Canadian-American bauxite transnationals, and by the stated intention of the government to participate in the industry along the lines of the earlier Chilean and Zambian examples.

All these events and fears of similar ones gave rise in the United States to the perception of a simultaneous political and economic "threat from the Third World,"[1] to use a now famous phrase coined in 1973 by an international economist who became a member of the Carter administration. Within the United States, however, there were differing levels and types of responses to the particular actions emanating from these Western hemispheric countries. The immediate hostility of U.S. companies and the federal government to the Peruvian and Chilean expropriations had, as is now well known, quite different outcomes.

The response to the Guyanese nationalizations and to the Jamaican bauxite levy was made in terms of what appears to have been an American perception of a general trajectory of radicalization of domestic and foreign economic and political policy on the part of the governments of these countries (though we might note that the acts of the two governments were separated in time). The response appears, therefore, to have been one of deciding to be generally unhelpful as far as providing American official economic assistance, encouragement of private foreign investment, and American influence in official international aid institutions were concerned. Jamaica, in particular, had been until 1974 a country the substantial development of whose economy in the 1960's had been crucially dependent on American private foreign investment.

On the other hand, both the U.S. government and private enterprise consider the Venezuelan nationalization of oil and iron ore facilities generally acceptable and part of an inevitable trend in the OPEC countries. The Venezuelans had, of course, engaged in extensive preparatory diplomacy, giving assurances of reasonable compensation, of a continuity of petroleum supply, and of a continuing place at a different level of operation for the American multinationals.

Finally, under the government of Luis Echeverría, Mexico appeared by 1974 to be reinforcing the trend in Latin America toward the nonalignment and economic radicalism stances of the Third World, and thus away from the traditional Latin American separatism vis-à-vis the postwar new nations. Echeverría's radicalization of Mexican domestic and foreign policy was taking place parallel in time to that occurring in the Caribbean, and particularly in Jamaica.

The events of October 1973 and afterwards in the international economic system had in fact a dual effect on the Caribbean countries. First, for most of these countries—in fact, with the simple exception of Trinidad and Tobago—and like the other non-oil-producing countries, the hike in oil prices was to have seriously deleterious effects on the balance of payments position and then on the general financial situations of the countries. This led to an immediate search, from wherever possible, for short term financial support. For Trinidad and Tobago, on the other hand, the increased petroleum prices had the beneficial effect of rescuing the country from the increasingly perilous (until 1973) foreign exchange and financial situation which had already been a contributor to domestic economic and political dislocation in that country. In terms of regional (CARICOM) political and economic relations, this increase in foreign exchange resources for Trinidad, of an order hitherto unknown, initiated an eventual change in status among the constituent countries. Where there had been relative equality in the status and contributions of the two pivotal states of the system, Jamaica and Trinidad, there now gradually occurred an imbalance in bargaining and, therefore, general diplomatic capabilities between them as the financial strength of Trinidad persistently increased and that of Jamaica persistently declined.

This takes us to the other side of the duality of effects to which we referred. In a sense the real effect of the petroleum price increases was, for countries like Jamaica, Barbados and Guyana, a *delayed* one. As is well known, the petroleum increases both followed and were the precursor of substantial rises in the prices of a number of commodities located in both the industrialized and developing countries, and stemmed from a particular pattern of behavior of the Western industralized countries and the centrally planned economies, in particular the Soviet Union.

Jamaica benefited from this by the opportunity to increase foreign exchange revenue by increased taxation on the bauxite levy, and also by the rises in free market sugar prices in 1975. But Guyana, Barbados and Trinidad benefited from this letter also. These countries, of course, are all poorer economies which, though small, are characterized by a certain diversity of resource bases, unlike many Third World countries.

It was, I suggest, the very severity of the situation induced by the oil price rises on the one hand, and the possibilities for exploitation of the resource dependence of the industralized countries, at a particular juncture on the other that provided the occasion and the necessary legitimacy for Jamaica to initiate the implementation of the idea of a collective bargaining institution for bauxite, the International Bauxite Association (IBA), and to gain the necessary confidence not simply for imposing the bauxite levy, but subsequently for engaging in a wide sphere of international diplomacy in respect of the reorganization of the international economic system which other Third World countries had previously been proposing. (We should note, however, that the IBA is not a simple Third World or underdeveloped country cartel, being composed of industrialized and underdeveloped, communist, and free market countries.)

It is within this general climate of flexibility induced by international economic instability or uncertainty that Caribbean countries participated and took, in certain instances, leading roles in the concerted diplomacy vis-à-vis the European Community that led to the so-called Lome Agreement in 1975. To this we shall return.

But while we concentrate on the impetus gained for the assertion of political and economic nationalism from the dynamic character of the international environment, some attention should be given to the impetus from the countries' domestic sociopolitical systems. The events of social rebellion in Trinidad in 1970, the persistent push for nationalist and socialist measures from the opposition party in Guyana, and the increasing unemployment and social disequilibrium (in spite of sustained economic growth in the 1960s) leading to change of regime in Jamaica in 1972 all suggested to the political elite the need for reconsideration of the strategy of economic development being undertaken by the Caribbean countries. The strategy was based on welcoming extensive foreign investment in, and ownership of, mineral resource locations and industrializaton on the basis of import substitution, again through the medium of private foreign investors. As is well known, the policy failed, from the point of view of employment creation, to keep pace with population growth in the face of declining agricultural production. Hence, the rise in the Caribbean, too, of populist nationalism, insisting on the indigenization of natural resource ownership in particular, comparable to such trends in other Third World countries, was legitimized at the level of the international system by the United Nations Declaration on Sovereignty Over Natural Resources.

Changes in Global Political-Economic Arrangements and Their Effects in the Caribbean

From the point of view of the Caribbean countries, the tendency towards normalization of political relations (détente) between the United States and the Soviet Union in the latter stages of, and after, the Vietnam war had two effects, one general and the other more specific. The more general, having meaning in the context of Caribbean radicalization of policy, was the appearance of a certain restraint on the part of the United States with regard to overt intervention in the hemisphere (the Congressional revelations concerning Chile further exacerbated this).

The second and more specific affect related to the suggestion of a normalization of United States relations with Cuba in the wake of (a) increasing mutual acceptance on the part of the U.S. and U.S.S.R. of certain rules of behavior—at least in respect to their claimed fundamental spheres of interest, (b) substantial economic relations between the two major powers, and (c) the American diplomatic opening to China and the unpredictability of expectations and role behavior that this created for America's small allies in particular. All these left open the possibility of sudden changes in American hemispheric policy, leaving the Caribbean, or other hemispheric countries, in the lurch, hanging on to an American Cold War policy now discredited by the United States itself. We will return shortly to this and other aspects of the U.S.-U.S.S.R. normalization process.

At the level of changes in global economic arrangements and

stances (that is, from the point of view of the diplomacy of international economic change), we can perceive especially after 1973, a dialectic between Third World demands for a New International Economic Order (NIEO) and the response of the industrialized north to this. From the Caribbean perspective, there were initially two diplomatic thrusts relating to this: first and more autonomously inspired, their continuing integration into the nonaligned movement, and acceptance through Guyana of responsibility for organizing the elaboration of the movement's Action Program for Economic Cooperation. Second, there was the diplomacy of the eventual Lome Agreement to which we have previously referred, involving, in cooperation with the African and Pacific countries, the reorganization of the framework of their traditional imperial or metropolitan economic relations.

Let us return, however, to the question of normalization of global political relations. The Caribbean countries (through the Prime Minister of Trinidad at an OAS meeting in Venezuela in 1970) had been early proponents of the so-called normalization of Cuba's relations with the countries of the hemisphere. This reflected a concern not only to ensure a controlled normalization parallel to that occurring at the level of the superpowers, but also to establish some system of diplomatic order among countries of the Caribbean archipelago, especially in the light of increasing popular awareness of the so-called Cuban development option, but also due to a concern to consolidate the incipient effort at harmonization of relationships among the countries of the post-1968 Commonwealth Caribbean integration endeavor.

An aspect of the post-Vietnam Nixon and Kissinger doctrine, emphasizing a less overt American security presence in the Third World, was the vigorous search for regional proxies, including proxies in the South American zone. This impinged on the Commonwealth Caribbean countries to the extent that two probable candidates for the "proxy" role, Brazil and Venezuela, exist on the fringes of the Caribbean Community system (and both have muted boundary problems with either Guyana or Trinidad). The increasing prominence of Brazil and Venezuela coincided (especially after 1973) with, on the one hand, Trinidad's concern with Venezuela's desire to define for herself a legitimate economic and diplomatic role in the Caribbean (reflecting an old concern with the area) and, on the other hand, a desire on the part of Jamaica to relocate herself diplomatically in the Caribbean Basin system.

When coupled with a certain U.S. insouciance with respect to Latin American international economic concerns, the import of all this is a degree of loosening of U.S.-Latin American relations which lead to possibilities for new alignment efforts with other Third World and

European countries. Peru's emergence as a center of nonaligned action allowed for Guyana's connection with a more radical Latin American country and, in the latter part of the 1970's, with a greater Guyanese concern with domestic affairs, while Jamaica began to assert herself in this direction vis-à-vis Mexico and Venezuela in particular. Jamaica's main concerns were with collective negotiation and the formation of government multinational companies as possible counters to the private enterprise multinationals.[2]

This observation of economic concerns allows us to return to our discussion of changes in global economic arrangements. The Third World, and therefore Caribbean trajectory, can be traced through the Action Program for Economic Cooperation that was a signal to, but had little resonance with, the industrialized countries, to the Algerian and post-OPEC inspired Special Sessions of the United Nations General Assembly on the program for a New International Economic Order, which the majority of Caribbean community countries supported. These sessions and the resolutions emanating from them have to be seen as creating normative legitimacy for these desired Third World demands, rather than as having short term operational (material) significance as far as developed country responses are concerned.

The Lome negotiations of ACP-EEC countries, on the other hand, were concerned with short term material benefits as well as those of the longer term, and allowed the Caribbean countries to cement relations with a wide variety of African and Pacific countries in specific, practical issue areas. And certainly a country like Jamaica which saw itself within what we might call the "Lome perspective" of pragmatic, issue-oriented diplomacy, would have been disappointed by the failure of the Conference on International Economic Cooperation (CIEC) in which it was a participant. This conference was another example of North-South negotiation born of the 1973 events, but in which, unlike the Lome negotiations, the major power of the Western world participated. But the apparent capacity of the industrialized countries, in the years that followed, to absorb the effects of increased prices and to accommodate at the same time the increased flow of petrodollars in the international monetary system reduced the already lukewarm Western acceptance of the need for a conference of this type, with the result that little has been produced by the CIEC.[3]

Subsequent doubts about the real benefits from Lome, when placed alongside the failure of the CIEC, raise to the Third World, and therefore Caribbean mind, the question of the operational relevance of the theme of interdependence. This phrase, an important American diplomatic slogan, can be said to have been given recognition by Third

World countries in the manner of their participation in the ACP/EEC and CIEC conferences, and is to be counterposed to what Western diplomats and scholars will have tended to see as the diplomacy of confrontation characterizing the U.N. Special Sessions and, in some measure, the UNCTAD Conferences.

The relevant point here is that the relative failures of the diplomacy of interdependence return us, in some degree, to the situation of North-South stalemate and relative Western indifference concerning Third World objectives on international economic issues that is characteristic of the pre-1973 period; a stalemate that was only broken by the diplomacy of confrontation of that year. This present situation of stalemate, if correctly perceived by this writer, may now be exacerbated by a feeling in the North that the bargaining capabilities of a number of important Third World countries (their capacity for exercising influence in what one writer has called the context of international civil power) are not now as substantial as they may have been in the 1973–76 period. We shall suggest some reasons for this, as far as the Caribbean countries are concerned, in some of what follows. For some of the Caribbean countries which have recently played, at various times, not insignificant roles in the arenas of confrontation and interdependence now suffer from crucial capability weaknesses.

Caribbean Domestic Politics and Their Location in World Ideological Trends

The recognition of apparent failures of political economy in the Caribbean by many of the political elite in the beginning of the 1970s, when coupled with the effects in the Caribbean of global detente, made for a search for alternative solutions—albeit ones appropriate to the framework of competitive party politics. This led, in consequence, and in spite of that country's political framework, to the increasing visibility and debate on the assessment of the social arrangements of revolutionary Cuba. This visibility was assisted by Cuba's own renewed attention to normalizing her relations with the Latin American countries and, by extension, the countries of the Caribbean subregion. The proffers of increased diplomatic contact by Cuba were reciprocated by the CARICOM (as by other Latin American countries) and sealed by diplomatic recognition, official visits to Cuba of the Prime Ministers of Trinidad, Venezuela and Guyana,[4] and favorable statements on their part on certain of the Cuban social arrangements. With a certain popular legitimacy growing for socialism, an increasing rhetorical commitment on the part of the political elite to the ideology of socialism of one or another variant became apparent—in a sense a reversion to a trend in commitment to socialist ideology that had characterized the politics of anticolonialism of the English-speaking Caribbean countries in the late 1940's and 1950's. We might note that this ideological commitment coincided with the countries' increasing movement in the international politics of nonalignment (to which we have already referred), where many leading Third World countries had been for some time protagonists of socialism and closer relations with the socialist bloc. In a sense, then, the domestic commitment to socialism also had an international relations function and rationale.

On the other hand, it can be seen that the ideological choices of particular countries in the region were based on specific domestic characteristics and elite perceptions of resource availability for development. Neither in Trinidad in the CARICOM area, nor in Venezuela, both beneficiaries of the petroleum price increases, was there a rhetorical turn to socialism (as with Guyana and Jamaica), although their consequent economic development programs envisaged substantial public sector expansion. Trinidad's vain attempt to enter OPEC, in addition, did not conduce a turn to nonalignment in tandem with other CARICOM countries; and Venezuela, while seeking to enunciate a diplomatic opening to the Third World (undoubtedly sensitive to Mexico's movement in that direction), attempted to elaborate an emphasis on the economics of nonalignment with as little as possible of the usual accompaniment of anti-Americanism. The Venezuelan emphasis on a Latin American place in the Socialist International should, however, be noted.

Herein lay the difference between these countries and those like Jamaica and Guyana, which accepted, at the level of public policy statements, the theses of Third World dependency and American transnational distortion of Third World countries' potential for development. Jamaica and Guyana accepted the possibility of American "destabilization" (after the Chilean pattern) of "progressive" Third World states and Third World interstate relations—the implication here being these governments' relations with Cuba in particular.

It needs to be emphasized that such perceptions marked a new turn in Commonwealth Caribbean countries' official perceptions of the workings of the American-dominated hemispheric system, even though they may have been previously prevalent elsewhere. And this rhetorical stance, which developed some popular resonance, was now accompanied by a widening of the countries' diplomatic contacts and relations with the major and minor countries of the socialist world.

When linked to the new interest specifically in Cuba, this orientation raised the question of the possibilities of aid from the socialist bloc, and the extent to which certain domestic and external political orientations might be prerequisites for the receipt of socialist bloc assistance.

The World System and the Caribbean in the Era of International Economic Instability

Beginning in 1975, the Ford-Kissinger administration adopted a policy that might be mildly described as one of general unhelpfulness as the economies of the increasingly vociferous Caribbean countries began to falter under the combined strain of foreign-exchange deficiencies and mass demands for increased welfare. But so, in large measure if for different reasons, could the response of the socialist bloc countries be described, at least as far as the Caribbean countries' short-term requirements for economic assistance were concerned. There does not appear to be much evidence that Caribbean governments had done much systematic preparatory exploration of the socialist bloc countries' position on the question of economic aid to Third World countries through the existing international institutions.

These two conjunctures of "unhelpfulness" (including U.S. hostility in international financial institutions) constrained the two countries progagating forms of socialism—Guyana and Jamaica—to stand their rhetoric on its head and subordinate themselves to the International Monetary Fund (IMF). This reversal mirrored the situation elsewhere in the Caribbean Basin where (in Mexico) President Echeverría had attempted a similar radicalization of policy, and in the wider Latin American region (in Peru). It suggested that the structural interlock into the Western international system, in which the Caribbean countries have historically been placed, remains the central parameter of policymaking. It might be suggested, in turn, that the notions of the countries' size, location, and ascribed significance in the context of detente would not, in the near term, induce assistance of a substantial kind from the socialist world. This seems to be the import of the policy and rhetorical statements emanating from both Guyana and Jamaica, even after the defeat of Gerald Ford and the advent of a Democratic administration. It is instructive that, apart from assistance under severe conditions from the IMF and allied institutions, the donors of substantial assistance of a short-term nature came from countries within the Caribbean Basin: Venezuela and Trinidad.

The U.S. Response

In an environment of constricted financial resources, the Caribbean countries have adopted a deal approach: the search for short-term assistance, together with the attempt to devote diplomatic resources to participation in the demand for reform of international economic relations (the NIEO and, in more specific and immediate terms, the UNCTAD Conference). The U.S. Government's views and policies with respect to both of these approaches will obviously be an important determinant of their evolution. As far as such views and policies have a bearing on the Caribbean, we can perceive three broad trends.

At the level of a developing policy theme with increasing academic legitimacy,[5] though not a formally enunciated policy line, is the view that Latin America, and by extension the Caribbean subregion, although an area of special interest and influence of the United States, has economic growth problems which, insofar as they are amenable to external solutions, should be the subject of "global" approaches by the U.S. In this regard, there should be no special hemisphere policy, since neither problems nor solutions are specific to Latin America.

Second, in the face of Third World and "liberal" American demands for an increase in U.S. official assistance (as a percentage of GDP), the role of private foreign investment as the motive force of development should be stressed.

Third, there is the effort at rationalization of official assistance by bringing this within a coherent multilateral strategy based on the OECD countries, though the element of bilateralism would be maintained at the specific donor-recipient level. This appears to have been the premise of the formation of a Caribbean Group for Cooperation in Economic Development, though contributions from the OECD and other countries involved have not been forthcoming to the extent expected by the American proposers of the system.

The policy implication of these three broad trends appears to be, from a metropolitan point of view, that there is a necessity for Caribbean countries to concentrate not on the NIEO as an alternative to prevailing arrangements, but on a recognition of the geopolitical framework of likely substantial transfers (private and public) to these countries, and on the interdependence of the elements within this framework.

The appearance of these general trends has coincided, as we have remarked, with the failure of economic policy in Jamaica, Guyana, and Mexico and their forced recourse to the IMF. Within the Caribbean itself, Cuban concern with the rationalization of her own economy after the 1975–76 drop in sugar prices, in spite of other types of technical assistance that she possesses, has substantially focused her resources on her domestic economic policy. The country's intervention in Angola has not negated this concentration, though on the other hand it may certainly have slowed the process of normalization of her relations with Caribbean Basin countries.

Implications for Caribbean Diplomacy in the Nonaligned and NIEO Arenas

The economic weakness of Caribbean countries, when taken together with the stance of relative inactivity on the part of countries like Trinidad and Mexico (which possess substantial financial resources), will certainly affect negatively their activist behavior in both the nonaligned movement and the search for the NIEO. In the Caribbean, this has already been affected by the fact that Cuba has assumed a leading role in trying to shape the nonalignment movement, precisely at the time that she has assumed an activist role in the liberation movement in Africa opposed by the United States.

In the context of this Cuban role there are signs that the United States seeks to weaken Cuban-U.S.S.R. support for regimes and movements at another level. It appears that the U.S. has decided to attempt a strategy of diplomatic intervention in an area where Cuba has gained a certain legitimacy in recent times, in the Third World movement. This takes the form of capitalizing on those currents in the movement which seek to delegitimize Cuba as a nonaligned country.

This has an obvious importance at the political level. But it also has another rationale, for Cuba is known to be active in the nonaligned movement, not simply at the political, but also at the economic level; that is, at the level of supporting Third World countries' diplomacy for a change of the international economic order. For the Cubans, this has two aspects: (a) a change of western capitalist-Third World country relations, but also (b) a change of relations within the Third World so that countries with new-found wealth adopt new policies concerning the allocation of and disposition of financial and material (oil) resources. If Cuba can be delegitimized, both of these thrusts, and in particular the second, will be weakened. It will be recalled that, also from the Caribbean, Manley had put forward in Algiers, in 1973, a plan for a Third World Fund to be drawn from the resources of the financially rich Third World countries themselves, thus lessening non-oil-producing countries' dependence on Western countries and Western-dominated international financial institutions.

So a delegitimization strategy deriving its motivation from a concern with Cuban-U.S.S.R. support for regimes in Africa comes to have a direct link with the nonaligned countries' plans for a NIEO for which Cuba provides important support. One can be sure that in the course of the elaboration of this strategy in the Third World, the U.S. will use both the political and economic instruments of diplomacy available to it. This is important for countries like Jamaica which, while being currently economically weak and dependent on the U.S. and U.S.-dominated financial institutions, are necessarily susceptible to differing forms of American pressure to act as "moderating influences" in the nonaligned movement.

There are, broadly speaking, two lines of strategy on this question of an NIEO. One which was more prevalent in the early post-1973 period speaks of a fundamental restructuring of international economic relations. A second, which may now well be the prevailing line, speaks of seeking U.S. and Western receptivity to a reorganization and adaptation of international economic relations to give Third World countries a better chance of attaining more stable and profitable gains from trade and production in systems dominated by the West (hence an emphasis on removal of tariff and non-tariff obstacles to trade, a commodities buffer stock, compensatory financing, etc). This constitutes, fundamentally, the diplomacy of UNCTAD. Cuba is one adherent of the first line of strategy, while countries like Nigeria and Jamaica are more prone to the second, though with differing emphases. Some countries see the second line of strategy as a principled, long-term one for gaining a better place in the Western-dominated system; others see it as a tactical line to be applied for a certain length of time in the present circumstances.

The link, however, between the two lines can be said to lie in the important question of control and sovereignty over strategic natural resources in Third World countries, giving as it would to Third World countries a right and a certain flexibility in the use and disposition of such resources. But this link is an ambiguous one, since sovereignty and control are taken in Third World countries generally to mean different things—complete ownership on the one hand and partial ownership of various levels on the other.

In the face, then, of trends such as we have just described, we conclude that the possibilities for any substantial benefits from pressures for NIEO for the Caribbean countries are not encouraging. The optimism of a few years ago that the financial and strategic commodity power of certain Third World countries would induce changes in Northern development policies is certainly now not warranted. In addition, at the level of regional and subregional collective policies for economic development and harmonization, the instabilities induced by the uncertainties of the movement of the international trading and financial systems have had distorting effects on the capacities of countries, including those of the Caribbean subregion, for systematic cooperation.

Political Parameters of U.S. Policy Toward the Caribbean

1. THE NEED TO ENSURE "ORDER" IN THE HEMISPHERE

The geopolitical concept of "order" has two aspects: (1) the relations between the hemispheric states, and (2) domestic order, with the United States seeing internal disorder as having the potential for international or regional disorder, and thus for negative effects on her own security. These two aspects are, therefore, inextricably linked in the American mind, as American administrations have always shown in their attitudes toward the older Caribbean states. The significance of this for particular Caribbean countries varies, in some measure, according to location. Jamaica, for example, is located among the countries of the northern tier of the Caribbean, toward whose domestic behavior the United States has always been particularly sensitive. (We refer here to Cuba, Haiti, and the Dominican Republic.) Along with the Bahamas, which are also structurally integrated at the economic level with the United States, this tier is considered a strategic subzone within the Caribbean region as a whole.

Although in this tier the American government has reluctantly accepted—within the policy of detente—the elaboration of closer relations between Commonwealth Caribbean countries and Cuba, it is undoubtedly the case that it is the content and level of these relations with which she is concerned. Kissinger had attempted to clarify this in 1976:

> I'd like to make the distinction between Cuba's military and Cuba's diplomatic activities . . . Our concern is military infiltration and movement of Cuban troops. And we have seen no evidence of Cuban organized military units within the Western Hemisphere.[6]

Kissinger was speaking here of "concern" requiring an American military response. An inference from the practice of American diplomacy would be that other kinds of Cuban presences, broadly characterized as "diplomatic," would require other forms of containment responses.

It is, in fact, with respect to this latter situation, that a particular line of economic policy on the part of Caribbean countries might be of particular concern. The basis of such concern would be the extent to which governments were indicating populist responses to local social and economic problems, responses which might lead to solutions other than those normally accepted within the conventional intellectual and political framework. This is the context in which the columnist James Reston could write, in an article on "Castro and the [American] Election":

> Now he is expanding his role to Africa and the world and exporting his troops to help the revolutionary Communist forces wherever they are. *This has clearly created a new situation in the Western Hemisphere, and particularly in the Caribbean, where economic, social and racial problems are almost out of hand.*[7]

2. THE NEED TO TREAT THE CARIBBEAN AS EXEMPLARY

This is often stressed by American policymakers, though often honored more in the breach, and it may be said to afflict Democratic administrations more than Republican ones. The Carter administration chose to emphasize this policy line. This approach was taken partly in response to the more visible Caribbean presence in forums dealing with the reorganization of international economic relations and partly in response to the search in this region for new solutions to local economic problems.

Clearly, the specific and operational modalities of the "exemplary" line of policy have not yet been finalized, and are an aspect of future U.S. relations with Latin America as a whole. The currently favored strand of thinking, however, would make an appropriate American response to Caribbean requirements for economic assistance contingent on a "proper" Caribbean political attitude and political response to what is seen as a legitimate American presence in this part of the world. There appears to be on the American side a sense that the gravity of Caribbean economic problems might well induce "appropriate noises"; but there will also be an awareness that such behavior is to some extent constrained by the volatility of politics in these parts. (One American expert witness to Congressional hearings in 1973, the academic Aaron Segal, described the region as "too small islands with too few resources and too many young people breeding too fast. That is what the Caribbean is all about.")

It is clear that the current discussions of bilateral vs. multilateral and regional approaches to Caribbean problems are taking place within this context of the "exemplary" approach. Clearly there will always be a bilateral aspect; but concentration on the multilateral and regional gives the United States the opportunity to widen the framework for the treatment of Commonwealth Caribbean problems at the geographic, economic and diplomatic level, bringing in the larger states of Mexico and Venezuela. The importance of this is that the scope and nature of relations involving these Basin states are still a subject of confusion within the Caribbean community itself. This, however, is something that requires a separate discussion.

3. THE NEED TO CONTAIN THE NEGATIVE EFFECTS OF RAW MATERIAL DEPENDENCY

This is a parameter of policy that has been emphasized for the United States in recent years as a consequence of the explosion of petroleum prices. But its particular Caribbean reference was the imposition of the bauxite levy by the Michael Manley government. There are, at least to this writer, indications of a perception of a greater need for diversification of bauxite-alumina imports at the level of the policies of the multinational companies, if not directly at the level of government. But we have already referred to the general sensitivity of government to business in that system. At the level of Jamaican government policy, on the other hand, the reorganization of ownership patterns in the industry (51 percent government ownership along with assurance of continuity of supply), were an historic attempt not only to meet national yearnings for "greater control of a wasting asset," but also to stabilize U.S.-Jamaican relationships and expectations with respect to foreign investment, particularly in an area where the U.S. recognized a certain dependency on a strategic material.

4. THE NEED TO ELABORATE A GENERAL LINE OF TRADE AND AID POLICY

This has been an important part of U.S. policy-thinking in recent years, spurred on by the more radical initiatives of certain Third World countries and taking advantage of the effects of the petroleum crisis and the general rise in commodity prices. In relation to the Caribbean, the United States had already begun to take cognizance of specific Caribbean needs during the negotiations between the ACP and EEC groups. But given continuing Jamaican and Caribbean difficulties, United States policy on the question of the possibility of new institutional relationships between the IMF, the World Bank, and American private foreign investment takes on added significance. This is the relevance of new notions of multinational consortia, the possibilities for cofinancing between public and private institutions, and of Joint Economic Commissions for the Caribbean. To revert to the earlier discussion, it is clear that, to the extent that some "exemplary relationship" approach does materialize, it will be colored by these notions.

Within these broad parameters, then, is a willingness on the part of the United States to allow excursions into experiments in the economics and politics of social democracy, partly because policymakers are cognizant of populist pressures in that direction, and partly because a more substantial balance in world relationships permits the availability of alternative sources of assistance to countries which, while nationalist, are noncommunist. In addition, most of the Caribbean economic systems, like those of many Third World countries, are still market-oriented ones, though in varying states of depression, in which both government and private enterprise avidly seek private capital inflows, however limited they may be.

But the operationalization of social democracy in an underdeveloped country, as Caribbean countries have learned in recent years, is hardly the same as that in structured societies such as those of the European countries. And it is the working out of the dynamics of this in response to which American policy will operate, within the broad parameters.

Can the U.S. tolerate a change in the balance (between private and public) in the economic system of Caribbean countries? If it can tolerate it, will it willingly support it? The U.S.S.R., it should be noted, is not averse to U.S. economic assistance to countries in the Third World in which it is itself engaged in rendering substantial amounts of aid. The Soviet analyst Ulyanovsky, for example, has argued since the early 1970s that *given that certain domestic conditions are fulfilled,* Third World countries can effectively trade and obtain aid from both "world systems." The assumption was made in some Caribbean countries in the early 1970s that environmental conditions were permissive of such an orientation. Whether this assumption still obtains so as to be meaningfully operative is an open question.

Notes

1. See Fred Bergsten, "The Threat from the Third World," *Foreign Policy,* No. 11, 1973.

2. I have discussed the orientation of Jamaica's foreign policy in some detail in "Issues and Trends in Jamaican Foreign Policy," in C. Stone and A. Brown (eds.), *Perspectives on Jamaica in the Seventies* (Kingston: Jamaica Publishing House, 1980).

3. See Jahangir Amuzegar, "A Requiem for the North-South Conference," *Foreign Affairs,* Vol. 56, No. 1, 1977, pp. 136–159.

4. Various interpretations have been given of the reasons for recognition. See Carl Parris, "Trinidad and Tobago's Decision to Recognize Cuba: A Case Study," and H. Gill, "The Decision of Guyana to Recognize Cuba" (papers prepared for a conference sponsored by the Institute of International Relations, University of the West Indies, May 1977).

5. See, for example, A. Fishlow, *The Mature Neighbor Policy: A New United States Economic Policy for Latin America*, University of California, Institute of International Studies, Policy Papers in International Affairs No. 3, 1977.

6. "Kissinger, in Mexico, Wary on Cubans," *New York Times*, June 12, 1976.

7. *New York Times*, March 3, 1976.

7

Cuba and the Contemporary World Order

NITA ROUS MANITZAS

In the contemporary world, no country can totally insulate itself against the play of international economics and politics. Even the most affluent and technologically sophisticated nations are swayed by international currents that are beyond their effective control. They can influence their international environment, but they cannot regulate and shape it to their own design. So long as they do not wish to commit nuclear suicide, they face real and restraining limits on their use of power in the international arena.

For small, underdeveloped countries, especially if they do not happen to be sitting atop a sea of oil, the constraints imposed by the international order are not only real, but often overwhelming. If major world powers are swayed by international happenings, their underdeveloped neighbors can be seismically jolted. Decisions made elsewhere, in distant foreign ministries or markets or lending agencies, can make their governments fall and their economies founder.

For much of this century there was a widespread assumption that the end of colonial rule would, in each case, automatically produce self-determination and genuine national independence. That assumption may have been valid for the North American colonies in 1776; almost everywhere else it has proved to be a fiction. In the last three decades, with the colonial powers in full retreat, a whole new vocabulary has come into common use—dependency, neocolonialism, destabilization, client states—to describe the reality left in their wake.

The dependent condition, moreover, is not a happy one. The problem is not solely a question of national pride and identity, although such factors assuredly have their weight. The crux of the matter is that

141

in an unequal world which seems to be growing more unequal as time goes by, countries that cannot generate a certain, sufficient measure of national autonomy, of power over their own political economy and civic society, do not do well.

To be sure, weak states may produce autocratic leaders who can accumulate more wealth and brute power over their fellow citizens than most world statesmen would dream of. They can also produce upper classes that share in advanced technology and affluent modern lifestyles. But such phenomena cannot be equated with national development or national well-being. When one applies a national yardstick, the empirical record of the last few decades is not encouraging. Aggregate economic growth rates notwithstanding, the absolute number of unemployed, underfed, and uneducated persons in the Third World is increasing, not declining. Such people become statistics, not effective national citizens.

Against this backdrop, a key question now confronting underdeveloped countries is how to accumulate sufficient power and autonomy over their own affairs to be able to pursue their special national developmental objectives. This question, in varying forms and guises, increasingly infuses the discussions of the United Nations, of the nonaligned bloc, of Latin America's economic council, the SELA, and of virtually all Third World forums. However, if the participating nations seem to agree that they share a problem, it is not so clear that they share any common understanding of its dynamics or, certainly, of ways to confront it.

In this context, the Cuban experience may be illuminating. Normative judgments aside, Cuba is one of the extreme cases that tests the limits of theory and practice. Few independent countries have been so blatantly subordinate to a hegemonic neighbor as Cuba was for much of this century. Few countries have been able to shift gears so abruptly and definitively as Cuba did in the early 1960s. Finally, few countries have managed so thoroughly, and in so brief a span of time, to reshape their national community and take off on a new, distinctive, developmental trajectory. All this was accomplished, moreover, in an international environment that was not only exceedingly complex, but also, on occasion, overtly threatening.

Precisely because of its velocity and its radical character, the Cuban experience throws into relief some of the more compelling elements that have shaped and infused the island's revolutionary trajectory. Similarly, because the international response to the Cuban phenomenon was so direct, so immediate, and so visible, it is possible to distinguish with relative confidence between those factors that were of superficial significance and those that were, and are, of major impact on Cuba's internal national affairs. One does not have to dig through dusty archives to find the relevant data; the Bay of Pigs invasion, the missile crisis, the economic boycott, and the massive infusions of Soviet aid are neither secret nor subtle occurrences.

Against that background, and with the data available to us, one can begin to advance a set of propositions about the impact of the international order on Cuba's national and international comportment. First, it would seem evident by now that, in the workings and impact of the international order on individual nation-states, the arrows never run one way. One can comprehend cause and effect only in terms of a dialectical stimulus and response, of a permanent interaction between what is national and what is international in origin.

Second, on the basis of the Cuban experience, one can suggest that the composition and configuration of a country's internal national community is one of the determining variables in the response that can, and will, be made to international events, constraints, and opportunities. Countries that have no national coherence or consensus can be readily "destabilized" from outside; countries that have succeeded in welding together a national community and citizenry will have more protection against the flow of international events and more possibility of responding with effective answers. They will certainly not be invulnerable to external pressures, but they will, at least, have more options at their disposal.

Finally, one can argue on the basis of the Cuban case that small states, even in a world dominated by superpowers, are not *necessarily* powerless in the international arena. Obviously, they are more vulnerable than the major nation-states to the ebbs and flows of the international economic and political order. Obviously, too, they operate under a number of inexorable constraints. But the Cuban experience demonstrates that under a certain confluence of circumstances they can find room to maneuver and to carve out their own "space."[1] The Cuban phenomenon, in this sense, challenges the "geographical fatalism" that suffuses so much of the Latin American literature. The issue it poses for us is not whether small states can generate power, but how.

If these propositions are valid, then the next question must address the factors in the Cuban case that have permitted the island to pursue its radically independent trajectory in the American hemisphere, to survive in an adverse international arena, to generate its own quotient of power and autonomy, and to advance as a nation. At a minimum, the following considerations would seem to be crucial: (1) the impact of historical experience on contemporary happenings; (2) the historical moment, in international terms, at which Cuba's revolution took place and which shaped the response of key international actors; (3) the texture and direction of national policy; (4) the nature of external assistance and alliances; and (5) the ideology and decisions of leading national actors in this complex web of historical, national, and international variables.

One should add to this list a number of geographical and physical "givens" which obviously must affect the play of economic, social, and political factors. For example, Cuba not only is a relatively small country, with a population of approximately 10 million, but it also is an island floating 90 miles off the U.S. coastline. That fact, in itself, must have special meaning and implications in a complex international setting. Cuba is also an island without major natural resources and, most important, without any indigenous source of energy. It cannot, in sum, go it alone. Its destiny is inextricably tied to the international web of trade, aid, and relations. Indeed, Cuba has historically lived off its international economic links, a situation that even revolution could not change.

The Historical Legacy

Few countries have been as subject to the whims and dictates of an external power as Cuba was for most of its history. To begin with, Cuba came late to independence in the Spanish-American hemisphere, ridding itself of colonial rule only in 1898, some 70 years after the other Latin American republics (with the notable exception of Puerto Rico) had broken loose from Spain. Moreover, Cuba's independence, culminating a 30-year history of insurrection and guerrilla warfare against the Spanish authorities, did not bring with it any real measure of national sovereignty. On the contrary, although nominally free, the Cubans in 1898 basically exchanged one imperium for another. If Cuba was no longer, technically, a colony, it was about as independent—as many authors have remarked—as Long Island.

Even Cuba's moment of independence was less than a truly national event. Three months before the war against Spain ended, U.S. troops entered the conflict. When the smoke cleared, they remained to govern the island for the next four years. Cuba might have its own constitution, it might have in subsequent years its own elections and governments, but the precedent for U.S. hegemony, for playing policeman on the island, was already set in concrete. The withdrawal of the U.S. Army in 1902 was a temporary retreat. U.S. troops returned to govern Cuba from 1906 to 1909. Later, squadrons of U.S. marines were landed in 1912 and 1916 to help settle internal Cuban political affairs.

In later years, political intervention would become less direct. It was nonetheless potent. Some 60 years after independence, a former U.S. Ambassador to Cuba could testify before Congress that "the United States, until the advent of Castro, was so overwhelmingly influential in Cuba that . . . the American Ambassador was the second most important man in Cuba; sometimes even more important than the president."[2]

Political hegemony, not surprisingly, was matched by economic influence and intervention. Until 1959, the Cuban economy was inextricably wedded to the needs and decisions of the United States. Like other underdeveloped countries, Cuba was essentially a monoculture; its economic fate was determined by sugar. The disposal of the sugar crop, however, was each year determined more by decisionmakers in the U.S. Department of Agriculture and the U.S. Congress than by any native Cuban agency. The annual U.S. sugar quota, while it protected Cuba from some of the more radical fluctuations in world prices, also gave the United States definitive influence over the rhythm and rate of Cuban economic development.

The sugar trade is only part of the story. U.S. influence and investment went well beyond the terrain of imports and exports. At the moment that Fidel Castro and his fellow insurrectionists landed in Oriente Province from the *Granma,* the weight of U.S. capital, technology, and management in the Cuban economy was extreme. U.S. companies controlled, for example, 40 percent of raw sugar production, 90 percent of telephone, light, and power services, 50 percent of the public railways, and a quarter of all bank deposits.[3] U.S. capital also dominated the refining and distribution of petroleum, the exploitation of Cuba's mineral resources, and a substantial portion of the island's manufacturing sector.

We could continue this litany at greater length, but it would only underscore the essential fact about Cuba's prerevolutionary situation: for all intents and purposes, the island was an economic and political appendage of its giant neighbor. This status was codified in such documents as the Platt Amendment, which for three decades officially sanctioned U.S. intervention in Cuba's internal affairs, and the Reciprocal Trade Agreement of 1934, which opened Cuba to a flood of U.S. exports and eliminated virtually all possibility of autonomous economic development on the island.

This historical legacy would have multiple and dramatic consequences for Cuba when the revolution got underway in 1959. In the first place, it would give a special tone and texture to Cuban nationalism. For decades, there had been latent in Cuba a sense of frustrated nationhood, of lost sovereignty, of overwhelming dependence on a rich, powerful, and intrusive neighbor. A revolution might send some Cubans running to the U.S. mainland, but the promise of independence and freedom from U.S. tutelage would also generate support across a wide spectrum of the community. In concert with other measures, a revolutionary leadership would be able to use Cuba's legacy of nationalism, with its special anti-U.S. content, as part of the glue to hold its citizenry together in the face of growing U.S. hostility and sanctions in the 1960s. The renewed sense of national pride and identity after 60 years of submission helped impede all attempts to subvert the Cuban revolutionary process from within. And when the United States finally resorted to overt invasion at the Bay of Pigs, the Cubans responded as a cohesive, national citizenry.

The history of Cuba's economic relations with the United States also had a decisive impact on the course of events after 1959, albeit in far different fashion. As the revolutionary process unfolded, and as confrontation with the United States escalated, the economy became Cuba's Achilles' heel. Locked into the mainland for 60 years, the Cuban economy was virtually "made in the U.S.A." Cuba's dependence on the United States for everything from foreign exchange to spare parts, from technological expertise to crude petroleum, was overwhelming. As economic sanctions escalated—culminating, eventually, in total economic boycott—the Cuban economy, together with the Cuban leadership, was inevitably pushed to the wall. One alternative, obviously, was to cede to U.S. pressure, to yield national autonomy in exchange for economic survival, and to revert to the former situation and status, albeit without Batista.

National revolutions, however, are not normally made for the purpose of maintaining the traditional status quo. As long as the Cuban leadership persisted in its nationalistic, egalitarian, and populist course, then its only other alternative in what was then a bipolar world was to seek the aid and protection of the Soviet Union. Whether ideological factors would also have helped push them, ultimately, into the socialist camp is a matter of speculation; the fact remains that without turning economically to the Soviets, the Cuban revolution would have collapsed.

The effect, of course, of the Cuban turnabout would be lasting and pervasive, coloring every facet of Cuba's subsequent evolution. It is a classic instance of the impact of the international order and international realities on the national trajectory of small, underdeveloped countries. It is also a classic example of the ways in which small, underdeveloped nation-states can exercise a certain measure of choice and autonomy over their own destinies in a great-power world. Their ability to do so, of course, does not depend solely on their own discretion. It depends, as well, on a convergence of variables at a given moment in historical time.

The Historical Moment

In a nationwide address on January 3, 1973, describing the new Cuban-Soviet economic agreements, Fidel Castro remarked to his audience that "the Cuban Revolution came forth at the very moment—and not a moment sooner—when the international balance of power and the big changes taking place in the world could make possible this reality."[4]

Castro was not the first to reach that conclusion. A number of observers of the Cuban revolutionary process have noted that its survival, in large measure, was a function of the Cold War. That assessment is generically correct, but insufficiently precise. If the Cold War provided the stage setting, it did so at a very special moment in historical time. Both of the major international actors, the United States and the Soviet Union, were at a juncture that permitted Cuba certain room for maneuver that it would not have had earlier, or later.

Although it is hazardous to speculate after the fact, it is possible to suggest that if the Cuban revolution had taken place in 1949 rather than 1959, the denouement would have been altogether different. The Soviet Union under Stalin was a Byzantine empire, but restricted in its objectives. Its primary concern was the survival of "socialism in one country." Its secondary concern, when its attention strayed beyond its own borders, extended no further than it had under the tsars, to the frontiers of East-Central Europe. Stalin's reach might intrude elsewhere, he might support communist parties worldwide, but their importance for him was relative. He would help them only so long and so far as they did not bring him into unnecessary conflict and entanglement outside his limited sphere of interest. One can deduce that much from the empirical record of his behavior in China circa 1927, in the Spanish Civil War, and in the civil strife in Greece after World War II. Three cases may not be conclusive evidence, but they are suggestive. On the basis of such historical testimony, one can speculate that Stalin's Russia would not have extended its mantle to Cuba during the early, embattled days of its revolution, and certainly would never have risked a missile crisis on Cuba's behalf.

Khrushchev's Russia was something else again. It was more of a mature, international actor. It was also a nuclear power that was beginning to flex its muscles not only in neighboring Central Europe but on the world stage. In this changed scenario, Cuba represented for the

Soviets more of an opportunity than a risk. Whether Khrushchev and his colleague knew what they were getting into when they first agreed to take the Cubans into their camps is, in retrospect, questionable. Certainly, the financial cost of keeping the Cuban economy viable over time must be more than they had anticipated. But the advantage of having a toehold, as well as a showcase, in the Americas evidently outweighed other, more practical considerations. And, clearly, it continues to do so.

The position of the United States vis-à-vis Cuba has been more consistent over the years. It is doubtful that the United States would ever have willingly tolerated the emergence of a socialist state on its borders. Indeed, in 1933, when Cuba's new president, Ramon Grau San Martin, tried to establish a strongly reformist and nationalistic government with radical social leanings, the Roosevelt administration made sure that his tenure in office would be promptly terminated. Twenty-six years later, when Fidel Castro and his troops descended from the Sierra Maestra, the U.S. reaction was essentially the same.

Nonetheless, even from the U.S. side, the historical moment in international time made a difference. The presence of the Soviet Union on the world horizon obviously entered into President John F. Kennedy's calculations in his actions vis-à-vis Cuba, a consideration that would not have had any weight in the Roosevelt era. The special characteristics, in sum, of the U.S.-Soviet confrontation in the early 1960s (or, if one prefers to dwell on the role of individual actors, of the Kennedy-Khrushchev confrontation) gave Cuba the necessary space to maneuver between the shoals.

To give historical time its due, one might wonder whether the response given by Kennedy, to refrain from engaging U.S. troops and the arsenal of the U.S. air force in the Bay of Pigs invasion, would have been the same a few years later under the Nixon-Kissinger administration. A duo that did not shrink from organizing a massive "incursion" into neutral Cambodia, or from plotting the overthrow of the Allende government in Chile, might not have been so restrained as Kennedy was when he inherited the Bay of Pigs war plan. The denouement might well have been different.

One can, of course, speculate endlessly about these alternative scenarios. One thing, however, is empirically certain: the very fact of the existence and survival of the Cuban revolution changed the shape of subsequent foreign policy and national developments in the American hemisphere. Among the more direct and visible results were escalated U.S. training of Latin America's military, especially in the techniques of anti-guerrilla warfare; the overthrow of the Frondizi government in Argentina in 1962; the overthrow of the Goulart government in Brazil in 1964; the invasion of the Dominican Republic in 1963; and, as Nixon himself has admitted, the so-called "destabilization" of the Allende government in Chile in 1973. In other words, the special historical moment that gave Cuba the necessary "play" to resist U.S. intervention and to pursue its revolutionary trajectory would not recur for the rest of Latin America's republics. The very presence of the Cuban revolution on the American landscape irreversibly changed the scenery and the surrounding political reality. Other Latin American and Caribbean countries would henceforth have to deal with a different international setting and a different array of available options.

The National Scenario

That the international economic and political order profoundly affected the course of Cuba's internal affairs and evolution is an obvious truism. At the same time, no country is simply a passive receptor of external stimuli. International currents, as they impinge on any country, are necessarily processed through a national filter. Their impact is conditioned by the configuration of any given national society. The intrusion of adverse international pressures may destabilize and totally fragment one country, while another may respond with considerable cohesion and resilience. External threats may send one country into chaotic disarray, while elsewhere the presence of an outside enemy will strengthen, rather than weaken, national unity.

There are, of course, certain obvious conditioners of a nation's response to international occurrences. An oil-rich state will react differently to an international energy crisis than a country without petroleum. An underdeveloped monoculture, trying to diversify its economic base, will naturally confront international economic realities that no amount of national will and effort can erase. Thus, Che Guevera's intensive drive in the first years of the Cuban revolution to industrialize the island and drastically reduce its dependence on sugar was derailed early on by the stark facts of the international marketplace and Cuba's own resources.

Such are the obvious realities. But there are also more subtle variables that will make a major difference in the ways in which a country will receive and respond to international currents. In the Cuban case, a key element clearly was the nature of the revolutionary process and its impact on the shape and coherence of the national Cuban community. Running counter to most orthodox theories of development, the Cuban revolution was initially focused on the social concerns and well-being of the nation, not on economic inputs and outputs. The earliest measures of the new leadership were directed to extending the boundaries of effective citizenship, giving Cuba's inhabitants a greater stake in their national patrimony rather than improving their productivity. Years later, facing a bleak array of economic problems, Castro himself would suggest that this order of priorities might have been too "idealistic." Nonetheless, it had a marked and lasting effect on Cuba's subsequent trajectory and on the ability of the island to survive in a highly adverse environment. It also provided an interesting example of the alternatives to standard models of "nation-building."

According to the conventional wisdom of contemporary development literature, the key to national progress, modernization, and all other civic and social good in a developing country is economic growth. Before anything else can happen, the economy must take off into self-sustaining flight. Once that occurs and a country is safely launched into healthy economic orbit, the other attributes of a good society will follow: educational opportunity, employment and social welfare, political participation, and the rest. The economy, however, is the motor. Until it is functioning well and growing sufficiently, all other national concerns should be deferred or, at least, subordinated to the requirements of economic advance. The accumulation of capital is the first order of business; the problem of its appropriate distribution can wait.

It is evident that Cuba's leaders today are as much preoccupied with capital accumulation and economic growth as any orthodox economist from the University of Chicago. In the first ten crucial years of the revolution, however, the *fidelistas* had other priorities. Social justice and social welfare took precedence over any immediate economic concerns. Nationalism and national sovereignty also weighed more heavily in their thinking that the economy, as Castro demonstrated when he was willing to run the risk of harsh economic sanctions from the United States rather than sacrifice Cuba's national autonomy. The economy, in sum, although it was never neglected altogether, nonetheless took a back seat in the Cuban revolutionary progression.

The first objective of the new leadership was to build a more equitable and truly national community, breaking down the gross barriers of class, race, rural-urban dichotomy, and cultural access that hitherto had shredded the fabric of Cuban society. In more tactical terms, their stated aim was to bring into the national mainstream the great mass of disadvantaged citizens who, until then, had participated only marginally in the goods and services of their own society. In keeping with that goal, the earliest measures of the revolutionary government were essentially social rather than economic in intent (although they had, of course, their economic consequences). Agrarian reform, urban reform, a nationwide literacy campaign, a major expansion of the primary school system, the extension of paramedical services to the more impoverished enclaves of the island, and a host of similar, redistributive programs followed in rapid succession. The primary concern of the revolutionary leaders was not how to accumulate more capital, but how to distribute their existing stock more equitably.

Obviously, such a policy has its finite limits, especially in an underdeveloped country. Nonetheless, even when Cuba's economic machinery became unduly strained and the Western economic boycott began to take its toll, the question of distribution was still paramount. Through a strict system of rationing, it was ensured that no citizen would be unduly favored while others starved and that the allocation of material goods, however meager, would be made on a national rather than a class basis. Even the reintroduction of material incentives in the 1970s has not changed the essential core of this policy. Some Cubans may now receive greater material rewards than others, but none is denied adequate caloric intake, access to the educational system, access to medical attention, and the chance of employment.

This strategy has had its cost. Part of the price, early on, was a massive exodus from the island of the former upper class and, far more important, of skilled managers and technicians who could not accept the rampantly egalitarian and increasingly socialistic course of the revolution. Their departure no doubt lessened the level of internal dissent and division, but it also left Cuba with a drastically depleted pool of professional talent. Another cost was major economic strain and inefficiency—although how much was due to the intrinsic strategy itself, how much to the economic boycott, and how much to the sheer inexpertness of Cuba's leaders in the early years would be hard to determine. In any event, the economy assuredly suffered, a process that reached its nadir in the grand debacle of Cuba's 1970 sugar harvest. If goods were still shared equitably, there were fewer goods to share.

The creation of a genuine national community has unquestionably strengthened Cuba's capacity to respond on its own terms to international pressures. That capacity was demonstrated most vividly at the Bay of Pigs, when the Cuban populace reacted as a national citizenry, effectively resisting invasion from without and subversion from within.

Nationalism, of course, does not have a solely defensive function. The *fact* of nationhood—as distinct from nationhood in name only— makes it possible for Fidel Castro to function on the world stage as a national, not a factional, spokesman. That attribute gives him more authority and independence of action than accrues to leaders who represent only a narrow, oligarchical clientele or some other, fractured constituency. It also enables Cuba to confront the international order and questions of foreign policy with a more secure and cohesive definition of "national interest" than is possible for countries that are essentially class-bound and, hence, nationally incoherent.

Nationalism, not as rhetorical posturing but as a shared, positive value, is in sum one of the major factors conditioning and filtering the impact of international affairs on Cuba's internal trajectory. It also is a key element in Cuba's ability to perform effectively on the international circuit, with a prominence that far exceeds its size and material base. At the same time, national unity, however important it may be in the total Cuban equation, would not have sufficed to keep the island afloat in an adverse universe had there not been other operating variables. Another essential ingredient, as Castro himself has frequently admitted, was the pattern and magnitude of external assistance.

The Nature and Importance of Soviet Aid

Fidel Castro's declaration in December 1961 that he was and had always been a Marxist-Leninist may well have caught Nikita Khrushchev by surprise as much as, or more than, observers in the United States. In any event, it is obvious that Castro's audacious leap into the Soviet camp, precisely at a time when it was in the Soviet interest to accept him, was a determining factor in the subsequent survival of the Cuban revolution. Whatever advantage the Soviets gained from the arrangement, the Cuban advantage has been substantially greater. For the Soviets, Cuba has been a strategic toehold in the American hemisphere, a showcase in the Third World, and, increasingly, a useful—though occasionally fractious—spokesman and surrogate in settings where the Soviets would not or could not act directly. For the Cubans, the Soviet Union has been their lifeline.

In the first place, the protective mantle of the Soviet Union has been important in forestalling any direct military incursion against Cuba by the United States. According to the public record of negotiations between Kennedy and Khrushchev at the time of the 1962 missile crisis, the Soviets, in exchange for taking their rockets back home, received certain binding assurances from the Kennedy administration about the use of military force against Cuba. These agreements, obviously, did not preclude in future years repeated attempts by the CIA at subversion, sabotage, and assassination in Cuba. What the Cubans were spared by the Soviet umbrella was any threat of direct invasion, of U.S. marines on their beaches and Boeing bombers in their air space. That guarantee, extended over time, has given Cuba in the last two decades a relative measure of tranquility that many Third World countries—from the Dominican Republic to Cambodia to Afghanistan—have not enjoyed.

While it is virtually impossible to put a dollar value on total Soviet aid to Cuba—which ranges from gifts of military hardware to important, long-term credits, from subsidized prices for sugar exports to technical training and services, from deferred loan payments to direct grants—it is clear that the magnitude of assistance over 20 years has been exceedingly large.[5] The minimal figure calculated by outside experts is $500 million per year, but there are recent, relatively educated guesses that put the figure as high as $9 million per day, if all tangible and intangible goods are taken into account. Whatever the absolute amount in dollars or rubles, it is a matter of record that the Soviet Union has channeled more aid to Cuba than the United States has ever apportioned to any single country in Latin America and the Caribbean.

The magnitude of assistance, however, is only part of the story. The nature and composition of Soviet aid have also been special and significant. Whatever may be the intrinsic motives of the Soviet Union, the structure and style of their assistance in the Cuban case helped rather than hindered the national trajectory of the revolution.

In the first place, the way in which Soviet assistance is granted, from government to government, gives Cuba's central authorities considerably more control over national economic development and more effective autonomy over national economic policy and decisionmaking than most developing countries now enjoy. When a substantial portion of the developmental "aid" package from abroad comes in the form of private foreign investment and loans, the net effect, more often than not, is actually to dilute the power of the central government and to remove effective national control from major sectors of the economy. The locus of decisionmaking lies outside the national sphere, in the hands of foreign companies, banks, and multinational corporations. Furthermore, the influx of private foreign investment can distort an economy, skewing resources in a direction that may not necessarily reflect the balanced needs of the host society. (The classic case, perhaps, is the automotive industry in Latin America, fueled by North American and European capital, in countries that still cannot sufficiently feed themselves.) Finally, the traditional pattern of foreign investment not only weakens the control of a given national society over its own economic destiny, but also creates competing poles of power and enclaves of citizens more tied to foreign than national interests.

By contrast, the Soviet style of aid-giving in Cuba has strengthened rather than weakened national control over the total, internal process of economic accumulation, investment, and distribution. The blessing, of course, is not unmixed. The current arrangement gives the Soviets a mammoth hold on Cuba—should they choose to exercise it. But they would then have to calculate whether a blatant show of economic blackmail against Cuba would advance their own interests in the rest of the Third World. Up to now, while they have certainly used their influence on Cuba, they have evidently found it more feasible not to put their relations with the island to any final, definitive test. Again, it is another instance of how small, underdeveloped states can, in a complex and multi-variant world, find a margin of relative "space" and independence even when the gross equation of power is radically adverse.

At another level, Soviet aid to Cuba, normally programmed over an intermediate or even longer term, gives national economic planners the possibility of elaborating their projections and policies within more reliable margins than most Third World countries can count on. A key case is sugar. While the Soviet Union has not appreciably helped Cuba to break out of its heavy traditional dependence on the sugar harvest, the Soviets have—through guaranteed purchases and prices— protected Cuba from some of the more radical twists and turns of the international commodities market. Moreover, the time horizon built into most Soviet-Cuban agreements gives the island a better fix on its "futures" than it could secure when it had to present its case annually to the U.S. Congress and the Department of Agriculture.

In some years, this arrangement with the Soviets prevented Cuba from raking in windfall profits when the international sugar market suddenly soared. In most years, however, it has kept Cuba from suffering the full effects of plummeting sugar prices. In either situation, Cuba has gained a measure of stability that, over time (and, coupled with other forms of Soviet aid), probably outweighs any short-term calculation of gain or loss. Obviously, since not all trade is confined to the Soviet Union, Cuba can still be seriously affected by sudden skews and shifts in the international market, but the relative margin of reliability is greater than the traditional norm.

Equally, if not more, important for a small country without energy sources, the Soviet Union has guaranteed Cuba's supply of petroleum and, moreover, has consistently charged Cuba less than the going OPEC price for this service. Also, Soviet military assistance, much of it provided free, has helped Cuba avoid the onerous burden of the arms race that visibly affects most Latin American countries, especially as one nears the Southern Cone. While one could continue this list at greater length, the message is already clear: the style and content of Soviet aid to Cuba has not only been crucial for the survival of the *fidelista* revolution, but also has been such as to strengthen, rather than dilute, the national composition of Cuban society.

As hinted earlier, there evidently are negative tradeoffs in this scenario. Cuba's overwhelming dependence on Soviet aid has its cost. If the Soviets have been far more tolerant with Cuba than they have normally been with their nearer neighbors, they nonetheless established certain rules of the game, especially in the 1970s. The first real message was sent in 1968, after a virtual decade of truculence and, at times, outright challenge by the Cubans. For one week, the Soviet Union cut off the island's supply of petroleum. Whether or not the full lesson hit home at that time is difficult to determine. It assuredly did hit home when the Soviets agreed to rescue Cuba from the mess it had made for itself with the 1970 sugar harvest.

Since 1970, the revolutionary elan that originally characterized the *fidelista* phenomenon has largely disappeared. The enchantment with moral incentives, if not totally dissipated, has given way to a strict system of material rewards. The army, which formerly awarded no rank higher than that of "major," now has varying gradations of generals and other accoutrements of a professional standard military establishment. The central planning apparatus, especially since it has been linked into the COMECON circuit, now conforms more tightly to the Soviet model than it ever did before. And Cuba's foreign policy, notable in the 1960s for its independence, unorthodoxy and generally refreshing flair, has come perilously close to conformity with the foreign policy of the Soviet Union.

Despite the above, Cuba still appears to have more relative autonomy over its internal affairs than most East European socialist states. Six thousand miles of geographical distance make a difference. Clearly, they limit the ability of the Soviets to intervene directly with military force. They certainly have limited any possibility of changing Cuba's top leadership at Soviet will. Moreover, the benefits to the Soviet Union of having an ally such as Cuba in the Third World probably outweigh the risks of disengagement, however independent the Cubans may from time to time appear. In the last analysis, the Soviet Union, heavy as its presence may be, probably interferes less in Cuba's internal comportment and its trajectory of national development than the United States has done—politically and economically—in the Dominican Republic and Nicaragua, among others, in the last 50 years. Aid is obviously important, but it is not, geopolitically, the whole ballgame.

Ideology and Choice

The final element in the Cuban equation is perhaps the most difficult to weigh and assess. It comprises the intermeshed conditions of ideology, values, and the autonomous choices of national actors. While these variables cannot be statistically quantified, their impact on the course of the Cuban revolution is certainly visible, both in the explicit rhetoric of the leadership and, more concretely, in the content and structure of national policy over time.

The roots of contemporary Cuban ideology can be traced back to Fidel Castro's famous statement, "History Will Absolve Me," delivered after his abortive attack on the Moncada barracks in 1953.[6] That document does not comprise any systematic or fullblown exposition of ideology. Its inspiration was certainly not derived from Karl Marx, but from Jose Martí, the hero and intellectual architect of Cuban independence. Nonetheless, for those who wish to read it closely, there are already visible some of the major components of subsequent *fidelista* values and ideological choices: national sovereignty and national community, social justice and social welfare, and a clear commitment to the great mass of disadvantaged Cuban citizens who, until then, had largely been marginalized from the mainstream of national society. These threads have continued to run through the Cuban ideological fabric, even with the formal transition to Marxism-Leninism. (Indeed, the Cuban reading of Marxist scripture has always been somewhat unorthodox and freewheeling, with Martí—and Fidel—vying closely with Karl for ultimate authority.)

On the national stage, the influence of ideology, however unsystematized at the outset, was clearly present in the architecture of domestic policy. It was reflected in such measures as urban and agrarian reform, the nationalization of foreign enterprise, and a host of other tactical, strategic, and policy choices that, cumulatively over time, set Cuba irrevocably on its current course.

National policy, obviously, has its international spillover. In the Cuban case, the repercussions were direct, immediate and dramatic. Each nationalist and redistributive move by the *fidelista* government in the initial months of the revolution brought Cuba closer to a collision course with the United States. It was precisely at this juncture that the options were most open and that the explicit choice of national actors became one of the key operating variables. Certainly, in 1959, Castro could have knuckled under and presided over a modestly reformist government, sufficient to keep his constituency reasonably quiet and the United States reasonably content. Alternatively, although probably suicidally, he might have chosen to go it alone. His decision—laden, of course, with other consequences—was to throw in his lot with the Soviet Union. Whatever may be the deterministic effects of history, internal and external structure, and the laws of political economy, there are always moments when human choice comes into play. Assuredly, this was one of those moments.

In confronting the international order, the Cuban decision to ally the island with the Soviet Union had certain immutable results. At the same time, there was a margin of difference and latitude in Cuba's ideology—in its world view—that has made Cuba qualitatively distinct from the typical East European client state. One element, of course, is the centuries-long influence of Western-Iberian-Catholic culture, which cannot be erased by mere fiat. Another, perhaps more important in terms of foreign policy and comportment, is Cuba's self-image as an underdeveloped country and its self-identification with the Third World. Whatever may be Cuba's gratitude to the Soviet Union or its friendship with the European socialist camp, there has always been in the psyche of revolutionary Cuba a sense of fraternity and solidarity with the south in any north-south dialogue. If its diplomatic and economic ties run mostly toward the Soviet Union, its affective ties have consistently been closer to Vietnam, Allende's Chile, Lumumba's Congo, and the Sandinistas.

Cuba's explicit sense of identification with the underdeveloped nations of the world has colored its reading of Marxist doctrine and, at a more practical level, inbued its international policies and comportment with a special flavor. A case in point is the current adventure in Angola. Those who see Cuba's present involvement in the Angolan situation, or elsewhere in Africa, as simply a surrogate mission for the Soviets are misreading the historical and ideological record. Obviously, Cuba's deployment of troops in Angola converges with Soviet policy interests in the African continent. But Cuba's involvement in Africa dates back to the early days of the *fidelista* revolution, long before the Russians thought it convenient to have the Cubans actively there.

The essence of Cuba's international behavior over time has been a mixture of ideology and opportunity, of values and *realpolitik*, of convergence and disjunction with the pulls and pressures of a great-power alliance. The catalytic agent in this complex mix has been rational choice, the ability of Cuba's leadership to perceive the finite perimeters of their space and maneuverability vis-à-vis the international order, and their ability to act accordingly. While the options and consequences may never be optimal, up to now they have not proved fatal.

Notes

1. Another example, of similar kind, would obviously be Yugoslavia over the last 30 years.
2. Testimony of Earl Smith, Ambssador to Cuba from 1957 to January 1959, before the U.S. Congress.

3. U.S. Department of Commerce, *Investment in Cuba*, U.S. Government Printing Office, Washington, D.C., 1956.

4. *Granma Weekly Review*, January 7, 1973.

5. See, for example, Edward A. Hewett, "Cuba's Membership in the CMEA," in Martin Weinstein editor, *Revolutionary Cuba in the World Arena* (Philadelphia: Institute for the Study of Human Issues, 1979).

6. Fidel Castro, *History Will Absolve Me* (London: Jonathan Cape, 1968).

8

The Commonwealth Caribbean and the Contemporary World Order: The Cases of Jamaica and Trinidad

PAUL W. ASHLEY

Penetration and Underdevelopment

The societies of Jamaica and Trinidad and Tobago (hereafter referred to as Trinidad) have been characterized as small, underdeveloped, highly penetrated, and structurally dependent states. However, the peculiarities of each society play an important role in coping with that phenomenon. This analysis aims to explore comparatively the impact of the international order on the process of national development in both of these island states. In particular, the patterns of penetration, the specific adaptations and constraints, and the overall significance for the development of democratic institutions will be highlighted. It should be recognized that to analyze the *total* impact of the international order on the national development (or underdevelopment) of these two states requires massive amounts of data which are not presently available for one reason or another. "National development" has many components: political, social, cultural, economic, and human, among others; and similarly, the forms of "penetration" are equally diverse and differ in their effects on the various components of "national development." Consequently, this analysis cannot be exhaustive, nor does it pretend to be; instead, the analysis is selective and is confined to that area of study referred to as "political economy."

Before dealing with the political economy of Jamaica and Trinidad, the relationship among "penetration," "influence," and "dependency" ought to be explored. Without entering into the definitional debates, we would like to suggest a sequential relationship, namely: *initial* penetration occurs usually without the consent of the victim; this penetration influences the victim in such a fashion as to facilitate greater penetration (this time with possible encouragement); greater penetration then leads to a state of dependency (structural or otherwise) in which the victim relies on the penetrant for its very survival. In this state of dependency, the penetrant has decisive influence on the victim precisely because of the structure, nature, and scope of the penetration that umbilically links the victim to the penetrant. Although the reliance of the penetrant on the victim may have been greater in the earlier stages of penetration, this is reversed in the later stage of dependency. Moreover, the development of the victim is critically influenced by the penetrant and takes place in such a manner as to increase that dependency. Autonomous development of the victim remains impossible as long as the umbilical cord exists.

THE CONTEXT

Historically, Jamaica and Trinidad, like all other Commonwealth Caribbean states, have exhibited external dependency on metropolitan countries in an extreme form—politically, economically, culturally, and even intellectually. These societies became virtual extensions of the metropolitan economy via the establishment of sugar cane plantations in the second half of the seventeenth century. These extensions were export-import oriented in the sense that their main economic activity was geared to external demand, whereas their basic needs had to be imported. Traditionally, large transnational corporations (TNCs) have been the main vehicles for the inflows of private foreign capital in both societies. Moreover, the TNCs have tended to dominate the economy and monopolize the most dynamic and profitable sectors. Accordingly, TNCs have been the prime motive forces in the Trinidadian and Jamaican economy. For example, Trinidad's growth in real Gross Domestic Product (GDP) increased by an average of 8.5 percent annually between 1951 and 1961. That increase was directly related to the TNC-dominated oil and asphalt industry.[1] Between 1951 and 1968, the Jamaican economy experienced substantial growth (averaging 6–7 percent per year). That growth was related to the TNC-dominated bauxite and tourism industries.[2] Other factors have also combined to facilitate those higher rates of growth, such as:

1. The strong level of external demand, which prevailed throughout the period, for the output of the economy.

2. The fairly high rates of capital investment inflows.
3. A general economic and political climate favorable to private foreign capital.
4. Governmental infrastructural developments to facilitate expansion.

Closer examination, however, will reveal the dominance of the TNCs in the external trade, the high rates of capital investment undertaken by TNCs principally in the mining sectors, and the substantial contribution of those TNCs to government revenue, which provided the financing of the infrastructural development. Although economic growth was rapid and sustained, the source of the dynamic was external—export demand and foreign investment. In other words, growth was a consequence of greater participation by, and subordination to, imperialist interests.

Growth in the economy must not be mistaken for national development, as substantial growth can be accompanied by severe deterioration in other socially significant areas such as distribution of national income and employment. For example, in Jamaica income distribution worsened: the share of the poorest 40 percent of the population earned money income declined from 7.2 percent in 1958 to 5.4 percent in 1969.[3] Moreover, the growth was highly skewed from high rates in the mining sector to negative rates in agriculture, with only modest rates of growth in the manufacturing sector.

Identification of TNCs as the main agents of economic growth within these economies, especially in the performance of the petrochemical and bauxite/alumina industries in Trinidad and Jamaica, respectively, should not obscure the fact that direct foreign investment had penetrated *all* the major economic sectors, and that recent government policy has led to collaboration in some public enterprises. This will be examined later. The various national manufacturing sectors have displayed little capacity to become autonomous determinants of growth, and private foreign enterprises (usually in partnership with local capital or their local subsidiaries) have tended to account for a large proportion of the output from that sector. Several factors have been advanced to explain the relative domancy of local manufacturing elites. Generally, the manufacturing sectors of both territories have been characterized by relatively low rates of net investment and an absence of any significant inflows of capital funds. Although there has been very limited import-substitution, the participation of the TNCs (or their affiliates) has overwhelmed modest local attempts. Hence the national entrepreneurial elites are more assured of their survival if they are complementary or appendaged to the TNCs. On the other hand, the participation of the TNCs has opened up other areas of opportunity to

the local manufacturing elites. However, there seems to be some inertia as these opportunities remain unexploited. Either the local elites are
not creative enough, undercapitalized, and lacking in entrepreneurial
abilities or the stimulus is not sufficiently strong to motivate them to
exploit those opportunities. Consequently, even in the wholesale and
retail trade, overseas distribution outlets such as Bata, IBM, and
Woolworth's are prevalent in both countries.

It can be argued with some justification that the initial penetration
was a prerequisite for national development as both Trinidad and
Jamaica did not, at the time, possess the necessary capabilities to
undertake such programs or exploit their natural resources. The issue
therefore turns to the capacities of these economies to achieve self-
sustaining economic growth. Of crucial importance, then, is the capacity of the Jamaican and Trinidadian economies to finance entirely from
domestic sources a rate and composition of investment sufficient to
effect a satisfactory long-term rate of growth.

The Jamaican economy has long exhibited an acute dependency
on private capital. For the economy as a whole, it was estimated in
1970 that 30 percent of the capital stock was foreign owned.[4] Between
1951 and 1968, gross investment formed a relatively high proportion of
GNP and totaled some 21.8 percent. For the period of 1950 to 1967, net
investment was approximately 15.3 percent of Jamaica's Net National
Product—a rate which Girvan notes is conventionally regarded as
more than sufficient for self-sustaining growth.[5]

A similar pattern emerged in Trinidad, where *direct* foreign investment has played a critical role in domestic capital formation. Unlike
Jamaica, which had a more vibrant tourist industry and a larger manufacturing sector, Trinidad's dependence on external sources of net
financial investment rests primarily on the oil industry. Between 1956
and 1962, direct foreign investment (new inflows and reinvested
profits) were equivalent to 74 percent of the post-tax profits of foreign-
owned operations in Trinidad. Moreover, during the period 1964 to
1968, 71 percent of direct investment consisted of reinvested profits of
foreign-controlled enterprises.[6] Thus there can be no doubt that the
economies of Jamaica and Trinidad in the 1950s and 1960s generated
enough surpluses to undertake self-sustaining growth.

But Trinidad and Jamaica have not embarked on such a course and
they have been no less dependent on the further penetration of external
capital than at the beginning of the postwar period. Capital inflows
have created the potential, but that potential has not been exploited.
The obvious question is why. It has been argued that the institutional
forms simply do not facilitate the exploitation of those surpluses for
national developmental goals. In fact, the arguments have been
stranger and have advanced the position that the institutional forms

(mainly the structure of the TNCs) frustrate the process of national exploitation of those surpluses. For although the surpluses are generated *within* the economy, the control and direction of those surpluses lay *outside* the national economy. The principal reason is foreign ownership *and* control of the principal sources of growth within these economies. The very structure of the TNCs precludes meaningful involvement of local capital in its operations, much less local directives. The surpluses generated by TNC activities within the national economy are not available to other sectors of that economy, but are subject to the global considerations of those enterprises. Due to its organizational structure and its goal of global optimization of resources, the activities of the TNCs bear little real relationship to the rest of the economy. By and large it remains a social, economic, and even political enclave characterized by an absence of backward and forward linkages with its environment. The TNC is not susceptible to national development planning, and its own local plans are distinct and separate from that of the rest of the non-TNC economy. Any gains accruing to the processes of national development from TNC activities are either peripheral, incidental, or welfare gestures designed to foster the "good corporate citizen" profile. This is not to say that the TNC does not contribute to the processes of national development; instead, it is the recognition that the *main criterion* in forming such a contribution is the further development of the TNC itself and not that of national development.

The pattern of ownership and control existing in Trinidad and Jamaica has other implications. For one thing there has been a significant outflow of investment income arising from direct foreign investment. The general situation of outflows exceeding inflows is a direct consequence of the reliance on (1) private foreign investment, and (2) the outflows continuing long after the cessation of investment inflows in the form of profits, royalties, and management and technical fees. For Trinidad, between 1965 and 1969 there were outflows of $185 million attributable to substantial investment earlier in the petroleum industry, giving rise to significant outflows of profits, interest, and dividends. More important, however, is that those outflows *exceeded* all other direct private investment in recent years. For Jamaica, there was an excess of outflows over inflows between 1966 and 1967; however, between 1968 and 1970 considerable expansion in the TNC-dominated bauxite/alumina industry accounted for the reversal.[7] Of course, the TNCs are in business for a profit, and, therefore, the foreign share of the total profits represents a leakage out of the economy. But even if the TNCs reinvested all of the surplus generated within the given economy, the result would be further entrenchment of foreign-controlled investment in the national economy—in other words, increasing alienation of the economy. In our view this is extremely undesirable, as *foreign* control and domination are the very antithesis of *national* development.

The effects of the TNCs on national development have been well ventilated by numerous scholars and very little purpose would be served by a restatement, although the analysis below grapples with some of the political and economic ramifications of TNC dominance in Jamaica and Trinidad. Even though TNC dominance is the *central* factor in the dependency of both island states, there are other associated factors that contribute to the vulnerability of these states to the vagaries of the international (external) environment. For example, foreign trade represents an overwhelming proportion of annual national income (approximately 60 to 70 percent for Jamaica). These economies export a very limited range of goods and services, with a few products contributing the major proportion of export earnings (in 1971, the petroleum industry accounted for 80 percent of Trinidad's exports, while bauxite, tourism, and sugar accounted for a similar percentage of Jamaica's exports). In addition, the geopolitical concentration of trading partners is very highly skewed, with the bulk of trade being confined to the major developed western nations such as the United States, Canada, and Britain. A similar pattern of financial and technical assistance sources exists, with a heavy dependence on the U.S., Canada, and international financial agencies such as the International Monetary Fund and the Inter-American Development Bank.[8]

What is of utmost significance in *all* of the external dealings is the noticeable absence of *control*. Even though the buoyancy of the entire economy (both public and private sectors) depends on the total volume and prices of the major exports, Jamaica and Trinidad have little control over either of the two. A similar situation pertains to the prices to be paid for imports. Although some control can be exercised over the volume and source of imports, this control is tempered by the high import content of the exports and by traditional lines of credit. The classic example of the former is Trinidad, which has to import twice its local crude production in order to engage in commercial processing. Hence, both Trinidad and Jamaica entered the turbulent seventies with very fragile forms of national development.

TRIALS AND TRIBULATIONS

The international economic conditions of the 1950s and 1960s—steady expansion and relative price and monetary stability—took a dramatic turn for the worse in the 1970s, with two major world recessions and price explosions in oil and most of the imports of developing countries, compounded by chaotic conditions in the international currency markets. As the international capitalist centers shook, the appendages, such as Jamaica and Trinidad, convulsed. Luckily for Trinidad, the principal mover in that economy was oil, which provided a much-needed cushion. Nevertheless, the halcyon decades of the fifties and sixties, which concealed the fragility of the national developmental paths undertaken, gave way to the turbulent era of the seventies which exposed the stark reality.

For Jamaica the exposure was frightening, if not catastrophic. The expansionary influence of foreign-financed investments in bauxite and tourism leveled off in 1971, and production in the former actually declined during 1975 and 1976, with dramatic reductions of tourist arrivals over the same period. The extent to which these declines are related to the Jamaican government's foreign and domestic policies and therefore indicative of foreign "destabilization" attempts, has not been effectively established.[9] The explosion in oil prices absorbed an ever-increasing proportion of Jamaica's decreasing export earning. Given the rapid growth in the import price index (139 percent from 1973 to 1976), the economy's capacity to import (export earnings divided by the price index) fell by 16 percent between 1972 and 1976. Private foreign investment and local investment contracted and eventually ceased, due mainly to adverse reactions to the government's "socialist" philosophy and the hysteria surrounding ulterior motives of communism. Gross investment declined over the period from approximately 32 percent to 17 percent of GNP and was accompanied by a decline of some 11 percent in the GNP.[10] The deterioration of the economy was ultimately reflected in the declines in the rates of growth and in the situation of high numerical values of *negative* growth which contrasted sharply with the high numerical values of *positive* growth characteristic of the 1950s and 1960s. The Jamaican situation was further exacerbated by government's borrowing on foreign commercial currency markets and utilization of lines of credit with exorbitant rates of interest. Given the depletion of the country's foreign exchange reserves (to the extent that the latter assumed minus values) and the official adventure into the international currency market, the debt service accounted for some 34 percent of the current foreign exchange receipts. Combined with the incessantly increasing fuel import bill, the consequences for national development are seemingly profound as national survival appears questionable.

Adaptation Mechanisms and Constraints

Various mechanisms have been utilized by the governments of Jamaica and Trinidad in an attempt to cope with changes in their international economic environment which have had dramatic repercussions in their national domains. These attempts have been met with varying degrees of success and share the common feature of refusal to alter fundamentally the relationship. Hence, the approach is one of accommodation and adjustment to the changes. In fact, the mechanisms employed have led to the perpetuation and deepening of the very structural dependency that is both the cause and the result of their national economic crises.

The mechanisms that have been employed may be differentiated according to those which aimed at accruing more of the surplus resulting from economic activities generated within the state's jurisdiction (revenue approach), those that tended to change the basis of ownership or control (nationalization/joint venture approach), those which aimed at altering the relationship between the center and the periphery (terms of trade approach), and those which were intended to alleviate the crises by extending financial assistance (financial resucitation approach). Of course, the categories are not mutually exclusive, and governmental activities usually involve a combination of approaches.

REVENUE APPROACH

Generally, the mechanisms used in this area usually attempt to plug loopholes against tax evasion by both domestic and foreign businesses. It is important to note that some of these loopholes were deliberately created by the local regimes in their concession agreements with the TNCs, and that the revenue contributions that the TNCs were making to the respective national coffers have always been a major tension point in the host government-TNC relationship. Although the host governments of Trinidad and Jamaica welcomed the exploitation of their national resources by TNCs (causing considerable growth in their national income in addition to accounting for the bulk of government revenue), the view has always been present that, given the size and profits of the TNCs, host governments were securing insufficient revenue from the TNCs, especially those involved in the mining industries. In a sense, this has been a direct consequence of the industrialization by invitation strategy whereby private foreign investment was "enticed" by overgenerous tax concessions in the hope that some of the revenue foregone could be recouped via income taxes extracted from the labor force involved. However, especially in the manufacturing sector, the employment generated has been relatively insignificant; in fact, unemployment in both territories has reached alarming proportions.

The major constraints on this approach are (1) the perception by the local regime of the need to "attract" private foreign investment via the indiscriminate application of fiscal and other incentives; (2) the penchant of the regimes for negotiations (in which they are hopelessly outclassed and ill-equipped) rather than resorting to their sovereign rights; (3) the severe handicap of lack of technical and nontechnical information about the TNCs, the international commodity markets, as well as their own local industry, thus crippling the governments' ability to negotiate seriously with the companies; and, (4) the TNCs' insistence that their revenue commitments should be fixed for very long periods of time.

NATIONALIZATION-JOINT VENTURE APPROACH

Nationalization—the acquisition of properties by the state on behalf of its nationals—as a key component of a strategy of development has been generally ignored by the regimes of Trinidad and Jamaica. Apart from the implications of the industrialization-by-invitation strategy, and the consequent image of a "favorable investment climate," nationalizations have occurred as if by default. Such nationalizations fall generally within the category of "salvage nationalizations" or "service nationalizations." In the former category, the main impetus for state acquisition is the consequent economic dislocation (especially in employment) of the phasing out or cessation of that operation; whereas in the latter category, the main impetus lies in the production of services (especially public utilities) on a subsidized or more efficient basis. In both cases, however, the joint venture approach is usually resorted to as the state perceives (1) that it has insufficient expertise to manage the operations effectively, and (2) the desirability of maintaining access to markets and technology.

   Both Trinidad and Jamaica have nationalized public utilities formerly owned and operated by private foreign interests. Nevertheless, these "service nationalizations" still depend on private foreign expertise which has been ardently solicited. Irrespective of the ideological orientation of the regimes, there have been experiments in the attempt to influence the development of the major public utilities in both countries. However, such nationalizations have not resulted in the desired control, since private foreign assistance (usually provided by large integrated TNCs) has managed to usurp control functions by virtue of their interlocking structure (subsidiaries providing finance, supplies, and services to the nationalized entity) and their being accorded strategic positions in the operations (e.g., General Manager, Chief Financial Officer, Chief Engineer).

   Although national ownership *and* national control are regarded as essential prerequisites for development within the region, the pursuance of this twin objective has wider implications for the international political economy. Let us assume, for example, that the necessary political will and underlying mass support exist and the relevant constitutional guarantees regarding adequate and prompt compensation could be satisfied or amended, what then are the objective international economic and political constraints? For Trinidad and Jamaica, certain constraints readily present themselves with regard to the petroleum and bauxite industries, respectively:

1. *The scale of the operations.* In both territories, the requirements (technical and managerial) of the industry far outweigh the national capabilities of the host government. Consequently, a gradual and selectively planned process would have to be implemented. In addition, the possibility of foreign assistance to supplement national capability has to be carefully investigated so as to prevent the occurrence of foreign domination under national disguise.
2. *The structure of the industry.* Not only are these "industries" national branch plants of a vertically integrated TNC network, but these plants' operations are confined to the lower scale of the production system (as in bauxite) or are dependent on the technological and managerial dictates of the TNC (especially in petroleum). In some cases, the operations are not viable autonomous units and the TNC linkage may prove critical.
3. *The market realities.* Assuming that the appropriate technological and other linkages could be reestablished, the market realities, notably the TNC's dominance of the international commodity markets, the vulnerability of an economy being overdependent on the earnings of commodity (being confined to the lower stages of production and therefore resulting in a reduced ability to cushion market fluctuations), and the diminishing importance of the country's output in relation to available world supplies, constitute serious constraints.
4. *The optimum deployment of resources.* In the financial area, such a policy would, in the short-term (and even if payments were tied to profits), alienate significant proportions of foreign exchange which could be used to develop undercapitalized areas of the national economy. In other areas, such a policy would entail an excessively skewed distribution of the country's limited resources, which might prove inimical to overall national development.
5. *The international political repercussions.* In the contemporary international political arena, there is not even the remotest possibility that U.S. imperialism would tolerate such an initiative in its

backyard. Oil and bauxite are still considered "strategic" resources in the production process of the metropolitan centers of
Western capitalism. Allende's demise in Chile is the most cogent
example of TNC–home government collusion. Moreover, the
vulnerability of the island's economies and politics to pressure
emanating from the international political economy is extremely
high.

The magnitude of the constraints does not necessitate abandonment of the twin objective of national ownership *and* national control,
but merely influences the strategies and tactics to be employed. The
joint venture approach has been the strategy favored by the regimes in
Jamaica and Trinidad. This involves the divorce of ownership *from*
control as government becomes in reality a "sleeping partner" extol-
ling, when required, the necessary legal and fiscal guarantees. It should
be recognized, however, that although joint ventures (with existing
TNCs, new TNCs, or other states) offer advantages in exploiting new
or existing potentials, there is the risk that the strategy may result in
the further entrenchment of private *foreign* capital which can be regarded as an indicator of the level of *national underdevelopment*.

One of the underlying rationales for the adoption of the joint venture approach to national development relates to the technological input of private foreign capital. Foreign capital is presumed to be
accompanied by a superior and more efficient technology which over
time will be imparted to locals, thereby raising the level of the national
capabiity. However, this perception has already attracted several
pointed criticisms, especially in the joint ventures in the petroleum
industry (Tesoro)[11] and telecommunications (Continental Telephone)[12]
of Trinidad. Currently, the whole assumption of access to technology
is being questioned, as well as the appropriateness and the terms and
conditions surrounding any transfer.

TERMS OF TRADE APPROACH

Being import-export-oriented economies producing little of what the
population consumes, both Trinidad and Jamaica have suffered from
the differentials in the movements of the prices of primary produce and
the prices of those products in the industrialized countries. Both
economies have experienced traditional neglect of the agricultural sector and are still heavily dependent on imported foodstuffs. Moreover,
the national manufacturing sector relies heavily on imported raw materials for limited import-substitution. In addition to very strong trade
union rivalry (more so in Jamaica than in Trinidad), the non-mineral

sectors are faced with the problems of increasing prices of imports, decreasing (or disproportionately increasing) prices of agricultural (and primary) commodities, and uncompetitive manufactured products due to low productivity, imported inflation, and work stoppages.

Traditionally, the strategy adopted by *all* Commonwealth Caribbean countries was one of selecting "protected" markets for their main agricultural produce (namely sugar, rum and bananas). The contemporary strategy aims at introducing a political directive directly into the international commodity economy via politically negotiated concession agreements as in Lome, the indexing of primary raw material to finished manufactured products, as well as stabilizing the drastic international price fluctuations for agricultural commodities. The contemporary situation is more critical for Jamaica than it is for Trinidad, due to the latter's influx of petrodollars. Hence Jamaica's active roles in international discussions on the New International Economic Order, the Common Fund, Third World debt, North-South dialogue, and leadership positions in negotiations between African, Caribbean and Pacific countries (ACP), and the European Economic Community (EEC) for Lome I and II. Whereas Jamaica has been very active in the arena of resource diplomacy, especially in the promulgation of producer organizations (notably the International Bauxite Association), Trinidad has adopted a passive, non-involved, distant stance, preferring to expedite her fortuitous gains in building an industrial base.

Apart from a very active resource diplomacy, the government of Jamaica has deliberately sought to diversify the country's trading patterns; ironically, the dependency on the traditional sources has been increased. Some of the reasons advanced for the failure are (1) the limited range and supplies of products the country offers, (2) the uncompetitive nature of that offered, (3) the reluctance of the manufacturing sector to establish linkages outside of the traditional geopolitical concentration, (4) the critical shortage of foreign exchange, and (5) the unreliability of the Jamaican exporter.

The increased state activity on the international scene has been accompanied by increased state activity on the national scene. Government has sought to (1) restimulate private enterprise, (2) broaden the productive sector, and (3) exert some control over the use of sparse foreign exchange reserves.

Restimulation of Private Enterprise. Various incentives have been made available and legislated, such as industrial and export incentives, the Export Industry Encouragement Act, and the Industrial Incentives (Factory Construction) Law. In addition, technical extension services, training for industry, and the financing and promotion of exports have been undertaken by various quasi-governmental agencies such as the

Jamaica Development Bank, the Jamaica National Export Corporation, the Jamaica Industrial Development Corporation, and the Jamaica National Investment Company, to mention a few.

Broadening the Productive Sector. In this area the government's strategy is twofold: first is the attraction of foreign investment (signified by its Foreign Investment Code and the creation of a free zone), and the second is land reform. The attraction of foreign investment seemed destined for failure due mainly to similar constraints operative in the restimulation of local private enterprise and the lack of any new natural resource demanded by the international capitalist system or the international socialist system. The land redistribution program was largely an unproductive misadventure because of the inadequacy of the necessary supportive services (such as managerial, financial, motivational, technical and scientific inputs).

Foreign Exchange Utilization Control. The most crucial constraint on immediate increases in production is the scarcity of foreign exchange which, among other things, has resulted in the unavailability of raw material imports. A rigid system has been implemented in an attempt to regulate and reduce the expenditure of foreign exchange (for example, drastic limitations on personal foreign exchange travel allotments, the creation of a Financial Intelligence Unit to detect foreign exchange smuggling, cessation of imports of "nonessentials," and import licensing). Although the system aimed at rationalizing current foreign exchange expenditure, giving highest priority to export-oriented and high labor content operations, the bureaucratic mechanisms have proven cumbersome and sluggish, resulting in (1) the further exasperation of those in the manufacturing sector who have not migrated and are willing to produce, (2) massive amounts of foreign exchange being "leaked" via a host of conventional and imaginative means, and (3) the mushrooming of a vibrant "black-market" in foreign currency (mainly U.S. dollars) and other scarce commodities.

FINANCIAL RESUSCITATION

This classification is reserved for states whose financial management falls under the aegis of an international financial institution with the national government acting as a conduit. Accordingly, this approach differs from the above-mentioned, since those were attempts by the local regime to adapt to their international environment. In the case of "financial resuscitation" the local regime has failed to adapt to the international environment; therefore, one of the system's readjustment mechanisms has been brought into play to realign the deviant. Jamaica is the classic example because, since 1977, the economy has been under the auspices of the International Monetary Fund (IMF). The IMF policies have been directed at four main areas: (1) stimulation of output and growth, (2) readjustment of relative prices without creating runaway inflation, (3) creation of adequate levels of public sector savings and investment, and (4) reorganization of the balance of payments and external finance.

The effects of the IMF policies on national development cannot be adequately analyzed in this chapter. Instead, we will merely note some of the constraints operative on the mechanisms employed.

First, there were massive devaluations of the Jamaican dollar in gradual stages (the crawling peg) and ad hoc sequences. The stated aim was to achieve "competitiveness" of Jamaican exports. This was predicated on certain questionable assumptions concerning the elasticity of supply and demand for Jamaica's exports. The devaluations also critically affected the capacity of the economy for growth, for growth is traditionally dependent on the capacity of the economy to import raw materials for the productive sector and the capital goods necessary for the expansion of productive capability.

Second, a prices and incomes policy was adopted which aimed at restricting the rise in wages to 15 percent, whereas price controls were totally removed. Hence the situation was one in which the workers' wages were supposed to decline in real terms. With the presence of very strong trade unions, such a policy was destined for failure. It should be noted that the aim of removing price controls was to ensure the generation of adequate surplus, which it was assumed would be the main source of finance for investment and expansion. Here, again, the basic assumption is questionable, as that "favorable investment climate" simply does not exist; in any event, indications are that it will require more than legislation for the workers to conform to those guidelines, given the precipitous daily erosion of their standard of living.

Third, the government sector was required to make a particularly significant contribution to the savings and investment effort by (1) undertaking massive and widespread cuts in its programs, and (2) operating the public sector enterprises on a strictly commercial basis. The former not only involved the nationalization of ministries and statutory bodies, but, more importantly, the reduction in public sector employment, and the severe scaling-down, cancellation, and cessation of government "people programs" which had a low productivity but high welfare component. During the period 1972 to 1976, the government administration and infrastructural programs accounted for the bulk of the jobs created during that time. The aim of this dictate was to reverse the trend and thereby divert labor to what is called the "productive sector"—a euphemism for private enterprise. The acceptance of such an IMF dictate clearly necessitated and, in fact, indicated the abandonment by the Peoples' National Party (PNP) regime of its philosophical approach (democratic socialism). Implicitly, the return of private enterprise to the position of main motor of economic development seemed imminent. Given the very high level of unemployment (estimated at 35 percent), possession of a job is considered a privilege; to remove that privilege seemed politically revolting. But the recognition of the private sector's role in the economy is only one side of the coin; that sector's willingness to perform that role under the PNP regime is the more crucial issue. The operating of public utilities (telephone, electricity, water, and urban mass transportation) on strictly commercial principles is desirable as long as it implies increased efficiency while not unduly sacrificing the welfare component. However, the imposition of substantially increased changes across the board without any indication of improved service has been reminiscent of the yet to be fulfilled promises of past governments, regardless of their ideological disposition.

Fourth, the key element in the reorganization of the country's external finances was the assistance of SDR 200 million (around $240 million) from the International Monetary Fund over a three-year period. In order to obtain its financial life support, the economy had to exhibit certain indicators determined by the IMF on a quarterly basis. Consequently, the IMF not only identified what it had considered to be the problems of the Jamaican economy, but the Fund dictated the corrective strategy to be pursued and established periodic tests to determine whether or not the tactics employed by the government were successful. In an attempt to ensure compliance, harsher conditions accompanied failure of a "test." Thus Jamaica's economic *survival* was viewed in terms of passing the IMF tests, with any implication for national development being peripheral and incidental. National social, political, and economic development was therefore subordinated to, if not compromised by, the preponderant preoccupation with economic survival under the aegis of the IMF.

Implications for the Development of Democratic Institutions

Any discussion of the development of "democratic institutions" must, of necessity, take into account the structure of decisionmaking within the institutions and the aims and objectives of such institutions. Generally, the term "democratic institutions" must imply some *determining* influence by the members on the institutions' objectives and the methods of achieving those objectives. In the Caribbean, especially in Trinidad and Jamaica, "democratic institutions" must be considered those instruments and organizations which facilitate the exercise of some element of *control* by nationals over their collective destiny. This does not preclude the participation of the state acting in the "national interest," although the class bias promulgated by the implementation of that concept is widely recognized. However, it must be emphasized that any attempt to democratize any institution necessarily involves a redistribution of *power* on a more equitable basis. Hence, the more equitable the distribution of power (and authority) within the institution, the more "democratic" the organization.

A penetrated system can be considered one in which representatives of a foreign polity participate *authoritatively* in the decision making processes of a state. The history of independent Trinidad and Jamaica is fraught with numerous examples of the participation—often invited—of non-nationals, usually with decisive influence on and in the decision making processes of those small ex-colonial societies. In a sense, the authoritative participation of non-nationals merely reflects the economic reality, as the levers of control are located *outside* of the territorial jurisdiction of the respective regimes. In the preceding section, we have noted the relative inability of the host state to control the TNCs; even in the case of national ownership, control has yet to be repatriated. One could cynically argue that for Jamaica and Trinidad it makes only marginal sense to speak of a *national* decisionmaking process when the plans for the major positions of the economy are formulated without the involvement of the host state. True, both territories periodically publish "Five Year Development Plans," but these publications merely incorporate the given plans of the TNC's with respect to their local operations, in addition to allocating the estimated revenue from the activities to the priorities determined largely, but not exclusively, by the national regime. In short, the TNCs' development plans and the government's are distinct and separate, despite the dependent relationship.

In the extreme case of financial resuscitation, the economy is under the management of an international financial institution in which Jamaicans participate minimally in decisionmaking processes. The overriding features are that the loci of decisionmaking are external to these states with respect to significant areas of their economies, and that nationals have very little influence on these external processes. Even in the extremely limited area where national decisionmaking is realized, the authoritative participation of non-nationals (or nationals representing foreign interest) is evident. From this standpoint, the nationals of Trinidad and Jamaica have little or no avenues for effectively shaping their economic destiny given the present structural relationships.

However, this is not to say that there have been no proposals to effect some influence by nationals on their collective economic and social destiny. Both Jamaica and Trinidad have committed to paper laudable concepts of worker participation, self-reliance, and cooperatives. The two nations have, at one time or another, stated their objectives of (1) accelerating the transfer of control of foreign-owned firms to locals; (2) ensuring that needed private foreign investment makes its maximum contribution to overall national development, in other words, in a manner consistent with the national goals and objectives; and (3) facilitating the development of local initiative.

The reluctance or incapacity of existing institutions to express and give substance to legitimate aspirations has very serious implications for the development of existing "democratic" institutions and the creation of new channels. The increased militancy has pushed the existing organizations onto a direct confrontational path with the state, which, in turn, has responded with a substantial increase in the utilization of its repressive apparatus. The increased militancy also accounts for the phenomenal growth in radical and militant groups which are passionately anti-imperialist.

For the nation-states of Jamaica and Trinidad there is a basic dilemma. On the one hand, the state, for one reason or another, has to rely on the efforts of private foreign capital for needed growth in the economy. On the other hand, the effects of the pattern of structural dependency are self-reinforcing and perpetuate conditions which can be considered inimical to national development. Internally, there have been growing pressures for the majority of the natives to have a stake in the economic activities that take place within the state's territorial borders, simultaneous with increased opposition (and even economic sabotage) by the small but economically powerful elites to the erosion of their privileged positions. In our view, it is the resolution of this dilemma that has the most direct bearing on the survival, development, or demise, of "democratic institutions" within these two islands. The words of Ralph Miliband have particular significance for small, underdeveloped, capitalist island economies in the Western Hemisphere:

Nowadays, however, it is not only with the power of their own business class that reform-minded and 'left-wing' governments have to reckon, or whose 'confidence' they must try and earn. Such governments must also reckon, now more than ever before, with the power and pressure of outside capitalist interests and forces—large foreign firms, powerful and conservative foreign governments, central banks, private international finance, official international credit organisations like the International Monetary Fund and the World Bank, or a formidable combination of these. Economic and financial orthodoxy, and a proper regard for the prerogatives and needs of the free enterprise system, is not only what internal business interests expect and require from their office-holders; these internal interests are now powerfully seconded by outside ones, which may easily be of greater importance.[13]

Notes

1. Frank Rampersad, *Growth and Structural Change in the Economy of Trinidad and Tobago* (Institute for Social and Economic Research, University of the West Indies, 1969).

2. *Jamaica Five-Year Development Plan, 1978–82*, National Planning Agency/Ministry of Finance, 1979.

3. Ibid.

4. Owen Jeferson, *The Post-War Economic Development of Jamaica* (ISER, 1972).

5. Norman Girvan, *Foreign Capital and Economic Underdevelopment in Jamaica* (ISER, 1971).

6. A. McIntyre and B. Watson, *Studies in Foreign Investment to the Commonwealth Caribbean, No. 1: Trinidad and Tobago* (ISER, 1970).

7. Paul Chen-Young, *Report on Private Investment in the Caribbean* (Kingston: Atlas Publishing Company, 1973).

8. Claremont Kirton, "A Preliminary Analysis of Imperialist Penetration and Control via the Foreign Debt: A Study of Jamaica," in Carl Stone and Aggrey Brown (eds.), *Essays on Power and Change in Jamaica* (Department of Government, Extra-Mural Centre, University of the West Indies, February 1976).

9. Vaughan Lewis, "Issues and Trends in Jamaica's Foreign Policy 1972–1977," in Carl Stone and Aggrey Brown (eds.), *Perspectives on Jamaica in the 1970's* (Kingston: Jamaica Publishing House, 1980).

10. *Jamaica Five-Year Development Plan, 1978–82*

11. Trevor Farrell, "In Whose Interest? Nationalization and Bargaining with the Petroleum Multinationals: The Trinidad and Tobago Experience," revised edition (Department of Economics, University of the West Indies, 1977).

12. Carl Parris, "Capitalism Unlimited: Trinidad and Tobago in Partnership with a Multinational? The Telephone Company, 1962–72—A Case in Point" (internal document of the Caribbean Public Enterprise Project, May 1978).

13. Ralph Miliband, *The State in Capitalist Society: An Analysis of the Western System of Power* (London: Camelot Press, 1969).

9

Caribbean State Systems and Middle-Status Powers: The Cases of Mexico, Venezuela, and Cuba

LUIS MAIRA

One of the important elements in formulating foreign policy in the Latin American countries with the greatest regional influence is the increasing preoccupation that has been noted in recent years with regard to the states that arose in the Caribbean in the sixties and seventies as a result of the ending of British colonial rule in that area.

In this chapter we shall try to establish to what extent there exists on the part of the nations that are closest to the Caribbean basin—Mexico, Venezuela, and Cuba—a set of systematic principles and actions directed toward increasing their influence in this zone. Our approach will be directed toward three topics that we consider to be important in elucidating the hypothesis posed: the estimation that the Latin American countries have of the state system that has arisen in the English-speaking Caribbean, the type of assertion by these Caribbean countries in the international system, the features of their foreign policies, and the contents of the policy formulations of the so-called middle-status powers of Latin America with regard to the Caribbean.

The Way Latin America Views the English-Speaking Caribbean

For centuries, and because of a process that has not yet been completely broken, the Latin American countries and the colonial enclaves that Britain, France, and Holland held in the archipelago of the Caribbean Sea were two separate worlds which took no notice of each other, in spite of their obvious geographical proximity. Separately, they each organized their national existence, having as axis a preferential relationship with the countries that fulfilled a hegemonic function with respect to them: the European countries and the United States in the case of the Latin American nations and their corresponding mother-country and, later, the United States and Canada for the Caribbean ones.

This lack of communication and ignorance only ended when, in the areas of former British rule, there started to emerge autonomous national entities, from the time of the declaration of independence of Jamaica and of Trinidad-Tobago in 1962. However, the appearance of the new states in the English-speaking Caribbean and their approach to Latin America is of use only in appreciating the obvious differences that separate them in the main fields of national affairs: a different economic organization, social structure, culture, size, and density of population, in addition, of course, to language.

In the final analysis, the key to understanding these two state systems resided in the features that accompanied the period in which these independent nation-states came into being. Whereas the Latin American countries appeared as the result of the breaking up of two empires (the Spanish and the Portuguese) which had no solid implantation of the capitalist system and implied the absence of the early Industrial Revolution, the lack of an imperial rule in earnest, and the strong predominance of the Catholic Church consolidated in the Counter-Reformation (which presented there more vitality than in any part of Europe), the new nations of the English-speaking Caribbean were the result of what has been called "the third blossoming of nationalism. They emerged from the uncontainable process of the breaking up of solid colonial empires that had managed to articulate efficiently the functioning of the economies that they ruled over, in agreement with their own production demands and, consolidating a closed system of relationship ("mother country and colonies") that turned out to be much more appropriate for transmitting their own guidelines of political organization and, in the final analysis, their view of the world and of history. Hence, if one must seek a logic both in the meaning and in the behavior of the Caribbean states, it is closer to that of the Asian and African states which also arose in the course of struggles for national liberation after the Second World War than to the reasoning that accompanied the appearance of the different Latin American republics at the beginning of the nineteenth century. As more than one analyst has pointed out, in these emerging states there is a much greater margin for new political experiments because the groups that were more influential during the British colonial administration have not inherited a power quotient comparable to that which enabled the landowning oligarchies of the Latin American nations to organize their prolonged internal rule. Likewise, the processes of radicalization in the countries of the English-speaking Caribbean are much more usual, as was shown by the significant experience of Cheddi Jagan from 1957 to 1964 in Guyana and in the line taken in that country and in Jamaica by the governments of Forbes Burnham and Michael Manley at the beginning of the seventies.

These elements, among others, form a part of the contradictory and complex view that the Latin Americans have of the new Caribbean countries which are, for them, a world that is both unknown and different. At first they considered them to be a threat to their control over the political regional organizations (OAS and the Inter-American Development Bank, among others) and ended up by considering them to be a challenge that they had to take on.

At first it was difficult for them to understand the political system in force in nations such as Trinidad-Tobago, Jamaica, Barbados, and Guyana, directly descended from the English parliamentary model of representative democracy that functions on the basis of a system of two relatively stable large parties in which are confirmed the existence of such prolonged leaderships of civilian statesmen of the type of Eric Williams, Earl Barrow, and the already mentioned heads of governments of Jamaica and Guyana, all of which have held power for a decade or more, and have legitimized their positions again by means of the electoral process. If one considers that phenomena of this kind were unknown in the first decades of the political development of the Latin American countries and that even today authoritarian forms and military governments make up an essential ingredient of the political mosaic of the region, one can understand how it is difficult for them to understand the functioning of political regimes of liberal democracy such as those that predominate in the English-speaking Caribbean.

Another factor that astonishes the Latin Americans stems from the speed with which the leading countries of the English-speaking Caribbean have begun to play a very important part among the forces of the Third World, especially because of their participation in the movement of nonaligned countries. That nations such as Guyana, which does not have a population of a million inhabitants, or countries such as Jamaica, which has a surface of less than 100 thousand square kilometers, plan an important role in world forums and have flourishing relations and trade with some Arab countries and with parts of Africa and Asia is something that escapes the "inter-American" concept that dominates the formulating of the foreign policy of practically all the Latin American governments.

Neither do they understand the problems posed by the social structure of many of the Caribbean nations and the ethnic contradictions which exist between the populations of Indian and African origin in countries such as Guyana and Trinidad-Tobago. The political and cultural contradictions that stem from this fact are also not grasped by Latin American countries. If they have problems of a racial nature, they are with indigenous peoples who lived in their territory before the arrival of the European conquerors, although normally there is a relatively advanced intermingling of races because of the long period of time since the time of the first colonization.

Finally, the lack of knowledge of the territory, the leaders, the cultural life, and the economic activity that predominate in the English-speaking Caribbean is an obstacle. Until 1963, when the new British Law on Immigration made it more difficult for workers from the Caribbean nations to enter Great Britain, the type of relations that these countries had were predominantly centered on Britain. The Caribbean started to take more notice of Latin America when it finally accepted the fact that it formed a part of its economic-political surroundings. This occurred, among other reasons, because of the economic needs that independence entailed and it became particularly imperative after Britain joined the European Common Market in 1973, a fact which implied, for the members of the Caribbean Free Trade Association, the loss of important tariffs and preferential agreements that England had accorded them up to that time.

The first attempts to approach Latin America by the leaders of the English-speaking Caribbean met with overt hostility and suspicion on the part of the Latin American governments. When at the Inter-American Conference in Caracas in 1954, the Guyanese leaders Cheddi Jagan and Forbes Burnham asked for permission to expose a case of violation of the constitutional rules in their country, permission was not even given to listen to them. In 1966, the application of Trinidad-Tobago to join the OAS was the object of a suspicious and cold reception, in spite of the fact that according to the statutes by reason of its geographical position it was enough for Trinidad-Tobago to promise, as it had already done, to respect the principles contained in the Bogota Charter. A special committee of five countries (Venezuela, Colombia, Argentina, Uruguay, and Guatemala) was set up to gather precedents before resolving the question. Finally, in 1969, Jamaica's application to join the same organization was the object of a veto on the part of the government of Bolivia, on the grounds that Jamaica had not finished breaking her colonial ties with England.

The concrete point is that the relationship between the Latin American countries and those of the Caribbean has been a difficult one, due to reciprocal ignorance or to the existence of political and economic bases that are very different. The foreign policy of Jamaica, Guyana, Trinidad-Tobago, and other new states first achieved identity by identifying with Afro-Asian demands against colonialism and racism. The states' first diplomatic missions were set up in this direction, as were the first contacts with other statesmen. Latin America was only a second step in their foreign schemes and this did not find, at first, either comprehension or support. Although things have changed in the last decade, we are far from being able to say that the duality of our worlds, which was the first feature of our mutual discovery, has been broken.

Beginnings of International Assertion by the English-Speaking Caribbean Countries

Although naturally the foreign policies of the countries that make up the English-speaking Caribbean have different features, there are common elements among them that define what could be characterized as the style of assertion by these nations in the world and regional systems.

A first element of this kind is the permanent search for a community of interests among them. For different reasons that have to do with the fact that the majority of their territories are islands (a factor which eliminates the traditional quarrels about where the frontier actually runs that have embittered the relations of the majority of the Latin American states), the predominant character of monoculture in their economies is based on the exploitation of primary resources, the small size of their domestic markets, which prevents them from being able to make scale economies that are adequate to undertake the industrial effort, and the long period during which they were all colonies. These factors have served to accentuate the identity of cultural and political ties, and have been factors that have placed the objective of regional integration as a goal to be reached from the time that they started to think about national independence.

The aborted attempt from 1958 to 1962 to organize a Federation of the West Indies was the most ambitious effort made on the political plane. In this attempt to secure the existence of one sole state unit among ten territories that included three of the four main states (Guyana did not participate in this effort) also served to make us realize the difficulties of achieving this goal. After having come with great difficulty to an agreement on Port-of-Spain as the seat of the capital of the federation, and after having agreed to a common government and parliament, Jamaica's decision to withdraw finally destroyed the entire effort.

In the absence of a wide political consensus, later attempts were directed toward creating economic associations destined to promote common interests. In 1965, thanks to the initiative of Barbados, Guyana, and Antigua, the Caribbean Free Trade Association (CARIFTA) was set up and was strengthened in the following years by the entry of several states. One should mention that although CARIFTA took as its model and inspiration the European Free Trade Association (EFTA), in which Britain was a partner during those years, the political attitude of its main promoters, Earl Barrow and Forbes Burnham, made it a first organic attempt to reinforce the subregional identity of the English-speaking Caribbean and, further, to secure a gradual link with Latin America.

The close contacts of the main leaders of the Caribbean are also expressed in the periodic attempts that its rulers have maintained since the first conference of Caribbean chiefs of state, which took place in 1963. In spite of all their problems, the quality of the communal links and the awareness of a common destiny have not ceased to be reinforced as new states have gained their independence. About 1973, following once more the example given by England in its relationships with the countries of continental Europe, the objective of a common market was defined by the heads of government of the zone, which set up the Caribbean Economic Community (CARICOM). The economic projects of this new entity are becoming much more ambitious and include a regional development plan based on a projection of the industrial, agricultural, and mining demands of the area; the establishment of a common foreign tariff; and the definition of a statute that would give differential treatment to the four main countries and the smaller states which, until they reached the number of thirteen, went to make up its structure.

Although normally the Caribbean specialists are extremely skeptical with respect to both the achievement and orientation that is behind the CARICOM, from a Latin American point of view such an attempt, beyond its obvious limitations, includes very important elements and achievements. A comparison of the latter with the equivalent Latin American achievements in the Central American Common Market or in the Andine Pact shows a comparable credit in favor of the attempts at integration that have taken place in the Caribbean. The number of efforts to set up a common policy for determining the prices of its main products and their agreement in organizations destined to support them, such as the International Association of Bauxite Producers (in which Jamaica and Guyana play a leading role because of their great impact in supplying the U.S. market) or the Multinational Marketing of Bananas (COMUNBANA) or the Multinational Shipping Enterprise of the Caribbean (NAMUCAR), confirm this judgment.

Within the very functioning of CARICOM one can find even more ambitious integration projects for which no equivalent is to be found on the Latin American scale. Such is the case of the agreement reached by the Ministers of Agriculture of the Caribbean region in March 1976 aimed to set up a multinational corporation for the production of foodstuffs in order to replace the volume of more than 600 million dollars annually imported from other countries. This initiative, which includes projects as varied as the development of farms for the cultivation of corn, soya, beans and other basic grainstuffs and the intensive production of fishing programs, is based on the organization of experimental stations the location of which remains subordinate to the technical conditions of the soil and the environment (in fact, it was decided that the first two farms should stay in Guyana).

As we shall have the opportunity of analyzing, when one reviews concretely the foreign policy of the middle-status countries of Latin America, the community standpoint and that of economic integration are, at least on the plane of principles, constant ideas in the speeches of the Caribbean leaders and contrast with the sometimes extreme and unceasing nationalism of the principal Latin American leaders.

Naturally, one cannot leave out of account the fact that many of the community structures that have been created fulfill the function of strengthening the characteristics of the social system that is predominant in the Caribbean and the capitalist character of its economic structures. Such is the case, particularly, of the Caribbean Development Bank which has played a leading role in the attempts to redefine economic and financial policy which have accompanied the most recent international readjustment of the nations that make up the Caribbean community.

Attempts by the Middle-Status Latin American Powers to Formulate a Caribbean Policy

In the last ten years, several Latin American countries and governments have "discovered" the Caribbean nations and have sought a closer relationship with them. The ever increasingly enforced coexistence with these countries in the economic and political organisms of the inter-American system has urged Latin Americans to behave in this way. When it is a question of countries of relatively greater development, this demand has been strengthened by the imperatives of widening their influence and meaning abroad.

This process, although it responds to interests and characteristics proper to the three countries that we shall analyze and determines varying results, cannot be understood without considering some of the global variables that condition—whether favorably or negatively—the efforts toward greater activism in their diplomatic apparatus with relation to the Caribbean subregion.

The first of these variables is the content of U.S. policy toward Latin America and the degree of its preoccupation with hemispheric affairs. In general terms, one could notice that to a reduction in the quality and intensity of U.S. efforts to form a Latin American policy there corresponds greater relative autonomy of the middle-status countries, an intensification of bilateral and multilateral relations between the latter, and a more certain attempt to drag the smaller countries into the international line that they have defined. These are the features of the period that opened with the second Nixon Administration at the beginning of 1973, when the converging of the factors of international crisis increased the space available for the regional leaders and their "Third World" policies. We thus notice that the time of greatest dynamism in efforts to influence the Caribbean correspond to a stage of "lack of policy" toward Latin America on the part of Washington. At the opposite pole, we find the situation which showed up from the arrival of the Carter government in 1977. The latter, by projecting a new scheme based on applying global, regional, and bilateral criteria to the different countries of the region, imposed on the leading countries of the area over whom it had influence that they act in coordination with U.S. policies and with the policies of confrontation which had predominated in the earlier stage.

A second factor interesting to consider is that of the shift in influences determined by the events on the global international scene during the decade of the 1970s in relation to the balance of forces of the Latin American region. If, in general terms, it is certain that the overcoming of the Cold War climate and the setting up of the policy of detente extended the opportunities and the margins of independence of the middle- and low-status states, the real possibilities of using this space were determined by more crucial factors in the economic situation. Thus the loss of dynamism of the U.S. presence in the region is a basic piece of the background but does not explain everything. The activism of the middle-status Latin American countries toward the Caribbean is explained, in addition, by their relative advantages in the new balance of political forces and, in the case of those that had closest ties of interdependence with the United States, by their more favorable situation with regard to the altering of the balance which had taken place because of the changes in the fuel market. Although it is paradoxical, Venezuela and Mexico saw that possibilities of leadership of the so-called Third World and of Latin America increased precisely because of a factor that separates them from the average condition of the other Latin American countries and removes them from the difficulties and new problems that they face, their reserves of petroleum. This determines that the international role that both countries play in the region is considerably greater than that which they played in the past, especially because they are able to participate in programs to finance initiatives that favor the countries most affected by the crisis. Although it is ironic, Venezuela and Mexico are a good example of countries which began to exercise more influence in the so-called "Third World" precisely at the time they seemed no longer to belong to it.

A third topic refers to the political options that draw together two of the main middle-status powers of Latin America (Mexico and Venezuela) and the more influential countries of the Caribbean region. They all have governments which tend to identify with the political proposals of social democracy and which are developing a stronger link with the organizations which belong to the Socialist International to break with its Central European character and widen its links with other regions, among which Latin America has a preferential significance. A whole model of the organization of the economy and society seems to accompany this new relationship. The fact that until the Vancouver General Conference of the Socialist International, the coordinator of the Latin American Policy Bureau was Michael Manley, and the fact that in different capacities the People's National Party of Jamaica, the National Congress Party of Guyana, the Acción Democrática of Venezuela, and the Partido Revolucionario Institucional of Mexico participated, indicates the need to delve more deeply into the points of ideological consensus that inspire the vigorous projects in the countries whose interrelationships we propose to consider.

VENEZUELA'S POLICY TOWARD THE ENGLISH-SPEAKING CARIBBEAN

In the strict sense of the word, Venezuela's foreign policy, understood as an effort toward active assertion in the region and in the world, dates from the restoration of democracy in 1958. After having had one of the most "internationalist" processes of independence in Latin America because of Francisco de Miranda's and Simón Bolívar's active efforts to gather resources for their cause in England and other European countries, the wide linking of their efforts with that of the Haitian patriots and some groups in Jamaica and the designing of a project of Latin American integration which had its concrete expression in the political project of Greater Colombia (which broke up in 1830), Venezuela lived through the involution of a parish-pump policy, dominated mainly by civilian and military strong-men who gave little opportunity for ephemeral democratic experiments and kept international relations within routine and not very imaginative guidelines. In most cases diplomatic positions were accorded as a resource for exiling from the country opponents who were dangerous for the leaders of the regime then in power. Since the beginning of the twentieth century the only leading thread in international affairs was to give preference to bilateral relations with the United States, normally on the basis of lending support to the preoccupations and projects of the State Department (remember as an example that Caracas was the place selected by Secretary John Foster Dulles for the conference destined to condemn communist actions in Latin America in 1954).

After the downfall of the Marcos Pérez Jimènez dictatorship, this tended to change rapidly, and Venezuela, both in the governments led by the Partido Acción Democrática (1959–1979) and in those led by the Partido Social Cristiano COPEI (1969–1974 and 1979–1984), has shown an active trajectory in the international field. Venezuela's position of leadership has been strengthened since 1974 (a year in which the country saw its income from petroleum sales quadruple, going from 2.5 billion to 10 billion dollars) with the ever increasing opportunity to support the needs of other countries in the region.

Within this constant, the foreign activity of the governments of Rómulo Betancourt, Raúl Leoni, Rafael Caldera, Carlos André Pérez, and Luis Herrera Campins show differing preoccupations and features within a general tendency to consolidate an ever increasing regional influence. Whereas the basic preoccupation of the first administrations of the period was the consolidation of the political model of liberal democracy, as this was strengthened it became the demand for the interests of the developing world against those of the large and developed capitalist countries. The turning point can be noted in the Christian Democratic administration of President Calerá. Whereas the first decade of Venezuela's contemporary democratic age can be understood from the point of view of its foreign orientation within an "East-West" logic, the second corresponds to a dynamic dominated by "North-South" relations. Although naturally the Caribbean became a preoccupation of major importance, only in this latter design do the events of the period immediately prior to it form an important background for understanding it.

Betancourt's foreign policy was based on a passionate conflict with two Caribbean nations: the Dominican Republic, led by the dictator Rafael Leonidas Trujillo, and the revolutionary regime in Cuba. In order to fight both of them, the "Betancourt doctrine" was postulated, according to which the existence of diplomatic relations on the part of the Venezuelan state was conditioned by respect for the principles and mechanisms of representative democracy on the part of the other countries.

Once the Trujillo regime had disappeared in 1962, the contradictions were concentrated on the Cuban government. An element that was particularly important in the conflict was the existence of an active guerrilla movement within Venezuela that openly challenged the continuity of government activities and the fact that Cuba gave these guerrillas active political support. Only under the administration of his successor, President Leoni, did the open struggle which had led Venezuela to assume an aggressive attitude in the applying of sanctions and the later expulsion of Cuba from the inter-American system start to attenuate and constitute a preparation of conditions for giving up the "Betancourt doctrine." At this time, when the attempts of the Armed Front of National Liberation had been upset, there began a breakup of national identity in the United States that during the Kennedy administration had made of Venezuela a preferred ally in the Alliance for Progress programs. On the other hand, the application of the latter to rightist regimes in Latin America, which has arisen because of military takeovers, determined the partial isolation of Venezuela in the region (under the Betancourt regime diplomatic relations were broken off with Argentina, Ecuador, El Salvador, the Dominican Republic, Honduras, Peru, Nicaragua, and Paraguay. Leoni broke them off with Bolivia, Panama, Argentina again, Peru and, after the military takeover of March 1964, with Brazil).

Things being what they were, with the Caldera government there began a definite change directed toward achieving détente in the conflicts and toward progressively widening Venezuela's diplomatic relations. In order to do this they raised as a new criterion of order "ideological pluralism," officially abandoning the "Betancourt doctrine." According to the new guidelines, the Venezuelan chancellery urged the establishment of diplomatic relations with all governments, whatever their origin or their ideological orientation, on the sole condition that they should not interfere in Venezuela's internal political affairs. In the international organisms and, in particular in the OAS, it also urged a policy of wide coexistence and participation. As its style the Caldera government attempted a discreet line which, without claiming leadership, enabled it to concentrate on the tasks of domestic development.

Very different was the position of Carlos A. Perez, who included among his personal aims extending Venezuela's international role by assuring it greater hearing in world forums and converting it into the subject of important calls for the defense of the interests of the developing world. It was at this stage, especially, that Venezuela's relations with its neighbors in the English-speaking Caribbean became more intense in the political context of the financial crisis of the latter and the Venezuelan boom that we have already described.

During the earlier administrations, and especially in the COPEI government, in which university professor Aristides Calvani was Minister of Foreign Relations, there had existed a preferential relationship with Trinidad-Tobago and a difficult situation with Guyana stemming from Venezuela's territorial demands which covered approximately five-eighths of the total area of that country, which amounts to 275 thousand square kilometers. Around 1961 Betancourt had reactivated old Venezuelan claims and stated that his country had sovereignty over a wide segment of Guyanese territory. Things had worsened by 1966, when the Georgetown government accused a group of Venezuelan diplomats of the Indian community in Guyana, indicating that this constituted a serious act of interference in the internal political affairs of the country. By 1969, however, there were new accusations against Venezuela; it was accused of supporting a secessionist attempt against the state of Guyana in the Rupununi regions.

All these antecedents induced the Caldera government to accept the mediation of Prime Minister Eric Williams and to sign a peace agreement with Guyana in 1970 in Port-of-Spain. By means of a special treaty, a situation of "status quo" was defined for the territory in dispute for a term of twelve years, with the parties agreeing to work toward the search for a peaceful agreement which would find a definitive solution to this quarrel.

The Carlos Andrés Pérez administration, which had begun in 1974, was the most important attempt directed toward conquering for Venezuela a vanguard position among the "Third World" countries based on intense diplomatic activity. This attempt made President Pérez a key figure in the North-South dialogue, gave Venezuela increasing influence in the criteria of OPEC, and strengthened its position in Latin America in defense of the line of economic and political coordination which it attempted to translate into the constitution of the Latin American Economic System (SELA) and which had as one of its major features the attempt to orient the activity of the two blocks of smaller countries which were Venezuela's immediate neighbors, Central America and the Caribbean.

In December 1974, Pérez met with the heads of state of Costa Rica, El Salvador, Guatemala, Nicaragua, and Panama in Guyana City. In the course of this meeting a "protective" attitude on the part of Venezuela toward the other states was formalized and a series of agreements was reached, several of which were of great importance for the countries of the English-speaking Caribbean. Among these one may point out the agreement by means of which the Pérez government, represented by the Investment Fund of Venezuela (Fondo de Inversiones de Venezuela [FIV], a public agency created to take care of financial utilization and the international aid programs based on petrodollars), accorded loans to the Central Banks of the Central American isthmus to help them to cover their deficits from import of petroleum. It also took on an obligation to finance investment projects that would contribute to the development of the natural resources of the countries of lower relative development as well as the promoting of their exports and the extension of trade in the subregion.

As a reflection of its policy of defending the prices of the countries that produced raw materials, the Venezuelan government agreed to accord loans to contribute to financing the holding back of a part of Central America's coffee production corresponding to the years 1973 to 1975, with the intention of regulating the supply of this product on the world market and guaranteeing fair and rewarding prices. But the most important aspect of the agreements reached was that Venezuela announced that it was ready for the FIV to sign an agreement with the Inter-American Development Bank in order to set up a trust fund aimed at financing the development of countries which had an insufficient market and a lower relative economic growth, this being put into effect by a later commitment to contribute 500 million dollars.

It is important to note that according to the Venezuelan view, all the countries that have a coastline bordering on the Caribbean Sea are a part of the Caribbean community. This was in contrast to the view of the Williams government in Trinidad-Tobago, which recognized as Caribbean countries and possessions only those which are a part of the archipelago of the Caribbean Sea. This apparent geographical discrepancy became a political struggle to the extent that Williams accused Venezuela of trying to achieve more and more hegemony over the zone. The reservations of the Trinidad-Tobago government increased with the constant visits paid by Pérez to the English-speaking Caribbean and his active ties to and support for the Prime Minister of Jamaica, Michael Manley, whom Williams considered his greatest rival within the state system of the English-speaking Caribbean, particularly after the wide political support that Manley received in the parliamentary election of 1976 and the municipal elections of 1977. Venezuela's diplomatic attempts to approach the Caribbean nations gave rise to a conflict that has contributed to preventing the full success of the operation, to the extent that it caused many of the states to have an attitude of distrust for Venezuelan proposals.

The Venezuelan government's active regional policy, one of whose basic purposes was to guarantee the union of the Latin American countries and those of the Caribbean into a single bloc in order to counterbalance the rise of dictatorships in South America included the latter's democratic impact, in addition to an active role in the Ayacucho Conference. At this conference held in Peru in December 1974, Pérez stood out as the main spokesman for "Latin American nationalism" and urged another extensive initiative that would be of influence in the Caribbean, the Amazon Pact.

Relations between Venezuela and Brazil in former decades had been greatly marked by competition and suspicion. To the consequences stemming from the breaking off of diplomatic relations, decided upon by Betancourt because of their origin in General Castelo Branco's government, one should add the jealous watch that the Caracas government kept on Brazilian attempts to extend Brazilian influence to the north of its frontiers, precisely in the Caribbean area. In 1968, Brazil had mobilized troops along its frontier with Guyana and had later worked out a preferential relationship with the government of Trinidad-Tobago. All this made it difficult for both countries to administer in common their interests in the Amazon region. During President Pérez's government, this tendency was considerably modified on the basis of direct contacts with the government of Brasilia. This permitted the setting up of a bloc of countries, led by Venezuela and Brazil, of which Colombia, Ecuador, Bolivia, and Peru were members in addition to the Caribbean states of Guyana and Surinam. After exploring the possibilities for cooperation concerning the development of the large Amazon territories that represent, without doubt, the most important reserve for agriculture and basic resources in the hemisphere, all of the bloc countries signed a Multilateral Cooperation Treaty in Caracas in May 1978 so that this reserve could be incorporated into the corresponding national economies. It is important to note that if the content of this initiative were made concrete, the real integration of the states of the English-speaking Caribbean in the Latin American political and economic context would be furthered, for what today constitutes a real wall of contention and an empty economic zone that strengthens the physical isolation of those states which arose from the process of liquidation of the British, French and Dutch colonial empires would disappear. Venezuela's decision to favor this possibility reflects a new attitude that probably confirms more than anything else the growth of confidence concerning its position and possibilities.

A final synthesis of the significance of the attempts undertaken by Venezuela with relation to the Caribbean subregion leads one to conclude that, in spite of the fact that its Chancellery lacks systematic policy projects, and even considering the very probable tendency that the Herrera government will have to lower the intensity of its international offensives, Venezuelan presence with regard to this area is very great and already places Venezuela in a preferential position among the countries that make up the international system with relation to the states located in the Caribbean Sea.

MEXICO'S POLICY TOWARD THE ENGLISH-SPEAKING CARIBBEAN

In the concert of Latin American nations, Mexico is a state which has for decades had an active position and considerable weight in the field of foreign policy. Unlike Venezuela and Cuba, Mexican international gravitation was an obvious fact in the period between the two world wars and has taken place since the end of internal conflicts brought about by the Mexican Revolution.

Mexico's international policy appears to have been historically determined in recent decades by two main factors. The first is the active utilization of actions abroad as an element of legitimation and counterbalance to the political system within the country. A careful reading of Mexico's contemporary history shows that foreign policy has tended to be more active in periods in which there were greater economic and political difficulties on the home front. The second factor is the use of global foreign policy decisions and comportments as an element to counterbalance what is the most important tie that Mexico has with a foreign country, its relations with the United States. This point is closely linked to the earlier one and leads one to point out that at the times when Mexico's bargaining power is increasing, it tends to guarantee its preferential link with the United States, and one notices a "low-profile" policy in its relations with the Latin American nations and with the rest of the developing world. On the contrary, in the critical stages, and at the same time as increasing tensions and eventual disagreements in its relations with Washington, the multilaterality of the international commitment and the strengthening of ties with the "Third World" are favored.

If we apply the criteria exposed to the most recent period of Mexican history, we find empirical confirmation. President Luis

Echeverría's administration, which corresponded to a period in which Mexico faced the impacts of a serious political crisis (loss of legitimacy of the Mexican political model stemming from what took place of Tlatelolco in 1968) and of a manifest economic crisis (the exhaustion of the so-called stabilizing development, which was at the root of Mexican industrial expansion in the framework of the import substitution process), was characterized by the extension and the ambitious designs of its international policy. The government of José López Portillo, in a more favorable context due to the new discoveries of gas and petroleum and the widening of PEMEX's production platform, tends to place Mexico among the middle-status nations with rising possibilities and does not openly identify with the Asian, African, and Latin American bloc of nations. The latter has as the basis of its international activity the bilateral negotiations concerning concrete objectives with the most important states of the capitalist world (the United States, France and Japan up to the present time) and of the socialist countries (the Soviet Union and the People's Republic of China).

Nevertheless, one must remember that, in general, the increase in Mexico's international activity started at the beginning of the 1960s. At that time the rulers of the country noticed that international economic development was not closely linked to international trade and to the conditions of financial exchange and technical assistance. This confirmation gave rise, first, to a strengthening of the economic and political ties to the other Latin American countries. Mexico's active membership in the Latin American Free Trade Association (ALALC), as a result of the Montevideo meeting in 1960, was a first landmark of this kind of preoccupation.

Nevertheless, Mexican interest in the new nations of the Caribbean was present only in an attenuated form during the 60s and was expressed only in the opening of formal diplomatic relations with countries such as Jamaica and Trinidad-Tobago. On the other hand, during the administration of President Díaz Ordáz (1964–1970), one could notice an obvious preoccupation about the Central American countries with whom special relations were kept up; close and personal contacts with their rulers and a whole program of economic aid and cooperation in development programs was planned.

The Echeverría period, on the other hand, included the Caribbean (and within this area the governments with a more progressive attitude, Jamaica and Guyana) as a key piece within its scheme of extending Mexico's international relations. The Mexican Chancellery, from 1971 on, embarked on a global rhetoric calling for trade interests and affirming the economic and political sovereignty of the poorer countries in the international field. It projected this rhetoric in forums such as UNCTAD III and the United Nations General Assembly. After 1972, all these principles were gathered together in the Charter of Economic Duties and Rights of the States for the approval of which an intense offensive was launched among the countries of the nonaligned movement. Mexico was not a member of the movement, although at this time it was always an observer at meetings.

The rapid and increasing ties between Mexico and the Caribbean countries, at this stage, thus had as their basis an identity of criteria and of political and economic revindications in the international field. Echeverría's government, together with Venezuela, promoted the constitution of SELA in 1975, but was much more active than the latter in implementing its initiatives, especially because Mexico was worried by the setting up of multinational enterprises on a regional scale. The Mexican government was the determining one in establishing the Multinational Shipping of the Caribbean, in reactivating the Latin American Energy Organization (OLADE), and in the policy of regional or global association of the producers of primary products of importance for the Caribbean (mainly bananas, sugar, and bauxite).

On the occasion of the establishment of NAMUCAR, Mexico's undersecretary of Foreign Relations Ruben González Sosa explained in a document on Mexico's position the general ideas that had inspired the initiative:

> The Caribbean countries are united among themselves by a series of relations of a geographical, historial and cultural nature, which make regional integration an irreversible process. These relations which have as indispensable juridical hallmark the respect of the principles of free determination, nonintervention and ideological pluralism, as well as the practice of international cooperation for development and solidarity with the peoples of the Third World, are at the root of the Mexican initiative.

President Echeverría, like his colleague Carlos Andrés Pérez, developed an intense personal diplomacy which included contacts with and visits to Jamaica, Guyana and Trinidad-Tobago in 1975 and thus heightened Mexican influence and presence in that area. A good example of the new position attained by Mexico in the Caribbean can be seen in the text of the joint communiqué signed by Echeverría and Burnham at the end of the former's visit to Georgetown in July 1975:

> The Prime Minister of Guyana manifested his satisfaction with the initiatives that the Mexican government has taken in support of the processes of integration that the countries of the region have created in the search for solutions to their economic and social problems and, especially with the agreement that Mexico has concluded with the Caribbean community in order to promote closer relations in the economic, cultural and techni-

cal field. While the Latin American region is trying to define its common needs and articulate its aspirations, one must recognize the importance with which the peoples of the Caribbean basin are acquiring an efficient infrastructure in transport and communications, *at the same time strengthening the subregion* as a progressive part of Latin America.

We consider that this last idea is very important in understanding the reasons for the Echeverría regime's approach to the Caribbean. Like President Pérez, the Mexican head of state understood very well that his "Third World" projects were encountering a suspicious attitude on the part of the principal South American governments. In some cases the negative attitude developed into open conflict, as occurred with the Chilean military junta with which Mexico broke off diplomatic relations at the end of 1974. Because of this attitude in the OAS and the inter-American organisms, support for Mexico's point of view from the English-speaking Caribbean bloc became a very important counter weight.

This probably explains the development of several rather ambitious operations that President Echeverría's government urged in the Caribbean, although it would appear that the range of these has not been studied zealously enough. A good example was the agreement signed by Mexico with the Jamaican government in November 1974 for the creation of a binational enterprise for producing bauxite, alumina and aluminum. This enterprise was supposed to build two plants with a total investment of 360 million dollars. In Jamaica they would put up an establishment for producing alumina, while on Mexican territory (on the Gulf of Mexico) they would make an aluminum refinery. The host countries of the plant would hold 51 percent of the capital, 29 percent of it would be subscribed by the other country and the remaining 20 percent would be open to third countries. At the time the agreement was announced, the Mexican government pointed out that thanks to the annual production of 120 thousand metric tons of aluminum in the country, an end would be put to the triangular trade which forced them to process Jamaican bauxite bought by Mexico in Houston. This bauxite came back into Mexico converted into alumina, and meant a significant saving of hard currency.

In spite of the above, in 1978 the new Mexican government announced that it was cancelling its participation in both plants after economic evaluation studies had shown that, because of changes in world market conditions, the cost of making alumina and of the aluminum in them turned out to be less than economical. Naturally, when the Jamaican government was officially informed of this resolution, their reaction was to consider it as the consequence of a change of line and a lowering of the ties and solidarity with the Caribbean nations on the part of Mexico.

But beyond the specific obstacles, the problem of the relationship between Mexico and the countries of the English-speaking Caribbean, like the case of Venezuela with respect to Guyana, has been rendered difficult in permanent terms by a territorial problem: the question of Belize. Although the dispute over this former British colony has mainly been raised by Guatemala, Mexico has appeared as a third country in the dispute, arguing, on the one hand, that during the colonial period these lands belonged to the Captaincy-General of Yucatan (a state which has since become a part of Mexico) and, on the other hand, that the 1882 border treaty between Mexico and Guatemala set up as the frontier between the two countries a line located on parallel 17° 49' which would run eastward for an indefinite length. This would include a segment of the area of Belize. Although Mexico has accepted the reality of an independent Belize, Guatemala remains antagonistic, and the possibility of an armed incursion cannot be ruled out, especially with the precedent of the Argentine occupation of the Falkland Islands in April 1982.

All of the above enable us to conclude that Mexico has toward the Caribbean a much less definite and complete policy than that which Cuba has and that which Venezuela is beginning to form. The main preoccupation with this region corresponded to a very definite stage, the Echeverría government, and fell within the latter's wide foreign policy objectives. Although a part of Mexico's territory borders on the Caribbean, both for its general geopolitical equilibrium and for its specific economic interests, the English-speaking Caribbean states as a whole do not have any fundamental importance for Mexico. We believe that this is what has made the government of President José López Portillo return to the line that had been predominant since the rise of those countries for which bilateral ties had had little intensity.

CUBA'S POLICY TOWARD THE ENGLISH-SPEAKING CARIBBEAN

Cuba's relations with the new Caribbean states are of a very different nature from those that determined Venezuela's or Mexico's, first, because Cuba is a state within the Caribbean archipelago, and these states, together with Puerto Rico, the Dominican Republic and Haiti, form immediate surroundings both in terms of security and of economic development. Disposing of a favorable balance of forces there thus became of fundamental importance for Cuba.

But in addition to this, one could point out that the experience of the Cuban revolution, for varying reasons, had an enormous impact on the neighboring states of the English-speaking Caribbean and received more widespread sympathy from them than from the Latin American countries. Cuba appeared in the eyes of many Caribbean leaders to be an example of national dignity facing the United States and demonstrating in its subregion that even the small nations could decide to set up a social system antagonistic toward the power that has historically controlled the Caribbean. The existence of various links because of migratory currents between Cuba, Jamaica, Barbados, and other islands, gave them a rather complete knowledge of the social, health, and education programs that the Cuban revolution had undertaken. Finally, the fact that Cuba appeared to be the sole country to have solved its problems of racial integration within the social structure (a question that still provokes great difficulties in many other Caribbean states) is of importance.

Things being what they were, the policy toward the Caribbean almost since 1959 has made up a fundamental segment of Cuba's regional assertion in the hemisphere. The fact that the independence of these nations took place after the establishment of the revolutionary regime led by Fidel Castro gave Cuban diplomacy the opportunity to explore in a systematic and opportune way the political tendencies of each of them. Also, the fact that the cause of independence in the British colonial possessions in the Caribbean gave rise to movements of a very wide character enabled Cuba to give solidarity to these processes without being accused at all of interfering in internal matters. At the time when the Cuban revolution had a more aggressive foreign policy (when in response to being expelled from the OAS), and when they decided to support guerrilla movements that were fighting in many places in Latin America against the military and rightist regimes, the countries of the English-speaking Caribbean were not included in that policy, and there were no known cases of links between the Havana regime and groups that were in revolt.

Cuba managed to be recognized as what we could call an "intermediary power" in the Caribbean region because of factors very different from those that had traditionally determined this concept (i.e., a strong economy, with a large domestic market, having petroleum and other sources of energy). The weight of Cuba in the Caribbean is explained by its growing military importance and capacity and by the active character of its foreign policy which, dominated by the confrontation with the U.S. government, appeared to be increasingly linked to the struggles for national liberation in all continents. Naturally, Cuban influence in the region was linked to its government's active participation in the movement of nonaligned countries in the so-called Group of 77 and in the most varied agencies and organizations in defense of the producers of raw materials and strategic resources. A very determining role in Cuban diplomacy was played by the direct work of Fidel Castro to link Cuba, beyond ideological choices, to the main leaders of the Caribbean. In the same way as happened with General Omar Torrijos, Fidel Castro's relations reached the plane of friendship with Manley and Burnham, with whom he maintained a frequent and cordial exchange of political experiences for a large number of years. Links of this kind helped Cuba in its effort to break the blockade imposed by the Punta del Este meetings. In 1972, the four main countries of the English-speaking Caribbean (Jamaica, Guyana, Trinidad-Tobago, and Barbados) all gave Cuba diplomatic recognition at the same time. Many of Fidel Castro's basic definitions were made on the occasion of visits to neighboring Caribbean states; for example, taking advantage of an attitude more favorable to dialogue on the part of the leaders of the Caribbean Evangelical Churches, it was on the occasion of a visit to Kingston in 1977 that the Cuban leader formulated some of his most important statements about collaboration between Christians and socialists.

The very content of the policy and the exchanges proposed by the Cuban government to its Caribbean neighbors was very flexible and variable: programs of technical assistance, collaboration on health or education, and mechanisms for political consultation or common action in defense of the value of export products made up the basic part of a line which the State Department viewed, more than once, as that of the mischievous activity of an older brother who passes on his rebellious habits and his experiences to the younger ones.

Naturally, a key to Cuba's greater hearing resides in the field opened to it during the Republican administration by the hard-line policy and the destabilization attempts applied from Washington against all those in the Caribbean who had aims of a rather greater international independence and justice. From this point of view, the time of the greatest success of Cuban influence in the English-speaking Caribbean corresponds to the years 1974 and 1975, exactly when, from another position, Venezuela and Mexico also saw their influence increase (many times acting in coordination with the Havana rulers). In 1975, Fidel Castro managed to get even Eric Williams to make a friendly visit to Cuba within a tendency which had no further developments in the following years. That same year the Committee of Development and Cooperation for the Caribbean of the Economic Commission for Latin America was set up with headquarters in Havana, at the express demand of the countries of the subregion. Cuba's active participation in the initial stages of the creation of the SELA was another fact that reaffirms the same tendency.

In later years, although neither the principles nor the political energies with which the Cuban government worked to obtain a favorable position in the archipelago and in the Caribbean region had changed, there appeared new factors that made it more complicated to achieve this objective. On the one hand, the presence of Cuban troops in Africa (initially supported in an active manner by the Burnham government, which authorized the expeditionary forces to land at its airports) introduced an unfavorable element into the Cuban image within the different countries and made possible the articulation of a line of conservative opinion that could present relations with Cuba as a threat to the security of those countries (as was the case of the position held by the Jamaican Labour Party, as well as that of the Trinidad-Tobago government).

A second element that complicated things for Cuban policy in the Caribbean subregion was the new line that the U.S. government inaugurated in 1977. The clever choice of liberal spokesmen such as Andrew Young to deal with the more progressive governments of the English-speaking Caribbean and the guarantees accorded by the latter in the sense that the U.S. would not undertake activities directed toward upsetting those governments, together with the offer of programs of economic aid to help them to face their financing needs, have opened up conditions which, of themselves, tend to lessen the regional influence of the Cuban regime.

A good demonstration of the fact that Cuban influence, although still high, is no longer at the point it was in the mid-1970s is the recent change of government in Grenada. The fact that the Prime Minister, Maurice Bishop, and his New Jewel Party, in addition to showing an overt sympathy for the Cuban revolution, raised the possibility of making use of military assistance from Cuba has roused a whole political movement in the Leeward and Windward Islands and has finally given rise to an official declaration from the State Department indicating that, for reasons of national security, the United States would oppose any such military assistance. After that declaration, further discussion about this point was suspended in Grenada, although the new international airport in St. George's, the capital, is being built with Cuban support.

In short, Cuba's position in the Caribbean places us in front of a third type of subregional policy in the English-speaking Caribbean. In this case, we may speak of a policy that is articulated and complete, with determined principles and efforts whose relative success or failure is conditioned by the general situations of international life and, in particular, by the orientations taken by Washington's policy toward the "intermediary power" that had the greatest successes in its relations with the new system of Caribbean states. Cuba is the nation that is most exposed to changes in its relative influence that do not depend on either the tenacity or the intelligence of its efforts.

Joint Actions of the Middle-Status Powers
Toward the Caribbean

We have pointed out on various occasions that the period of greatest international "activism" by Venezuela, Mexico, and Cuba with regard to the English-speaking Caribbean corresponded to the stage which ran from the petroleum crisis of 1973 to the beginning of the work of the Carter administration early in 1977. This has led us to supplement our view of the "middle-status powers" of Latin American under this heading by relating some of the joint actions that they undertook and contrasting them with the type of activity that they are developing at present.

In 1974, after an interview between Presidents Pérez and Echeverría and a journey made by the Venezuelan Chancellor Efraim Schacht, the objectives of a joint political action destined to change the axis of the Latin American countries from the political field to economic problems were defined. Policy was changed from joint handling with the United States to the exclusive linkage of the nations of the "Latin American bloc." The rhetoric of that time, at the level of both chancelleries, was inspired by the idea that the Latin American countries should complete their political independence by effective economic independence and that, in order to achieve this, they should work together in organisms in which the United States was not a member and where the basic aim was increasing the capacity of the members to defend their own interests. With this in mind, the constitution of the so-called Latin American Economic System (SELA) was conceived; this was an initiative toward which Brazil, Argentina, and other important countries of South America were extremely skeptical from the outset. All this forced the governments of Mexico and Venezuela to deploy a series of steps and initiatives with the object of interesting a number of countries that would guarantee a certain viability to the new organism. In these attempts they encountered, in the larger Caribbean countries, an excellent disposition and open support. Finally, at the beginning of August 1975 in Panama City, and with the participation of 25 countries of the region, this regional economic system was put into effect. A very important role in this initial stage was played by the Cuban delegation, which was headed by the Minister of the Economy and Trade, Marcelo Fernández Font. The group that had come together had to work on the basis of reaching "unanimous consensus." After a heated debate, it was agreed to set up a "permanent system of intraregional cooperation and of consultation and coordination of the Latin American positions in the international economic organisms and forums, as well as in relation to third countries and groups of countries."

The Panama meeting, which took place at the ministerial level, was only able to set up "a beginning of creation" of the SELA because of the cautious attitude of the main South American countries. For the same reason, agreement was reached on the functioning of a high-level working group, open to all countries, which would be in charge of the preparation of the statutes of the new organization and of a program of work to be undertaken right away. This procedure enabled them to put into the proposals the favorable disposition of the countries that particularly wanted the creation of the SELA (Mexico, Venezuela, Cuba, Panama, Jamaica, and Guyana). But this probably resulted in considering strategic objectives that a good many of the members did not share.

After the meeting setting up the SELA there was the creation of the Committee of Development and Cooperation Caribbean, from October 31 to November 4, 1975, at a meeting in which the countries were again represented by ministers. The group included all the Caribbean nations which were in the CEPAL office in Port-of-Spain, plus Cuba, Haiti, and the Dominican Republic. In an important constitutional declaration, after characterizing the Caribbean as a "multi-state archipelago," the countries expressed their political will on 23 points, including their express wish to strengthen the SELA. Concretely, they indicated their decision to assist in the development of activities and projects that transcend the framework of the committee in the field of the Latin American Economic System and to undertake actions and projects in the framework of this in order to *"further a more complete identification of the positions and interests of the Caribbean countries with the rest of Latin America, recognizing it as the proper framework, on the level of the region as a whole, for exercising cooperation, consultation and coordination among the member countries."*

One could visualize at least two immediate objectives for the SELA. Venezuela and Mexico particularly stressed the creation of multistate enterprises destined to take on the most urgent needs of the members of this economic system in the case of production and services in the line of increasing their links. They also stressed the definition of a common position of the "Latin American bloc" in the main international meetings. With this in view, the rapid creation of the Multinational Shipping of the Caribbean (NAMUCAR) (formally organized at a meeting which took place in San José, Costa Rica in December 1975, with the initial participation of Mexico, Venezuela, Cuba, Jamaica, Nicaragua, and Costa Rica) constituted an important landmark in fulfilling the objectives established. However, difficulties were not long in appearing and were evident, especially in the apathy of the South American countries, which lowered the level of their representation in the following meetings. Thus, at the ministerial-level meeting that took place in Caracas in April 1977, only eight of the 25 member countries had ministers at the head of their delegations. As in December 1976, when there had been a change of government in Mexico and the new government's foreign policy did not put as much emphasis on the tasks of leadership of the Latin American group, the initial political dynamism of the SELA tended to drop even more.

Since then, this initiative has readjusted itself in terms that enabled it to fulfill some important tasks, though no longer within the perspective of being the great Latin American cooperative organization. As was duly pointed out in a recent comment in *Business Latina America:* "Although it has not yet become a catalyst for coordinated regional action as proponents hoped, the body is far from moribund. SELA has developed a number of far-reaching projects that bespeak its seriousness in tackling development problems. Even though its plans may look like pie in the sky at this early stage, companies should beware of dismissing them too lightly. A look at SELA's project list might offer insights for use firms' own long-term planning for Latin America."

The existence of SELA, though consolidated, has not permitted it to play a fundamental role, even less to be the new organic agency for accelerating Latin American integration and designing alternative forces to those urged by the United States. This readjustment has rendered possible a relative reactivation of SELA in recent times, this time on the basis of the preoccupation that the growing protectionism of business in the developed capitalist countries poses for the Latin American and Caribbean countries. Thus, when the fourth ministerial council of the SELA met in Caracas in April 1978, one of the major issues was the need for the Latin American countries to act more as a unit in the main international forums. This time Mexico, represented by Minister of Foreign Relations Santiago Roel, adopted once again a more active position and supported the formation of new multinational marketing enterprises for commodities and the idea of presenting a common line to the multinational financial organizations.

A second field of efforts in the period of greater preoccupation with the Caribbean area and the definitive integration of it into the Latin American bloc was in the Latin American Energy Organization

(OLADE), which comprises 20 of the region's 26 countries. In September 1975, due to a joint Venezuelan-Mexican initiative, the countries attempted to render the organization more dynamic because of the problems posed in the trade balances of poorer countries after the rise in petroleum prices. A concrete aim was self-sufficiency in energy within Latin America, and they worked to obtain a political consensus which would include the exchange of energy resources through interstate agreements of a bilateral or multilateral nature. With the active support of the main English-speaking Caribbean countries, the Permanent Secretary of the OLADE (whose headquarters is in Quito, Ecuador) was urged to prepare two basic plans: the study of an information system on hydrocarbon markets, in order for the region to receive enough of them from preferential exchanges guaranteed by the petroleum-producing countries, and the establishment of a financing organization, a kind of bank for financing energy programs, which would assure that the countries receive resources for developing projects destined to exploit new sources in a direct or multilateral way.

At the following meetings neither of these objectives materialized in the terms proposed, precisely because of the political factors we have mentioned. OLADE had both points on the agenda at the eighth and ninth annual meetings, which took place in Quito and in Mexico City in 1977 and 1978, but did not advance beyond a more precise technical formulation and a definition of three main alternatives under the heading of financing: the formation of a preinvestment fund for energy projects, the association of efforts in this line with the IDB and the World Bank, or the channeling of these programs through the SELA (a position strongly defended without great success by the Venezuelan government).

On the subject of joint efforts, one can thus clearly distinguish two stages; in the first one, Mexico and Venezuela, together with Cuba and the Caribbean countries, sought to develop very ambitious programs and excluded the United States from participating in them. From the beginning of 1977, Washington recovered an active international initiative in this area and established the Caribbean as a subregion of specific importance in its new programs of policy toward Latin America. This resulted in a "coadministration" of the problems of the English-speaking Caribbean which united the efforts of the United States, Venezuela, and Mexico, together with other developed countries, but without Cuban participation being considered. At this stage, it was also suggested that new organizations be set up to take charge of the development problems of the Caribbean. The most important of these is the special working group for the Caribbean that was set up within the World Bank in December 1977.

The increasing preoccupation of the U.S. government with the English-speaking Caribbean countries was expressed, beginning in January 1977, in very different ways. Besides a diplomatic offensive which included tours by high-ranking State Department officials, one should especially note the visits to the region made by Terence Todman, Assistant Secretary for Inter-American Affairs, a U.S. citizen born in the Virgin Islands and, therefore, from the Caribbean. Todman furthered the approach of U.S. businessmen to their colleagues in the Caribbean area and to that area's political leaders. To this end, two important business conferences on the Caribbean were organized in the state of Florida: the first took place in Tampa in June 1977, and the second in Miami in January 1978. While representing the U.S. State Department at the first of these events, Todman described the Caribbean region as "a vast area which offers ample possibilities for a commitment to democracy and development." On an official level they proceeded to redesign the line to be followed with regard to the Caribbean governments and, in particular, the orientation of the assistance programs that should be prepared for them. The Carter administration resolved to further a program that would strengthen the tendencies toward a community of subregional interests. In favor of this decision was the consideration that none of the Caribbean states had economies on an appropriate scale for full industrial development. An objective was fixed, that of encouraging better relations among the Caribbean countries themselves, as a means of avoiding the influences of a different foreign power (basically Cuba).

In regard to the supplying of aid, the U.S. government rejected both direct bilateral aid and multilateral assistance accorded by the governments themselves. The first was rejected due to consideration of what could be a bad U.S. image because of its positions in the Caribbean in the period immediately prior to this one, while the second was rejected in order to accentuate a more technical handling of the problem. Finally, the task force designated to evaluate the policy toward the Caribbean in the State Department opted for a close coordination of four international financing institutions, the International Monetary Fund, the Inter-American Development Bank, the Caribbean Development Bank, and the World Bank. It was decided to put the latter in charge of the direction and coordination of the programs on the basis of a working team which would include the United States, Canada, Great Britain, Japan, and a group of developed countries (Venezuela and Mexico among the middle-status nations on Latin America, and the beneficiary countries of the Caribbean themselves).

Since the establishment of this special committee on the Caribbean in December 1977, it has been possible to appreciate a different attitude on the part of Mexico and Venezuela. Mexico's attitude changed because of a delicate financial situation that it underwent at the end of 1976, which forced the government to practically double the value of the dollar in its parity with the Mexican peso, together with the breakdown of the North-South negotiations. Mexico was therefore determined to concentrate on solving its own financial problems and not to participate temporarily in any form of multilateral aid. Venezuela, on the other hand, following the line that had been implemented in recent years, participated in this effort and made the corresponding contributions.

In any case, what is of interest here is that from 1977, the readjustments made by the Democratic administration in its Caribbean position, together with the local conjuncture, opened up for the U.S. an important political field for its initiatives. Faced with U.S. dynamism, the efforts made by the middle-status Latin American countries toward the Caribbean, which vary in intensity, turned out to be much less relevant than in the preceding period. But the Reagan era may witness a very different turn of events.

10

Social and Political Obstacles
to Economic Development
in Haiti

FRANCISCO E. THOUMI

This chapter is a byproduct of a work assignment for the Inter-American Development Bank. Beyond that, however, it was inspired by the great impact which Haiti had on the author, who has never felt more disarmed as a professional economist. Haiti is a country of many paradoxes, and in many ways it is incomprehensible to a Westerner, particularly to an economist used to analyzing the markets of other American countries. In Haiti capitalism operates in a way in which the power structure overwhelms the competitive market forces; therefore, many of the normal economic analyses fail to be validated by the facts, and economists' recommendations fail to be implemented.

In this chapter, an attempt is made to understand some of the main forces that operate in the Haitian economy. The conviction that the relations described here are valid was developed through the study of the assembly subsector which links the Haitian economy to the outside world and which provides a great inflow of new ideas, processes of production, and other elements of social change.

This work is impressionistic in nature. The hypotheses presented are not tested in a statistically or econometrically rigorous way. There are two main reasons for this; the first is simply the lack of solid data in

The opinions and ideas expressed in this chapter are the author's and do not necessarily reflect the policy or position of the Inter-American Development Bank. The author wishes to thank Hugh Schwartz for his valuable comments during the preparation of this chapter.

Haiti. Most of the information used was obtained from interviews with entrepreneurs, government officials, international civil servants, and diplomats. These interviews were used to construct or estimate many of the relevant figures used in the study. The second and more profound reason for the impressionistic character of the study is the importance that is given within the study to the power structure. Economists have failed to deal with power because it is not testable in a positive way. In other words, the data is used to describe the power structure because a power structure cannot be hypothesized theoretically, then tested rigorously. In spite of these limitations, it is hoped that this work contributes, at least marginally, to a better understanding of the Haitian economy.

General Background

Haiti is the poorest country in the Americas. It has a per capita income of only $217 at current prices, which is just 39 percent of the per capita income of Bolivia, the second poorest American country. Haiti also has the highest illiteracy rate of the continent (75 percent), one of the highest infant mortality rates (149.1 per thousand live births), and one of the lowest life expectancy rates at birth (52.2 years).[1]

Though the country does not have reliable population estimates, current population is "guesstimated" at being between five and six million. Due to a birth rate which is rather low by "less developed country" (LDC) standards (2.7 percent), the high mortality rate (1.45 percent) and the substantial emigration from the country, the population growth rate is remarkably low among the American LDCs (1.7 percent). In spite of this low population growth rate, Haiti is greatly overpopulated. A large proportion of the country has been eroded, and currently only one-third of the country's surface is made up of arable land, which means that there are between 245 and 295 persons per arable acre. This situation is bound to get worse because infant mortality rates are expected to decline as a result of a significant effort being undertaken to improve the potable water supply. One of the most striking and frightening aspects of Haiti's current situation is the realization that a country with such dramatic overpopulation and food supply problems has not yet had the population explosion common to LDCs which have improved sanitary conditions in the way in which Haiti will have to improve them in the near future.

The great population pressure in the rural sector has increased migration to the cities, and especially to Port-au-Prince, which is growing at the very fast rate of over 6 percent per year. Unemployment is extremely high; while no data are available, employees of multinational agencies place the open unemployment level in Haiti at the 25 percent level or above. Given these circumstances, the need to generate employment in urban Haiti is one of the most important issues in Haitian society today. It is in this context that the assembly manufacturing industries could play a very important role in Haiti's economy.

The Assembly Manufacturing Subsector

As mentioned above, the manufacturing sector has been the most dynamic element in the Haitian economy. Most of this dynamism has been due to the growth of the assembly manufacturing for export.[2]

MAGNITUDE, PERFORMANCE, AND STRUCTURE

The subsector is comprised of approximately 200 factories which employ approximately 40,000 workers. If one can assume that three or four people are supported by each worker, then the assembly industries support approximately 18 percent of the population of the Port-au-Prince metropolitan area, where all the assembly operations are located. Employment since 1974 has increased by approximately 50 percent, despite the fact that the electricity cutbacks of 1977 (brought on by the drought) led to a virtual moratorium on growth for nearly a year. Employment in the electronics and miscellaneous group of assembly industries has doubled since 1974, and there has been an increase of about 50 percent in baseballs, toys and other sporting goods. In clothing, however, the largest branch of the assembly subsector, employment has remained constant since 1974 due to the slowdown in the rate of output expansion required to comply with the U.S. quota on textiles and garments.

Employment in the assembly sector fluctuates through the year, as international demand for some of its main products, such as baseballs, peaks during the summer, and as the annual clothing quota tends to be fulfilled by October. Thus employment during the second half of the year tends to be approximately 5000 workers lower than in the first half. These fluctuations have been smaller than what might be expected, however, because the United States has allowed some clothing exports at the end of the year to be made under the next year's quota.

As in many other Latin American countries, the assembly operations employ a very large proportion of women.[3] This large female employment is said to cause social problems in other countries, as the male ego tends to be hurt when the women become the main breadwinners in the family.[4] However, this characteristic of assembly operations is not likely to cause as many social problems in Haiti as in other Latin American countries because the traditional structure of the Haitian family gives more importance to the female than is true of other Latin American countries and allows her the role of breadwinner. Furthermore, Haitian assembly operations tend to employ a larger proportion of males than the same operations in other Latin American countries, as males are more likely to take jobs which in other countries are considered exclusively reserved for women, such as sewing clothes.

Wages in the assembly subsector are paid on a piecework basis in most factories. The wage paid for each piece is determined by dividing the minimum legal wage in that industry by a norm determined by what is considered to be the normal productivity for a day's work. The minimum wage laws set standards which vary according to the presumed skill level of the activity. Thus, the minimum wages in "high" skill assembly operations such as electronics are now $2.00 a day, while they are $1.80 a day in "medium" skill operations such as baseballs, and $1.60 a day in "low" skill operations such as clothing. Entrepreneurs claim that under the piecework system, most workers make a wage which exceeds the minimum legal level by about 10 to 20 percent. The law allows a plant to pay a salary of only $1.00 a day to aprentices during the first 90 days of employment, and some government officials maintain that many factories use the apprentice regulation to pay lower wages for up to 90 days and then fire the workers and hire another "apprentice" who is likely to have worked in the same trade before. While this may occur, no hard evidence was found showing that the practice is widespread. Given the low wage level and the piecework system of payment, the disruption to production that would result from frequent firing to avoid the minimum wages and high worker turnover that such a practice would entail would not likely be in the entrepreneur's interest.

Haiti has a system of various taxes and levies which increase legal labor costs by approximately 50 percent. Full payments are not made by many firms, however, as the workers do not perceive a real benefit from joining the social security system and thus do not request entrepreneurs to enroll them in it. Many workers feel that the medical and insurance services provided by the government are simply not worth the 2 percent salary contribution which they are required to pay if they join the system. The last figures from the social security institute indicate that only 21,000 manufacturing workers are affiliated with the system; as Haiti's manufacturing labor force is likely to be about 60,000, this means that approximately two thirds of the manufacturing employees who should be part of the social security system do not belong to it. That does not mean that fringe benefits are nonexistent in the many plants which do not belong to the social security system; some provide their own fringe benefits, such as in-house medical service, transportation, Sunday pay for a six-day work week, and an annual monthly wage bonus in December. The high avoidance of the social security payments means simply that fringe benefits in many plants are likely to be 25 to 30 percent of the wages rather than the 50 percent that the law requires. Average annual labor costs for 1978 were estimated at $527 in clothing ($1.88 a day assuming 280 work days); $708 in baseballs and toys ($2.53 a day); $789 in miscellaneous products ($2.82 a day), and $999 in electronics ($3.57 a day). These labor costs have increased at an average annual rate of 8 percent during the last six years, which indicates that in real terms they have been approximately constant.

The wage levels in Haiti are among the lowest in the assembly operations of Latin America. Managers of visited plants believe that the actual labor costs per unit of output are the lowest because labor productivity is very high in spite of the fact that a very large proportion of the labor force is illiterate. Labor productivity is very high because the Haitians are particularly creative with their hands and have an outstanding level of dexterity. Furthermore, there are no labor organizations, and the workers are traditionally submissive and willing to follow orders and perform repetitive manual tasks.

In spite of the low wage levels, the minimum wages are above the shadow wage rate as indicated by the following facts: (1) every time there is a job opening for an unskilled position, at least five applicants are found within a day; (2) many workers are willing to walk to and from work even if it takes over an hour in each direction, to save the 9 cents of a ride in the "tap-tap" (modified pickup trucks used for public transportation); and (3) workers in some of the artisan operations make substantially less than in the assembly plants. In one artisan enterprise it was estimated that wages were as low as 70 cents a day. Thus the shadow wage rate in Port-au-Prince for unskilled work is definitely below the minimum wage level, and probably in the $1.00 to $1.25 range for factory work.

Wages for skilled workers are substantially higher than those for the unskilled. A welder or foreman makes between $180 and $300 a month. These workers are somewhat scarce, as many of them emigrate to other countries in the Caribbean or the U.S., where they can find higher paying jobs. However, while migration has been high among qualified personnel, their scarcity has not been great enough to curtail the growth of the assembly subsector. As the subsector continues to grow, one can foresee an increase in the real salary of qualified personnel, unless the annual supply increases or the obstacles to emigration become more difficult to conquer.

As in other countries, the assembly subsector is the labor-intensive subsector *par excellence*. Total fixed capital investment per worker, including land and buildings for the subsector as a whole, may be placed at about $2500 to $3000. In general, fixed investment in clothing, electronics, and baseballs and toys is somewhat lower than in the miscellaneous category which processes some local raw materials such as sisal, rush, cotton, and wood. However, even in this "high" fixed capital assembly process, total fixed investment per worker is less than $4000. In some cases, the investment per worker is so low that it would be financially advantageous to increase it, for example, by the installation of central air conditioning tents to increase worker productivity to a point that would make the introduction of air conditioning profitable. This is particularly true in some electronic assembly processes which require some heat generating steps such as soldering, and make it extremely uncomfortable to work in the hot Haitian environment.

However, many of such increases in productivity are not made since the high profits environment discourages efforts to achieve marginal improvements, particularly if there is any risk at all involved.

As in most LDCs, accurate profit figures in manufacturing are almost impossible to estimate. However, it is remarkable that entrepreneurs state that profits are high, that they will not undertake projects yielding less than 30 to 40 percent annually, and, in some cases, that profits exceed the total payroll by over 100 percent. The ability that entrepreneurs have to repay large bank loans used for expansion purposes in periods of three to five years confirms these statements about high profit levels.

Total value added generated by the assembly operations includes labor costs, profits and the value added contributed by the use of some local inputs such as utilities, buildings, services, and a few domestic raw materials, notably sisal and cotton. While the precise level of profits, and thus also the value added per worker, would be extremely difficult to estimate, our educated guess is that value added per laborer ranges between $2000 and $3000 annually in the assembly subsector.

Haitian government officials acknowledge the importance of the assembly operations in the country but lament that those industries do not generate many backward linkages in the economy inasmuch as they do not use many domestic materials. This seems to be used by some officials to show a preference for import-substituting industries over the assembly export plants. There are several interesting points which should be noted, however.

First, some import-substituting industries use largely imported raw materials and intermediate components and thus do not create any more backward linkages than the export manufactures. Some, indeed, are little more than assembly operations for the domestic market which generates less employment per unit of investment than the assembly export plants.

Second, one of the most easily attainable backward linkages that the export assembly plants can generate is in the textile industry—and government cotton and textile policies[5] appear to have played no small part in the failure to capitalize on this opportunity, though less than aggressive domestic enterpreneurship is surely to blame as well.

Third, it should be noted that there has been an appreciable degree of backward linkage in a few product lines, notably baseballs, where Haitian value added has risen to 50 percent. In addition, the assembly export industries have had a notable demonstration effect on several of the exporters of traditional light industry products based on local inputs.

The composition of the assembly exports has changed somewhat in the last four years, though mainly at the product level. Clothing remains the principal category, accounting for just under 40 percent of the sales value. The imposition of a U.S. textile and clothing quota (affecting the overall level of exports and most articles on an individual basis as well) curtailed, but did not put a halt to, the growth of clothing exports. The quota fostered a measure of product diversification— toward some of the medium-priced commodities, and toward those articles not designated with an individual quota. There still is relatively little market diversification; although a European-owned assembly operation has now been established and one U.S. company is exporting 70 percent of its output there, Haitian entrepreneurs have not made any serious efforts to investigate sales possibilities in Europe.

Toys and sporting goods are the second most important category of assembly exports. Baseballs and softballs have been the dominant product, and Haiti now supplies 90 percent of the U.S. market. In the last few years the addition to output has been in a wider array of sporting goods as well as in stuffed toys. Electrical and electronic assembly is likely to forge ahead of clothing during the eighties. In the light industry group, artisan manufactures such as embroidery, banana bark furniture, sisal lamps and wall hangings, fishing lures, and leather skin pieces are among the products with growing export potential.

Only 10 percent of the assembly plants are wholly owned subsidiaries of multinational corporations, while 25 percent are joint ventures and 65 percent are entirely owned by Haitians. This ownership structure is drastically different from that of the assembly subsector in other Latin American countries, where there is much higher foreign participation. This difference will be discussed below.

The assembly subsector is Haiti overlaps with the artisan industry. There are assembly operations which include a factory process and a subprocess which takes place outside the factory, in the workers' own homes. Also, there are "factory" operations which are basically large numbers of artisans under one roof. An example of this is the embroidery of samples which are then shown in U.S. and European stores where embroidery sets are sold. Also, the assembly sector includes some processes which are normally not classified as part of the manufacturing sector, but which have all the characteristics of assembly processes such as the assortment of the food coupons collected at U.S. supermarkets.[6]

EVALUATION OF THE EVIDENCE AND FUTURE PROSPECTS

As mentioned above, the assembly manufacturing subsector has grown quite rapidly in the recent past. Haiti's success in the assembly industries has been due to a combination of three main elements: extremely low wages by international standards, closeness to the U.S. markets, and a very disciplined and dextrous labor force. Since these elements continue to be present in the Haitian environment, since urban unemployment and underemployment are still very high, and since profits continue to be remarkably high, one may wonder why the assembly subsector has not grown faster in the past and whether it can grow faster in the future. While no quantifications are really possible in a rigorous econometric sense, what emerges from the evidence collected is the sense that the three positive factors mentioned above have prevailed over other negative elements in the past, but that the latter have limited the growth of the subsector. These negative elements are the lack of infrastructure, the nature of business relationships and entrepreneurship in Haiti and of the government's intervention in the economy, and the import restrictions on clothing in the United States. The prospects for the assembly industry depend overwhelmingly on what happens to these constraining factors.

In a way, the easiest constraint is the lack of infrastructure, since assembly operations do not really need much more in the way of expensive infrastructure. Good port and airport facilities exist in Port-au-Prince, if not in other cities, and there are low-cost industrial buildings and a reliable supply of electricity in the capital.

The nature of business relationships and entrepreneurship, as well as the government's ways of operating, depend on very deeply rooted elements of the Haitian culture about which a foreigner is not qualified even to speculate. However, the fact remains that the success of the assembly operations in the future depends on the ability of the subsector to diversify its markets, and especially to tap the European market;[7] on its ability to grow beyond the confines of family owned and operated enterprises; on the ability of the government to establish rules which apply to every firm in the same way, thereby eliminating the need of a personal connection to the power structure; and on the ability to diversify the products exported, as the baseball market is not expected to grow and there appear to be major impediments to substantially increasing participation in the U.S. clothing market. In order to grow at a faster rate, which the assembly subsector is capable of doing, a social and political infrastructure which provides more flexibility and depersonalizes the economic relationships in Haiti would be desirable. While economists can make suggestions such as the creation of a free zone and the establishment of tariff drawback and temporary imports systems, only the Haitian government leadership can implement the needed institutional changes. Without that, the legal incentive measures will have little impact on the employment and well-being of the masses of Haitians who live in subhuman conditions. Such a shift in institutional arrangements will require a number of changes, most prominent among them the decreasing of the tight personal controls under which industrial development takes place. This would encourage rather than hinder entrepreneurship and the attractiveness to local and foreign investors of investing in Haitian industry, and so promote Haiti's future development.

The last constraint, the U.S. quota on textiles and garments, is a restriction to Haitian exports which is leading to a curtailment of expansion plans in that component of the assembly industries. These restrictions clearly limit the potential for growth and for providing productive employment to the poor, which are among the principal development objectives pursued by the U.S. government. Perhaps the U.S. will give particular consideration to this when it renegotiates the textile and clothing quota with the Western Hemisphere neighbor which has by far the lowest level of per capita income.

Sociopolitical Constraints to Manufacturing Development in Haiti

As extensively mentioned above, the most important constraints to the rapid growth of the assembly industries in Haiti are not of an economic nature but of a sociopolitical one. In the eyes of the economist, all the market elements for a much faster growth and for the achievement of greater levels of employment are present: very high profits, very low wages, a very dextrous and hard-working labor force, no meaningful labor organizations, and close proximity to the main markets. Therefore, a valid economic question is what is preventing Haiti from increasing total employment and therefore having equilibrium in the labor market? While a partial explanation can be found in the lack of infrastructure and in the U.S. textile quota, those are obstacles which other countries have conquered even though they had smaller market incentives to do so. For this reason, the answer to the previous question has to be found outside the realm of the pure market analysis. Therefore, it becomes of the utmost importance to understand the social and political environment in which Haiti's business activities take place.

The most striking characteristic of manufacturing and other branches of the Haitian economy, which pervades all economic activity in Haiti, is the importance of personal relations. Haiti is a society in which it is necessary to have adequate personal connections in order to operate a business successfully. While it is true that personal relations help in every economy, in the Haitian environment they are of vital importance.

In order to describe and understand the importance of personal relations in Haiti, let us describe some elements of the legal framework in which economic activity takes place in Haiti. First, laws are very frequently written in a way that either allows a variety of possible interpretations, which puts a fair amount of discretionary power in the hands of an individual or group of individuals, or does not permit adaptation to the changing and modern environment in which manufacturing plants operate. For example, the land law requires of a foreigner one year of residence in the country before he can buy real estate, and there is no mention in the law of the treatment of either foreign corporations or mixed capital firms. Another example is provided by the requirement to obtain a franchise to waive import and export tariffs on components before an assembly operation can be established. In both cases the law does not produce a rule which specifies what may or may not be done in a general way, but creates a system in which individuals can make discretionary decisions about what may or may not be done.

In other words, the law does not draw a general policy guideline, but establishes a system by which decisions are made, or, as with the land law, it leads to situations in which the law cannot be used to set policy, and it thus becomes necessary for a group or an individual to do so in a discretionary way.

Second, the actual implementation of the laws and policies depends on the bureaucracies of the various government branches. These bureaucracies, as in many other countries, operate more or less efficiently, depending on the personal relations of the private person whom they are supposed to serve. For example, a particular commodity can clear customs in one day or two months, depending on who the importer is. In order to do business successfully, it is necessary to be able to work with the bureaucracy; that is, to make sure that the bureaucracy does not become an obstacle to production and management in a plant.

Third, political and economic power tend to be complementary to each other in all countries in the world. This complementarity is particularly striking in Haiti. As the legal system and policy implementation give great discretionary power to various elements within the government, these elements can exercise both political and economic power to their benefit. Any private enterprise stands to gain a great deal by obtaining the capability of affecting the decisions of the government and its bureaucracy, and any politician and government employee also stands to gain by establishing a connection with the private economic sector. In this environment, where the implementation of policy and the interpretation of law cannot be predicted accurately, the private sector enterprises, in order to minimize their risks, seek a connection with the political power structure so that they can guarantee that the interpretation of the laws and the implementation of policy will benefit them, or, at least, so that they will not become an obstacle to the private firm's growth.

The need that private entrepreneurs be linked with the political power structure introduces some very interesting complications in the art of successful entrepreneurship. First, as profits depend very strongly on the government's policy interpretation and implementation, a successful entrepreneur has to devote a large part of his time to dealing with those elements. Explicitly, a successful entrepreneur is characterized not necessarily by being an innovator in the Schumpeterian sense, but by being a person with the appropriate connections to the power structure operating in the capital market and in the government bureaucracy; that is, economic success is associated with appropriate connections, not with risk-taking and innovation. Second, because connections in a country with as small an elite as the one in

Haiti depend heavily on family relationships, managers also build their connections around their families. This element produces a few peculiar characteristics in the manufacturing sector:

1. There are no corporations in an operational sense in Haiti, just as there is no organized stock market; therefore, a private citizen cannot buy into a firm.
2. Almost all private sector firms owned by Haitians are family enterprises.
3. There is a tendency to keep management within the family of the plant owners. Thus the growth of a firm can be limited by the lack of available managerial talent. A family with many young males can expand its business at a much faster rate than a family with no young males. Remarkably, sons-in-law are not perfect substitutes for sons, as they are not always trained properly to undertake managerial roles. The Arab business and industrial minority, however, does consider managerial potential as one of the positive characteristics of a potential marriage candidate, particularly when he is a new or potential immigrant to Haiti. Very few private sector Haitian-owned plants were found in which ownership and management were separated (i.e., that were run by a professional manager). However, most of the professionally run Haitian firms are new, a fact which is indicative of the change which is taking place in Haitian society.[8]
4. Most of the foreign manufacturing firms in the country operate in partnership with a Haitian who uses his connections to eliminate problems. Not surprisingly, among the assembly operations visited, the ones having the most problems getting materials through customs and being sued for labor code violations were operations run by professional American managers with no ties to Haitian groups.

The characteristics of the Haitian manufacturing sector indicate that personal relations in the Haitian economy actually create a bottleneck for the economic growth of the sector. In order for Haiti to develop and modernize, it is imperative that the economic relationships of the country become depersonalized. To achieve this goal, certain policies may be suggested:

1. Laws have to be revised, and many new ones will probably have to be written, so that they can be adapted to the requirements of a modern society. This is true of tax laws, tariffs, income tax legislation, etc.

2. Laws and policies have to be designed to minimize the discretionary power of government officials and the generation of rents through government restrictions (e.g., export monopolies should be abolished, tariffs should be set at reasonable levels and be collected instead of being set at higher levels and then waived for some people). In general, once policy is set, the market forces and not the government officials should decide what resources are allocated to which ends.

Conclusions

This analysis of the assembly manufacturing sector in Haiti has shown that despite the recent success and growth of this sector, there are great social and political obstacles to its more rapid development which are also obstacles to the development of other types of activities. The main obstacle is found in the power structure of the country, which concentrates decisionmaking in a few power centers and individuals. These power centers are not accustomed to delegating authority and using the price mechanism to make decisions about the allocation of resources in the country. Because the time that the individuals in power can use in this comprehensive decisionmaking process is limited, they can easily become a great bottleneck to Haiti's further growth. A situation similar to that of a congested switchboard readily develops. To do business successfully in Haiti it is necessary to have a line connected to such a switchboard; however, as all lines are occupied, further business growth is limited to the new switchboard lines that can be developed. The process by which the number of lines grows, and by which the market takes some of the functions concentrated today in the power centers, becomes a prerequisite to economic growth. However, this process depends on the foresight and ability of the centers of power to relinquish some of the functions they have had in controling economic life in the country. This chapter makes some suggestions about which policy measures could lead the economy toward a depersonalization of economic relations. These suggestions could look to some Haitians like the kind of policy recommendations that only a very naive foreigner could make. While this is possibly true, it is also true that if the economy fails to generate more employment quickly, the Haitian society in general, and its power centers in particular, will face a very rough future.

Notes

1. Inter-American Development Bank, *Economic and Social Latin America, 1977 Report* (Washington, D.C., 1978), p. 267.
2. The early success of this subsector has been studied by Morrison; see T. K. Morrison, "Case Study of a 'Least Developed Country' Successfully Exporting Manufactures: Haiti," *Inter-American Economic Affairs*, Vol. 29, No. 1, Summer 1975.
3. Assembly operations require great manual dexterity, patience, and ability to work with small parts. Normally, the productivity of women at this type of work is higher than that of men, inasmuch as women have smaller hands and are used to doing repetitive tasks at home.
4. A detailed study of the assembly-for-export subsector in other countries has been made by Sharpston; see M. Sharpston, "International Subcontracting," IBRD Staff Working Paper No. 181, September 1974.
5. Once a major export product, cotton now needs to be imported on occasion to satisfy the demands of local textile producers, which satisfy partially the domestic market, and which supply only a minor fraction of the inputs of the clothes assembly plants. Even though production increased substantially in the early seventies, reaching a new post 1930s peak of 5,300 metric tons in 1973, it leveled off in 1976 and dropped sharply in 1977. Cotton fiber if now only a minor export item, and exports of cotton cloth (primarily denim) have come to an end. Only a relatively low level of exports of carpets, bedcovers, and miscellaneous cotton products remains.
6. These coupons are flown to Haiti to be sorted out and then forwarded to the various manufacturers who issued them. This process requires a certain level of skill, as workers have to be literate, and is carried out on an air conditioned building lest the wind blow and mix already sorted coupons.
7. This has been done successfully by other Latin American countries such as Brazil and Colombia.
8. Also noticeable is the cliquish nature of some of the non-family-owned plants. For instance, when an entrepreneur was questioned about the nature of the relationship with his partner, he answered plainly: "he is like my brother."

PART 3

Democracy and National Development

11

Democracy and Development: Policy Perspectives in a Postcolonial Context

IRVING LOUIS HOROWITZ

One of the great myths of our age, paid homage to by both free enterprise and state planners, is the relationship between economic systems and their political structures. Depending on the belief system at work, the illusion that democracy is a consequence of either capitalism or socialism (but not both) continues to be maintained in works too numerous to cite.[1] Yet capitalism coexists with democracy in Holland, and dictatorship in South Korea; and socialism characterizes democracy in Yugoslavia as well as dictatorship in North Korea. It becomes apparent that any mechanistic formula of "base" and "superstructure" cannot supplant the need for a realistic evaluation of democracy in the world at large.

The mystification of democracy in the First and Second Worlds is understandable: each wants to establish the claim that its economic system is prerequisite to establishing a democratic order. But upon investigation, each can be seen to have idiosyncratic elements in their notion of democracy that negate the possibility of agreement about the character of democracy. As a result, analysis of democracy as a variable gives way to a theory of political democracy as a libertarian product of capitalism in the West, and a similar theory of social democracy as an egalitarian product of socialism in the East. In both worlds, democracy is held to be linked to special economic conditions which evolved in earlier historical circumstances. Such a vision of democracy is probably not relevant to present-day Third World structures; indeed, it may not even be meaningful to First and Second World structures.[2]

The subject of democracy has been widely written about, in great detail. But in relation to the Third World, the tendency has been to abort serious discussion of democracy, either through a sense of embarrassment or perhaps through a sense that the subject is irrelevant with respect to the development process. For example, one widely held view is that "world systems are the only real social systems." As a consequence, it becomes meaningless to discuss Third World democracy without discussing the history of entrepreneurial civilization, the origins of the European world economy in the sixteenth century or, even more modestly, the rise of American eminence in the late nineteenth century. In such global sweeps, policy problems are magically eliminated and hard choices nicely skirted.[1] Dealing forthrightly with democracy represents an important stage in development theory, and may facilitate the evolution of democracy itself.

Deeper thinking about the possibilities for democracy in the Third World is suggested by Guillermo O'Donnell, who suggested in a recent essay that "the issue of democracy is important not only because it contains the Achilles heel of this (bureaucratic-authoritarian) system of domination, but also because it contains a dynamic that can be the unifying element in the long-term effort to establish a society that is more nearly in accord with certain fundamental values." While he does not elucidate this normative structure, O'Donnell observes that the contradiction between the goals of democracy and the realities of daily life is "a key to understanding the weaknesses and profound tensions of the present system of diminution. It is also an indication of the immense importance of what remains implicit behind the superficial appearance of those societies who, on the one hand, are the focus of any hopes for achieving legitimacy and yet, on the other hand, are a Pandora's box that must not be tampered with."[4] Let us examine these tensions and contradictions.

There are at least three levels at which the concept of democracy has meaning. First is a simple taxonomic statement about properties of social systems that can be described as democratic. These range in type and character from personal freedoms of action to public choices on behalf of the common good. Second, there is a policy context: two basic types of democratic "system"—one political, the other economic—dominate analysis. One essentially has to do with individual liberty, the other with social equity. It is fair to say that whatever we mean or do not mean by democracy, at a policy level our definitions embrace notions of extending liberty and equity. A third way of examining democracy might be called normative. Questions about democracy are related to fundamental premises of democratic civilizations and peoples: the place of obligations in a world of freedom or, conversely, the place of freedom in a world of obligations; questions about constraints upon action and the responsibility of conscience; and issues relating to the role of authority in the behavior of citizens. These classical issues are well known, if not necessarily resolved.

For purposes of analysis, I shall stay at the second level of discussion about democracy, concerning questions of policy as it relates to democracy. The creation of a new taxonomy is essentially formalistic; it may add more indicators or variables for consideration, but shed scant light on operational or historical issues. The third, philosophic and normative, level of analysis fails to address everyday possibilities. In staying at the policy level of analysis, I undoubtedly betray personal bias no less than intellectual preference, but democracy as a question of policy rather than of language or metahistory offers the best hope for clarifying the terms of action, no less than theory. As developing regions reach beyond the broad concept of a Third World to develop more substantial and tangible manifestations of their identity, policy issues become paramount.

Notions of political and economic democracy have been juxtaposed so as to make each a repository of the First or the Second World. Such mechanical views hold that questions of liberty and political democracy are characteristic of the Second World. Why is this so? In the First World, questions of liberty have arisen in relation to the organization of political and party life. Not only have serious issues arisen concerning the quality of differences served by differing parties, but the capacity of such parties to mobilize citizenry has been called into doubt. Pluralization has turned into fragmentation, as interest groups displace organized mass parties in the conduct of national political life in the advanced Western bloc. Hence it should occasion little surprise that the relationship between parties and politics in the Third World is less than perfect. Indeed, more surprising is that multiple parties have remained a factor in a considerable majority of Third World nations.

The Second World tends toward reification. It erroneously assumes that economic democracy is uniquely characteristic of socialism and of planned societies and the planning factor. Stratification within the Second World is accentuated by political favoritism. There are such variations within social sectors from one nation to another that even the assumption that economic democracy is linked to Soviet socialism is subject to severe scrutiny. If factors of race, ethnicity, and sex are added to those of class, it becomes apparent that there is no automatic correlation between democracy and the Second World.

Devotees of the Third World have been certain that somehow the Second World would synthesize political democracy and economic democracy. The dilemma is that this synthesis simply has not come about. Quite the contrary, throughout much of the Third World, the basic structure of the regime remains military, the basic administrative form remains bureaucratic and authoritarian, and the basic ideology has become nationalism.

Locating sources of democracy in the Third World is no easy task. It is no more the case that democracy is consonant with political forms of rule in the First World, or economic forms of rule in the Second World, than that democracy characterizes military forms of rule in the Third World. Each world has different revolutionary origins. The bourgeois system was established in the First World long before consensualist or parliamentary curbs to the laissez-faire economy were undertaken. Economic changes in the Second World were wrought by parties dedicated to the establishment of some kind of socialist systems; in this world, economic change followed but did not precede political revolution. In many parts of the Third World, changes came about through military intervention and military movements from below as well as from above. Economic development and political systems were largely subjected to military rule. To assume an automatic correlation between the Third World and the democratic system is obviously no more the case in the Third World than in the older systems.

Political democracy is no more a bailiwick of the First World than economic democracy is a monopoly of the Second World. Democracy is neither antagonistic to nor supportive of any specific economic order. It is no more true that there exists a high level of economic democracy and a low level of political democracy in the Second World than it automatically follows that there is no search for economic democracy in the First World. The exercise of liberty and the preservation of freedom in the First World have led to a search for economic democracy as well. Democracy is a unitary phenomenon: it tends to hold together the selection of factors that make for free choice and human rights. It is a serious error to assume that democracy is parceled like goods and services. Bearing this in mind, the question of democracy in relation to the Third World must be considered anew, if indeed it is to be considered realistically.

Up to now we have had a strange adaptation by Third World authoritarians of the Huntington thesis that the costs of democracy are too high for the developmental impulse to bear. It has been assumed that high levels of development require high levels of authoritarian control or military rule. There has been a strong relationship between the military factor and the developmental impulse. But the literature also indicates that there are many cases of high levels of militarization and low development. Some forms of military rule admit of higher levels of democratic participation in the social system than theories of military domination would admit.

Increasingly, military dominion remains the policy impulse in the Third World, while there are increasing demands for democratization of the substructure. If one looks at Latin America, Southern cone countries, Andean bloc countries, Central American countries, and Caribbean countries have all tended to show increased demands for democratic procedures at the political, economic, and social levels while at the same time admitting that the military factor should remain central to the developmental impulse.

Quite apart from rhetoric, the Third World shows no simple relationship between militarism and dictatorship. Militarism and democracy coexist everywhere. Democratic norms are observed both in relation to demands for personal freedom and to demands for economic justice consonant with military rule. If there can be democracy under single party rule in the Second World, or multiparty democracy in the First World, then there can be democracy under military rule in the Third World. Once we understand that democracy is an archetypical norm, covering many strata of society, then the form and the origin of revolutions in the Third World recedes in importance, and the antagonistic juxtaposition of militarism and democracy can be replaced by a more accurate model.

Demands for democracy are ascendant within many areas of the Third World, despite the military origins of many Third World revolutions. Absolutist rule is no longer feasible precisely because military rule is now seen as a remarkably successful *stage* in the developmental impulse, rather than a negation of liberty or equity. In many nations (although not all) under military rule, levels of development have risen steeply and sharply. Countries like Brazil, Peru, Mexico, or even Argentina, in a global context, make plain that as demands of development are met, as economic growth has been a social norm, concerns increasingly shift from raw aggregate growth to the equitable distribution of material goods and services. With these come increased demands for democracy, because whatever else it signifies, democracy has to do with distribution of goods and services and the right to express dissatisfaction over existing forms of inequity. The success of military rule in the Third World has not satisfied some social strata, but has only intensified contentions for political ascendency and accentuated the "crisis of credibility" Carl Stone has written about with respect to the Caribbean region.[5]

As a function of rapid development, the Third World is moving toward, rather than away from, democratic rule. As a nation develops, demands for democracy become louder and clearer. There are, to be sure, nations that do not reveal such tendencies: the two Koreas in Asia, Paraguay and Cuba in Latin America, and Libya and Iran in the Middle East. Curiously enough, while some of these nations show developmental patterns and others show stagnation, the ideological commitment to one or another bloc seems to play little role or display slender linkages to democratic rule. While demands for a wider distribution of goods and services seem constant, such demands cut across specific forms of state power. The general impulse of the Third World is for widely disbursing goods and services. Less evident is the demand to disburse power and authority in a similarly holistic manner. While there is some correlation between the more advanced sectors of the Third World and democratic forms of rule, this is certainly not a uniform tendency, much less a social "law."

What necessarily must check assumptions about the relationship between democracy and development in the Third World is the special role performed by the military as the chief architect of social and national integration. Given this subculture of military rule, the Third World has historically had a political base that has at least made democracy possible—democracy has not been easily done away with. Throughout its history, the Third World has had a strong democratic impulse toward personal freedom. The peculiar history of Latin America has been to move from personal concepts of democracy toward military concepts of justice. Especially in the advanced countries of Latin America, the question of democracy has reasserted itself now that the impulse toward development has yielded fruit.

The Third World is faced with a set of false options. It is not simply a choice of taking from the First World its political democratic models, or from the Second World its economic distributive models, because these models have not been completely realized in either of these two worlds. The Third World must contend with militarism as the substantial base of all organization of life. The relationship of that military cluster to the practice of either economic or political democracy remains central.

An entire level of democracy is not addressed by politics or economics, but has to do with health, education, welfare, and the social uses of the public domain. The military has not been able to address such social considerations in a direct form. Hence the drive for democracy in the Third World has to be judged in terms of social democracy no less than political or economic democracy. Areas of public domain are entirely twentieth-century in character. The forms of such social democracy have been worked out in the capitalist West and the socialist East with varying degrees of success. Questions of democracy can parallel questions of development. For the first time, in Latin America we have the same issues that confront those who are operating in North American terms: how much democracy can a society absorb, and at what level of growth? The policy issue is no longer an absolute choice between development and democracy (or dictatorship or democracy, or militarism or democracy), but rather the peculiar stresses and strains that come from developing a democratic order in societies that imperfectly realize their economic and political goals through military means. How the exercise of democracy takes place despite the existence of the militarism that has inspired many developmental changes in the latter half of the twentieth century is both the critical question and the unique opportunity.

Democracy is a unitary concept even though it has tripolar policy expressions. We may isolate political, social, and economic factors, but ultimately we are dealing with a unitary concept. It is a considerable blunder to view democracy as if it were parceled out. The exercise of personal freedom issues into ever-increasing demands for economic justice and equity. Similarly, as economic equity and economic justice are obtained, there is increasing demand for personal liberty. Certainly new demands within the Soviet Union and China for personal freedom of expression illustrate just this fact. Students of the Third World, and of Latin America in particular, must appreciate the extent to which the concept of democracy is volatile because of its unitary nature. It is not merely a managed policy; democracy is simply not something one can have in one area but curb in another area of public affairs.

Not only intellectuals, but the military as well, have exhibited a failure of nerve. In many parts of the Third World, neither group appreciates the degree to which small numbers of people cannot simply regulate democracy as they can levels, forms, and tempos of economic development. A political leader cannot curb personal freedom or demand a reduction of egalitarian demands without having a deep impact on economic development. It is also a mistake to think that democracy must necessarily take the form of multiparty regimes on the one hand, or Leninist-type single-party regimes on the other. Neither tendency has really altered events in the Third World. What has happened is that military rule and democratic thrust have become parallel. Further, the military has become decreasingly involved in the total rule of a society, and increasingly involved in the management of the small chunk in which power prevails. In other words, the military has become more like policymakers, like politicians, in fact, and more like economic managers. They have allowed wider—far wider—areas of democratic demands to surface.

The examination of democracy cross-sectionally in the Third World would reveal a continuation of military forms of domination and democratic expressions of authority. This contradictory and uncomfortable situation best expresses what Third World democracy has come to mean. It is a profound error to insist that the Third World is a garrison state with no democracy, but only militarism; one must not miss the dynamics of change and the taproots of political motivation. It is also a profound error to talk about the Third World as a place without local autonomy, or unable to act on its own and for its own. The mistakes of the dependency model in this respect are inadvertently notorious. First, this model falsifies what the Third World stands for; and second, it falsifies the levels and the range of free expression in each nation of the Third World. The dependency model introduces a note of dangerous sentimentality in which a powerful First World (or Second World) confronts a powerless Third World. The balances not struck between the major powers and the energy suppliers indicate how volatile the development patterns are, and how archaic and outdated models become.

The Third World has raised a new problem: can democracy exist when regimes are military rather than civilian in character? For the first time we are confronted with a situation in which neither multiparty nor single party economic vanguard states is as decisive as a manifestly military regime. A syndrome evolves wherein you have military rule guaranteeing high levels of economic development and yielding a democratic process rather than dictatorial outcomes. That becomes both the interesting challenge and the fact of all Latin America and much of the rest of the Third World at this time.

One of the dilemmas in the literature on the Third world is a tendency to cast democracy as either distributional (economic) or individual (political). This is a gross oversimplification. The distribution of goods and the choice of ends are both basic to development. What is "distributed" is never simply economic goods, but also political power. Hence, democracy in fact has the same structural characteristics throughout the three worlds of development.

As has been observed in relation to the Caribbean and Latin America, and is also true for large sections of the Middle East and Asia, the class system of the Third World itself is relatively weak. Political life holds on tenaciously, not simply because of egalitarian or libertarian impulses, but because no specific class sector is able to come to power without opposition. A relatively weak and highly differentiated bourgeoisie confronts a relatively weak and undifferentiated proletariat in the game of politics, while large (even majority) portions of the population remain outside the political process. In the Third

World economic classes remain relatively small and divided; political participation is restricted to such classes by the exclusion of broad popular masses; and politics becomes an increasingly important "game" for the participants, often to the exclusion of other potential players. The character of electoral involvement reflects the fragmentary nature of democracy in the Third World.

Institutional legitimacy that derives from mass participation is relatively absent. It may be artificial when, for example, high electoral numbers are sought in meaningless exercises to sanctify acceptable officials. The ritualization of the political process in the Third World means that democracy itself becomes formalistic. Safeguards against such formalism often inhibit international growth. For example, much of the Third World consists of small nations with limited economic potential and equally limited geographic potential. And while these factors yield small power versus big power sentiments, they also promote democratic possibilities. Participation accords better with the sort of direct involvement possible in small nations than with the sort of symbolic, massified politics of very large nations.

In discussing the possibilities for democracy in the Third World, one must not overlook tendencies that trade a weaker international role for a stronger national sovereignty. Small states have been so self-conscious about the weakness characteristic of smallness for so long that some of its more attractive features in terms of system maintenance and capacity have escaped attention. For example, a personal element can be retained in political participation; participation can remain high; economies of scale can readily be managed; and small states are exempted from at least some of the major international tensions that grip big powers.[6] In a political universe divided between big powers, negotiations of political order are sometimes made possible by big-power schism. Democratic societies may emerge where none existed in an earlier, colonial era.

Scholars in the Caribbean region, where small nations abound, have been particularly sensitive to the possibilities of Third World democracy in a highly developmental economic climate. On the basis of a careful analysis, Edwin Jones has pointed out that administrative effectiveness and structural change can only take place if the region's small size is conceived of "first as a resource and only secondly as an obstacle." The other point, too easily overlooked, is that size and democracy correlate best when a motivated leadership is highly responsive to populations that care. Hence small states may lead to "a developmentally relevant ideology or mobilizational system which would lead to the institutionalization of problem-solving techniques equal to the problems of a neo-colonial economy, distorted social at-

titudes and institutional irrelevance."[7] Even if one discounts the long-
ings of developmentalists for the actualities of broad masses, the fact
remains that a new impetus has been given to the interrelationship of
democracy and development by the bursting forth of the so-called
ministates, which until recently have been more patronized than perceived.

The structure of present-day world power is quite distinct from the
structure of power in the era of colonial rule. Bipolar struggles characterize this period, while colonial western hegemony characterized the
earlier period. It may seem simpler to focus on the history of western
imperialism, but it is truer to events of today to appreciate that the
Soviet Union has also developed a variety of imperialism. Those who
urge a closer economic and political linkage with the Soviet Union
need only examine the relationship of COMECON nations to each
other and their structural similarities to western varieties of core and
periphery relations. The point is that democracy is easier to maintain in
a bipolar climate than in a unitary world systems climate. The strategy
of nonalignment is thus instrumental to the installation of democratic
structures. This is a lesson increasingly understood by Third World
nations as they chart their courses between the Scylla of the West and
the Charybdis of the East.

The Third World has come to appreciate that democracy is not just
a system, but a strategy. Like other development strategies, democratic strategies are adopted to the degree that they do not result in
total chaos at one end or total stagnation at the other. If democracy
means a collapse of leadership and organization, then the process of
development ceases to be meaningful. But just as certainly when democracy becomes a technique to supply basic needs without providing
for growth, or worse, a method for achieving equality by lopping off
the heads of the opposition in a paroxysm of leveling, the overall
growth needs of a society become imperiled. At that point, the same
sort of risks exist in pushing the egalitarian button as exist in pushing
the totalitarian button.

Third World leadership is in the position of constantly monitoring
and evaluating the cost-benefit ratio of democratic vis-à-vis authoritarian strategies of development and does so in a context of a scarcity of
managerial skills and personnel. The leaders must also be careful not to
separate the developmental process from democratic impulses, since
to do so will demoralize a society and eventually create sources of
rebellion and reaction. Masses, after all, do not engage in insurrection
in order to develop; they will, however, rebel for democratic ends.
Leaders must be careful not to confuse the dialectical relationships
between democracy and development with the mechanical relation-

ships between anarchy and behemoth. And here the need for evaluation research and policy studies in Third World contexts becomes paramount.

Even though democracy cannot properly be considered a "stage" of development, it is no accident that advancing countries such as Nigeria, Brazil, and China are capable of movement in this direction, while more backward states are not. As Gino Germani recently pointed out, in both market and planned developing economies, democracy must create full employment conditions as well as a variety of opportunities, even if this means employing people, goods, or services above and beyond the optimum required in terms of the available technology.[8] Indirect social welfare, largely determined by political concerns (welfare has the latent function of decreasing income redistribution), is characteristic of democratic societies. Of course, the problem is one of generating sufficient surpluses to "pay off," in either a patronage or client system, those pressure groups and interest groups clamoring for the further extension of egalitarianism. As Huntington has warned: the decreasing ability of democratic societies to offer such rewards in the future may jeopardize the developmental process itself.[9] Again, the degree to which democracy, like development, is a matter of policy rather than invisible forces and/or hidden hands, becomes manifest when examined in a comparative context.

At the risk of an overly optimistic conclusion to a properly pessimistic decade, one should take note of large scale shifts in the political structures of major Third World powers. Comparing the beginning of the 1970s with that of the 1980s, researchers must note strong democratic tendencies in many Third World nations. A decade ago Nigeria was reeling under a recently concluded civil war, with a military regime that seemed ensconced for years to come. China was in the throes of the last stages of the Maoist gerontocracy, seemingly to be replaced by warlords intent on maintaining the fiction of development at the expense of real growth. Egypt was under the leadership of an intransigent regime intent on proving its equality only on the field of battle. But Egypt did just that and then went on to extraordinary diplomatic breakthroughs abroad and serious reforms at home. Brazil combined its "hard line" in politics with an economic miracle at terrible expense to the masses, but has since been thoroughly revitalizing its political system and reorienting its economic priorities.

These have been abbreviated descriptions of immensely complex regimes. Further, this has also been a period in which countries such as Chile have become enamored of development without democracy. Still, on balance, the prospects for democracy are encouraging; moreover, it is a tough minded democracy that takes seriously the need for development and reduced stratification. In mentioning Third World powers such as Nigeria, China, Egypt, and Brazil, we can better appreciate how autonomous political systems are derived, in short-run terms at least, from supposed economic bases. The economic systems of these four countries are profoundly varied; the levels of social stratification are also quite different; and finally, the levels of military penetration of the political process are noticeably varied. Thus large, pace-setting nations within the Third World have begun to turn their attention to the question of democracy; and they have also begun turning theory into practice.

Can we speak of democracy, as we speak of development, as having a tripartite response to the twentieth century? Certainly, in my own work I conclude that economic development may be achieved through basic modes of the political process, basic modes of the economic process, and mixed strategies of both through the military process.[10] This is not the case in terms of democracy: that is to say, democracy may reflect strategic twentieth-century responses to the problem of development, but it is a unitary concept. It takes specific forms in different nations of the Third World vis-à-vis the First and Second Worlds. However, the question of democracy cannot be viewed mechanically as being different organically or substantively in the three worlds of the developmental process. The level of democracy may differ, and policy impulses may be altered, given different levels of economic development. But the Third World has not invented or achieved unique processes of democracy. Rhetorical excesses aside, democracy remains the same kind of problem in the Third World that it does in the First and Second Worlds. It is basically an issue of paired distribution: first, of goods and services; second, of power and dominations. If interdependence is to replace dependence as a basic mode of policy operations, relationships based upon hierarchy, status, or charity must be replaced by a notion of the democratic process that extends the same kinds of equity in goods and powers to nations that it does to peoples.

Notes

1. See Ernest W. Lefever (ed.), *Will Capitalism Survive?* (Washington, D.C.: Ethics and Public Policy Center of Georgetown University, 1979), especially pp. 3–14, 54–57.

2. Ali Maruzi, "The New Interdependence," in *Beyond Dependency: The Developing World Speaks Out,* edited by Guy F. Erb and Valeriana Kallab (New York: Praeger, 1975), pp. 38–54.

3. Immanuel Wallerstein, *The Modern World-System: Capitalist Agriculture*

and the Origins of the European World-Economy in the Sixteenth Century (New York: Academic Press, 1974), pp. 350–357.

4. See Guillermo O'Donnell, "Tensions in the Bureaucratic-Authoritarian State and the Question of Democracy," in *The New Authoritarianism in Latin America*, edited by David Collier (Princeton, N.J.: Princeton University Press, 1979), especially pp. 314–317.

5. See Chapter 3 of this book, "Decolonization and the Caribbean State System," by Carl Stone.

6. Robert A. Dahl and Edward R. Tufte, *Size and Democracy* (Stanford, Cal.: Stanford University Press, 1973), especially pp. 110–117.

7. Edwin Jones, "Bureaucracy as a Problem-Solving Mechanism in Small States," in *Size, Self-Determination and International Relations: The Caribbean*, edited by Vaughan A. Lewis. (Kingston: Institute of Social and Economic Research, University of the West Indies, 1976), pp. 73–97.

8. Gino Germani, *Marginality* (New Brunswick, N.J.: Transaction Books, 1980), pp. 42–43.

9. Samuel Huntington, "The Democratic Distemper," in *The Public Interest*, No. 41, Fall 1975, pp. 9–38.

10. Irving Louis Horowitz, "Social Planning and Social Science: Historical Continuities and Comparative Discontinuities," in *Planning Theory in the 1980s: A Search for Future Directions*, edited by Robert W. Burchell and George Sternlieb (New Brunswick, N.J.: Center for Urban Policy Research, 1978), pp. 41–68.

12

Democracy and Socialism in Jamaica: 1972-1979

CARL STONE

Conceptual Framework and Historical Background

Reduced to its essential principle and divorced from the ideological forms through which it is expressed, democracy can be defined as a process which seeks to redistribute power from centers of power concentration to the majority of citizens in a political system. The channels through which that process is articulated are invariably determined by the cleavages and conflicts between social interests, the competition for power between contending elites and counter-elites, the social ideologies through which competing interests are articulated, and the institutional forms which govern political life. This chapter will attempt to assess how these interrelated factors influenced the unfolding democratic process in Jamaica in the period between 1972 and 1979.

In order to analyze democratic development in Jamaica during this period it is necessary to establish a conceptual framework within which to locate the significance and meaning of these operative forces as well as to identify the historical continuities between contemporary trends towards democratization and earlier political developments in Jamaica. This is especially so because democratic theory is entangled with a confusing historical legacy of liberal ideology and because the contemporary ideological forms through which concepts of democracy are articulated in Jamaica distort the political and social traditions out of which they have emerged.

The central question I seek to answer relates to the impact of socialist tendencies during the period under review on the unfolding democratic process in Jamaican politics. More specifically, I should like to appraise the extent to which the dominant socialist tendencies of the contemporary period have advanced or retarded the progress towards greater democratization in the Jamaican political system.

The complex multiplicity of political tendencies that have been dominant on a global scale since the nineteenth century can be reduced to three basic elements: populism, liberalism, and authoritarianism. All political systems represent a varying mix of these basic elements. Political change both in the Caribbean and elsewhere has to be understood as a dialectical process whereby contending social interests seek to alter the balance and mix among these basic elements. Political stability is attained when a political system is able to achieve a synthesis of these antagonistic elements after cycles of conflicts and contradictions. In each period or historical epoch, identifiable social interests act as the means by which particular basic elements are articulated as the dominant political tendency around which to seek that balance, mix, or synthesis of the three competing elements. Political instability is the consequence of a failure of dominant or ascendant social interests to achieve that synthesis. The capacity to achieve synthesis hinges largely on how far the dominant political tendency being promoted is able to meet and resolve the material and social demands made on the state by the articulate, organized, and active interests in the political arena.

What precisely are the distinguishing features of these basic elements? Populism, first of all, is a political tendency which seeks to elevate and raise the status, power, and interests of those social groups that are located at the bottom end of a social hierarchy and to assault and attack interests and groups that are highly placed at the upper end of the social hierarchy. The populist political tendency is therefore *redistributive* in its focus, seeking to resolve social conflicts, cleavages, and tensions by policies, programs, ideologies, and symbols geared to elevate the power, status and interests of the lower strata at the expense of the privileged strata. Populist tendencies can be articulated by revolutionary movements and ideologies such as Marxism, by reformist movements such as Social Democratic political parties, or by cultural, racial, or religious movements that assume a political character. The distinguishing feature of global political trends since the nineteenth century has been the pervasiveness of the wide variery of populist tendencies that have been manifest at the local community, national, transnational, regional, and global levels of political life. Populist principles emphasizing the redistributive ethic have achieved an almost universal appeal and moral legitimacy on a global scale and have been accompanied by intense moral fervor, especially in the Third World.

The populist political tendency has been variably tempered, restrained, and controlled or managed by its antithesis, the political tendency of authoritarianism. Authoritarianism, or elitism, seeks to build a strong authority system which locates command positions of power and control over a political and social system in the hands of political actors or institutions that are controlled by and loyal to interests at the upper end of an old, new, or emergent social hierarchy. Authoritarianism seeks to develop hierarchies of power, ideological principles, and symbols that legitimize those hierarchies; minimal levels of concentrated power exercised by decisionmakers that are minimally insulated from nonelite pressures; and to promote both technical and technocratic competence and ideological conformity as the main criteria of leadership recruitment. All systems of managing state power manifest authoritarian tendencies, but to varying degrees.

Liberalism historically represents an attempt to resolve the contradiction between populism and authoritarianism, but it represents only one of several alternate syntheses of that contradiction. In its essential principles, it seeks to restrain and control both populism and authoritarianism. As a political tendency, liberalism involves attempts to limit and restrain the authority and power of those who govern by making them subject to electoral accountability, the rule of law, public opinion, and entrenched rights relating to individual political freedoms and protected domains of private power. Liberalism restrains populism by trying to apply brakes on the power of majorities, on behalf of minorities and of the individual rights and freedoms endangered by mass populist pressures. Liberalism is historically a creature of parliamentary government and the delicate balance of social forces that emerged in advanced capitalist societies. Liberalism emphasizes the protection of individual rights in contrast to the populist emphasis on the redistribution of power status and social resources.

Communist political systems represent an expression of revolutionary populism that destroyed bourgeois hierarchies and feudal hierarchies only to build a strong bureaucratic state based on authoritarianism while preserving its populist ideology in the synthesis achieved in revolutionary consolidation. Liberal democracies in the North American and European variants democratized rigid feudal and colonial hierarchies by populist-reformist political movements that were diffused by liberalism only to build new hierarchies around private domains of power over industrial capital and corporate empires that have been restrained by liberalism and the residue of populist forces in the political arena. Single-party systems in the Third World represent a synthesis of populism and authoritarianism, but lack the elaborate bureaucratic apparatus of system management developed under communism. One-party-dominant systems and military regimes in the Third World represent divergent authoritarian tendencies.

Parliamentary politics, as it has evolved in the former British colonies of the Caribbean and in Sri Lanka, India, and Malaysia, has been based on competing populist party movements where populist tendencies have not been diffused by liberalism. In these political systems, liberalism seeks to restrain authoritarianism with variable results, depending on the strength of the private domains of power. The result is a continuing tension between liberal and populist notions of democratic practice and principle and cycles of populist resurgence that threaten political stability. Authority systems are inherently weak, with the result that governments are weak and lose credibility where they are unable to deliver on populist demands. Unlike the industrial parliamentary democracies, the private domains of power are either weak or subject to constant harassment and the erosion of power over time by strong populist tendencies.

Democratization in Jamaica must therefore be seen as partly reflecting the articulation of populist tendencies seeking to elevate the power, status, and interests of lower socioeconomic groups by a displacement of privileged interests; as partly reflecting the efforts by private domains of power to bring liberalism to bear as a constraint on the political directorate; and as partly manifesting the degree of responsiveness of the political system to the material and social demands and needs of the majority of the country's citizens.

Before the emergence of these populist political forces in the 1930s, the Jamaican colonial state system was under the ascendant influence of the local white and light-skinned planters and merchants in a political economy where propertied, private domains of power enjoyed a high degree of autonomy from state control. After the emergence of the People's National Party (PNP) and the Jamaica Labour Party (JLP) as competing populist power contenders, between the 1930s and independence in 1962, these private domains of power expanded by diversification of the economy into urban service and manufacturing sectors. The monopoly of power held by these private interests gave way to a sharing of control over state power by emergent urban bourgeois interests, traditional planter and merchant interests, and the emergent brown and black political directorate representing the interests of the overwhelmingly black population.

The PNP was the more radical of the two populist forces. it advocated state control of the economy, cooperatives, greater democratization of the political system, a more explicit nationalist position, and socialist ideas geared to popularize egalitarianism. The JLP, on the other hand, defended the virtues of free enterprise, did not support the PNP's advocacy of sweeping structural changes in the society and the economy, and merely promised better living conditions for the working class and the peasantry while symbolically championing the cause of the socially oppressed.

Populist based programs and policies achieved certain clear gains during this period. A strong and competitive trade union movement was established to bargain for workers, with the main objective of maintaining the rate of increase in wages, and farm associations[1] were established to represent a broad cross-section of mainly small and medium-scale farm interests concentrated mainly in export agriculture. Farm sector policies and land settlement schemes were developed to serve the needs of the petty commodity small farming sector. The proportion of farmers owning land increased from 60 to 77 percent between 1943 and 1958. The number of primary schools, which had not increased since 1926, was expanded by over 100 percent between 1945 and 1964, and school enrollment of youth of primary and secondary school age increased by 178 percent and 50 percent respectively, over that period. The infant mortality rate dropped dramatically as health standards improved. The tax burden was spread more equitably over the period as the ratio of direct to indirect taxes increased.

Voting and partisan activity were the main forms of political participation for the majority of the citizens, with voting levels varying between 60 and 80 percent in most communities and party activism engaging approximately 20 percent of citizens. Over and above actual activist membership in local party groups, clientelistic ties between party leaders, intermediaries, and citizens seeking patronage benefits and favors provided the most extensive network of participatory ties in the political system that brought over time some 60 percent of the electorate in sporadic or continuous contact with lower, middle, and upper levels of party leadership across the country.

The political parties provided the main channels for the articulation of individual and collective interests in search of responses by the state. As the political parties matured, they increasingly frowned on nonpartisan activism and sought to coopt and incorporate all such pockets of activism and harass some that resisted. They attempted to establish territorial hegemony over defined community zones, using violence and patronage as a carrot and stick combination to preserve that territorial hegemony. Bourgeois interest groups representing a relatively strong class interest were the only organized interests permitted to operate nationally without efforts at penetration and cooptation by the political parties, while fear of the Rastafarian movement as an antisystem tendency restricted the efforts at party absorption which, when later attempted, were unsuccessful.[2]

A class division of labor evolved in the channels of participation. Bourgeois and middle-class interests had direct access to the political directorate through school ties, family connections, tightly knit social networks, professional and occupational ties, and class privilege. Many operated from within the state as advisors, technocrats, and public officials. Similar ties and avenues of access existed with the top bureaucrats. On the other hand, the parties were the only channels open to the poorer classes.

As the political system evolved up to and after independence, the main power structure in the society continued to be the private domain of power based on property and the ownership of wealth. However, a rival power structure in the domain of public power controlled by the populist party leaders emerged around the party organizations, their networks of alliances, clients and brokers, and the increasing dependence of all classes on resources and policies controlled by the state through the political directorate.

The populist and authoritarian tendencies competed for ideological ascendancy. Authoritarianism was dominant in the workplace, where owners and managers treated workers as low-status underlings to be constantly reminded of their social inferiority. The educational system reinforced the hierarchical values of the old social order that existed from prior to the 1930s up to independence, promoting unbridled snobbery and discrimination against the lower socio-economic groups and the black majority. The established churches reinforced that old social hierarchy. Racism against blacks and class-color snobbery and discrimination were rampant in the society up to and after independence in all major public and private institutions and agencies of employment, although the tendencies were strongest in the private sector.

The social interests seeking to reinforce authoritarian values did so on behalf of preserving an old, decaying, and paternalist social order that had its historical roots in the old plantation and slave history of the society. They were inherently opposed to creating a meritocratic society in which elitist values would predominate but where the criteria of upward mobility into the hierarchy would be based on achievement, competence, professionalism, and competitive traditions of recruitment into managerial and top administrative positions. Such a system would minimize and reduce the class and color privileges which allowed a small ethnic minority to dominate the command positions in the economy to the virtual exclusion of the black majority. Because the social order that Jamaica had up to independence associated all forms of authority with class and racial oppression[3] and with exploitation by racial and class minorities, postindependence forms of dialectical antagonism between populism and the residues of the old social and racial-class hierarchy had the long-run effect of undermining all forms of authority and thereby making the society more difficult to govern, as populism was later to escalate to levels of anarchist absurdity.

The internal life of the political parties was organized along very hierarchical and authoritarian lines. The maximum leaders of the parties ruled the organizations like monarchs presiding over kingdoms. A few top party leaders who deviated from the authoritarian model found that they were constantly challenged by second-level leaders. The high level of dependence of activists on patronage and the focus on that as their prime participatory objective meant that political leaders had immense power with which to manipulate and control party followers, especially where political gunmen and mercenaries were available to enforce party discipline. The elaborate participatory forms[4] that have been developed inside the party machines facilitated participatory rituals designed to strengthen party leadership and did not really allow for any effective rank and file participation in policymaking, the definition of policy options, leadership selection, or leadership accountability to the rank and file. What internal democracy there was within the political parties was based on intense factionalism between middle and lower-level leadership over office, policy directions and options, patronage resources, competition for the favor of the maximum leader, and conflicting and competing political generations, ideological tendencies, and social ideologies. Heightened levels of mass participation were encouraged in periods when these factional disputes intensified.

The resurgence of populism toward the end of the decade between independence in 1962 and the 1972 election set the stage for renewed demands for advancing the democratization process along populist lines.

During that decade two important developments emerged to set the stage for the terms on which the issue of democratization was posed in the 1970s. First of all, a new generation of urban and urbanized youth came to their late teens and early adulthood facing increasing levels of unemployment. These youth were influenced by the growing popularity of the antisystem ideology of Rastafarianism, which defined the power structure as an oppressive "babylon" and were influenced by currents of racial militancy in the United States, having been socialized by the growing populist street culture of the hardened and deprived urban ghetto communities.

This new militant generation increasingly sought to articulate issues relating to racial and class exploitation under the influence of emergent radical organizations led by the middle-class intelligentsia. The reaction of the JLP government was to try to tighten the reigns of control by repressive measures, which created for the opposition PNP the issues of civil rights, police brutality, freedom of speech and movement, and abuse of power by the JLP government. Black Power and leftist literature was banned and leftists were harassed.

By the end of the decade, increasing state regulation and direction of the economy, and a growing high profile role of the state in economic management under the JLP, established the institutional infrastructure to shift the political economy from a free enterprise system to one of emergent state capitalism. The leaders of the radical populist movement of the late 1960s who were absorbed into the PNP after its 1972 victory increasingly sought to define the democratization issue in terms of expanding the role of the state beyond state capitalism to a state-controlled political economy[5] in order to serve people's needs more effectively and to weaken the power base of the bourgeois interests.

In spite of the heavy emphasis placed on the political rights issue by the PNP in the 1972 election, public opinion surveys[6] confirmed that only a small minority of the electorate in the middle class and upper sections of the working class regarded the issue as a salient or important one. Mass sentiments on this liberal issue of free speech and political rights were ominously weak at a point when antigovernment sentiments were running quite high. Public opinion, beyond the articulate upper- and middle-income minorities, had not developed a high sensitivity for such political issues. The centers of the public domain of power were defined by the majority of citizens as the legitimate preserve of the elites, the powerful, and the privileged interests higher up the social hierarchy. The only openly accessible power domain was the political party in which citizens participated on terms defined by the political leaders. Government and the state operated at a distance from the people, and the electorate was concerned mainly with the performance issue of how the political directorate delivered social and economic improvements; and even here, the majority of judgments were mere echoes of partisan allegiances.

By the end of the decade after independence, the public domain of power represented by the state became the dominant center of power to which the private domains of power became subordinate. The bourgeois class increasingly preserved its class ascendancy by establishing client relationships with members of the political directorate, by penetrating the state apparatus, and by protecting and advancing their class interests from leadership positions within public institutions such as statutory boards and corporations.

Certain clear trends therefore emerged in the period leading up to 1972 as regards the democratization process. Elitist and authoritarian principles remained dominant in the main public and private institutions that represented the nerve centers of private and public power. The bourgeoisie sought to hold on to the traditional privileges it enjoyed as the inheritor of the private domain of power of the planters and merchants under the old and decaying social hierarchy. The dominant populist political party movements concentrated on delivering welfare and social benefits to client classes, but did not threaten the status quo. On the contrary, they contrived to exercise tight agenda management of public issues in order to keep explosive class and racial issues off that agenda. Militant populist tendencies reemerged outside of the mainstream of the two-party system and were met with repressive reactions by the governing political directorate. The state began to loom large in the management of economic life, but on terms of close collaboration between the bourgeoisie and the political directorate. State power continued to be exercised at a considerable distance from the people, as militant populist demands for greater popular control over the private and public domains of power were articulated by militant urban minorities on the fringes and outskirts of mainstream, two-party politics.

PNP Democratization, 1972–1979

After the PNP came to power in 1972,[7] it sought to define itself as a vanguard party force charged with a mandate to advance and accelerate democratization by extending greater popular control over all the domains of power in the society. The PNP took over and absorbed the newly emergent and militant populist political tendencies that surfaced in the decade prior to 1972.

The PNP defined its democratization goals between 1972 and 1979 as embracing the following central areas:

1. Broadening the base of ownership of capital and promoting greater worker participation[8] and influence over the production process.
2. Establishing greater internal democracy in its internal party machinery.
3. Deepening and broadening political awareness through programs of mass political education and politicization, using the ideology of democratic socialism as the basis for this mobilization.

4. Democratizing the political process at the local level by expanding local government autonomy and creating new institutional forms, such as grassroots community councils, as the vehicles through which to articulate local democracy.
5. Democratizing the educational system by bringing students and workers into the joint management of these institutions.
6. Bringing citizens into the machinery of law enforcement through Home Guards that would work alongside the police in fighting crime on the local community level.
7. Promoting popular participation in the processes of planning and economic decisionmaking.
8. Promoting forms of community and popular ownership of land and agricultural production.
9. Promoting social legislation designed to raise the level of equality realized by disadvantaged groups.
10. Establishing popular control over the mass media, using state ownership as a mechanism through which to move to more broadly based ownership.
11. Removing the restrictions on literature of a political character imposed by the earlier JLP government.
12. Engineering basic constitutional changes designed to make the fundamental laws of the land more in tune with popular control of the political system.
13. Isolating the privileged bourgeois interests as enemies of the people and harassing these class and minority racial interests as obstacles to progress and exploiters of the masses.
14. Extending government control over the economy and especially its commanding heights to further the cause of the people's interests.
15. Bringing the party machinery and party activists into direct involvement with the implementation of sensitive areas of public policy.

It can be readily gleaned from the above list of democratization tasks that the PNP government was seeking to take on a very comprehensive program of populist democratization. Each of these areas was in itself a mammoth task when measured against the background of the elitist traditions of politics in Jamaica. Their success required high levels of organization, high quality activists, a wide range of leadership resources, a reservoir of intellectual skills, a mix of ideological commitment and technocratic competence, and a climate of public opinion that was sensitive to the central value and importance of democratizing political life as an end in itself, over and above the concrete forms of welfare benefits that accrue to client classes from state initiated policies and programs. Tactically, the PNP chose to define the opposition JLP as an agent of reaction and conservatism, which meant that democratization did not have bipartisan blessing and would become a center of partisan controversy. The JLP's reaction was not to fight democratization per se, but to concentrate on administrative weaknesses, the abuse of power, corruption, economic failures, and political mismanagement, as those were seen to arise from particular policy initiatives.

The PNP democratization process had a number of factors guaranteeing it as a favorable initial reaction from the electorate. The people felt distant and alienated from the exercise of state power when the PNP assumed office. Populist social philosophies disseminated by leftists, Rastafarians, politicized minorities among the youth, and the radical intelligentsia were becoming more and more popular as the affluent ethnic minorities retreated into isolation from random and sporadic attacks from these activist minorities. The bourgeoisie was easily intimidated by the expanding domain of public power represented by the state, because it depended on state protection, promotion and support, as well as on clientelistic ties with key members of the governing political directorate. The oil crisis and consequent economic dislocations further weakened and eroded the private domains of power and provided a justification for the state's assuming greater management control and direction of the economy. The growing levels of unemployment and detachment from the means of production by persons unable to find legitimate sources of income provided a warmly optimistic climate for radical solutions. The party's leader, Michael Manley, rose to levels of popularity between 1973 and 1976 that the opinion polls showed to be in the region of two-thirds of the electorate acknowledging him as the outstanding leader of the country. He had become a symbol of populist demands for fundamental changes in the social order. The socialist symbolism captured the mood of the country and articulated the underlying and popular misgivings and distrust of the dominant ethnic minorities, as well as resentment at their evident affluence and control over the economy. The socialist theme tapped a deep popular aspiration for an end to the old decaying order and the creation of a new and just society.

On the other hand, there were some clear danger signals that problems would develop between conceptualization and actual implementation. The major problems had to do with the thin layers of leadership, the limited technocratic skills and intellectual resources, the lack of discipline among party cadres, the dangers of rampant corruption and patronage excesses, and the weaknesses in the areas of planning and implementation. Most fundamental, however, was the assumption and risk involved in taking it for granted that the democratization issue had really entrenched itself as a high priority item on the agenda of public opinion expectations and desires over and above the traditional preoccupation with welfare and patronage benefits. This factor was to assume major proportions and should have been carefully monitored in view of the likely economic dislocations that would flow from political contentions between leftist ideologues and the bourgeoisie.

Two fundamental misconceptions pushed the PNP into seeking accelerated progress toward advanced forms of democratization. The ease with which large sums of foreign currency could be borrowed up to 1976 to maintain higher levels of public spending than the economy could sustain and the psychological and ego-boosting impact of successfully imposing the 1974 levy on the transnational bauxite companies created a false sense of economic power. The PNP misread the impact of promoting rampant populism in a society in which authority symbolized class and racial oppression. Unbridled populism was soon to define all forms of authority as oppressive, which means that experiments in democratization would collapse into indiscipline and semi-anarchy when organizational controls could not be established. The PNP also seemed to not grasp the fact that some of the dispossessed and opportunist middle strata groups warmly backed forms of popular control and participation without any regard for the consequences.

Tactically, therefore, the PNP attempted to deal with too many areas of structural changes toward democratization with meager organizational resources, with the result that most of these areas of democratic change either failed to get properly off the ground, or faded for lack of success. Additionally, the assumption made about the basic changes in public opinion exaggerated the demand for democratization and failed to sufficiently recognize that democratization was a low-priority item of popular expectations that came far behind the traditional concerns for improved social and material benefits. The implication was that once those benefits were perceived as dwindling, inadequate, and insufficiently distributed among the client classes pressing demands on the political directorate, the democratization issue would lose its salience. Most critically, the drift toward a blind populist hostility to all forms of authority spelled doom to any hopes of achieving effective management of popular participation in economic activity, and it accelerated disorganization within production generally and labor relations specifically.

What precisely was the fate of these democratization initiatives? Some initiatives were mounted with positive results, others produced negative or zero results while another category of democratization initiatives never really moved much beyond the conceptualization stage.

On the side of positive gains, the PNP made considerable advances in raising the level of intensity of participation by its rank and file activists and in arousing heightened levels of activist interest in matters of party ideology and public policy. Ideological factionalism between leftist and centrist positions in the middle and upper levels of party leadership also stimulated higher levels of rank and file participation in these issues. Dialogue and communication between party leaders and rank and file activists increased to a level where some leaders came under pressure from rank and file articulation of policy and ideological issues following cues from competing factional middle and top leadership groups. Varied parallel groups were formed as supportive arms of the party, with the objective of reaching homogeneous target groups such as women, leftist youth, young farmers, and middle class professionals. The PNP brought the radical university intelligentsia, the communists, and the ghetto militants into the mainstream of Jamaican party politics in contrast to the earlier strategy of the JLP, which sought to isolate them. Revitalization of the party machinery under new and vibrant management gave the party a life of its own, where traditionally a party in power tended to be a mere shadow of the party in government. PNP parliamentarians and government ministers were increasingly accountable to internal party pressures.

Public opinion polls showed that the Home Guard established as a supplementary security force was accepted by a majority of the population, although a significant minority concentrated in the urban areas was concerned about cases of abuse of power and political use of the force against citizens supporting the opposition JLP. The high levels of petty crime and theft, estimated by opinion surveys to be in the region of a 30 percent proportion of victims in the society, provided support for this policy.

Many areas of social legislation, including maternity leave for women, a minimum wage, removing the legal stigma and disadvantages of bastardy, providing a law protecting workers against unfair dismissal, and protecting tenants from the arbitrary powers of landlords, attracted the support of organized labor, lobbies representing mass interests, and rank and file citizens. Conversely, these initiatives met with criticism from privileged interests. The PNP also removed summarily the ban on political literature imposed by the JLP government it replaced.

This is as far as the positive initiatives towards democratization carried. One unanticipated effect, which was facilitated by the removal of the ban on radical political literature and the increasing politicization of the PNP, was that public opinion became a more important factor in Jamaican political life, influenced by the efforts at mass mobilization, ideological propagandizing, and the constant flow of salient and major issues that were debated back and forth in the mass media and at the community levels throughout the country between 1974 and 1979. The PNP had brought the public fully into an exposure to an ongoing debate on political matters in the society that assumed top billing on the agenda of public interest between 1974 and 1976. The proportion of activists in the electorate rose to approximately 30 percent, and the younger generation, hitherto alienated and excluded from mainstream party politics, was brought fully into the political process by a lowering of the voting age to 18 years (from 21 years) and by the overall networks of political mobilization. The youth had become a political force to reckon with, and they provided a vanguard force advancing populist demands.

Some of this politicization was aided by the PNP embrace of Marxist minority political tendencies, which formed alliances with high-ranking leftists inside the PNP and got a cover of governing party protection. Under this umbrella of protection, the mainly university-based radical intelligentsia organized and politicized cadres of young, middle-class professionals who were carefully streamed into sensitive positions in the mass media, teaching, and the public service, as well as some areas of the service professions and the private sector.

On the negative side of the balance sheet, a number of initiatives either failed miserably or created counterproductive effects that neutralized the small gains achieved. The attempt to mobilize popular participation in the creation of a production plan in 1977 turned out to be a grand public relations gimmick that neither legitimized the plan in the eyes of the public nor provided important inputs into what was eventually put forward as the national plan. In May 1977 only 40 percent of the electorate supported the plan fully, and in September 1977 the polls showed that only 36 percent of the electorate thought that it had generated any positive results. The plan itself did feature one or two of the ideas put forward in the mass participation through mass rallies and smaller gatherings as well as letters, but this was more for cosmetic political effect since the main content of the plan was the work of a few technocrats.

Expanding state control of the economy backfired in the long run, as many citizens blamed the 20 to 30 percent drop in living standards between 1972 and 1978 for most groups as having been aggravated by excessive bureaucracy, government red tape and bungling, corruption, and maladministration by the state sector. Opinion polls consistently recorded the low levels of support for state ownership as the economy was gripped by declining production, declining employment, shortages, and massive increases in the cost of living. A poll in 1977 showed that 59 percent of the electorate opposed further government acquisitions of private enterprises, while only 39 percent were in favor. Some corruption issues, such as the alleged multimillion-dollar fraud by a public official (Dexter Rose), provided propaganda ammunition for interests opposed to state ownership. As government became more and more restrictive in its regulatory policies over trade, foreign exchange, and wage controls, socialism emerged less as a populist device to liberate the oppressed and more as an oppressive arm of an ever-expanding bureaucratic monolith.

Popular participation in ownership and production in agriculture turned out to be a disaster. Expensive state-run farms called Food Farms expended $3 in cost for every $1 of food crops produced as a result of labor indiscipline, political intimidation of technocratic controls, the overmanning of labor supply to service party patronage purposes, theft of crops by undisciplined labor, and low levels of production. Worker-run cooperatives in the sugar industry maintained the production levels of earlier forms of management, but produced at costs that were 50 to 60 percent higher than the cost levels of similar capitalist cane-producing farms because of weak financial control, excessive bureaucracy, waste and corruption, and organizational indiscipline. Much publicized projects such as the Pioneer Farms for youth produced very little, attracted trivial support, and declined rapidly over short periods of time. The Pioneer Farms, for example, placed 363 persons, which number rapidly diminished over time to 198, having put only 116 acres into production from the 1,417 acres of arable land available to the project from 11 farms.

After a promising beginning, which yielded gains already identified in the internal life of the party, the program of political education lost touch with the mood of the country after the 1976 election, when the increasing crisis in the economy shifted the agenda of public opinion concerns from populist ideological demands for change to pragmatic preoccupation with mundane day by day economic survival. As unemployment mounted to 250,000 out of a labor force of 700,000, and as the government seemed less and less able to cope with the deteriorating economic situation (made all the more difficult by tight International Monetary Fund controls over wage increases), socialist symbolism became tarnished with the image of failure between 1976 and 1979, while the ideological propaganda continued, isolated from the nonpartisan mass audiences throughout the country. As this trend developed, government ownership of three of the four main mass media channels (including two radio stations and a newspaper) was exposed to liberal attacks on alleged misuse of state power to promote party purposes, particularly as at least two of the government owned media articulated a strong left position that, by 1979, was supported by a minority of the electorate. Similar charges were levelled over the involvement of party activists in public policy and government projects through the Ministry of Mobilization, which was really the party secretariat, brought into the state machine under the guiding hand of the minister, who was the PNP's General Secretary.

Community councils came up against stiff resistance by local government elected officials who felt threatened by the proposal. The necessary legislation giving statutory recognition to the councils was put through, but the expectations in terms of a massive buildup of community participation through the councils did not materialize. What they in fact provide is a vehicle for community action by government supporting local level activists. Starved of funds to do anything that brought bread and butter benefits to the communities, their impact has been trivial and, except for isolated community areas, the entire proposal is a grand bureaucratic program without sufficient mass support to give it significant impact on national politics.

As the mood of the country shifted from majority support for the governing PNP party in 1976 to majority support for the JLP opposition party in 1979, a number of democratization areas became casualties abandoned or scaled down to insignificance due to lack of strong mass support. These included worker participation, constitutional change, local government reform, democratization of educational institutions, and broadening the base of ownership in the economy generally. By 1979 the momentum of acceleration for democratization ran out of gas, and the PNP shifted from promoting such basic changes in the distribution of power to beginning in earnest to try to recapture lost mass support in the hope of overcoming the buildup of popular support for the opposition JLP party. Consolidation of party support took over the agenda of political action for the PNP, and this brought to an end initiatives to carry forward the democratization process beyond the minimal gains already achieved.

There were some predictable conflict issues that emerged over the period, which remain unresolved. The PNP is divided between tendencies that respect the liberal rules of the game of two-party parliamentary politics and tendencies that have sought to isolate, demolish, and absorb the opposition JLP party. Without the dramatic decline of the economy, especially since 1977, Jamaica would probably have become by 1979 a one-party dominant system. The single party tendencies in the PNP are strong among the leftist cadres and leaders, and they produce extreme intolerance of criticism, harassment of critics, censorship of at least one of the government owned media, misleading propaganda about "CIA-imperialist" conspiracies as a smokescreen behind which to hide policy failures, the abuse of state power in the use of security personnel and powers against the opposition party, and crude manipulation of the government owned media. The JLP and vocal antigovernment groups and interests in the society have used the liberal principles of free speech, freedom of association, and freedom from arbitrary state power to mount damaging criticisms against the PNP government. These criticisms captured the mood of the electorate in the face of two major scandal issues involving the shooting of citizens supportive of the JLP by police and soldiers in circumstances that aroused tremendous anger and rage among partisans and nonpartisans alike. High levels of crime, countered by militarized police vigilance that invariably spills over into abuse of power and police harassment of the poor communities, project the government in the role of a babylon, in much the same mold that the JLP was cast by its reaction to political radicalism and increasing criminality in 1972.

The initiatives toward democratization were weakened by the populist tendencies towards indiscipline, by the association of all authority with oppressive manipulation, and by corruption and weak leadership cadres. The general weakening of authority systems in schools, production, public institutions, and political life led to the increasing resort to violence and intimidation as the ultimate means of resolving personal and group conflicts. Democratization efforts encourage anarchic tendencies where weak authority systems prevail.

Liberal tendencies of the democratic ethic confronted populist notions of power in a situation of political stalemate where neither has been able to establish dominance, and the absence of authoritarian controls encouraged nonbargaining approaches to issues that dissipated energies in unending and prolonged conflicts.

The marginal gains toward democratization are matched by negative political trends that increase the problems of governing the society. The PNP proved incapable of finding a synthesis around which to blend liberal, populist, and strong authority elements, and the party's control over these contrary political tendencies weakened to crisis levels as the economic problems unfolded over the years. In particular, class confrontation with the bourgeoisie dislocated the economy, with the result that Jamaica weathered the economic crisis of the 1970s very badly. Whereas living standards over the 1972 to 1978 period improved in other small middle-income countries in the region such as Costa

TABLE 1 / November 1978 Public Opinion Poll Results

Question: What do you think was the best move the PNP made since it was reelected in 1976?

	Kingston (%)	Rural Parishes (%)
Housing and protection of tenants	18.2	13.5
Minimum wage	16.2	4.9
Trade and foreign policy	5.5	0.0
Adult literacy	5.4	10.2
Equal rights for women	4.5	1.3
Others	6.3	9.5
Agriculture	0.0	10.4
Tourism, etc.		1.6
Nothing positive since 1976	28.5	22.7
No views	15.4	25.9

Question: What do you think was the biggest mistake the PNP made since it was reelected in 1976?

	Kingston (%)	Rural Parishes (%)
Communist ties	15.3	7.8
Cost of living	9.0	10.7
IMF policies	8.1	2.0
Security (Green Bay and Massop killings)	7.2	2.7
Mismanagement	6.3	5.2
Intimidating businessmen to migrate	5.4	9.9
Criticizing the U.S.	2.3	2.0
Dexter Rose issue	5.1	3.8

Rica, the Bahamas, Barbados, and the Dominican Republic as their economies expanded despite the world economic crisis, living standards deteriorated in Jamaica.

Wage labor came in for increasing difficulties as wage controls, coupled with rapid rates of increases in prices, reduced the purchasing power of the working class drastically over the period.

In the face of all these trends the issue of democratization died by 1979 and was pushed off the agenda of concerns in national public opinion. A public opinion poll carried out in November 1979 indicated that, among the policies for which the electorate gave the government most credit, there was a conspicuous absence of any reference to most of the democratization initiatives listed earlier. Only the protection of tenants, equal rights for women, and the minimum wage, which are all social legislation areas with anticipated concrete benefits, attracted any significant rating in the public's mind. The survey results set out below also indicate that among the listing of the most negative policies some of the democratization issues emerge. These include the alleged abuse of security power in the Green Bay and Massop killings,[10] leftist political trends that inspired the mass media and political educational efforts, corruption in government ownership (the Dexter Rose issue), government mismanagement that arose as one response to increasing government ownership, and the attacks on the bourgeoisie which were part of the populist political line of the PNP.

The poll findings (Table 1) make very clear the error made by the PNP in assuming that a basic shift had taken place in political values whereby democratic changes per se would elicit strong public support independent of perceived benefits from the economy, the state, and the patronage networks.

Finally, the PNP was caught in the pressures that came from the active public opinion its political mobilization aroused. More than at any other time in the country's history, citizens talked politics, assessed issues, read political commentary in the newspapers, and took positions on controversial issues. This raised the impact of opinion shapers in the media and made the government more and more vulnerable to public criticism. This had negative results for the government when, in such areas as foreign policy, its increasing alignment with Cuba, and its anti-U.S. posturing, its positions ran counter to the mood of the country in 1979 and generated waves of popular support for the opposing positions adopted by the JLP. Indeed, the most emotionally charged issue of 1979 was a quarrel between the Cuban Ambassador and both the JLP and the local newspaper *(The Daily Gleaner)*, which were criticized by the Ambassador for promoting anti-Cuban propaganda. The issue led to a demand by the JLP for his expulsion from Jamaica. The polls showed that 53 percent of the citizens in the capital supported the JLP line and were critical of the PNP's defense of the Ambassador, while 52 percent of the citizens in other parishes supported that line, with 12.7 percent and 13.2 percent, respectively, having no views.

Conclusion

This analysis of the developments toward greater democratization in the Jamaican political system between 1972 and 1979 has argued that the main developments in this area have to be seen as efforts by the PNP to act as a vanguard force implementing populist demands for a greater amount of popular control over the private and public domains of power in Jamaica. Although these populist demands took the initiative in defining the course of democratic development over the period, populist democratic gains were not fully achieved because the PNP exaggerated the strength of popular demand for them. The attachment of democratization to the political fortunes of socialism as an ideological package meant that the strength of the support for democratization disappeared as socialist management of the economy was seen as deteriorating. By the end of the period, the agenda of public concerns had shifted from ideology to economic survival. In addition, the PNP attempted too many structural changes with inadequate organizational resources, and completely lost sight of the fact that in a two-party parliamentary democracy the engineering of basic changes in the distribution of power cannot be imposed by law or fiat but involves prolonged processes of interest bargaining, accommodation, and the reconciliation of conflicting interests. Populism took the initiative, but liberalism was reasserted through the opposition party, anti-PNP tendencies, and independent pockets of public opinion. This counteroffensive gathered momentum as PNP credibility in economic management declined. PNP populism created an active public opinion in political life in the country that by the end of the period asserted itself against PNP tendencies that had lost touch with the mood of the country.[11]

Notes

1. See Carl Stone, "Political Aspects of Postwar Agricultural Policies in Jamaica," *Social and Economic Studies,* June 1974.

2. The PNP attempted to co-opt the movement later in 1972 but failed.

3. See Rex Nettleford, *Mirror, Mirror: Identity, Race and Protest in Jamaica* (Kingston: Collins & Sangster, 1970).

4. An excellent discussion of early party developments is outlined in Trevor Munroe, *The Politics of Constitutional Decolonization, 1944–62* (Kingston: Institute for Social and Economic Research, University of the West Indies, 1972).

5. A detailed analysis of varieties of Third World political·economy is contained in Carl Stone, *Understanding Third World Politics and Economics* (Kingston: Earle Publishers, 1980).

6. All surveys and polls referred to in this chapter were carried out by the author using national samples varying in size between 550 and 900 respondents. The polls were done quarterly on behalf of *The Daily Gleaner*.

7. See Carl Stone, *Electoral Behaviour and Public Opinion in Jamaica* (Kingston: ISER, 1974) for a detailed analysis of the 1972 election.

8. The author served on a committee set up by the government to make recommendations on worker participation in Jamaica and was a member of the statutory board established to oversee the introduction of sugar cooperatives.

9. Between 1972 and 1978 the level of public spending as a proportion of the GNP increased by more than 100 percent.

10. Both killings were extensively reported in *The Daily Gleaner* and have become the subject of legal proceedings.

11. For a comprehensive analysis of Jamaican society, party politics, public opinion and public policy, see Carl Stone, *Clientelism and Democracy in Jamaica* (New Brunswick, N.J.: Transaction Books, 1980).

13

Cooperativism, Militarism, Party Politics, and Democracy in Guyana

J. EDWARD GREENE

Social scientists have found it very difficult to think about "moving societies" in the process of transformation. It is difficult enough to perceive whole societies and see them through the mind's eye; it is much more difficult to visualize societies both in the round and in the process of change. Thought about social change has therefore been greatly facilitated by the use of "before and after" models (i.e., sociological snapshots that outline the dimensions and configurations of social space at a particular point in time). Insight into the transformation of societies can be obtained by conceptualizing models or ideal-types of historical societies and comparing them with contemporary ones. The differences in the dimensions and configurations of the models will constitute a rough measure of the amount, type, and direction of social change that occurred during the time period involved. Utilizing such an approach, social change becomes the movement of societies from one classification to the next.

There are, of course, both dangers and difficulties with such an approach. There is, in the first place, the danger of what has been referred to as the "fallacy of the golden age," that is to say, the tendency to reconstruct models of previous societies that incorporate the idealistic and subjective images of the analyst. There is also the opposite danger of constructing models of past societies which incorporate selected aspects that have negative connotations. There is a second danger that is more clearly methodological, the "fallacy of retrospective determinism" (i.e., the tendency to assume that past social

258   J. Edward Greene

structures could only change in the direction and manner that they did in fact change. As Bendix puts it, "we must conceive of the future as uncertain, in the past as well as the present . . . The fact is that the eventual development of past social structures was uncertain as well."[1] In other words, our models of the historical development of real societies must be probabilistic rather than deterministic, and we should recognize that there is scope for considerable variation in the configurations that societies may take as they pass through time. Awareness of this fact will allow us to understand how any two societies which appear to start from the same beginning might very well transform themselves into quite different social units.

Attempts at reconstructing models of historical societies are also hampered by the state and nature of historical research into such societies. Not only may historical research into some societies be imperfect or incomplete, as is often the case; it may also rest so completely on the implicit, but nevertheless significant, "thought model" of the historian that further attempts to utilize the data in the construction of alternative models may prove futile. Indeed, the "facts" that are contained in historical research are very often not objective events recorded by historians but items in reconstructed histories or "conceptual translations" of the past.[2] When, therefore, we assess societies in terms of levels of democracy and development it is important to take into consideration the conceptual biases as well as the problems of applying these concepts rigorously from one political system to another.

In this chapter we examine certain specific characteristics of the contemporary developments in Guyana, such as cooperativism-militarism and the nature of the party system, the particular social bases underlying these principles of social organization, and the impact in the forms and effectiveness of democracy.

Democracy and Variants of Socialism

From the overwhelming amount of literature on the subject, a simple model of the key elements of democracy or, at least, those normally considered significant, would include the following:

1. Citizen involvement in political decisionmaking.
2. Equality among citizens.
3. Liberty or freedom granted to, or returned by, the citizenry.
4. A system of representation.
5. An electoral system the basic principle of which is majority rule.[3]

There are many philosophical justifications and arguments associated with each of these characteristics. But these need not detain us here, except to say that since countries of all social, economic, and political persuasions recognize "democracy" as a virtue, it is one of those "ideal types" that is identified with nationalism and national liberation struggles. In other words, there is a widespread tendency for national and revolutionary goals to be identified with the key elements of democracy. More important is that the possibilities for rational social action are seen by nations to depend on a choice among grand alternatives—communism, socialism, and capitalism, or some combination of these. What this implies is that democracy is generally viewed as the symbol of mobilization and the operative mechanism of different economic systems. There is a growing tendency among Third World countries to propose some variant of socialism as a norm toward which they ought to strive. In 1970, for example, the Guyana government declared the country a "cooperative socialist republic." Similarly, in 1974, the People's National Party, under Michael Manley, pronounced Jamaica a "democratic socialist society." These declarations raised old questions both within and outside the respective Caribbean countries about the compatibility between democracy and socialism.

The fundamental assumption linking these two concepts is that participation in political decisionmaking should be extended to economic decisionmaking. Democratic socialists argue that since the economy and politics are so closely interrelated, citizens should be able to control their economies through some form of collective self-reliance under the management of the state. To them, the democratic capitalist system gives too much power to individuals and groups. In addition, democratic socialists contend that the capitalist system has failed to solve the fundamental problems of poverty and underdevelopment. The developing countries in particular view democratic socialism as a noncapitalist path to development. The main reason for this is that under the capitalist system the interests of the dominant class do not necessarily coincide with those of the people; and only when economic systems are controlled by the people will solutions to these problems be possible. The major characteristics of democratic socialism may therefore be identified as follows:

1. A large proportion of property in the state is to be held by the public through the democratically elected government, including all major industries, utilities, and transportation.
2. A limit to the accumulation of private property.
3. Governmental regulation of the economy.
4. An extensive welfare system.[4]

There is considerable variation in practice between countries which profess democratic socialism, in particular in their pattern and nature of government ownership, private enterprise, and social welfare. One of the main determinants of the successful application of democratic socialism is the class which takes power in the postcolonial state (i.e., the bureaucratic and military oligarchies that staff the state apparatus). Shivji[5] has shown that in the Tanzanian experience the bureaucratic class benefited from the state's appropriation of a significant part of the economic surplus which was used for bureaucratically directed economic activity. This led ultimately to conflicts between the working class and the bureaucratic bourgeoisie. To counteract these tendencies, the ruling class normally manipulate class alliances in order to form a national democratic state. To sustain the state in this form the class alliances must be committed to a shared objective. Otherwise a class factionalization persists whereby some form of authoritarian control of the main instruments of state is the only guarantee of power to the ruling class.

There are also factors partly outside the control of the state bureaucrats which may sponsor or militate against the development of specific objectives. One is the level of economic dependency and the other the international political alliances contracted by the postcolonial state. With respect to the former, practices of democratic socialism can be nullified to the extent that policies of the dependent state are incompatible with those of the dominant economy. Related to this is the withdrawal of sponsorship of a dependent state by the dominant international powers. Then, too, the dominant international powers can, as it were, destabilize nation-states, in particular those in which class factionalization is most acute. This is illustrated in the case of Salvador Allende's downfall in Chile. In the words of de Vylder:

> The strategy behind the whole Chilean road to socialism was based on the underlying assumption that it was possible to divide the bourgeoisie into two separate and well defined parts: one monopolistic sector which should be fought and expropriated and one non-monopolistic sector which in no way should feel threatened . . . but which instead should and could be won over to the side of the popular forces (or at best neutralized).[6]

If Allende's Chile offers any lessons, they include the difficulties of blending competitive electoral politics with the transition to socialism; the problems of gaining control of an economy when vital sectors are locked into the advanced capitalist system, and the insecurity of a regime when the domestic capitalist class is organized in a strong political lobby backed by international capitalist interests. In the case of Guyana, the persistence of racial divisions and the factionalization of the elite, the radicalization of the political system and differences in strategic approaches to socialism, the pronouncement of cooperatism, and the antidemocratic practices have tended to distort the process of evolving a noncapitalist path to development. Cooperatism, militarization and the party system in the 1970s have all facilitated this paradox of democracy and development in Guyana.

"Cooperative Socialism" as a Rational Norm

In February 1970, Guyana became a republic. The constitution was amended to provide for a president who replaced the Queen as the symbolic head of state. More significant than the legal change of status—from monarchy to republic—was the philosophy of "cooperative socialism." By this Burnham envisaged a republic in which the cooperative would become the instrument for making "the small man a real man." In his own words:

> A just society cannot be achieved unless the majority of the people, the masses, the little men, have a full share in the ownership and control of the economy, a share which corresponds realistically with their political power. The small man in Guyana today, through adult suffrage, holds the reins of political power but the substance of economic power rests in other and fewer hands.
>
> A rearrangement and redirection of our economic and social systems are therefore necessary and urgent in order that the worker, the little man, may be able to gain substantial control of the economic structure, concomitant with his political influence and participation. . . .[7]

What had been proposed for Guyana is by no means new; cooperative movements have existed since earliest times whenever people have worked together in large or small groups to attain social, religious, or economic objectives. The underlying social philosophy of the cooperative movement was formulated during the first half of the nineteenth century by such writers as Robert Owen[8] in England and Charles Fourier[9] in France. Owen regarded the formation of human character to be of prime importance. The happiness of each depended upon the character of all. Under the system of free enterprise, bad characters were formed because avarice was encouraged. All were trained to seek pecuniary gain, and the best feelings of human nature were sacrificed to the love of accumulation. Competition and the pursuit of profit resulted in the exploitation of labor, unemployment, increasing poverty, misery, and crime.

Owen's ideas were extended by Sidney and Beatrice Webb,[10] who saw cooperatives as part of a wider social movement that was aimed at transforming Britain into a social democracy. To them cooperatism, by itself, could not replace capitalism. Cooperatism was mainly a form of social ownership, facilitating the ownership and control of productive agencies by consumers, and was complementary to state ownership.

The philosophy of "cooperative socialism" in Guyana is no doubt predicated on the normative assumptions of Owen and the Webbs, but it also has its roots in Guyanese history. Rawle Farley[11] shows how, after emancipation and as a way of protecting their interests against those of the plantation, the Africans formed cooperative villages and engaged primarily in the farming of ground provisions and the raising of pigs. Rice cultivation, according to Rodney,[12] was the Indian laborers' way of escaping from the sugar plantation. The rice industry began as a subsistence sector, based on Indian immigrants whose indenture had expired and who chose to remain in Guyana. although the industry expanded rapidly, especially after the sugar crisis of the 1920's, capitalists showed no interest in rice producing or rice milling. The introduction of the Mahaicony Abary Rice Development scheme in the 1950s and its successor, the Rice Development Company in the late 1960s (with a central mill, drier, blender, and other agricultural machinery) has helped not only to raise the technology of the rice industry, but also to preserve its structure as a small peasant's industry. Eusi Kwayana's analysis[13] of the rice industry arrives at the conclusion that the developments within the industry so far may have prevented the growth of cooperatives for the purpose of marketing. In fact, the main use rice farmers have found for cooperatives has been in the field of credit and the acquisition of agricultural machinery.

Ideal-type and historical factors therefore combine to provide a formula which ought to distinguish the objectives of cooperative socialism from those of capitalism and totalitarian regimes, respectively. First, in extreme cases economic organization may be formulated under a system of free enterprise or one of state control (more recently the idea of the mixed economy has been espoused, especially among developing systems). The idea of the cooperative as a third sector of the economy is one of making the traditional comparable to the modern sector. Thus it is aimed at rationalizing the traditional precapitalist sector in such a way as to make it competitive with the private sector. Second, the cooperative is an attempt to whittle away the economic control wielded by the bureaucrats and the oligarchy in the private sector. In capitalist systems, control and ownership factors are monopolized by the business oligarchy (i.e., the large companies and multinational corporations). In totalitarian systems the workers are subordinated to state monopolies. Only in theory do workers own the state; in practice, the state is controlled by the bureaucracy. Cooperatism promotes the idea that workers ought to participate at the level of policy decisions; that workers ought to have a greater share in and control of the economic wealth of the nation.

As a strategy for change, cooperative socialism, in principle, offers a solution to the endemic problem identified by one economist as follows:

> The problem confronting Guyana today may be described in its historical setting as a problem of slow and arrested growth of the modern sector in the face of continuous population growth in the traditional sector. This did not provide a corresponding increase in employment opportunities, a situation in which income per head remains low.[14]

Hence the key to economic transformation is perceived as follows:

1. To improve the ratio between capital accumulation and a rise in population growth.
2. To produce a linkage effect between the modern sector's investment activities and the demand for output of the traditional sectors.
3. To mobilize capital and technology in the modern sector so as to provide increased efficiency and productivity in the traditional sector.

The cooperative sector as a third sector offers to promote transformative changes in the following ways:

1. *Structurally*, by providing backward and forward linkages with the other sectors.
2. *Functionally*, by expanding the zone and diversifying the range of activity within the sector.
3. *Normatively*, by creating an overriding ideology which promotes integrative planning between the cooperative sector and the public and private sectors both individually and collectively.

The introduction of cooperatism coincided also with the extension of state participation in the economy. The government sought to take the trading activities out of the hands of the private sector by establishing the External Trade Bureau and by acquiring (Guyana) Gadraj Ltd. Through these enterprises, the government had hoped to diversify its sources of supply of goods and to ensure economies of scale by being able to engage in large purchases. Neither of these aims has so far been achieved, partly because of dependence on external brokerage facilities and partly because of the increasing lack of foreign exchange balances required to pay for new sources and for taking advantage of cheaper sources of supply. Between 1970 and 1976 the number of public enterprises increased from 13 in 1970, to 23 in 1973 and to 42 in 1976.[15] These include a large number of productive enterprises in sugar, mining, forestry, fishing, and manufacturing. The majority of these enterprises had been foreign-owned monopolies, while the others (mainly commercial enterprises) were locally owned. In some cases government takeover of certain enterprises was effected to prevent them from being closed.

Among the main features of the expansion of the state sector were the establishment of the Guyana National Cooperative Bank in 1970 as part of the process of miniaturization of foreign banks: and the nationalization (1971) of the Demerara Bauxite Company (DEMBA), a subsidiary of Alcan Ltd., Reynolds Mines Ltd. (1974), and the Booker Group of Companies (1976). In the case of the latter, the government assumed total control of the sugar monopoly, including its relatively large industrial and commercial complex. The expansion of the state sector also has had implications for output and employment, insofar as the public sector by 1978 was estimated to be responsible for 80 percent of the GNP and 80 percent of total employment.[16]

The expansion of the state sector has also increased the state bureaucracy and the need for technical and managerial skills in this sector. This problem is exacerbated by the relatively high level of migration of skilled personnel. According to Sackey there is a continuing exodus of approximately 25 percent of such skills from Guyana, and those skills are not replaced.[17] Related to this are the competing bureaucracies in the military and in the governing party.

Militarization

The rapid expansion of the state sector also coincided with the proliferation and growth of military institutions in Guyana. This tendency, as we shall see, has become part of a process to entrench the party government of the People's National Congress (PNC) under the leadership of Forbes Burnham. Prior to independence in 1966, there were three types of military institutions: the volunteer force, the police, and a special service unit. The latter was formed in 1964 as a response to the need for additional trained personnel to cope with the upsurge of civil unrest and political violence experienced in the 1960s. These formed the basis of the military and paramilitary forces in Guyana at the end of the 1970s. The special security unit became the Guyana Defence Force in 1965 and is recognized to be the professionally trained army with

TABLE 1 / Estimates of Military and
Paramilitary Forces*

	1964	1966	1977
Guyana Defence Force	500	750	4,000
Police Force	1,635	1,881	3,751
National Service	–	–	4,000
People's Militia	–	–	10,000
	2,135	2,631	21,751

Source: George K. Danns, "Militarization and Development: An Experiment in Nation-Building," Transition Vol. 1, No. 1, 1978, p. 30. Estimates of the
Government of Guyana, 1973–77.

responsibility for the external defence and security of the state. In 1975
the government created the Guyana National Service and in 1976, the
People's Militia. These may be classified as paramilitary organizations,
insofar as they consist of civilians who received military training for
purposes of national defense. Table 1 shows the rapid expansion in
military and paramilitary personnel between 1964 and 1977, while
Table 2 shows the levels of expenditure in the 1970s.

Since its inception, the Guyana Defence Force has been active in
external defence insofar as Guyana has been involved in a series of
border disputes with its neighboring territories of Venezuela and
Surinam. When Burnham instituted the cooperative republic in 1970,
he redefined the role of the army. Not only did he take over the offices
of Minister of Defence and Chairman of the Defence Board, but he
called on army and police officers to give unconditional loyalty to him.
Both the army and the police became involved in expediting cooperatism, the former providing a large reserve of manpower in building
roads and airstrips in the hinterland areas, and the latter establishing
several cooperative projects, especially in farming and housing.

TABLE 2 / Expenditure on Military Institutions*

Year	National Budget ($1.00 Guyana = $0.45 U.S.)	Total Defense Budget	Percentage of National Budget
1973	290.6	22.5	4.2
1974	358.5	38.1	5.9
1975	580.7	79.0	8.2
1976	795.2	113.1	12.0
1977	885.4	132.1	14.1

Source: George K. Danns, "Militarization and Development: An Experiment in Nation-
Building," Transition Vol. 1, No. 1, 1978, p. 30. Estimates of the Government of
Guyana, 1973–77.

By 1975, however, the cooperative enterprises failed to generate the level of mobilization or production anticipated by the government.[18] In addition, class factionalization, the racial issue, and growing industrial unrest began to indicate that the ruling PNC had not been able to consolidate the process of transformation that cooperative socialism professed. The Guyana National Service was set up as a paramilitary organization. National service is seen by the government as a duty of all citizens. People at all levels and occupations, including students, have been required to perform national service which ranges from three weeks to one year and involves instructions to develop a national consciousness, a socialist orientation, and a commitment and loyalty to the government.

A complementary device for mobilizing the citizens is the People's Militia, set up in 1976 with the slogan "Every citizen a soldier." The People's Militia is largely drawn from the membership of the party and was established to perform the following functions:

1. Provide a framework on which, during a period of rising tensions, mass preparations for emergencies can be carried out.
2. Support the People's Army in all of its functions when called upon to do so.
3. Assist the People's Police in the maintenance of law and order when called upon to do so.
4. Provide a reservoir of trained recruits for the army.
5. Contribute to the life of the community by engaging in productive work and providing a labor rescue organization in an emergency.[19]

The People's Militia is obviously an extension of the ruling PNC party. The GDF, the Police, and the GNS are used as part of the machinery that helps to sustain a government in power when all rational indicators suggest a decline in popular support and widespread disaffection with its rule. In other words, the increasing militarization of Guyanese society is one of the devices used to sustain a regime whose legitimacy has declined. It is a device to manipulate the symbols of democracy and socialism but, like cooperatism, is part of an attempt to institutionalize the PNC as a party state.[20]

Class, Politics, and a Party State

In Guyana, as elsewhere in the Caribbean and the Third World, the colonial policies of the First World powers—in this instance, Britain and subsequently the U.S.—were as much responsible for creating the racial divisions as for the class structure which in most cases paralleled the ethnic divisions in the society. First through slavery and indenture, then through the consolidation of monopoly control over key sectors of the economy (in Guyana, bauxite and sugar), the British-U.S. hegemony manipulated race and class in such a way that the local political leaders and their followers became pawns in the international struggle for economic supremacy. The historical details of this interplay of forces as they relate to Guyana are well documented in other studies.[21] Suffice it here to say that while racial and class factors need not be incongruent in a process of social transformation, in Guyana, especially since 1961, racial cleavages have been the more prominent of the two factors in mobilizing the electorate.[22] This has manifested itself in a form of political cleavage which continues to pose one of the greatest impediments in the transformation to socialism to which both Burnham and Jagan have expressed their commitment. By the time the 1973 elections were held, right-wing groups such as the United Force and the Liberator Party coalition still persisted, but were electorally insignificant.[23]

Between 1968 and 1973 the PNC government introduced several progressive policies, of which three are of special importance: the attainment of Republican status in 1970, the nationalization of the former Canadian-owned bauxite company in 1971, and the official adaptation of "cooperative socialism" as a philosophical basis for bringing about transformative change. While republican status did not fundamentally alter the structure of politics, it shifted the symbols but not the substance of power away from the Westminster model and toward the local regime and those in authority. This change was accompanied by such acts as the abolition of appeals to the Privy Council in Britain, the reform in official dress, and the sponsorship of an international policy of nonalignment. The major consequence of localizing the political symbolism is that it places greater pressure on the local regime to accept culpability for any social and economic dysfunctions within the system rather than, as in former times, to transfer these responsibilities to a colonial power or imperialist sponsor. This is especially so when, as in the case of Guyana, political symbolism was followed by a policy of nationalization. The takeover of DEMBA, the Canadian-owned bauxite company (now called GUYBAU), in 1971 underscored the direction of public policy toward the ownership and control of local resources by the state. Subsequent nationalization and expansion of the state sector seem to reflect the government's policy that, with regard to resource-based industries and particularly mining, the government has a right to majority ownership and control. At the time, the act of nationalization in Guyana was a relatively radical step, judging by the reaction of most other Caribbean regimes. Most notably, the ruling Jamaica Labour Party and the government of Eric Williams in Trinidad sought to assure metropolitan business interests that their investments were guaranteed against similar takeovers. In fact, ownership and control of the commanding heights of the economy seemed very consistent at the time with the professed aim of the Burnham government to establish a society in keeping with the concept of cooperative socialism.

A plausible interpretation of the government's policies between 1968 and 1973 is that they reflected a strategy of winning a wide cross-section of support in which elements of both right- and left-wing persuasions could be mobilized to support the PNC. Hence cooperative socialism was originally vaguely defined as "a system in which the cooperative sector will be the mechanism for making the little man a real man."[24] In practice, it seemed to be an accommodation between capitalism and socialism. Its trisector economic model proposed the formula whereby private, public, and cooperative enterprises would be complementary to the development process. As an electoral device it offered all things to all men and therefore seemed justifiable. The competitive electoral model is one in which the political parties attempt to maximize their support by attracting broad-based rather than specific interests. The PNC's presentation of cooperative socialism to the electorate in 1973 made sense in view of its dominant objective not just to win but, according to its leader, to get a two-thirds majority in Parliament. However, in ideological terms, the meaning of cooperative socialism was less clear, even with the rationalization from a chief PNC spokesman that "the development of the cooperative is an instrument of transforming the society and a thrust toward socialism."[25]

Cheddi Jagan, clearly opposed to this view, states that:

> L.F.S. Burnham has designated Guyana a "Co-operative Republic," under which "the small man will become a real man!" The PNC puppet regime has declared demogogically that it is socialist and that co-operatives will be the means by which socialism will be brought to Guyana, and not vice-versa as the People's Progressive Party holds; namely, co-operatives and cooperativism can succeed only in a socialist society, supplementing the dominant public sector.[26]

Even more specific about the differences in the interpretation of socialist practice between the two parties is Ranji Chandisingh, at the time one of the main Marxist theoreticians in the People's Progressive Party (PPP):

In short, the imperialists put the PNC in power and they are serving foreign interests, as well as helping themselves. This is not the society we want. We want to build a land where people can grow up—free from fear, poverty and hunger; where man to man is no longer wolf, but friend, brother, comrade.[27]

Whatever the subsequent election results would be, it was clear from the campaign that both the PPP and PNC had accepted a socialist path to economic development but differed not only about the means to achieve this end but also about the end itself. It was, for example, evident that within both parties the consciousness of the rank and file membership at least accepted, if not comprehended the social contradictions for which socialism may be, theoretically, the solution. In practice, however, it was less evident that the rank and file electorate had actually made a transition from the cleavages of racial voting.

That class politics had begun to reassert itself is nowhere better illustrated than at the level of organized labor. It is largely true to say that the trade unions provide mass support for the two major parties. That the Guyana Agricultural Workers' Union (GAWU)[28] and the Manpower Citizens' Association (MPCA) represent the sugar workers, exclusively, cannot be dissociated from the fact that their leadership is predominantly Indian. Outside the sugar belt, trade unions are monopolized by African politicians and workers.[29]

The trends toward class politics as we have identified them have more or less accelerated since the 1973 election. They are responses to and influences on the policies of the PNC regime. The PNC's gradual move to the left since its accession to power in 1964 had culminated 10 years after (December 14, 1974) in a policy statement by Burnham known as the Sophia Declaration. Burnham not only declared the PNC a "socialist party committed to practicing cooperative socialism," but summarized the main features of the new party constitution as a framework within which socialism could be achieved in Guyana. The new constitution was:

1. To ensure and maintain through the practice of cooperative socialism, the interests, well-being, and prosperity of *all* the people of Guyana.
2. To pursue a commitment to the Socialist ideal and, more particularly, to ensure that the people of Guyana own and control for their own benefit the natural resources of the country.
3. To provide every Guayanese the opportunity to work for and share in the economic well-being of the country, and to ensure

that there is equality of opportunity in the political, economic, and social life of the country.

4. To motivate the people of Guyana to improve by their own efforts and through the party, the communities in which they live.
5. To pursue constantly the goal of national self-reliance.
6. To work for the closest possible association of Guyana with her Caribbean neighbors and to maintain a link with international organizations and agencies whose aims and objectives are consistent with those of the People's National Congress.[30]

The declaration acted as a catalyst for the gradual ideological rapprochement between the PNC and the traditionally socialist PPP, which had proclaimed itself a Marxist-Leninist party in 1968. Instead of the policy of "civil resistance and noncooperation" adopted after the 1973 election, the PPP in 1975 was prepared to give "critical support" to the PNC government with the aim of encouraging a transition to "real socialism" in Guyana.[31] In turn, the government apparently made a concession to the PPP in November 1975 by agreeing to recognize the Guyana Agricultural Workers Union as the sole bargaining agent for the sugar workers. This union, founded by Jagan in 1953, was hitherto not recognized by the British colonial authorities or by the postindependence PNC governments. It had previously used its representation strength—90 per cent of the labor force—within the sugar industry to launch two damaging strikes in 1975 in order to press its claims for recognition.

Ideological rapprochement was further consolidated by February 1976, when Burnham announced that the government was to take control of the sugar industry's main employer by nationalizing the local subsidiaries of the British Booker McConnell Company, which in 150 years of operation in Guyana had established itself as the country's largest single employer and biggest foreign exchange earner. Its agricultural, industrial, and trading interests accounted for an estimated 40 percent of the country's gross national product. Dr. Jagan, whose party had long advocated such a nationalization, fully endorsed the government's action, which brought nearly 80 percent of the national economy, including almost all foreign exchange earning activists, under state control. In addition, however, Jagan called for new and more radical measures, including nationalization of all remaining foreign interests, and for the closest relations in all fields of the world socialist community headed by the Soviet Union.

The PPP's "critical support" had therefore been a response to its perception of the PNC's increasing move toward socialism. But in so doing it upset the balance, if not the growth, of the "ultra-left" movement. The rest of the Working People's Alliance, which was formed in 1973, were skeptical toward Burnham's pronouncements on socialism. The PPP's announcement of its new policy, without notice to its allies in the Working People's Alliance, created chasms in the anti-Burnham lobby. But in the context of Guyana, Burnham's political tactics have always tended to break up a coalition of interest wherever it appeared to consolidate an anti-Burnham lobby. Between 1958 and 1964 Burnham effectively absorbed and attracted the moderate elements of the United Democratic Party led by John Carter; then, between 1964 and 68 he attracted the conservatives in the United Force. Since 1968 he has so far been relatively successful in absorbing the members of the left wing; most significant were the defections from the PPP to the PNC of Teekah Singh, former Minister of Education in the 1961–1964 PPP government, and executive member and party ideologue Ranji Chandisingh.[32] These two were among the most articulate spokesmen within the PPP for the pursuit of Marxist-Leninism. When defections are viewed as a more general trend, the PNC's caricature of the PPP as a "vanishing party" is not altogether unfounded. Of the founding members of the original People's Action Committee of 1952, only Cheddi Jagan and his wife, Janet, are still members of the PPP. Joycelyn Hubbard resigned from the Party in 1969; and Ashton Chase gradually became inactive, as did Rudy Luck before he finally resigned in 1969. Brindley Benn, following a dispute with Jagan over the chairmanship of the Party, resigned in 1964 and formed the Peoples Vanguard Party;[33] Cedric Nunes, Chairman of the Party from 1964 to 1966, migrated to England; and Miles Fitzpatrick and Moses Bhagwan also left the Party, the latter being expelled for left-wing deviation after criticizing the policies of the PPP in 1964. Others, such as Lillian Branco, Eugene Stoby, Leonard Durant, and Harry Madrimootoo, are examples of the array of former PPP activists who have joined the PNC since 1968.

These alignments and realignments provide numerous implications for the future of party politics in Guyana. However, what concerns us most are the structure and functions of both the PNC and PPP that have emerged as well as the effects these would have on future elections. Significantly, the organizations of both parties have been generally modified to reflect more fully the model of democratic socialist parties. In 1968, the PPP had declared itself a Marxist-Leninist party and had reorganized the party to reflect "the structure of the Bolshevik party and the Leninist principles which guide all the communist parties in the world."[34] The Sophia Declaration, in 1974, announced that the PNC would "assume unapologetically its paramountcy over the Government which is merely one of its executive arms."[35] One year later,

at the first Biennial Congress of the PNC, Burnham clarified this view
further:

> For some time now, we have been enunciating the thesis of the
> paramountcy of the Party over the Government and other agencies and
> institutions. But only in recent months has this thesis been seriously
> regarded by many within and without the Party. Even now as we review
> the last year particularly, we can observe that the concept is not fully
> understood, or in some cases completely misunderstood by Party mem-
> bers and non-members alike.
>
> That the Government is subordinate to the Party should be obvious. It is
> the Party that mobilizes, educates and appeals to the people on the basis
> of its programme. It is the Party that then selects the members of the
> political government to execute the former's policy which has been care-
> fully debated and then presented.[36]

The significance of the 1973 election had less to do with the results
than with the obvious institutionalization of left-wing politics. The nature of factionalism, the demise of the conservative interests associated with the United Force and the Liberator Party, the demands
by radical groups such as the Working Peoples Alliance and the Association for Social and Cultural Relations with Independent Africa, and
the "critical support" by the PPP forced Burnham to define socialism
more clearly and to reorganize the PNC to meet the challenges of his
stated socialist objectives. In this regard, Burnham appeared to have
responded to political demands inherent in a society which, since 1953,
has been increasingly radicalized.

Factionalism and the Party-State

This can be more easily illustrated by looking at the interests and
alliances which challenge the PNC electorally and ideologically. Challenging the two main political parties in the 1973 election were several
political factions; some actually contested the elections with little hope
of winning, while others mainly functioned as interest groups by raising
issues, highlighting grievances, and hoping indirectly to influence the
way people vote. There were essentially three factions in the elctoral
contest, along with the PPP and the PNC. The United Force (UF), the
Liberator Party, and the People's Democratic Movement were from
the onset given little chance of significantly affecting the electoral results. In many respects, the vibrance of the "third force" had diminished with the resignation of Peter D'Aguiar from the United Force in
1969, a party which he led since 1961 and which briefly (in 1964)

justified one of the rationalizations for the introduction of proportional representation in Guyana (i.e., to promote third parties and to forge coalitions among interests on other than racial grounds). That the UF may have exacerbated rather than muted the racial factors has been discussed elsewhere, but by 1973, without vibrant leadership and with a depleted party organization, it merged with the Liberator Party to contest the election.

THE LIBERATOR PARTY

The Liberator Party itself represented a merger between the Guyana Anti-Discrimination Movement (GADM) and the United Force. GADM was formed in 1971 around a band of professionals, mostly lawyers of Indian descent, to combat the allegedly growing discriminatory practices of the Burnham government. Acting as a pressure group, GADM printed a weekly bulletin, *The Liberator,* which articulated a number of grievances and acted as a catalyst around which its middle class Indian leadership hoped to mobilize support based on a stand which, though anti-Burnham, was not pro-Jagan. GADM further developed a close association with the Guyana Council of Indian Organisations (GCIO), which claims to speak for Guyanese of Indian descent. GCIO, formed in 1972, was the "Indian" answer to the Association for Social and Cultural Relations with Independent Africa (AS-CRIA). Even though its mass membership could not be easily identified, unlike ASCRIA, it was intent on maintaining the cultural viability of East Indians and argued that a separate but cooperative approach to the dominant cultures would enrich the cultural basis of the society.

THE PEOPLE'S DEMOCRATIC MOVEMENT

The People's Democratic Movement (PDM) mushroomed at election time under the leadership of Llewelyn John, former executive member of the PNC and a minister in the Burnham government. Of its 53 candidates, John was the only nationally known political figure. Ironically, as Minister of Home Affairs between 1964 and 1968, he was responsible for the conduct of the 1968 general election. It was therefore easier for him than for most others to anticipate any unfair practices by a ruling party intent on maintaining itself in power. John's party was nondescript, however, in that its membership was ill-defined, but comprised mainly Afro-Guyanese who had either become disenchanted with the PNC or formerly supported D'Aguiar's United Force. John himself had become alienated from the PNC when his attempts to win the vacant position of party chairmanship received no support from the party leader. After the retirement of Winefred Gaskin, who became Guyana's ambassador to Jamaica in 1969, John, who was then vice chairman, saw himself as the natural successor. Burnham, however, supported Robert Jordon for the post. In a straight fight between John and Jordon at the 1969 conference, the latter won by a very slim majority, a fact which demonstrated the strength of John's support among the rank and file delegates, notably the women's auxiliary and the youth arms of the party.

Like the Liberator Party, the PDM lacked both the leadership and organizational penetration that are required to mobilize electoral support, especially in a system of proportional representation where it is not sufficient to consolidate support among small communities. Under the plurality system, a small third force can concentrate its efforts on specific constituencies in the hope of creating the necessary electoral swings needed for victory. But when nationwide votes rather than localized seats are at stake, it is not difficult to comprehend how the requirements of public relations can stretch the resources of small parties beyond their capacity to perform effectively. In addition, the only identifiable issues raised by these two electoral groups were a belief in the free enterprise system and an opposition to corrupt practices by the government.

ASCRIA

The Association for Social and Cultural Relations with Independent Africa, though not competing in the election, articulated some of the most critical issues through its founder-leader Eusi Kwayana. To understand the importance of ASCRIA's role it must be recognized that from when it was formed in 1964 until 1971, it acted as the cultural arm of the PNC. Among the major aims of ASCRIA were the revival of African culture in Guyana through a program of educational reform to project African history, politics, and philosophy and to stimulate pride in African heritage by knowledge of and association with the activities in Black Africa. From 1968 to 1969 ASCRIA greatly increased the efficiency of the structure and organization of its movement across the country by its regular recruitment drives and cultural programs. Especially in the rural areas, there was a great overlap between membership in ASCRIA and membership in the PNC. In collaboration with the Young Socialist Movement (YSM), the youth arm of the PNC, AS-CRIA built a road from Tumatumari to Konowarcik in the North West District. ASCRIA was among the chief advocates of a cooperative republic, one which emphasized self-sufficiency and the distribution of lands in Guyana among groups and individuals so as to encourage both small and large agricultural ventures among Afro-Guyanese. Its members organized a cooperative settlement in Southern Rupununi which was closed down by the government. Kwayana was also dismissed as the chairman of the Guyana Rice Marketing Board.[37] The official split between ASCRIA and the PNC was announced by the former in April 1973.[38]

By 1973, therefore, ASCRIA challenged both major political parties on ideological grounds. Not only did it accuse the PNC of thwarting the development of socialism by "establishing and teaching the ideology of Burnhamism," but it also charged that the PPP "falsely calls itself Marxist-Leninist."[39] ASCRIA's open criticism of both dominant parties acted as one of the main catalysts for intensifying the ideological debate and the challenge of new alliances of the left.

NEW LEFT COALITION

The Working People's Alliance, formed in September 1973, was originally a coalition of groups committed to socialism. It included AS-CRIA, the Movement Against Oppression (MAO) led by radical academics, the Indian Political Revolutionary Organization (IPRO) led by Moses Bagwan, and the PPP, which had refused to take its seats in the legislature after what it claimed to be massive fraud in the 1973 general election. The main reasons for its formation were to consolidate the need for a national patriotic front and an antidictatorial alliance. It recognized that the task of transformation "can best be achieved in the context of a united front of revolutionary democratic parties or groups both Marxist and otherwise."[39]

Since 1955, after the break-up of the PPP-PNC coalition, the WPA offered the first possibility of a class-based alliance cutting across the main Afro-Indian cleavages that have been the basis of the political alignment in Guyana. The implications of this alliance were that it challenged the ideological credulity of the PNC government but, more important, that if permitted to grow it would, through the ASCRIA-MAO factions, undermine the main areas of support on which the PNC depends—the black unemployed and the black youth. Within the alliance, the IPRO represented, to a large extent, the professional and middle class Indians, while the PPP represented the Indian working class and the Indian peasantry. In any future electoral contest such an alliance could make it difficult for the PNC to rationalize electoral malpractices on the scale of the 1968 and 1973 general elections.[40] Under these circumstances, the PNC government has used its monopoly over the state apparatus to erode the key principles we have identified with the democratic process, in particular, those related to "freedom," "representation," and fair "electoral practices." It has denied the opposition access to the media, which are almost totally under the control of the government; refused permission to the main opposition to import or accept gifts of newsprint to facilitate the publication of its weekly paper, *The Mirror;* and has denied opposition groups permission to hold public meetings.

In spite of protests from a wide cross-section of political parties and pressure groups within the country, the PNC government passed a bill in the National Assembly, in April 1968, which removed the referendum clause enshrined in Article 73 of the Guyana Constitution of 1966.[41] In a national referendum held in July 1978 to decide the issue, the government won the issue by a landslide. The results were widely acclaimed by observers to be another example of the PNC's abuse of the electoral machinery for its own ends. Several organizations and their supporters boycotted the referendum, but the fact remains that all the fundamental rights listed in Article 73 can be changed by a two-thirds majority in the National Assembly, a majority which the PNC received in the 1973 election. Under the amended Article 73, the PNC passed another bill, in July 1979, postponing the general elections which were constitutionally due in December 1978.

Without the benefit of attitudinal data, it seems fair to say that the electoral malpractices of the government, in particular the reported abuses associated with the referendum, have undermined the legitimacy of the Burnham regime. The crisis of legitimacy in Guyana is further heightened by the contradictions created by the regime: its failure to establish a broad coalition of socialist groups in spite of its claims to be socialist, its failure to generate a higher quality of life in spite of its claims to generate economic self-sufficiency and, most of all, its failure to comply with the minimum requirements of democracy, such as guaranteeing representation by interests.

The Working People's Alliance declared itself a political party in September 1979. According to its manifesto, it is guided by the principles of Marxism-Leninism and is committed to the establishment of the "People's Democratic State." The main significance of this party is twofold. First, it has close ties with the PPP, whose commitment to Marxism-Leninism has been long established and whose support by the East Indian working class remains unassailable. Second, its close ties with ASCRIA gives it an effective means of entrance to the PNC's core support in the African community. In addition, several professional and working class groups have openly opposed the antidemocratic policies of the Burnham government and provide the possibility of a swing in support from the PNC to the new left coalition.

Conclusions

These trends in Guyana have amounted to a setback to the PNC's attempt to create a party-state. In this regard, the PNC has been a victim of its own desires to monopolize rather than to democratize the state. In 1976, it refused to accept a proposal by the PPP for a national patriotic front government of which, as the governing party, it was to have the dominant share of representation. While the precise details of such a front were not known, its formulation would no doubt have preempted factionalization of the left in the way that it has presently manifested itself. We have already pointed to the fact that the gradual radicalization of politics in Guyana had by 1973 totally eliminated the rightist groups. Paradoxically, of the three main political groupings—PNC, PPP, and WPA—it is the PNC which now appears to be on the "right." Whereas in the 1960s the PNC was able to absorb the right-wing groups in its struggle against the PPP, in the early 1970s it seemed capable of accomplishing the same absorption, but of the left.

After 1973, the Guyanese government pursued closer relations with the socialist bloc and increased its diplomatic and trading linkages with Cuba, the Soviet Union, East Germany, North Korea, and Yugoslavia. Guyana's close relations with Cuba, for example, led to a shift in support from UNITA to the Cuban-backed MPLA in Angola. However, it failed to attract bilateral and other forms of aid from the U.S.S.R. At the same time, between 1966 and 1972 and between 1973 and 1977, the U.S. provided 62 percent and 51 percent, respectively, of all loans for purposes of development. Financial aid is only one of the many general indicators to small states like Guyana of the possible sources of economic support in the event of crisis. The internal economic crisis in Guyana since 1974 has no doubt sensitized the Guyanese government to the international options available to salvage the regime. Therefore, on account of the U.S. reactions to nationalization in Latin America, for example, in the 1970s in Chile and Peru, the Guyanese government made no attempt at further nationalization between 1971 and 1974. Also, the U.S. had significantly increased its aid to Guyana between 1974 and 1975, but decreased it by 1976, no doubt on account of Guyana's policy of supporting the MPLA.

In addition, Guyana's relative silence in recent international forums may be a further indication of some form of rapprochement with the U.S. The implications of these trends both for democracy and development are by no means clear. Nevertheless, it must be recalled that the PNC government originally came to power with the assistance of the United States. There is no reason to believe, given the Marxist-Leninist options, that the People's National Congress cannot persist as a government, again with the aid of the U.S. In this case, both the key principles of democracy and the development of a party-state along socialist principles will be delayed. Whether this is a reasonable price to pay for the possibilities of development is a subject for further research.

Notes

1. Bendix Reinhard, *Nation Building and Citizenship* (New York: Wiley, 1964), p. 3.
2. See Raymond Aaron, *Introduction to the Philosophy of History* (Boston: Beacon Press, 1975).
3. For a full discussion see Lyman Tower Sargent, *Contemporary Political Ideologies: A Comparative Analysis* (Homewood, Ill.: Dorsey Press, 1978), Chap. 3.
4. Sargent, pp. 62–63.
5. Issa G. Shivji, *Class Struggles in Tanzania* (London: Monthly Review Press, 1976).
6. S. DeVylder, *Allende's Chile: The Political Economy of the Rise and Fall of the Unida Popular* (London: Cambridge University Press, 1976), p. 84; quoted in Joseph L. Nogel and John W. Sloan, "Allende's Chile and the Soviet Union: A Policy Lesson for Latin American Nations seeking Autonomy," *Journal of Inter-American Studies and World Affairs,* August 1979, p. 344.
7. L. F. S. Burnham, "A Vision of the Co-operative Republic," in L. Searwar (ed.), *Co-operative Republic: Guyana, 1970* (Georgetown, 1970).
8. Robert Owen, *A New View of Society: Socialism in Great Britain* (London: Everyman's Library, 1906).
9. Charles Fourier, *Le nouveau monde industrial et sociétaire* (Paris, 1841).
10. Beatrice Webb and Sidney Webb, *The Decay of Capitalist Civilization* (New York: Harcourt, Brace, 1923).
11. Rawle Farley, "The African Peasantry in Guiana," *Social and Economic Studies* 4 (1955), 5–21.
12. Walter Rodney, *West Africa and the Atlantic Slave Trade* (Nairobi: East Africa Publishing House, 1967).
13. Eusi Kwayana, "Economic Relations in Pre-Republican Guyana," in L. Searwar (ed.), *Co-operative Republic: Guyana, 1970* (Georgetown, 1970).
14. Wilfred David, "The Third Sector," in *Essays on the Cooperative Republic of Guyana,* The Critchlow Labour College Lecture Series Publication No. 2 (Georgetown, 1972).
15. See Helan McBain, "The State, Foreign Relations and Non-Capitalist Development in Ex-Colonial Countries," unpub. M.Sc. thesis, University of the West Indies, 1979, Appendix III, pp. 282–86.
16. Maurice Odle, "Guyana—Caught in an IMF Trap," *Caribbean Contact,* October 1978, pp. 10–11.
17. See Jim Sackey, "The Migration of High Level Personnel From Guyana: Toward an Alternative Analysis," *Transition,* Vol. 1, No. 1, 1978, pp. 45–58.
18. For an indication of the high expectations about the contribution of the cooperative sector, see *Government of Cooperative Republic, Second Development Plan 1972–6* (Georgetown, 1976), p. 120.

19. *The Guyana People's Militia* (Georgetown, 1976).

20. We obtained a reasonable set of information by compiling a list of top army personnel in the period 1970–78.

21. See, among others, Ashton Chase, *133 Days Toward Freedom in Guyana* (Georgetown, Guyana [n.d.]); Cheddi Jagan, *Forbidden Freedom: The Story of British Guiana* (London: Lawrence & Wishart, 1954); *The West on Trial: My Fight for Guyana's Freedom* (London: Michael Joseph, 1966); Peter Newman, *British Guiana: Problems of Cohesion in an Immigrant Society* (London: Institute of Race Relations/Oxford University Press, 1964); R. T. Smith, *British Guiana* (London: Oxford University Press, 1962).

22. See J. E. Greene, *Race vs. Politics in Guyana* (Kingston: Institute for Social and Economic Research, 1974).

23. In that election the PNC won 37 seats, the PPP 14, and the UF.-LP coalition 2.

24. People's National Congress Broadcast by L. F. S. Burnham, Guyana Broadcasting Corporation, July 14, 1978.

25. Ptolemy Reid, People's National Congress Broadcast, GBS, July 10, 1978.

26. Cheddi Jagan, "The Caribbean Revolution: Tasks and Perspectives," opening address to the Caribbean Anti-Imperialist Conference, Georgetown, Freedom House, August 1972.

27. People's Progressive Party election broadcast by Ranji Chandisingh, Guyana Broadcasting Service, Wednesday, June 27, 1973. Mr. Chandisingh subsequently quit the PPP in March 1966 and is now a member of the PNC and Principal of the Cuffy Ideological College, the educational arm of the PNC. The reasons for his decision to leave the PPP after 18 years are outlined in "Ranji Chandisingh, Why I Quit the PPP," *Sunday Chronicle,* Georgetown, Guyana, March 28, 1976, p. 9.

28. The conflict for recognition between these two unions was not resolved until 1975, when the Burnham government accepted the GAWU (which supports the PPP) as the main bargaining agency for workers in the sugar industry.

29. In 1969 the Trade Union Council prepared an alternative bill known as the "Jackson proposals." But the government refused to accept those which sought to reduce the powers of the minister in addition to regulating prices and accepting strikes as legal after a minimum period of negotiations.

30. See *Declaration of Sophia,* address by the leader of the People's National Congress, Prime Minister Forbes Burnham, at a special congress to mark the 10th anniversary of the PNC in government, December 14, 1974 (Georgetown: Guyana Printer, 1974). An article in *The Financial Times* (June 5, 1975) referred to the declaration as Guyana's "Little Red Book," an analogy to the collection of Chairman's Mao Tse-tung's thoughts published in China in the 1960s.

31. See "Jagan to Give Critical Support to PNC Government," *The Chronicle,* Georgetown, Guyana, August 12, 1975, p. 1.

32. For a fuller discussion of the earlier shifts in alliances and the policies of absorption by the PNC, see Greene, Chapter 3.

33. Brindley Benn ran against Ashton Chase in 1961 for the chairmanship of the party, and was originally declared the winner. After the intervention of Cheddi Jagan, party leader, the decision was reversed. Benn resigned from the party and subsequently formed the People's Vanguard Party, which espouses a pro-Chinese line. However, the membership of this party is not very vocal, and

its popularity has never really been tested as it has yet not competed in any of the elections since its formation in 1965.

34. See introduction to *Party of a New Type* (articles in *Granma*) Georgetown, Educational Committee of the People's Progressive Party, 1974.

35. See *Declaration of Sophia,* p. 11.

36. Forbes Burnham, *Leader's Address at the First Biennial Congress of the PNC at Sophia,* Georgetown, August 18, 1975, p. 4.

37. Kwayana was appointed to this position after the 1968 elections.

38. See "ASCRIA's Statement on the Negative Directions in Guyana," Coordinating Council of ASCRIA, April 1, 1973, p. 5.

39. See "Statement by Working People's Alliance," Georgetown, December 1973.

40. For analysis, see J. E. Greene, *Race vs. Politics in Guyana* (ISER, 1974) on the 1968 elections and "Guyana: Class vs. Race," in *People and Politics in the Caribbean* (London, Institute of Commonwealth Studies, 1981).

41. Article 73 contains basic rules concerning the system of government. For example, it deals with the supremacy of the constitution, the composition of parliament and its tenure, elections and their conduct, the ombudsman, and the role of the presidency.

14

Decolonization and the Authoritarian Context of Democracy in Antigua

PAGET HENRY

The importance of democratic institutions derives from the fact that they are attempts at solving the problems of individual freedom and individual participation in collectivities of various sizes and types. These problems stem, in part, from two basic characteristics of collectivities. The first is that most collectivities are stratified. As a result of this stratification, rights and privileges, and hence the capacity to be free and to participate, are not uniformily distributed. The second is that in most collectivities the activities and responsibilities of leadership are often delegated to or appropriated by a few. One consequence of this delegation or appropriation is that there develops a need to establish, legitimate, and routinize definite patterns of interaction between the leaders and the led. With regard to this relationship between the leaders and the led, democratic institutions have three primary functions: (1) to serve as a check on the arbitrary use of power, (2) to ensure that decisions on public issues are the result of rational discussion, and (3) to ensure popular input in the decisionmaking process. With regard to class and other social inequalities, democratic institutions have aimed either at their elimination or toward the ensuring of individual rights in spite of these social differences. To the extent that a society gives over a portion or portions of its institutional space to the exercise of the above practices, it be considered a democratic society.

However, in spite of the importance of these practices, only relatively small areas of the institutional space of societies are usually democratized. Often these are areas that are specially set aside for

281

such practices, while social life in other institutional areas takes place in a comparatively undemocratic fashion. In other words, democracy as a principle of social or institutional organization is always found to be a part of a larger institutional context whose principles of organization are essentially nondemocratic.

If this is indeed the case, then it should come as no surprise that the relationship between democratic and nondemocratic institutions within societies has been a rather uneasy one. The uneasy nature of this relationship is indicated by the constant contractions and expansions that occur in the size of the institutional space that societies democratize. In many societies there have been periods in which this space has been completely absorbed by a nondemocratic social praxis, only to return after a period of struggle or the collapse of the previous order. This periodic elimination of the practice of democracy often stems from crises of goal attainment in other institutional areas. However, for these crises to result in the elimination of democracy, a dominant group, elite, or class has to act successfully on the belief that a solution must include a reduction in the current level of democratization.

In this chapter, we will attempt to examine the major expansions and contractions in the practice of democracy in a peripheral capitalist society, Antigua. However, before proceeding with this analysis, it will make matters clearer if some additional theoretical issues are thematized and made explicit. In particular, the following remarks will be aimed at clarifying a number of relationships between democracy and peripheral capitalism.

Democracy and "Peripheral Capitalism"

In several of the attempts that have been made to clarify the social foundations of democracy, it has been suggested that there exists a close relationship between capitalism and democracy. For example, Milton Friedman has argued that "capitalism is a necessary condition for political freedom."[1] This relationship, Friedman argues, results from two peculiar features of capitalist societies: (1) the noncoercive nature of economic coordination in these societies, and (2) the check which independent economic power places on state power. Much more cautious in his claims is social historian Barrington Moore. In Moore's view, capitalism is accompanied by democratic institutions only if its emergence occurred under very specific conditions. These are (1) a balance between the power of the state and the power of the landed aristocracy, (2) the growth of a strong and independent bourgeoisie, and (3) the avoidance of an aristocratic-bourgeois coalition against the peasants and workers.[2]

In spite of very important differences, both of these explanations place great emphasis upon the limited and institutionally bounded nature of state power. The power of the state is confined primarily to the task of securing the structural prerequisites (laws, police, administration of justice, etc.) of a capitalist process of production. In other words, the state does not engage in economic production, but secures the general conditions necessary for production. These limitations on the role of the state make possible the institutional space in which economic elites can function with a minimum of governmental interference or regulation. It is the existence of this space that is for our two theorists an important structural condition for democracy in capitalist societies. However, for Moore there must be at least one other condition, one that Friedman's analysis overlooks. The limitation of state power is not enough; for although it reduces the possibility of state domination by a political elite, it frees the economic elites to engage in class domination for purposes of surplus extraction. Hence, there must be a balance of power between the classes before we can conclude that economic relations in capitalist societies are noncoercive in nature. So in Moore's view, the social conditions for democracy in capitalist societies rest on two important pillars: a balance of power between the state and the economic elites on the one hand, and a balance between these elites and workers on the other.

In providing us with these two structural conditions for democracy in capitalist societies, Moore's thesis is extremely useful. However, a number of critical remarks are in order. First, the ideal typical status of the model needs to be pointed out. The model presents a set of ideal conditions that democratic capitalist societies approach but never reach. Similarly, it presents an ideal set of conditions that nondemocratic capitalist societies approach but never reach. However, because of the idealized manner in which the model is formulated, these two sets of conditions remain static and unrelated to each other. As a result, they are never applied to the same society simultaneously. Secondly, there is no clear characterization of the levels of democratization or de-democratization that accompanies the realization of these ideal conditions. For example, does the former set represent the conditions for the elimination of all forms of nondemocratic rule, or are they the conditions for the highest levels of democratization that can be practically instituted? In more positive terms, what is needed is a model that de-idealizes democracy—one that deals systematically with varying levels of democratization and sets these varying levels in a dynamic relationship with the levels of authoritarianism found in the surrounding nondemocratic institutional context. In short, a model is needed that allows us to see how democracy is conditioned by and conditions its institutional context.

Within such a framework, we may reformulate Moore's thesis in the following manner. In capitalist and other types of societies, democratic institutions have arisen in largely undemocratic settings. These undemocratic settings are constituted by an unequal distribution of power between the classes or other social groups. More specifically, in capitalist societies the greater the inequalities in the distribution of power between the state and the dominant economic elites on the one hand, and between these elites and the working classes on the other, the more authoritarian will be the institutional context of democracy. Changes in this unequal distribution of power are often the result of group struggle or the collapse of the old order. The institutionalization of democracy often helps to effect and to routinize such changes. Consequently, it can make the day-to-day use of coercion a more difficult task and so lessen the degree of authoritarianism characteristic of its institutional context. However, the extent to which it will be able to do this is determined by the size of the portion or portions of the society's institutional space that is actually democratized. But the size of these spaces are in turn determined, in part, by the nature of the changes in the distribution of power. Hence we must speak of levels of democratization that are always accompanied by their (hopefully weakening) shadows—levels of authoritarianism. Finally, the practice of democracy, together with other forces, may help to further lessen the imbalance of power and so lessen the degree of authoritarianism available for use in other institutional areas. However, this trend is always reversible, as these processes of democratization and de-democratization are related in a dynamic way. This, in brief, is the statement of the generalizable relations that exist between capitalism and democracy. We have now to examine these in peripheral capitalist societies.

In the modern period, the process of peripheralization can be divided into two broad phases: the first was largely a product of European hegemony, while the second was a product of U.S.-Russian hegemony. During the former, peripheralization took the form of colonization, while in the latter it takes the form of satellization or quasicolonization. However, in spite of this distinction, peripheral societies—especially in their colonial periods—tend to be further from the ideal conditions of balance when compared with central capitalist societies. In other words, if they are at all democratic, democracy is practiced in an essentially authoritarian context. This is so for several reasons. First, in these societies the state tends to be a more pervasive and militarized institution, as most of these societies were forcefully incorporated into the capitalist system. Second, in these societies there tends to be a greater imbalance between the classes, as workers in these societies are often of a different racial or ethnic group and have the status of a conquered people. Third and finally, in peripheral capitalist societies there tend to be greater opportunities for the use of state power by the economic elites, opportunities that enhance an already advantageous power position. These factors will be developed in greater detail as the analysis proceeds.

From this characterization of the distribution of power in peripheral capitalist societies, two important conclusions are drawn: (1) that if democracy is institutionalized, it will operate in an essentially authoritarian context; and (2) that reductions or eliminations of democratic spaces in these societies are most likely to occur as a result of crises of goal attainment in two institutional areas, the economy and the state. Only in these two areas have elites accumulated sufficient power to carry out such authoritarian solutions.

The crises arising in these two areas and the responses to them have differed in important ways in the two periods of peripheralization distinguished earlier. In very general terms, however, they may be characterized as follows. In the political arena, crises leading to authoritarian actions are usually rooted in problems of goal attainment on the part of the political elites. In most cases this elite is made up of a political directorate responsible for the maintenance of an overseas "empire," together with its local counterpart. Take the case of the imperial directorate: as a part of the political elite, it is engaged in processes of political management and political accumulation. That is, it is interested in increasing its decisionmaking power, its resource base, and the power and size of the empire. Developments that thwart these aims must be dealt with, sometimes in a coercive manner. The desire of the colonized or the satellized not to be a part of the "empire" has often been such an untoward development. In the economic arena, the possibilities for the reduction or elimination of democratic practices stem from the ability of the economic elites to use force when facing crises of capital accumulation. The accumulation of capital, as Marx has shown, is a process that includes the extraction of surplus labor from the working classes. Very often, this process runs into difficulties for a wide variety of reasons; however, when these difficulties do occur there is a tendency to solve them by increasing the exploitation and domination of labor. The extent to which this can actually be done, however, is determined by the power that is available to the economic elites. In peripheral capitalist societies, the economic elites often have the necessary power because of their control of resources and available opportunities for the use of state power. Other scenarios are possible, of course. For example, the working class could rebel and set up a nondemocratic regime. However, in the Caribbean this has less often been the case. So in sum, the distribution of power in peripheral capitalist societies is such that it makes it possible for the dominant elites to carry out programs of de-democratization as part of a solution to crises of political and capital accumulation.

In what follows, an attempt will be made to apply these theoretical formulations to the study of democracy in Antigua. The analysis takes place in three phases. The first two, the phases of plantocratic democracy and of colonial authoritarianism, took shape in the period of European colonization, while the third, a period of abridged democracy, is taking shape within the framework of American satellization. From these analyses we hope to show (1) that in each of these periods the authoritarian context of Antiguan democracy was largely determined by the authoritarian responses of ruling elites to crises of goal attainment; (2) that these responses were largely responsible for the expansions and contractions that democracy has experienced in Antigua; and (3) that in the contemporary period, the movement for decolonization—by changing the distribution of power between the classes—has in part been responsible for current levels of democratization.

Plantocratic Democracy in Antigua

Democracy began its career in Antigua by being the exclusive privilege of the elite in an essentially authoritarian society. Paradoxical as it may appear, the established institutions of democracy were themselves an integral part of a larger system of domination, the colonial/plantation system, that the elites themselves had created. To understand this paradox, it is necessary to situate Antiguan society within the framework of the world capitalist system. It is only after it has been situated in this system that the larger nondemocratic context of plantocratic democracy will become clear.

Like most other peripheral capitalist societies, the introduction of the capitalist mode of production in Antigua was the result of conquest by one of the more developed of the European capitalist societies, Britain. It is possible to divide the history of the British empire into four phases: (1) the old colonial empire (1600–1784), (2) the second British empire (1784–1867), (3) the period of British hegemony (1867–1930), and (4) the period of decline (1930 to the present). These four phases are marked by important changes in British colonial policy, some of which in turn had important consequences for democracy in the colonies.

As social systems, empires have very definite principles by which they assign specific roles and status to the various groups and nations that they conquer. Looking back at the construction of the first or old colonial empire, it is possible to isolate a number of important economic, political, and cultural principles that guided the thinking of the directing elites. In the political/military sphere, conquered nations had to accept British rule, a political status that was less than full national sovereignty, and to cooperate in the defense of the empire. In the economic sphere, the basic principles that guided incorporation were mercantilist; that is, colonies were "to supplement the stock-in-trade of the national shop by furnishing products which the mother country could not herself produce. Thus fortified, the latter could sell more to foreign rivals and buy less from them. The 'balance of trade' would then move in her favor and the foreigner would be obliged to remit the difference in hard cash, which was regarded as real wealth."[3] In strict mercantilist terms, these were the economic benefits that were to be derived from colonies. Finally, in the cultural sphere, the policy was one of establishing and maintaining the dominance of the British way of life. This was usually achieved through processes of deculturalization, on the one hand, and carefully limited assimilation on the other.

It was to conditions such as these that Antiguan society was subjected when it was incorporated into the old empire in 1632. These general requirements were largely responsible for the manner in which the society was reorganized in the effort to make incorporation functional. As this process of reorganization got underway, the indigenous Indian population was quickly subdued, and British rule was established. Under the protection of the imperial state, and with the labor of a subdued population, economic activity was started. Within the larger mercantilist framework of British economic foreign policy, Antigua and the other Caribbean islands that had so far been incorporated were assigned the role of supplying the imperial power with sugar and a few other tropical goods. With these facets of the reorganization process accomplished, the primary concerns of the ruling elites now become clear: (1) the permanent political control of the island, and (2) the use of its land for the commercial production of sugar. In what follows, we hope to show that both the authoritarian context and the nature of democracy in this period of Antiguan society were a direct result of the manner in which these projects were executed by the relevant set of elites.

With the assignment of a specific economic role organized on capitalist principles, commercial agriculture was well on the way by the last quarter of the seventeenth century. Antiguan planters began the serious cultivation of sugar in the 1660s. This they did with assistance from Dutch merchants eager to pick up the carrying trade that would develop. The Dutch introduced Antiguan planters to a method of sugar cultivation they had learned from the Portuguese, who had already been cultivating sugar in the Atlantic Islands and Brazil. The peculiar feature of this system of production, for us, is that the labor force it used was made up of a small number of salaried artisans and a large number of slaves. So, starting around 1674, Antiguan planters began importing their new labor force from Africa. This decision to employ a slave labor force is important to our argument for several reasons. First, it was the manifestation of a decision to use the power to reorganize the society, to create an authoritarian and not a democratic society. Second, it implied a decision to maintain this colonial monopolization of power, as this was a condition for slavery. Third and finally, it represented a decision to use that power to institutionalize a system of surplus extraction that was based essentially on force. These decisions were part of a larger set that would determine the social conditions under which sugar would be produced and capital accumulated. But this particular subset was especially important in determining the levels of institutionalized coercion that would characterize the institutional context of democracy.

As a result of these decisions, the turn of the eighteenth century saw the production of sugar on large plantations employing slave labor become the dominant form of economic activity. These developments represented the beginning of the era of the big planter—"the golden age" of sugar. This golden era lasted until 1775; until then, profits were not hard to come by and Antigua fitted admirably into the mercantilist scheme of things.

Around this authoritarian organization and execution of the plantation production of sugar there crystalized a set of class relations that were founded, in part, on the relations of domination contained in this authoritarian system. At the top of this class hierarchy were the big planters, members of the political elite, and the top professionals. Below them were the poor whites (artisans and small planters) and whites with different religious beliefs. Below the poor whites were the free coloreds, and, at the bottom of the class hierarchy, the African slave labor force. The boundaries between these class/color groupings were rigid and clearly marked—almost to the point of being castelike. The social position of each of these groups—their rights (or lack of rights) and privileges—were all clearly defined by custom and law.

Thus, in accordance with the mercantilist view of colonies, the local economy was reorganized and commercial agriculture established. However, it was executed in a manner that created and required social structures that were inconsistent with high levels of democratization. Built into this system of production was a structure of domination that was founded upon the method of surplus extraction chosen—slavery. The choice of this method implied the creation of a society with deep and fundamental inequalities between the major social groups. It also implied the creation of secondary structures of racial and class domination to maintain these inequalities—structures that are inconsistent with high levels of democratization. Consequently, this system of production very quickly came to constitute one of the major authoritarian pillars of the society.

Having examined the manner in which the economic project was executed, we now have to examine the manner in which the political project was executed, in the effort to secure and routinize the incorporation of the society. That is, we will now examine the nature of the colonial state that had the day-to-day responsibilities of maintaining the above authoritarian order, on the one hand, and of maintaining institutional space for the practice of democracy, on the other.

We have already seen that in the effort to make Antigua a part of the empire, the indigenous population was given the political status of a conquered people. This imposition made the relations between the imperial state and this population authoritarian and militarized in nature. As the indigenous population was soon eliminated, their place was taken by an imported labor force which was subjected to the same authoritarian, militarized form of rule. But the imperial elite had to deal with more than just the indigenous population; it also had to deal with local Britishers who were claiming the same rights as their fellows at home. So in addition to maintaining the conditions necessary for the above system of production, the colonial state also had to secure the rights of these individuals. It was here that democracy found a place in this essentially authoritarian colonial/plantation society. Finally, the imperial elite had to deal with its own relations with the colonial state it was creating. It had to grant the local elites representative institutions yet, at the same time, maintain its imperial authority. This, we shall see, was an important source of friction between these two sets of elites. These were some of the major problems that the colonial state had to solve, and hence were important in shaping the nature of its institutions.

During the period of the first empire, the system of government worked out to meet all of these concerns was the so-called old representative system. It was set up in all of the West Indian territories that were incorporated during this period. The basic elements of this system were a governor, an executive council, and a legislative assembly. The governor was the local representative of the imperial elite. He received his authority and his instructions from this elite and not from the local set. The executive council was recruited through the governor's powers of nomination and performed two primary functions: it served as an advisory council to the governor and also as the upper house of the local legislature. The governor had the power to dismiss councillors as long as he submitted reasons to the imperial elite.[4] Finally, there was the elected legislature, which was to be the seat of popular input. However, slaves were legally barred from this body, while property restrictions excluded all but the wealthy. Through these devices, the elites were able to maintain their monopoly of power in spite of this process of democratization. Together, these three elementary structures constituted the center of colonial government in Antigua. For example, the laws of the society were enacted by these bodies. Bills had to be passed three times in each house before being presented to the governor. The latter would assent only if they did not contradict the terms of his commission or his instructions. Through this acceptance of an appointed governor, a compromise was reached between the local and imperial elites. Through the legislature the local elites were able to act "responsibly" on their own behalf and maintain their rights as British citizens. However, through the governor, the imperial elite was able to subject the actions of the local elite to its scrutiny and approval.

This, then, was the nature of the colonial state. Through the figure of the governor, the authoritarian relationship between the imperial state and the indigenous and imported populations was reinforced. Also through this figure, the subordinate status of the local political elites was reinforced. Through the imposition of laws and property qualifications that restricted voting, the authoritarian relationship between the local elites and indigenous and imported populations was reinforced. As a result of this mode of institutionalization, democracy became a functioning part of the second authoritarian pillar of the society, the colonial state.

The Rise of Complete Colonial Authoritarianism

The institutionalization of plantocratic democracy described above lasted from the 1660s to the 1860s. Between 1868 and 1951, it was de-institutionalized and its regular practice eliminated. The institutional space that it occupied was taken over by the exerise of imperial rule, thus ushering in a period of complete colonial authoritarianism. To understand this elimination of democracy, we will have to examine the crises of goal attainment that the imperial political elite was now facing—crises that it would solve by completing its already essentially authoritarian rule.

The crises facing the imperial political elite were on two fronts: (1) those stemming from difficulties with local colonial governments, and (2) those stemming from difficulties in constructing and securing "the second empire." Let us begin with the first. As noted earlier, colonies like Antigua that were incorporated during the first empire were given constitutions that permitted the establishing of representative institutions. However, there was always a great deal of ambiguity surrounding these constitutions: local elites and their imperial counterparts could not agree on the exact manner in which imperial authority was to be exercised.[5] As a result, bitter conflicts often ensued over this issue. The members of the West Indian assemblies were well known for their recalcitrance and their demands for greater autonomy for their parliaments. However, it was in the American colonies that the most dramatic confrontations occurred. Rejecting the British interpretation of the matter, along with British mercantilist policy, the Americans revolted and declared their independence in 1776. This loss brought to a head the potentially explosive nature of the relations by which the colonies were governed. Consequently, the imperial political elite was forced to entertain new ideas concerning their future governance.[6] However, immediately following the American Revolution no major changes are observable, except for the more cautious and conciliatory attitude of the imperial elite in its relations with local colonial elites.

Of greater importance at this time was the set of problems that had been created by the construction of the second empire. This task created problems for the imperial directorate because it forced them to come up with new forms of colonial rule in the new territories that its military forces had been acquiring. These new forms were necessary because the new colonies were territories that had been taken from other European powers, particularly the French. In these colonies, in addition to the indigenous and imported populations, the imperial directorate now had to establish British rule over recalcitrant French men and women. By the end of the eighteenth century, as parts of the expanding empire, the British had taken and held for varying periods of time the islands of Grenada, St. Lucia, Martinique, Guadeloupe, and San Dominique from the French, and Trinidad from the Spanish. The problems of governing these islands were made all the more acute because this was the revolutionary period in France. Revolutionary republicanism was alive in these territories (particularly Haiti) and brought the British face to face with a political force that had already shaken their monarchy and contributed to the loss of the American colonies. Between 1795 and 1797, two attempts were made to seize Trinidad for Republican France.[7] The need for new forms of government in these territories was made even more evident by the experience of Grenada. There the French had been granted the basic rights of the old representative system, with disastrous results. In 1779, the French colonists assisted France in reoccupying the island. After the British recapture in 1783, the French colonists again revolted in 1795.[8] In brief, it was the explosion of revolutionary republicanism in the region, together with the presence of non-British Europeans, that created new problems of governing for the imperial directorate.

The response of this section of the British political elite was to establish more authoritarian regimes in these colonies. Martinique, in 1794, represented one of the first departures from the pattern of granting constitutions that embodied representative institutions. However, the British did not hold on to this island for very long. Consequently, the first really significant case of the establishment of complete colonial authoritarianism was Trinidad, in 1801.[9] After its imposition there, colonial authoritarianism became the pattern in other newly conquered territories. Because government under the old representative system was an oligarchic democracy, the structure of government under the new or Crown Colony system was not all that different. The latter had the same three crucial elements as the former—a governor, an executive council, and a legislature. The major difference was that the legislature was now a nominated body, and no longer an elected one. This extension of the governor's powers of nomination increased his control over the legislature, which in turn increased the power of the imperial elite in these colonies. However, the position of the planters did not change that much, since the governers were often advised in their instructions to recruit the membership of the two houses from that class.[10]

Having resolved the problems of incorporating new territories through the imposition of Crown Colony government, the imperial directorate was still left with the problems arising from the ambiguities in the constitutions of older colonies like Antigua. Important members of this section of the British political elite were divided on a solution to these problems. Some favored the generalization of a revised representative system, while others favored the generalization of the Crown Colony system. But, as the elite debated the issue, events were taking place in the older Caribbean territories that would soon force their hand. Most important was the decline in the profitability of sugar, which started around 1776. This decline occurred for several reasons. First, in 1776 the territories lost their supplies of cheap foodstuffs from the American colonies. Second, by this time slave rebellions had become a dreaded reality, and opposition to the slave trade had grown. In 1804 the trade was outlawed in British colonies, and slavery itself was outlawed about thirty years later. Third, the profitability of sugar was further affected by competition from other islands (Cuba in particular), Britain's replacement of mercantilism with free trade, and, later, competition from European beet sugar. The importance of this decline for us is that it forced a substantial reorganization of the industry. This reorganization involved changes in patterns of ownership, technologies employed, methods of labor control, and surplus extraction. Although we cannot go into detail here, this reorganization resulted in sugar becoming profitable once again and in the reconstitution of the industry on less authoritarian principles. Consequently, the system of production still remained an important authoritarian pillar of the society.

Of more immediate concern, however, is another important result of this reorganization. This was the reduction it produced in the number of plantation owners that it left in the islands. This reduction was important in that it reduced significantly the size of the class with which the imperial elite had allied itself and through which it ruled. The reorganization also resulted in the reduction of the size of the white population as a whole. These reductions came at a time when the size of the black and colored segments was increasing, and these segments were no less militant because their people were no longer slaves. It was the potential for black or colored rule implicit in this demographic shift that became critical in the last years of the old representative system. Events came to a head in 1865 with the Morant Bay rebellion in Jamaica. It gave the imperial elite the opportunity it needed. By this time, the local elites in most of the islands were eager for increased imperial protection. The imperial elite was confronted with essentially two demands: (1) continue to support and rule through the local white elite; or (2) enfranchise the coloreds or the coloreds and the blacks. It rejected both, arguing that either one of these would lead to racial domination. So, after declaring the local elites and classes incapable of ruling, it proceeded to establish its own rule. This it did by generalizing the system of Crown Colony government from the newly conquered territories to the older ones between 1865 and 1878. The major exception was, of course, Barbados, where local resistance had always been consistent. It was as a part of this larger set of events that the institutional space occupied by democracy in Antigua was absorbed by an expanding practice of colonial authoritarianism in 1868.

In sum, the rise of colonial authoritarianism was a response to problems of political accumulation and political management in two areas: the establishing of British rule in the new colonies, and the defining of the scope of local power in the old colonies. The imposition of this more authoritarian form of rule was routinized by a change in the distribution of formal power between the imperial elite and the local white elites. This change increased the capacity of the imperial elite to command, and so increased the level of authoritarianism available to it when dealing with local groups. Finally, this increased level of authoritarianism is important in that it is against this level that the impact and the extent of later redemocratization must be measured.

Decolonization, Nationalism, and the Rise of Mass Democracy

As noted earlier, the period from 1865 to 1931 was the period in which British hegemony established and maintained itself. The last quarter of the nineteenth century marked the zenith of British imperialism. In particular, the period witnessed the incorporation of various portions of Africa and Asia into the British and other European empires. The essentially unchallenged manner in which these acts of seizure were carried out was itself quite revealing. It was suggestive of a world in which European expansion went essentially unchecked, a world in which agreement over the incorporation of subject peoples was determined largely by the balance of power between a small number of European political elites. To grasp clearly the phenomenon of decolonization, it is necessary to understand, among other things, the decline and eclipse of the European-dominated world order which had occurred by the 1930s. Important changes had been taking place in other parts of the globe that dramatically altered the international position of these elites. This changed international position was to be one of a number of important factors leading to the decolonization and redemocratization of colonial societies like Antigua.

The decline and eclipse of the European-dominated world order was the result of sociohistorical forces that had been gathering momentum over many years. The first was the gradual but continuous growth of the U.S. and the U.S.S.R., both internally and externally. In both of these countries, the experiment with modernization that had been pioneered in Europe was being repeated on a much larger scale. As a result, by the early decades of the twentieth century, both of these countries emerged as super powers that not only dwarfed Europe, but soon succeeded in making the rivalry between themselves the dominant concern of world politics. Both the U.S.S.R. and the U.S. were, because of their own national interests and ideological outlooks, opposed to the European system of empires and to the managing of world politics around the maintenance of a European balance of power. This opposition of the super powers significantly weakened the position of the European elites and so became an important factor in the decolonization of the Third World.

The second factor contributing to the decline of the European dominated world order was the continued competition between the European powers themselves. This competition reached near suicidal proportions in the two world wars, which finally placed the leadership of the world into the hands of the Americans and the Russians.

Third and finally, there was the revolt of the colonized against European domination. At the turn of the twentieth century, European domination was at its zenith in the Third World. Yet just seventy years later, only its vestiges would be left behind. In the period after the Russian Revolution and the First World War, movements for national liberation were gathering momentum in Asia. After the Second World War, similar movements were well on their way in Africa and the Caribbean. In 1955, these two waves of nationalism found new confidence and solidarity in the Afro-Asian conference at Bandung. From this point on the tide had irreversibly turned.

Faced with these changing circumstances and increasing international pressures, the European political elites had little choice but to dismantle their long established empires. Given their weakened position, it would have been impossible for them to forcibly put down the many simultaneous revolts that were occurring in the colonies, and, at the same time, to deal with the pressures that were coming from the two super powers. The particular technique employed by the British political elite in the dismantling of its empire was that of constitutional decolonization. Through the processes contained in this technique, not only was dismantling accomplished, but also the containing and directing of the paths that the nationalist movements in the colonies would take.

Constitutional decolonization was the process through which formal political power within the colony was slowly transferred from the control of the imperial elite to local elites. However, it was not to the elites of former times, but to the leaders of the nationalist movements that this power was transferred. This transfer took place through a series of progressive constitutional changes which eventually led or will lead to formal political sovereignty. The various stages on this path and the model of nationhood to be institutionalized were already worked out, as by now there were several independent nations within the British empire. Canada, Australia, and the other so-called "white dominions," had attained independent status within the empire. The achievement of this status was in part the culmination of processes that were set in motion by the loss of the American colonies. Consequently, as this stage-wise process of decolonization had already been worked out, for the imperial elite it was largely a matter of extending it to the colonies that were still governed through the assembly or crown colony systems. The model of nationhood implicit in this process of decolonization was one that included institutional space for the practice of democracy. This space would be made available once again by making the legislative councils elected bodies and by removing all restriction on the franchise. By taking this path, therefore, these societies would be not only decolonized but also democratized.

In Antigua, the movement for national liberation started gathering momentum in the 1930s, as sugar production was experiencing another major crisis. As noted earlier, the reorganization of sugar production in the second half of the nineteenth century did essentially two things: it preserved the high levels of authoritarianism characteristic of the industry and restored its profitability. However, in spite of these successes, things were never the same. First, although the industry was still very authoritarian, the shift from slavery as a method of labor control to a contract act reduced the ability of capitalists to employ coercion.[11] Second, although profitability was restored, it was not steady, with the industry showing little or no growth.[12] Thus the world depression of the 1930s was another severe blow to an already stagnant and moribund industry. Consequently, the ensuing economic dislocations were quite severe. As these dislocations began to take hold of the Antiguan economy, worker discontent began making itself felt. By 1935, violence had erupted in several of the islands. This violence was directed, as we shall see, at existing social conditions and their inability to meet the basic needs of workers. To avoid similar eruptions in Antigua, two important concessions were quickly agreed to by the imperial elite between 1936 and 1937. The first was the making of five of the eleven seats in the legislature elected, as opposed to nominated, seats. The second was the elimination of the contract act, which further weakened the legal underpinnings of the authoritarian social relations that governed colonial capitalist production. In addition to these, development and social welfare plans were drawn up, including an economic "recovery program" for Antigua.

These concessions, however, only temporarily delayed the struggle that was to come. Around the turn of the century, two distinct traditions of protest were observable throughout the region. One was oriented toward the problems of racial domination and peaked with the Garvey movement. The other was oriented towards the problems of working class domination and peaked with the trade union movement of the thirties and forties. The shift from the former to the latter occurred in Antigua around 1939. By this time, strikes and other forms of labor unrest were once again on the rise: and out of this particular set of struggles came the second major attempt at the unionization of the working classes. Earlier attempts had failed, in part because of the nature of the legislation surrounding the practice of trade unionism. This legislation was changed in 1939, and it made the formation of the Antigua Trades and Labour Union (AT&LU) much easier.

Even though in the early days the union understood itself in democratic socialist terms, its ideology is better described as laborism than as any form of socialism. This is so for the simple reason that the union was much more concerned with improving the position of labor within the existing society than with the socialist reorganization of the society. However, it was a contradiction in which many of the leaders were caught without fully realizing it. Although this commitment to redressing the balance between capital and labor has been a constant with the union, its strategy for realizing this redress has often changed. In the early years, the strategy was one of partnership between capitalists and workers. After 1943, a position of state capitalism was pushed, and after 1951, the strategy that was later to be known as industrialization by invitation. Along with this laborist position, strong anticolonial and anti-upper-class sentiments were expressed. The anticolonial position was a comparatively mild one—never really approaching revolutionary dimensions. It centered around a negotiated settlement of the issue of self-government and the ending of the dominance of the planter class.

Fortified with this ideological outlook, the union began representing workers in 1940 and experienced its first success with the securing of small wage increases for workers at the Antigua Sugar Factory. From this start, the union moved on to successfully represent estate and waterfront workers. By 1946, after a number of additional successes on the economic front, the union's leadership decided to enter the political arena. As elections were being held that year, the leadership decided to contest the five seats in the legislature that had recently been made elective. To do this, the leadership quickly formed a political committee which was later to become the Antigua Labour Party (ALP). This committee selected the five candidates, all of whom were members of the union's executive, and ensured that the necessary property qualifications were met. All five of the union's candidates were elected—a feat the union would perform several times again in the future. In parliament they pushed their laborist programs cast within a framework of state capitalism. However, on these matters they met with little success as they were outnumbered by nominated members drawn from the planter and upper middle classes. Here the leaders were caught in the dilemmas of parliamentary laborism in a peripheral capitalist society without fully realizing it.

From these experiences of political and economic representation, the union, by the late forties, had developed a very specific set of demands. The more important of these included the following: (1) universal adult suffrage and the removal of all barriers to the polity, (2) self-government, (3) land and security of tenure for peasants, and (4) an eight-hour day as opposed to a twelve-hour day. Throughout the second half of the 1940s, the union, along with its political committee, fought resolutely for the realization of these demands. A breakthrough on the first and second issues came in 1951 with a substantial change in the Crown Colony constitution. This change was to be the first of five steps through which Antigua would have to pass on its way to independence. The new constitution increased the number of elected seats in the legislature from five to eight and introduced both universal adult suffrage and the committee system of government as a preliminary to the ministerial system. The union contested the 1951 election under these new conditions and won all eight seats. The second step in this process of constitutional decolonization occurred in 1956, with the acceptance of a constitution that introduced the ministerial system of government. As a result of this change, the union's top executives became the island's first ministers. The third step was taken in 1961, with the increase in the number of elected seats from eight to ten (leaving one nominated seat) and the appointment of a Chief Minister. The union's chief executive, Mr. Vere Bird, was appointed to the latter position, while the union once again contested and won all ten seats in the new elections. The fourth step came in 1967, with the achievement of associated statehood. Under these constitutional arrangements, a fully elected legislature was introduced. Also realized under these new arrangements was the formal transfer of final responsibility for national affairs (except for defense and external relations) to the new local political elites. Finally, in 1981, this process was completed and formal independence realized.

The "New Elitism" and Democracy in Postcolonial Antigua

The institutionalization and practice of democracy in the years since 1951 can be divided into periods. The first, which extended from 1951 to 1967, was a period of growth for democracy. As we have seen, it was a period in which the franchise was widened, the legislature slowly made more elective, and greater responsibility for national affairs placed in the hands of elected officials. As these changes took place, the institutional space occupied by democracy increased, and so did its influence on other institutional areas. In short, significant inroads were being made in the authoritarian framework of the period of complete colonial rule. This continued increase in the level of democratization was the result of the momentum that the movement for decolonization had generated. The leaders, then in the process of becoming the government, were still close to the people they had led; the two were still joined together by a unity that had been forged in the struggle to expel the colonizer. It was the continued existence of this pro-independence solidarity that provided the motive force for the growth of democracy during the period between 1951 and 1967.

The second period, which extends from 1967 to the present, has been one in which the above trend towards increasing the level of democratization of the society has been arrested. Not only has this trend been arrested, but the regular practice of democracy has been abridged and is often manipulated in a variety of ways. Since 1967, democracy has gained no new institutional territory, and it could be argued that it has been forced to yield some of its own. What is less debatable, however, are the numerous ways in which its practice has been both legally and illegally abridged. The most serious legal abridgements have been those that have circumscribed the rights to free speech and assembly (the Public Order Act), a free press (the Newspaper Amendment Act), and the right to unionize (Industrial Court Act and the Labour Code Act). The illegal practices that further abridge the practice of democracy have largely been the result of the breakup of the pro-independence solidarity and the formation of permanent opposition groups. These practices have taken the form of "victimization," with the result that job discrimination against members of the opposition has become a widespread practice. This discrimination has made party competition more intense and sometimes violent. These trends are closely related to subtle but important changes in the composition of the local elites, and the distribution of power between them and between themselves and other social groups. Therefore, to understand them fully we must now turn to an examination of these changes. In the contemporary period two important changes have taken place in the composition of the elites: the emergence of a new white (predominantly American) economic elite and a local black political elite. It is the hegemony of these two that constitutes the basis of the new elitism. We will begin our examination with the first of these two sets of elites.

The New Foreign Economic Elites

It would be highly misleading to assume that the destruction of the European centered world order resulted in the creation of a new order in which the new nations of the Third World have been able to function as fully independent states. In fact, the opposite has been the case. In place of the world order dominated by a European balance of power, a new order has been established which is dominated by a U.S.-U.S.S.R. balance of power. As with the old order, the new confronts the nations of the Third World with claims and demands of its own on their sovereignty. The rise of both the U.S. and the U.S.S.R. to the status of super powers was, in part, the result of continental conquests up to the end of the nineteenth century, and overseas quasi-colonization or satellization in the twentieth century. This process of overseas satellization ushered in a new phase in the peripheralization of the Third World. It differed from the European pattern of imperial domination in that it recognized the formal sovereignty of the nations penetrated. Consequently, strategic institutional control (economic, political, and military), which leaves the formal trappings of sovereignty in shape, has become the primary strategy of the satellization process. This is not to say that outright overseas conquest or colonization has been unknown to the super powers, but that it has been the exception rather than the rule.

With the exception of Cuba, the Caribbean region is slowly passing from a condition of European colonization to one of American satellization. The process of satellization began with the gradual establishment of a hegemonic position within the economic and military spheres of Caribbean societies. In the former British Caribbean, American economic penetration began with the securing of control over the bauxite reserves of Guyana by Alcoa between 1912 and 1925.[13] In the fifties further economic penetration took place, with other American companies acquiring the rights to bauxite reserves in Jamaica[14] and oil reserves in Trinidad.[15] Finally, in the sixties, it was access to precious beach lands and the establishing of tourist industries in most of the islands. Military penetration, which took the form of bases, came during or after the Second World War. Most of these penetrating ventures were undertaken with British cooperation—that is, while the region was still colonized—but without challenge to British rule. As national leadership passed into local hands, this form of penetration only increased, thereby establishing the process of satellization and the presence of new foreign economic elites.

In Antigua, American economic penetration came in the areas of oil refining, garment manufacturing, and tourism, but primarily in the latter area. Military penetration came with the establishment of two bases, one for the air force and one for the navy. As these ventures presented no direct threat to local sovereignty, they fit easily into the plans of the new local elites, since they provided jobs for many of their supporters. That they were viewed in this manner was not an entirely mistaken view. It was a recognition of opportunities that existed within the framework of American satellization that were excluded by the conditions of British colonialism. Also, the local political elite was still locked in a struggle with the last remnants of the planter class and, though they did not become directly involved, the competition for local resources (labor in particular) that the presence of the new capitalists generated became an important factor in the final demise of the planter class. Through the better wages they made available, the new industries generated an exodus of labor from the plantations to the hotels— so much so that the planters were often forced to import labor. These difficulties, together with the secular trend toward stagnation characteristic of the industry, led to its final collapse in 1971. In 1975, oil refining came to a similar end, which left the economic arena to those investing in tourism. Thus American satellization contributed indirectly to the final collapse of British economic incorporation and the reorientation of the Antiguan economy. This transition resulted in the switch from an agrarian economy based on sugar production and European ties, to a service economy based on tourism and North American ties.

The primary concern of the economic elites in the new service economy, like that of the old elite, is capital accumulation. They are in the business of supplying a service to an international market for a profit, just as the planters supplied sugar. Hence they, too, are interested in maintaining favorable conditions of profit realization. However, inspite of the similarities in the role and positions of dominance that both of these elites have occupied, their actual capacities to dominate—that is, forcefully extract a surplus from labor—is very different. This is so for several reasons. First, because of the youth and the high rate of turnover characteristic of the tourist industry, the new elite is not a tightly knit and cohesive one. Members are interested in quick profits and so are reluctant to put down roots. Hence the industry as a whole has more of an enclave status, which was not the case with sugar. Second, the new economic elites do not have control over the local state apparatus to as great a degree as the planters did. Third, the new economic elites have to confront a stronger working class that is now unionized, enfranchised, and more self-conscious. Fourth and finally, relations between the members of the new elite and their home state are not as intimate as those between the planters and their home state. Nonetheless, the American government remains a force that the new elite can fall back on if relations between it and the local state deteriorate. However, this reduced capacity to dominate does not mean that this elite has been unable to function. On the contrary, it has been able to exact from the state the right to extract and repatriate surplus under very favorable conditions. These conditions can be seen in the concession agreements under which foreign industries are set up.[16] Also, in the day to day competition to influence state decisions, this elite often gets its way.

The New Local Political Elite

Paralleling the growth of the new economic elites has been the growth of a local black political elite. The growth of this elite, which consists primarily of top party officials and members of the upper reaches of the civil service, judiciary, and other state operated institutions, is a part of the growth of the politico-bureaucratic elements of the middle class. This growth has largely been the result of local control of the state. To understand clearly the growth of this elite, we must now examine another facet of the movement for decolonization that has so far remained unaddressed. This facet is the organizational dimension of the movement and the dynamics for elite formation that it contained.

Movements for social change seldom last very long if they remain at the level of elaborating a critical alternative. To attain the momentum needed to change the old order, they must acquire an organizational base. However, such an organizational base usually has dynamics of its own that, if not carefully understood, could thwart or even come to eclipse the goals of the movement. These tendencies toward elite formation are rooted in a number of structural contradictions between normatively oriented movements and the processes of large-scale organization given their classic expression by Michels. For Michels, large scale organization and normatively oriented movements are incompatible, in that the nature and the requirements of the former are such that the leaders will have a near monopoly over the resources through which power is accumulated and exercised. For example, leaders of large scale organizations often have near monopolies over finance, channels of communication, personnel, leadership skills, and the opportunities for acquiring such skills. The more securely and tightly controlled is the monopoly over these resources, the greater will be tendencies toward elite formation. With such advantages accruing to the leaders, the chances for the emergence of an active legitimate opposition are reduced, while those for the further entrenchment and social improvement of the leaders are increased. Hence the tendencies toward elite formation which, in turn, create the possibilities for elite domination or manipulation.

All mass movements that have taken on an organizational base must confront these problems. "Organization," says Michels, "implies a tendency to oligarchy."[17] This tendency is of course more acute in the cases of democratically oriented movements, as they are faced with an instrumental short-circuiting of their primary goals. However, this tendency is not as automatic as the above statement would suggest. Rather, the tendency varies with the internal structure of the organization and, in particular, with the hierarchy of authority and how access to it is controlled. So for example, the tendency should be weaker in organizations with higher levels of internal democratization than in those with lower levels. Consequently, the extent to which leadership has been democratized or "authoritarianized" becomes an important determinant of the process of elite formation and of the tendency for organization goals to replace movement goals. Thus even though it is true, as Michels has argued, that internally nondemocratic organizations can support and function within a democratic polity, the problem does not end there. It is not that simple, because the elitist structures of power that the movement created do not cease to function after the movement has attained its goals. Rather, they become a part of the nondemocratic institutional framework that helps to determine the scope and effectiveness of democratically determined action. From this perspective, the level of internal democratization that a democratically oriented movement institutionalizes becomes extremely important, for it will help to reduce the level of elitism that its organizational base will introduce into the society and so reduce the chances of an organizational short-circuiting of its primary goals.

In the case of the movement for decolonization in Antigua, we saw that the primary organizational instrument was the Antigua Trades and Labour Union. The leaders of the AT&LU very quickly became responsible for managing, planning, and directing the course of this movement; they were, so to speak, its executives. What is important for us here, is the internal structure of the organization that took the responsibility of managing and directing the movement. The internal structure of this union was not very democratic; it was much less so than the political order it was advocating. It was essentially bureaucratic in nature, with a charismatic leader at the top—a pattern of organization that resulted in a rather low level of internal democratization. Consequently, as the years went by and success attended the movement, these tightly controlled positions of leadership were subjected to processes of elite formation. The structures of power that these processes generated were subsequently to become a part of the authoritarian context of the democratic praxis that the movement would introduce. Let us examine these processes in greater detail.

As noted earlier, the worsening economic conditions of the 1930s were the more immediate factors that gave rise to the movement for decolonization. As events gathered momentum, unemployed and distressed workers gathered around individuals who were able to articulate clearly their grievances and stand behind them in their struggles with the planters. In short, leadership was based on oratory and other charismatic qualities. However, these charismatic leaders did not spring from nowhere, nor were these growing movements completely without an organizational base. Most of these leaders were drawn from the lodges and friendly societies, which were the only mass organization that were permitted for a long time. However, as these organizations were legally barred from being explicitly political, they could not provide the appropriate base. Much more appropriate was that base provided by the AT&LU. For many years, being engaged in the struggle was the primary concern, and this created strong bonds of unity and solidarity. Calling effective strikes, hard bargaining, and wage increases kept workers and leaders together. However, as early as 1943, there emerged clear signs of intense disagreements at the top. Because of the low level of internal democratization, these disagreements quickly resulted in an intense struggle for power. At the end of this struggle, Mr. Bird and a group around him emerged as the new leaders of the union. From this point on this faction, through a variety of means including hard work and purges, has been able to retain its control of the leadership.

However, as the strategies for retaining and accumulating power were employed, the ranks of those who became disaffected with Mr. Bird and his administration swelled. This growing number of dropouts and castouts soon allied themselves with the union's major competitor, the Antigua National Party. This was the party of the upper middle class, and its members opposed much of what the union stood for. Because of this conservatism, the party was unable to attract a very large following, and so posed only a minor threat to the union.

Because it was still the most progressive of the political forces erupting on the island, and because of the lack of viable alternatives, the union and its leadership continued to dominate the movement in spite of growing dissatisfaction with the oligarchic tendencies developing within it. With every new worker it represented, and with every new seat it won in parliament, the union grew stronger and stronger, as did the power of the leaders. These cumulative increases in the power of the leaders were examined in the earlier analysis of the process of constitutional decolonization. There we described the increases in the power and prestige of the leaders that came with the successes of the union and the various constitutional changes. More specifically, the power, prestige, and wealth of the leaders increased on two fronts: (1) they were in complete control of a growing union which had virtually monopolized the organization of labor, and (2) they were gradually extending their control over the decisionmaking capacity of the state. This process of political accumulation reached its zenith in 1967 with the achievement of statehood. With this achievement, the leaders were now the executives of both the union and the state, with little formal opposition.

However, the monolithic system of power that as being constructed was more apparent than real, for within it, much resistance had been growing to this increasing monopolization of power by Mr. Bird and his administration. This resistance resulted in another purge of the union, just three months after statehood in May. In this cleanup operation, the general secretary, Mr. George Walter, and two other important field officers were expelled. However, this purge was to be very different from the big purge of 1949. This time the fired officials took with them large numbers of followers and formed a rival union, the Antigua Workers Union. The union's chief executive was Mr. Walter, the fired general secretary. After a long and bitter struggle with Mr. Bird in his role as premier, the new union finally gained legal recognition. In the course of this struggle, the union had already become part of the anti-Bird movement which had been gathering momentum. With the help of the union, this movement soon turned itself into a rival political party, the Progressive Labour Movement (PLM). The PLM, with Mr. Walter at the helm, contested the 1970 election and won, giving the Bird regime its first defeat. Mr. Walter had now repeated what Mr. Bird had done: he formed a union and, on the basis of the power it generated, took control of state power. Both the AWU and the PLM were laborist in outlook, and took great pride in their internal democratic structures. However, the level of democratization institutionalized was not much higher than that in the ALP and the AT&LU. So not surprisingly, the PLM/AWU combination soon came to be a mirror image of the ALP/AT&LU combination. Many of the same tendencies toward oligarchy and toward the embourgeoisement of the leaders found in the latter were soon evident in the former. In short, once again, a nondemocratic pattern of managing a democratic movement had generated inequalities similar to those it was trying to eliminate. As a result of these conflicts and processes of elite formation, the new local political elite is now split into two competing, but almost identical, halves. These halves are in competition for the control of state power, each claiming that it can do a better job at the political helm.

The processes of elite formation just described have been largely responsible for the more important of the current changes that have taken place in the Antiguan class structure. They have resulted in the rise of a white service-oriented economic elite and in the rise of a black political elite. The former, through law and custom, has established for itself the right to extract economic surpluses and hence possesses a potential capacity to dominate. The latter, through their organizational control of the movement for decolonization, have acquired almost complete control of the society's capacity for collective decisionmaking and for the legitimate use of force. Hence they, too, possess a potential capacity to dominate. It is the manner in which these elites have used the rights and resources they command in the pursuit of their respective goals which constitutes the new elitism that conditions the current practice of democracy. To see this, we must now examine the relations betwen the economic and political elites, those between the political elites and the masses, and finally, those between the two factions of the political elites.

Relations Between the Foreign Economic Elites and the Local Elites

Relations between the foreign economic elites and the local political elites are best understood as a case of what happens when a democratic laborist or socialist party comes to power within the political system of a peripheral capitalist society. These parties usually come to power on the promise of redressing the balance between capital and labor. However, coming to power under the above conditions, these parties are subject to a number of sociological forces that push them in the direction of moderation, compromise, or even capitulation, and thus away from their goals. The most important of these are that members of the party become political colleagues of their opponents and, as such, are subject to the socialization and to the levers of power still controlled by those committed to the existing order.

As we have already seen, the local political elites became colleagues of their capitalist opponents as early as 1946. Thus it is possible to divide the relations between the economic and political elites into two phases: the first is that dominated by relations with the planters and the second is that dominated by relations with the new service elite. In their relations with the planters, the new local elites were aggressive; their basic attitude was one of limited confrontation with very specific redistributive aims. The party's strategy for dealing with the inequality between labor and capital moved in two directions. One was to use its influence in parliament to force planters to sell lands to the government which the government would rent or make available to peasants. The other was to push for a fairly wide ranging program of nationalization. However, in both cases the planters were able to limit the party's actions. The sale of lands was stopped after a point, and nationalization was limited to the area of public utilities. This general retreat before the power of capital was very clearly summed up by a party official: "While therefore, according to socialist policies the nationalization of essential services and certain basic industries is accepted as a *sine qua non,* trade union leaders in Antigua had to study the implications of full policy of nationalization within a program of (foreign) industrialization that was so essential to the island. They had to consider whether or not the programs and policies of the British Labour Party could be used, and after careful consideration rejected most of them."[18] Consequently, whatever improvements did take place in the social position of labor left the hegemony of foreign and local capital very much intact. At first these compromises were hard to make; but with the gradual bourgeois drift of the leaders, they became easier to accept and rationalize. So by the time the new service elites had begun investing, the local political elites had become enthusiastic supporters of capitalism.

In the second, or contemporary, phase of the relationship between the economic and political elites, the tension between capitalism and the interests of labor virtually disappeared from the life of the parties. Its place has been taken by an extremely cooperative relationship, in which the local political elites—irrespective of which party is in power—play a subordinate role. This subordinate role grows out of the externally dependent nature of the institutions of peripheralized societies. Foreign economic elites, by contrast, are willing to invest if profits can be made. Consequently, in this relationship, the local political elite—through its control of the state apparatus—guarantees a number of basic property rights and conditions of capital realization and expatriation, all in an effort to make capital "feel at home." In a large number of cases, since the government has acquired the remains of the defunct sugar industry, cheap land has become a part of the offerings of the political elite. In return, the political elite gets several things. First, it gets the opportunity to legitimate and prove its ability to manage the affairs of state. Second, its network of patronage widens. That is, members may acquire money or contracts for themselves or for their friends or party members. Third, foreign investments provide jobs for workers which often go to party supporters. It is through this pattern of job creation that the political elite has sought to deal with pressing problems of unemployment. In sum, a system of economic concessions, legitimacy needs, investment needs, patronage, and corruption has come to define the relationship between the foreign and local elites. Structurally, these interactions may be described as the institutionalization of a set of what O'Donnell has called "privatist relations" between the state and civil society. They are privatist in that they entail "the opening up of institutional areas of the state to the representation of the organized interests"[19] of the new foreign economic elite. This opening up is specific to this class and has not been generalized to other classes. Reinforcing these privatist relations has been the institutionalization of a number of "statizing" measures between the state and the working class. They are statizing in that they entail "the conquest and subordination by the state of the organizations"[20] of this class. Again, these relations are specific to this class and have not been generalized.

This pattern of cooperation between the two sets of elites has resulted in a gradual improvement in the capacity of the foreign economic elites to extract surplus, and a corresponding decrease in the capacity of labor to continue appropriating larger shares of the surplus. This improvement in the conditions of profit realization has been one of the primary demands of the new economic elites. Because of the dependent nature of the economy, and out of fear of losing possible investments, the political elite has often given in to such demands. Having made such concessions, this elite has been able to make them real through its control of the decisionmaking process in two areas, the union and the state. Through its control of the unions, the political elite has been able to exercise control over wage increases and other union demands; and through its control of the lawmaking function of the state, it has been able to redefine the role of unions and the relations between capital and labor. It is in this context that the Labor Code and the Industrial Court acts must be interpreted. The represent an attempt to redress and routinize the conflict between capital and labor in a manner that has gradually increased the power of the former. This shift permits an increase in the amount of coercion that is sometimes or routinely used in the process of surplus extraction. This increase in the use of coercion, which is in part based on the above acts, is one of the crucial factors in the current abridgement of democratic practices.

Relations Between the Local Political Elite and the People

Another factor affecting the current practice of democracy is the changed relationship between the political elite and the people. A number of factors have contributed to this change. The first is that the leaders are in power and have been for some time. This has created distance between the two. Second, the privatist relations that the political elite now have with the economic elites have further increased this distance. The third factor affecting the relationship between the local elite and the people is that of patronage. As the former has continued to pursue its policy of close cooperation with foreign capitalists, its members have had increasing amounts of patronage to distribute. This increasing amount of patronage, together with the above distancing, has largely transformed the relationship between this elite and the people from one of solidarity in struggle to one of clientilism. The people have come more and more to perceive politics in terms of the material rewards that it can bring, while the leaders increasingly use the distribution of such rewards as a basis for control and support. Fourth and finally, relations between the elite and the people have been affected by the institutionalization of the two-party system. This has resulted in the division of the working class and elements of the middle class into two rival union/party combinations. Although officially the two-party system is recognized, neither party has in fact been able to accept the existence of the other. A *modus vivendi* in which party competition has been routinized in a peaceful manner has not been worked out. Consequently, with the increasing amount of patronage to be distributed, victimization assumes larger and larger proportions; more and more of the members of the PLM/AWU combination are replaced when the ALP/AT&LU combination is in power, and vice versa. The result of all this is that a strong element of hostility has come to characterize the relationship between one faction of the political elite and the people following the other faction.

This element of hostility, which has manifested itself primarily in victimization, is a product of the new elitism conditioning the current practice of democracy. For the masses, it places the whole process of voting within a context of intimidation. Thus, in addition to selecting a government, elections have also come to mean a loss of jobs for members of the defeated party and jobs for loyal supporters of the victorious party.

Relations Between the Two Halves of the Political Elite

The third and final factor affecting the current practice of democracy is the relations between the two factions of the local political elite. As just noted, a practice of peaceful party competition has not accompanied the institutionalization of the two party system. Consequently, competition between these two halves for the control of state power has become a very tense affair. Slander, lies, character assassinations, disruption of meetings, and acts of sabotage have become a part of the competitive process. The use of these techniques has locked government and its opposition in rather wasteful see-saw battles that have left their relations in a chronic state of crisis. Often leaders of the opposition will do things to embarass the government or undermine its credibility; for example, they may encourage the government workers to strike or they may disrupt a public government function. The government often overreacts to such events. On other occasions, it is the government that starts the ball rolling, by interpreting a legitimate action of protest by the opposition as an attempt to overthrow it. To such actions the opposition will then often overreact. It is the highly charged nature of this competition that has led governments in power to use the law, and sometimes force, to constrain the ability of the opposition or other opposing groups to organize and demonstrate their opposition. The enactment of the Public Order and Newspaper Amendment Acts came as part of the efforts of governments to secure their positions by reducing the firing power of the opposition; so also did the use of "special policemen" by the PLM government and, now, the use of a beefed up regular police force by the Bird government. The former set of actions were the legal basis of attempts at curbing the activity of the opposition, while the latter were the basis for more forceful attempts.

These legal and forceful attempts at curbing the activities of the opposition constitute a third element in the new elitism that currently conditions the practice of democracy in Antigua. Just as the relations between the local elites and the masses introduced an element of intimidation into the democratic process, so the relations between the two factions of the local elite have introduced an element of violence. Thus, on account of the nature of the competition between these two factions, democracy has come to involve not only high economic and occupational risks, but high personal ones as well.

Conclusion

In this chapter we have been concerned with two primary issues: the identification of the structural bases of the authoritarian context of democracy in Antigua, and the impact of the more recent movement for decolonization on that authoritarian context. With regard to the former, the structural bases were identified as being rooted in the distribution of power between the classes and between dominant elites within these classes. In all three periods examined, we saw that the basic components of the class structure were the same: a foreign economic elite, a local or foreign political elite, a small local middle class, and a large local working class. Although many factors went into the making of the relations between these components, the most important, we suggested, for an understanding of the changing authoritarian context were the changes in the distribution of power and the possibilities these created for the institutionalization of authoritarian solutions to problems of goal attainment. Thus, when power accumulated in the hands of the imperial elite and away from locals, colonial authoritarianism became a possibility. Similarly, the accumulation of power by local classes in the contemporary period is largely responsible for the lessened degree of authoritarianism. Therefore, with regard to our first issue, we can conclude that the distribution of power between the crucial collective actors in the society has been, and will continue to be, an important determinant of the authoritarian context of democracy.

With regard to our second issue, we have shown that the movement for decolonization introduced a number of changes in the composition of the classes and the distribution of power between them in the contemporary period. It is the amount of coercion that this changed situation permits that defines the authoritarian context of democracy in the current postcolonial period.

Finally, we may ask: what lies ahead for democracy in Antigua? Within the framework of the present compromise and the class relations flowing from it, it would seem reasonable to expect the continued accumulation of power by both the economic and political elites. This, of course, may mean a thickening of the elitist context in which democracy is currently situated. However, there are two factors pointing in the opposite direction. First is the failure of present postcolonial arrangements to cope adequately with existing social and economic problems. Second is the fairly widespread resentment of the domination contained in the practice of satellization. Opposition groups such as the Antigua-Caribbean Liberation Movement (ACLM) which attempt to address these problems are confronted with two major obstacles: the fear on the part of many of the socialist alternative they propose, and fear of the possibility that they, too, will only repeat what other leaders have done, but under a different label. Given these conditions, it is quite likely that present trends will continue; hence we can expect a thickening of the elitist context of democracy in the forseeable future. Whether this elitism will come to be dominated by the clientelist-corporatist elements it contains will be important to watch for in the future.

Notes

1. Milton Friedman, *Capitalism and Freedom* (Chicago, 1971), p. 10.
2. Barrington Moore, *Social Origins of Dictatorship and Democracy* (Boston, 1967), pp. 430–32.
3. Vincent T. Harlow, *The Founding of the Second British Empire 1763–1793*, Vol. 1 (London, 1952), p. 159.
4. Elsa Goveia, *Slave Society in the British Leeward Islands at the End of the Eighteenth Century* (New Haven, 1965), p. 56.
5. D. J. Murray, *The West Indies and the Development of Colonial Government, 1801–1834* (London, 1965), p. 5.
6. Ibid., p. 65.
7. James Millette, *The Genesis of Crown Colony Government* (Curepe, Trinidad, 1971), p. 156.
8. Ibid., p. 156.
9. Loc. cit.
10. Goveia, p. 71.
11. Under this act workers were required to work for at least a year on the plantations in exchange for housing, medical care, and sixpence a day. See Douglas Hall, *Five of the Leewards* (Barbados, 1971), p. 38.
12. Paget Henry, *From Underdevelopment to Underdevelopment,* unpublished Ph.D dissertation (Cornell University, 1976), p. 105.
13. Norman Girvan, *Corporate Imperialism: Conflict and Expropriation* (New York, 1976), p. 106.
14. Loc. cit.
15. Eric Williams, *The History of the People of Trinidad and Tobago* (New York, 1962), p. 247.
16. For a discussion of the concession agreement under which the oil refining industry was set up, see Paget Henry, p. 211.
17. Robert Michels, *Political Parties* (New York, 1962), p. 70.
18. Novelle Richards, *The Struggle and the Conquest* (London, 1967), p. 55.
19. Guillermo O'Donnell, "Corporatism and the Question of the State," in James Malloy (ed.), *Authoritarianism and Corporatism in Latin America* (Pittsburgh, 1977), p. 48.
20. Loc. cit.

15

Resource Ownership and the Prospects for Democracy: The Case of Trinidad and Tobago

CARL D. PARRIS

The title chosen for this chapter reflects a growing uneasiness among elements of the North American intellectual, political, and economic establishment about recent events and future trends in the Caribbean region. As seen from this perspective, these events and trends represent "social turmoil" and "possible communist domination" and necessitate quick remedial action in the form of economic aid as well as the establishment of a permanent Caribbean joint military task force at Key West, Florida, the United States toe in the region.[1]

It should be made clear at this stage that this writer is of the view that the concern of the United States for this region, dubbed as it was by former Secretary of State Cyrus Vance "one of the world's leading trouble spots," derives not only from the strategic importance of the region to its southern flank but, more importantly, from the fact that the United States depends on it for up to a quarter of its oil supplies which pass through export refineries and transhipment terminals in the area.[2]

It is because of this fact—that Trinidad is the home of one of the largest of these refineries, and, according to recent figures, has had nearly $3 billion in foreign assets within its shores—that a concern for the Trinidad and Tobago government's attitude toward resource ownership and the prospects for democracy become relevant. The task of this chapter is to throw some light on the interrelationship, if any, between these two processes. We will attempt, first, to map as accurately as possible the Trinidad and Tobago government's attitude toward resource ownership and the model of development chosen. Second, some of the consequences of that choice will be explored, and third, these consequences will be related to the prospects for democracy in the country.

Modernization or Development?

In 1956, the Trinidad and Tobago government, led by Dr. Eric Williams, faced the choice of which of two paths to the future it should take. The first path we shall call "modernization" and the second path "development." Modernization, like development, is a model of historical transition. Modernization consists, above all, in the adoption of patterns of behavior and consumption, ways of life and values, ideas and attitudes typical of the more "advanced" societies without any structural change in the institutional framework and economic subordination of the country. Development, on the other hand, consists in the creation of forms of organization and management and patterns of responsibility appropriate to the possibilities of the country concerned.

It is not surprising, given the fact that the prevailing intellectual orthodoxy of the time postulated that the problem of economic transformation rested on the modernization of the "backward" countries by means of their introduction to the technologies of the North Atlantic world, and given the fact that this orthodoxy was legitimated in the region by the writings of the West Indian scholar Arthur Lewis, that the Trinidad government in 1956 chose to transform the country by embarking on a scheme of industrialization which involved the borrowing of resources from the "developed" world. This model of development explicitly assumed that there was a shortage of capital and assigned to the state the task of attracting it—capital being seen as a package of inputs involving entrepreneurship and, to some extent, even markets.

With respect to the question of ownership of the country's resources, if the country's 1956 elections manifesto and the government's attitude toward Texaco's further investment in its oil resources are sufficient indicators of a position, then it can be clearly stated that the government in 1956 preferred to allow its resources to be developed by private initiative, both local and foreign. This being the case, our contention is that changes in the government's position on this question resulted from a process of narrowing options, as the pattern of post-1956 economic modernization polarized classes and created new local elites. Relating this now to the future prospects for democracy, we shall contend that the increasing gap between the new national power system and the rest of the nation will lead unavoidably to the emergence of the "strong regime," today so favorable in the new nations, and is part of the price to be paid for a "better" integration in the power system prevailing in the international society.

Trinidad, 1956–1964

By the mid-sixties, the government of Trinidad and Tobago found itself faced with increasing demands from organized labor for strong governmental action with regard to ownership and control of the country's national resources, as well as for drastic changes in income distribution.[3]

In the budget speech for 1964, the then Minister of Finance demonstrated that he understood the implications of these demands for the strategy and thus the role of the state:

> There appears to be a developing "strike consciousness" on the part of labour which is inhibiting the impetus to grow. . . . Unsatisfactory industrial relations during the past two years have struck at the root of confidence of investors, rapid wage increases are reducing the competitiveness of local labour. These factors combined are tending to nullify the various incentives offered by the Government to attract investment. . . . The process has already gone too far. Any continuation of this state of affairs into 1964 will permanently injure our industrialisation effort and damage our international reputation.[4]

To all intents and purposes, the strident demands of organized labor represented a clear sense of its own and its government's loss of economic control to metropolitan corporations. Recognizing as they did that metropolitan capital in the form of direct investment was not engendering the much-vaunted entrepreneurship which the government had claimed that it would, but was in fact engendering retrenchment and, in some cases, little employment, the unions were demanding as well that the government assume the burden of job creation. That government had, in fact, lost control can be seen from as early as 1963. At that time, its finance minister, reflecting on the role of the foreign commercial banks, noted that

> [They] run their business in a way that is not in the interest of the population . . . their policies have always been dictated by their head offices and consequently in the interest of foreign and metropolitan powers . . . [The]

insurance companies are not making their contribution to the community. . . . They are net exporters of capital . . . and the amount of capital which is exported from year to year has been increasing rather than decreasing. . . .[5]

With respect to oil, he pointed out:

It accounts for almost 44.5 per cent of our imports . . . so immediately you are faced with a situation where you do not want to tax the raw material because it is not the policy in a country which is industrialising to tax the raw materials of industry. You are therefore faced immediately with a situation where 44.5 per cent of your imports are not taxed, which is crude oil. That leaves a matter of 55.5 per cent and out of that you have to take away concessions granted to pioneer industries such as duty free machinery, plant and equipment and of course, they are granted concessions in respect of income tax, depreciation allowance and so on . . . what I want to make clear is that . . . if everybody wants concessions in order to produce then . . . somebody has to make the contribution to government's revenue.[6]

But who was to play what role in the strategy of development, and what mechanism was available to the government, given its attitude toward the development of its resources? The government could either get tough with labor and so preserve the climate for investment or attempt, in the light of its understanding of the real purpose of both foreign and local private capital, to get the latter to play a more dynamic role in the economy. But the corporations, entrenched as they were in the commanding heights of the economy, sugar, and oil, quite adamantly refused to curtail retrenchment and to assist in the diversification of the economy arguing, as one leading corporate manager stated, that "our primary objectives are best contained in producing, refining, shipping and marketing of oil. . . ."[7]

It is in this context of the polarization of opinion on who should play what part and, most importantly, who should reap the rewards and in what "climate," that the government faced in 1964 the question of public ownership versus private ownership of its natural resources and announced that in the future it would pursue "a middle way between outright nationalisation and old fashioned capitalist organisation backed by the marines and the dollars of the United States of America."[8] When translated, what this in fact meant was that the government would, in time, enter into joint ventures with foreign firms for the development and exploitation of its natural resources.

What is important to grasp at the outset about this joint-venture strategy as practiced in the period, is that it is in no way in conflict with the premises of the "industrialization by invitation" model, premised as it is on the need for foreign "capital" inflow into the domestic economy.

As the Second Five-Year Development Plan clearly points out, the boundary of state involvement in the economy was still clearly limited to the "prudent investment of public funds in the improvement of such public facilities as education, electricity, transport and communications, health, water and drainage. . . ."[9]

At the same time, it hoped that private enterprise would take advantage of the opportunities which the government was creating by means of its incentive scheme. In short, the joint-venture strategy was initially a rescue operation in the context of growing unemployment. In fact, as the government itself points out, up to 1968, "questions relating to Government participation in or acquisition of assets formerly operated exclusively by private enterprise were decided empirically."[10]

It was not, therefore, until 1968, with the publication of the government's Third Five-Year Plan and its open admission of the failure of local and foreign capital to play the part designated in the strategy, that a further statement on the role of the state in the economy was articulated. It stated: "The public sector will . . . not hesitate to enter either alone or in partnership with foreign or local private capital into the productive fields of industry, tourism and agriculture."[11]

But in this period, as we have documented elsewhere,[12] the government was neither financially nor politically able to substantially initiate the new position; and by 1969, beginning with the strike at the government-owned bus company, a process of strident delegitimation set in. The year 1969 saw organized labor openly accusing the government of continued bias toward foreign capital and ushered in, as it were, the conflagration of 1970, led by the youth and the unemployed demanding, as they put it, the "whole cake and nothing but the cake."

The government found itself in 1972, after a full sixteen years of a program of bringing in modern technology and modern business and developing the industrial sector, faced with an unemployment rate of 13 percent by official statistics, not counting the underemployment of those working less than thirty hours a week and an income distribution situation which was worse than it was in 1957–58. In fact, according to comparisons of household surveys for the two periods, the top 10 percent had improved these positions by 4.5 percent, and the top 20 percent had gained 8 percent more of the national income, whereas the bottom 20 percent lost 1.2 percent of their share, dropping as it was from 3.4 percent in 1957–58 to 2.2 percent in 1971–72.[13] Just as importantly, the government found itself faced with a foreign reserves position which, though not as alarming in 1972 as it was to become in 1973, was one that had begun to evaporate.

It was the stark realities of the consequences of the model and the inability of the government to implement in this period the joint-venture strategy that gave rise in 1972 to the following statement on private foreign investment:

1. We welcome new foreign investment which brings in expertise, new technology and access to export markets to assist and supplement national efforts in our development.
2. No new 100 per cent foreign-owned enterprises will be allowed in key sectors of the economy and national participation in joint-ventures involving new foreign firms must be of meaningful proportion.
3. Alienation of land will not be permitted.
4. Existing foreign-owned enterprises must take steps to facilitate national participation including in particular worker participation.
5. Certain areas of our economy are reserved exclusively for national effort.
6. All firms, whatever the structure of their ownership, must in their operations give ample opportunity to transfer to nationals the skills, knowledge and expertise required to run the business.
7. Government will take a leading part, including the use of direct participation to expedite national control and ownership.[14]

What this new policy in fact signaled was a continuation of the government's dependence on foreign investment, while at the same time signalling an intended increased role in the economy for the public sector. But as we have indicated earlier, the period from 1969 to 1972 in Trinidad was not the most propitious for direct foreign investment. Such a climate had to be created. This the government sought to do by the institution of "rule by force."

Rule by Force, 1970–1972

So massive was the challenge to the government beginning, as we stated earlier, in 1969 that the government in 1970 declared a state of emergency and introduced the first of a series of antidemocratic pieces of legislation. The Public Order Bill, introduced in August of 1970, sought, among other things, to:

1. Regulate public meetings and marches.
2. Penalize persons inciting others to racial hatred or to violence.
3. Prohibit the organization of training of quasimilitary organizations and unlawful oathtaking.

4. Allow entry to the police for the purpose of search.
5. Enable the minister to make detention orders.

Faced with mass public outrage at the clearly intended rape of citizen rights, the government withdrew the bill.

Undaunted, however, by the massive act of defiance shown by the public, the government in November 1970 introduced and passed in Parliament what is now known as the Firearms Act.

Justifying the need for this bill, the leader of government business in the Senate argued that

> the Government are forced to take adequate measures to stamp out this tendency to violence, to arrest the spread of illegal arms in the country and restore a feeling of security, and safety to all law-abiding citizens. The Bill aims at the preservation of law and order and fixes stiffer penalties for those who break the law.[15]

There are two important observations to be made about this bill. First of all, a very close reading would reveal the reintroduction under a new guise of several sections of the withdrawn Public Order Bill.[16]

Second, despite the clear intention of the government to protect itself and those who were at the top of the income ladder, the bill failed to allay fears of imminent regime collapse, even among those it clearly intended to protect. For example, the Senate representative for private sector agriculture stated:

> I do not want anyone to say I am accusing the ship of sinking, but it is certainly leaking very badly and this is another instance where, in my view, we are merely plugging a hole. A Bill of this type is nothing but a short term deterrent which may be quite unwarranted in normal times.[17]

And, by December 1970, one of the government's staunchest supporters was arguing that "the ineptitude and inefficiency of this government is so legion that I can go on for hours . . . you are on your way out."[18] That these views were widespread is evident also from the results of the general elections of 1971. Here, faced with an official opposition party boycott of the elections, the ruling party, though retaining legal power, secured only 28 percent of the popular vote.[19]

Opposition to the government continued unabated. Strikes, work stoppages, cries of illegitimate government and the need for constitutional reform, and new elections filled the air. But the government had already made its choice. It had declared its intention to preserve law and order. Thus, when the American firm, Badger, ceased operations and airlifted its senior personnel out of the country, the government (on October 20, 1971), arguing that "we therefore face once again a serious threat to law, order, economic stability and peace of mind . . .,"[20] declared another state of emergency, arrested the leaders of the opposition groups,[21] and announced that Parliament would be summoned to introduce legislation on the following subjects:

1. The demarcation of jurisdiction of unions.
2. The regulation of strikes and "go-slows."
3. The control of processions and demonstrations.
4. Revision of the law relating to seditious utterances with emphasis on the preaching of racial hatred.

The outcome of this by November 1971 was the introduction of the Sedition Amendment Bill.[22] Within this piece of legislation, "sedition, whether by words spoken or written or by conduct, is a misdemeanor indictable at Common Law and punishable by fine or imprisonment."

Under the act, once a seditious publication is found in any place or thing over which a person has possession, custody, power, or control, he is guilty of sedition.[23] There can be no doubt that the act was intended to protect the minority White, African, and Indian high-income elite. After all, the American firm Badger had informed the government that before it re-entered the country "the company has to be assured by all concerned that its expatriate employees and families are welcome to work and live in Trinidad. . . ."[24] Thus Section 4 of this act describes as seditious intention "any intention to advocate or promote with intent to destroy any part of an 'identifiable group' distinguished by race or colour, religion, profession, calling or employment."

By December 1971, the rights of citizens were further curbed. The government introduced yet another piece of legislation, the Summary Offences Bill. Accordingly, "If you want to hold a public meeting you must, subject to the exceptions in the Bill, notify the police . . . if you want to have a march or procession . . . you must apply for a permit."[25] What had happened in Trinidad and Tobago by December 1971, therefore, was that the rights of citizens who initially had been told "march where you like" had been effectively curtailed. But the institution of rule by force in no way increased the legitimacy of the government. What in fact happened was that by late 1971 there appeared in Trinidad and Tobago a group called the National Union of Freedom Fighters, espousing (1) the ideology of Marxism-Leninism[26] and (2) the strategy of guerrilla warfare. Two aspects of this organization, in our opinion, speak directly to the question of the extent to which the process of delegitimation had set in and the extent to which the state had become militarized.

First, among its alleged members were to be found the offspring of that generation of school teachers and civil servants which had initially been the backbone of the ruling party. Second, it was said to contain within it the seeds of a generation of Trinidadians who had clearly decided it was their right and duty to reclaim their country.[27] But to a government committed to the preservation of law and order, the existence of such a group could not be tolerated. Its army was mobilized and was told: "You may find yourselves out in the hills for a week or two. You are going out there to bring back law and order. Your duty is to do what you are trained to do." Sensing, no doubt, the ambivalence of the soldiers, the army commander continued, "Do not at any time let your thoughts waver from your aims. Your aims are clearly written out. There are rules and regulations which you must follow."[28] But the response of the regime, which we have characterized as rule by force, was not solely due to internal political factors. It was a response, as well, to internal economic factors. In short, the shift to the right was also the response of a regime in the context of a weak and faltering economy.

During the period 1969 to 1973, the public debt had increased by 59.4 percent. From a total gross public debt of $370.4 million in 1969, it had risen to $625.9 million in 1973.[29] Second, the country was faced with the problems of continuing high unemployment, with a rate fluctuating, according to official figures, between 13 and 15 percent. Third, after a period of moderate price increases between 1968 and 1971, domestic prices escalated during 1972 and rose sharply in 1973.

How was the economy to be saved and thus allow the government to implement its new role for the state, that of prime mover of the national economy? The answer, of course, comes in the form of the dramatic oil price increases of late 1973.

Trinidad, 1974–1980: Prosperous Dependence

The period 1974–80 can perhaps best be summarized in the words of the Prime Minister himself:

> Amid all the ferment in the Caribbean area, unprecedented in territorial scope, ideological content and political intensity, Trinidad and Tobago pursues the even tenor of its economic ways. The key to it all is its hydrocarbon resources. In the eleven years 1963–73 total revenue from oil amounted to TT$786 million. The latest revenue estimate for the year 1975 is TT$1,184 million.[30]

Therefore, Trinidad found itself in 1974 one of those favored petroleum producers earning vast quantities of foreign exchange from the sale of oil since the energy crisis which began at the end of 1973. In a sense its range of choice, contracted as it had been by 1973, suddenly opened, and the option of modernization versus development was posed once again. What is interesting to grasp is that even in the face of the stark results on the 1956–73 period, option one, modernization, was again chosen, and in the budget for 1976 the government announced proposed public expenditures on eleven colossal projects involving fertilizers and steel polyester-fiber, phosphorus, natural gas expansion of aluminum smelter, joint petrochemical ventures with Texaco and Amoco, and a number of supporting infrastructural projects for water, telephones, and ports. The total annual expenditure involved in the energy-based projects (in Trinidad dollars) was estimated as follows:

> 1976: $455 million
> 1977: $549 million
> 1978: $801 million
> 1979: $525 million

The total for these four years for the energy-based industries alone, $2,439 million, exceeds the total public sector spending for the period from 1969 to 1973 of $2,271 million. The announcement of these projects and the role of "foreign capital" indicated, forced the government, through the Prime Minister, to put on the table the rationale for the maintenance of the strategy of development chosen:

> I want to deal with the question of national ownership involving the question of trans-national corporations and show some of the realities in this matter which explain the stand of the Government. . . . I am going to deal . . . with some of the examples of genuine nationalisation which we are aware of . . . and which we reject. . . . It starts off with Europe, the East European countries . . . these countries whose basic feature in respect of their economic activity and development is increasing indebtedness to countries that are not nationalised. . . . If genuine nationalisation therefore is to be so defined as not only to permit but to demand an increasing dependence upon the profits, the savings, the funds . . . of countries that are not nationalised, then I say we on this side have certain apologies to make in respect of our definition of genuine nationalisation.[31]

In short, Trinidad, through a policy of export-oriented industrialization, would not seek to take advantage of the new international division of labor in which, for the first time, peripheral countries such as Trinidad were becoming sites for world market-oriented manufacturing industries.[32]

According to the pronouncements of several government ministers, the establishment of these export-oriented industries is supposed to function in such a way as to advance the solution of three problems:

1. The creation of jobs and the reduction of unemployment.
2. The training of a skilled industrial labor force and the transfer of technology.
3. An increase in foreign exchange inflows with a consequent amelioration of balance of trade and balance of payment difficulties.

There is no doubt that these goals, given the levels of public expenditure, are only modest. In fact, they differ in no way from those espoused by the government in the period from 1956 to 1973.

Let us now, therefore, in the absence of hard data, speculate as to the likely outcomes of the just-mentioned objectives.

Unemployment

As is evident from the example of other world-market-oriented industries such as oil refining,[33] export production is for the most part limited to partial production within the frame of a transnationally organized manufacture. This means the production of components of particular products in a number of factories at different locations throughout the world. Such production itself is integrated into the respective national economies through the utilization of infrastructure and labor force. The employment structure in export production is marked by a profound imbalance. These factories practice a particular system of selection from a practically unlimited source of unemployed labor. The criteria are lowest wage cost and highest performance and productivity, using unskilled and semiskilled labor. If this pattern of employment takes place, then one would hardly expect this unbalanced employment structure to make a dent in unemployment among the economically active population.

Transfer of Technology

Again, using the oil industry in Trinidad, export-oriented production leads only to the very limited training of skilled industrial workers; it does not entail a significant transfer of modern technology. On the contrary, the utilization of modern process technology, consisting as it does in the decomposing of highly complex production into elementary operations, has the effect that the unskilled labor force in the underdeveloped countries is predominantly engaged in simple tasks which in no way raise qualifications or require higher skills. Nor are there any grounds for expecting that industrial export production in the development countries will lead to a continuing transfer of modern product and process technology or to training in the organization and management of industrial large scale technology.

Net Foreign Exchange Inflow

As demonstrated by balance of payments trends in other underdeveloped countries which have already traveled the industrialization export production route, this strategy contributes little, if anything, to their net foreign exchange earnings. There are several reasons for this. Exports are usually offset to a considerable extent by the costs of raw material imports. Necessary infrastructure is built with foreign loans, which have to be serviced for years to come. In the specific case of Trinidad and Tobago, following closely on the heels of the 1976 budget and the announcement of its colossal projects, the government announced its intention to initiate a program of heavy external borrowing on the Eurodollar market, in keeping with a report of its coordinating task force, which estimated that the development of these industries would require an injection of about $4 billion.

In general, it would appear that export-oriented production of the kind envisaged by the Trinidad and Tobago government manifestly perpetuates the historical process of dependent development and gives rise once again to uneven regional, uneven sectoral, and uneven social development.

We see this kind of political development as a direct consequence of the rapid industrialization which, in Trinidad and Tobago, has devastated agriculture, denied development to manufacturing based on indigenous knowhow, and generated massive unemployment. More important, however, the most devastating impact of this policy has been on the political system. The whole base of a democratic political system has withered away. The extermination of independent craftsmen and small businessmen, the dominance of multinational corporations, the almost total reliance now on foreign skills to "develop" the country, and the continuing growth of the public sector have eliminated those in the society who could have constituted an independent focus of political activity. Indeed, there is now in Trinidad and Tobago what one commentator has aptly described as "a pervasive sense of political paralysis."

Conclusion

If the conclusion at the time of writing that politics in Trinidad and Tobago can be described as being in "a state of paralysis" is correct, then we would argue that to the extent that certain elements in the United States are concerned over the future of democracy in the region, Trinidad and Tobago deserve to be looked at more closely.

Notes

1. Official Text of President Carter's remarks, October 1, 1979.
2. See Horace Sutton, "Caribbean in Conflict" in *Saturday Review*, March 1, 1980, p. 14.
3. For a detailed analysis of this period, see Carl D. Parris, *Capital or Labour: The Trinidad and Tobago Government's Decision to Introduce the Industrial Stabilisation Act, March 1965*, Working Paper No. 11, Institute of Social and Economic Research, University of the West Indies, Mona, 1975.
4. Ibid.
5. Ibid.
6. Ibid.
7. See statement of Texaco's representative to Tripartite Talks on Employment and Unemployment in Oil and Sugar. Verbatim Record of Discussions, Government Printery, Port-of-Spain, 1964.
8. Eric Williams, "Trinidad and Tobago, International Perspectives" in *Freedomways*, Summer 1964, p. 333. Also see his contribution to the debate on the government's Second Five-Year Development Plan in Trinidad and Tobago Official Report, Parliamentary Debates (Hansard), House of Representatives. Debate on Second Five-Year Development Plan, Vol. 3, p. 257.
9. *Trinidad and Tobago Second Five-Year Development Plan, 1964–1968*, Government Printery, Port-of-Spain, p. 3.
10. *White Paper on Public Participation in Industrial and Commercial Activities*. Government Printery, Port-of-Spain, 1972.
11. *Third Five-Year Development Plan*, Government Printery, Port-of-Spain, 1968.
12. See Carl D. Parris, "The Trinidad and Tobago Government's Decision to Recognise Cuba," unpublished manuscript, Department of Government, University of the West Indies, St. Augustine, Trinidad, 1977.
13. Ralph Henry, "A Note on Income Distribution and Poverty in Trinidad and Tobago," *Central Statistical Office Research Papers, No. 8*, October 1975.
14. *White Paper on Public Participation in 1972*, p. 5.
15. See Debate on the "Firearms Bill" in Parliamentary Debates (Senate) Hansard, Vol. 10, 1970–71. Tuesday, November 10, 1970, p. 11.
16. See, in particular, clauses 29–30.
17. See Debate on Firearms Bill, p. 36.
18. See Debate on The Appropriation Bill, in Parliamentary Debates, p. 223.
19. For an analysis of this election, see J. E. Greene: "The 1971 General Elections" in T. Munroe and R. Lewis, *Readings in Government and Politics of the West Indies*, Department of Government, University of the West Indies, Mona, Jamaica, 1972.

20. *Trinidad Express,* October 20, 1971.

21. Mainly the leaders of the Oilfield Workers' Trade Union and the National Joint Action Committee.

22. For all the provisions of this piece of legislation, see "Sedition (Amendment) Act No. 36 of 1971," Government of Trinidad and Tobago, Port-of-Spain, 1971.

23. See Section 2(b) of the Act.

24. See *Trinidad Express,* October 18, 1971.

25. See Debate on Summary Offences (Amendment) Bill in Parliamentary Debates, Senate, December 14, 1971.

26. The existence of this group provided the opportunity for a lively debate to take place between a local French creole University Professor and two African lecturers. See the *Trinidad Guardian,* October–November 1973.

27. The letter of Beverly Jones, slain at the tender age of eighteen, reflects undoubtedly these sentiments. See *Trinidad Express,* October 24, 1973.

28. See speech of the Army Commander to the December 1973 Graduation Class, *Trinidad Express,* December 13, 1973.

29. See Review of the Economy, Government of Trinidad and Tobago, Port-of-Spain, 1973.

30. Eric Williams, "Oil as the Basis of Economic Development and Political Stability," *Trinidad Guardian,* April 4, 1976, reprinted from the *Washington Star.*

31. "PM Cites Examples of so-called Genuine Nationalisation," *Trinidad Guardian,* October 17, 1976.

32. For this view, see especially, the speech by the Prime Minister at the start of construction of the Iron and Steel Complex at Point Lisas, October 18, 1977. Office of the Prime Minister, Public Relations Division, Press Release No. 584.

33. See, especially for the Caribbean, the work of Trevor Farrell, *The Multinational Corporation, the Transfer of Technology and the Human Resources Problem in the Trinidad and Tobago Petroleum Industry,* unpublished report to the Caribbean Technology Policy Studies Project, University of the West Indies, Kingston, Jamaica, 1977.

16

Dependent Capitalism and the Prospects for Democracy in Puerto Rico and the Dominican Republic

RUBÉN BERRÍOS MARTÍNEZ

The intimate relationship that exists between the economic and political structures of any given society has become an undisputed "truth" or "myth," depending on whether a dialectical or a mechanical relationship is assumed by modern political economy.

But the acceptance of so evident a relationship is a relatively new phenomenon, and the old modes of thinking—which establish a practical separation between the economic and political structures—seem still to prevail in the actions of many policy formulators. Thus they embark upon economic policies which can only lead to the development of political structures which run counter to their expressed democratic political aspirations. Such is the case with dependent capitalism and democracy.

To corroborate this thesis, with particular reference to the Dominican and Puerto Rican experience, it is first necessary to present the value judgments and premises from which we depart.

Democracy

Individual liberty is not only the right to choose between good and evil—what is called free will—but it is, moreover, the power to resist evil and to produce goodness. Democracy is to the society of individuals what liberty is to the individual. Consequently, democracy encompasses not only the right to choose between alternatives, but the right to choose, coupled with the power to participate in, all decisions that affect the community.

Departing from the inextricable relation between the economic and political spheres, we thus conceive democracy as the right of all members of the society to choose and to participate in all political and economic decisions which affect the society. We further believe that if such concepts are to transcend the merely ideological realm, they will have to find their application in the alteration of class and production relations prevalent in most present day societies.

Democracy at the very least, from the purely political perspective, demands the full respect of what has traditionally been known as civil or human rights. It also demands the existence of national sovereignty and independence. Such a structural framework is necessary (as long as the nation-state is the fundamental basis of the international community) for the existence of a body politic composed of free citizens, capable of electing their government so that the laws which regulate the life of citizens have as their origin the people themselves. The collective right of national independence, the existence of a free electoral system within the context of that national sovereignty, and the full respect of individual rights are the minimal requirements of what has traditionally been termed political democracy.

On the other hand, the right to choose and the power to participate cannot be limited to the political sphere if democracy is to acquire its full meaning. Llorens Torres, a Puerto Rican poet, used to state ironically, referring to this limited political concept of democracy, that "the poor enjoy the freedom of speech of recounting their sorrows to each other." The enjoyment by workers of the product of their work and the existence of democratic economic enterprises constitute minimal requirements of what has been termed economic democracy.

Unfortunately, the scope of the term democracy has been mostly limited to "political democracy," with no regard whatsoever to "economic democracy." From this perspective, it is obvious that capitalism—dependent or national—and democracy are intrinsically incompatible. But we shall demonstrate that dependent capitalism and even political democracy—which many tend to confuse with real democracy—are also, in the long run, incompatible.

Dependent Capitalism

Dependent capitalism encompasses a very complex set of activities, structures and relationships which are difficult to understand utilizing the traditional categories available in the social sciences. Dependent capitalism has to be analyzed, not only in terms of those macroeconomic variables usually used in evaluating development experiences, but those in terms of its impact on social, cultural, and political structures.

It entails a particular manner of relating to the world capitalist economy. Basically, it implies a development model which assigns to foreign capital a leading role in the development of the modern sectors of the economy, particularly in industrialization, and in the transformation of traditional activities and attitudes.

The proponents of dependent capitalism see in foreign investment a way of compensating for a number of deficiencies in local society: its incapacity to save, its technological backwardness, the absence of local entrepreneurs, and others.

But the relationship to world capitalism goes beyond the importation of capital. Embedded in foreign capital is foreign technology, which derives from the nature of the products being produced and from the nature of production processes in the highly industrialized capitalist countries. But this technology has little to do with factor proportions or resource endowment in the receiving country. Thus, often the imported technology is capital intensive while the receiving countries are labor surplus economies.

Furthermore, the economy is open to imports from abroad which cover the whole range of goods, from consumer nondurables to capital equipment. Although the first stages of dependent capitalism in Latin America entailed a period of limited import substitution, that is no longer true. In effect, the principle of comparative advantage is the guiding principle in determining development strategy. Moreover, investment in industry has been accompanied by an increasingly important penetration of foreign transnational capitalism into other sectors such as services and communications.

With the importation of technology, the importation of goods, and the penetration into services and communications, comes the importation of culture and values, so that consumption patterns among certain sectors of society become similar to those of their counterparts in the advanced countries. The aspirations of the masses are framed in terms of these consumption norms. What begins as the importation of capital for industrial production becomes the importation of a way of life, of a set of values and norms. Local culture and society are thus reoriented and transformed to serve the needs of transnational capitalism. The assumption that a country could integrate its economy to world capitalism and isolate its impact only to the economic sectors has been shown to be untenable.

The Cases of Puerto Rico and the Dominican Republic

Puerto Rico and the Dominican Republic have been subjected to foreign capitalism for a very long time. Therefore, it could be argued that there is nothing new in the present situation. But foreign capitalism in the Caribbean was initially linked to the plantation economy, and only in the postwar years has foreign investment been oriented primarily to industrialization and related activities and attracted by low wages or government incentives of various types. It is during this period that one can identify conditions which can be characterized as typical of the dependent capitalist model.

Our analysis will thus concentrate on the postwar years and particularly on the last two decades, for it is in this period that the Puerto Rican and Dominican economies are faced with a different breed of capitalism, with very different impacts on both countries. Present conditions—the transnational corporations as the dominant institution, the wider scope of activities encompassed by them, and the global character of capitalism—make for the differences that go beyond superficial distinctions between pre- and postwar capitalism.

We shall place a greater emphasis on the experience of Puerto Rico because its dependent capitalism model predates that of the Dominican Republic and, in many ways, has served as its model. It is useful to remember that for many years Puerto Rico was the model proposed and promoted by the United States and many of the international development agencies for the underdeveloped world. In the Caribbean, the "industrialization by invitation" strategy popularized by Arthur Lewis was based on the Puerto Rican experience.

THE PUERTO RICAN MODEL

What has come to be called the Puerto Rican model started around 1947. Up to that time there had been at least two easily identifiable stages. The first, starting with the American occupation in 1898, saw Puerto Rico begin a transformation from the hacienda economy to the plantation economy, with heavy emphasis on sugar cane. This system went into a crisis in the 1930s and gave way to a short and, in many respects, most interesting period. From 1940 to 1946 the Puerto Rican government attempted to establish an industrial base through public ownership of productive enterprises accompanied by substantial social reforms and modernization of the state apparatus.

This is not the place to consider the reasons behind the adoption and demise of this approach; but by 1946, sectors within the ruling Popular Democratic Party were calling for a different approach. There were also considerable pressures from the United States for Puerto Rico to abandon its so-called "socialist" experiment. Nevertheless, two factors need to be recalled: that war conditions permitted the island a greater leeway in defining its own possibilities, and that the change in 1947 came at a time when United States capitalism was once more expanding. Thus a model like the one developed in Puerto Rico from 1940 to 1946 was no longer welcomed.

Be the reasons why they may, the fact is that in 1948 legislation was approved which created an industrialization program based on the attraction of foreign capital to the island. The main attractions of Puerto Rico were three: a very generous tax holiday program, low wages, and free access to U.S. markets. This program, with minor changes and modifications, has persisted until today.

By the mid-sixties it had become evident that the initial expectations of the industrialization program were not to be met. Net employment gains were minor, and the increased competition from other countries made Puerto Rico a less attractive location. The nature of world capitalism had changed in the direction of making capital much more mobile than before, thus raising the possibility of having a wider choice of locations and forcing the competing countries to try to outbid each other in attracting investment. Many factories closed operations in Puerto Rico and moved to more suitable locations.

Puerto Rico's reaction to the initial signs of the approaching limits of the labor-intensive industrialization program was to embark on a heavy industry strategy based on foreign petrochemical enterprises. The presumption was that these basic industries would generate secondary industrial processes and, through these, large numbers of jobs. After fifteen years of petrochemicals, the results have been very disappointing. Investment in the industry totalled some $1.2 billion but, at its peak, the employment generated never amounted to more than 7,000. This was accomplished at extremely high costs in terms of pollution, misuse of resources (particularly water) and heavy costs in terms of subsidies to the major petrochemicals. For example, in the period since 1965, only three of these plants absorbed close to 20 percent of all the increased power generating capacity on the island. If one considers that investment in this activity was close to $450 million, this means, *grosso modo*, a subsidy of some $90 million. This strategy was further hampered by, among other things, the increased price of petroleum and changes in the United States legislation concerned with oil imports.

By 1973 the rate of growth which had been maintained through the sixties and early seventies by external indebtedness and public investments decreased substantially as did employment (by 1976 government employment constituted close to a third of all employed persons). At

the same time, social decomposition indexes reached alarming proportions, and Puerto Rico became one of the world leaders in drug addic-
tion, criminality, alcoholism, and emotional disturbances. As the 1970
decade came to an end, Puerto Rico, which had been the model of
neoclassical success, had become the extreme example of the failure of
the dependent growth model.

THE DOMINICAN MODEL

In the Dominican Republic, the process of incorporation of the dependent capitalist model can be traced from 1965. In fact, the intervention
of the United States in that country establishes something of a landmark in this regard. There are several salient factors which deserve
mention. Foremost is the dependence on foreign, mostly U.S., investment. As in the case of Puerto Rico, there is a government incentive
program, and low wages provide an attraction. In both programs industrial production is the basic economic sector and is geared toward the
exports market, although in the Dominican Republic the mining sector
is of somewhat greater importance. A difference which is worth mentioning is the fact that in the Dominican Republic—contrary to Puerto
Rico—much of foreign investment has been channeled through one
company, Gulf and Western, which has been active in a wide range of
activities which encompass everything from sugar cane plantations to a
beauty contest. This is a reflection of many factors: changes in the
nature of the large capitalist enterprise from a vertically integrated one
to a horizontally diversified entity, the absence of restricting legislation, and the fact that this particular enterprise came into the country
fairly early in its process of industrialization.

THE IMPACT OF DEPENDENT GROWTH IN PUERTO RICO AND THE
DOMINICAN REPUBLIC

There are many ways of measuring the success or failure of a development program. Classical or neoclassical economists have, for the
most part, used the rate of growth of income and production as the
measure par excellence.

It has become increasingly clear, however, that these criteria are
radically insufficient. The success of an economic program, as we have
already pointed out, has to be gauged in terms of its social and political
impacts, and not just in terms of GNP growth. It is increasingly recognized that a country can experience sensational growth of its capitalist
sector while, at the same time, experiencing increasing impoverish-
ment of large sectors of its population, and that what had previously

been hailed as the process of modernization can also be seen as disintegration of the society's traditional structures, a process with results which can be extremely negative.

Thus in evaluating the Puerto Rican and Dominican model, we will not be concerned so much with the economic growth aspects of the process—which can be considerable, particularly under circumstances like those prevailing in Puerto Rico in the postwar era—but rather with these other dimensions.

Employment and Income Distribution. With respect to employment, the experience in Puerto Rico has been disastrous. Between 1950 and 1975, while the population was growing from 2.2 million to 3.1 (40%), and the working age population increased from 1.3 to 2.1 million (60.1%), those employed increased only by about 24 percent, from 600,000 to a bit less than 740,000. In the meantime, the official rate of unemployment increased in the period from around 10 percent to close to 20 percent. In absolute numbers, the unemployed increased from 88,000 to close to 150,000.[1]

What is more significant, however, is that the rate of participation in the labor force, never high in any case compared with other countries, fell from 53 percent to a little more than 40 percent. As can well be imagined, with employment figures like these the distribution problem is quite serious. But these figures, bad as they may be, hide even worse conditions. For example, in Puerto Rico, unemployment among the age group from 16 to 24 is 35 percent, even with a participation rate of only 32.4 percent.

There are no reliable recent figures on income distribution, but the figures from the 1970 Census do not provide much ground for optimism in that respect. The figures then reflected a situation in which the poorest 40 percent of the families received 8 percent of the income, and the richest 10 percent received 35 percent of the total income.

For the Dominican Republic the figures are not any better. Unemployment hovers around 24 percent, and it is estimated that underemployment affects 60 percent of the employed labor force. Regarding income distribution, in 1975, 72 percent of the families received 30 percent of the income, while on the highest end of the scale, 10 percent of the families received close to 40 percent of the income.[2]

Migration. The migration process to the United States during the past two decades has been one of the most important concomitants of the development process in Puerto Rico and the Dominican Republic.

In the case of Puerto Rico, between 1954 and 1976, close to one million persons left the island for the United States. This is approximately one third of the island's population at the present time. In the Dominican Republic the process of emigration has also accelerated dramatically since the mid-sixties, and it is estimated that the number of Dominicans who had migrated to the United States by 1979 exceeded 600,000.

With migration figures like these, questions concerning the beneficiaries of the development process arise. Certainly much of this migration was a result of explicit government policies—although these were not recognized or acknowledged—which recognized migration as an escape valve to reduce the social tensions developed as a consequence of the model itself.

External Dependence. There are many criteria for measuring external dependence, but we will limit ourselves to mentioning two. The first is the external debt of the countries. Between 1965 and 1976 the external debt of Puerto Rico's public sector increased from $909 million to 5.6 *billion*. For the Dominican Republic the increase was just as dramatic, though on a smaller scale, with debt increasing from $100 to $700 in the same period.

With respect to the current account in the balance of payments, the situation is as follows: in the Dominican Republic the current account has not had a surplus since about 1967, with the latest deficit figures hovering around $100 million. In the case of Puerto Rico, the deficit in the current account for 1979 exceeded $4 billion.

CONTRADICTIONS OF THE MODEL

The dependent capitalist model, as exemplified in the cases of Puerto Rico and the Dominican Republic, gives rise to a number of contradictions. These contradictions will, in turn, inevitably produce a number of explosive social and political tensions. The first contradiction, one which has been amply documented in the recent literature on development, has to do with the displacement of traditional activities such as agriculture, and the consequent unemployment generated. The new activities, being capital-intensive, do not generate the required number of jobs. We have seen how this effect is amply demonstrated by the employment statistics of both Puerto Rico and the Dominican Republic.

A second contradiction arises from the need which the dependent capitalist model of development has, on the one hand, to maintain low wages and, on the other hand, to provide a market for the products of industrial capitalism. The Puerto Rican postwar antilabor policy consisted of the following elements: the discouragement of local labor organization, the importation, together with factories, of tamed United States' unions, and the vehement government opposition to the application of U.S. minimum wage laws to Puerto Rico. As regards the

Dominican Republic, suffice it to note that the average daily wage in 1973 was $0.45 per hour, with purchasing power decreasing about 33 percent in the period 1972 to 1975.[3]

A third contradiction arises, particularly in the smaller countries like Puerto Rico and the Dominican Republic, because of the need to import not only most of the inputs for the production processes but also the capital equipment. This leads to serious balance of payments difficulties which, as noted, are typical of the Puerto Rican and Dominican economies.

As a result of these contradictions, the costs of maintaining the viability of the dependent capitalist model, both in Puerto Rico and the Dominican Republic, are continuously increasing. For both countries to maintain an advantage in attracting foreign capital in the face of increased competition from others, they must attempt to keep wages low and to provide additional incentives in the form of infrastructure investment, tax advantages, and subsidies of various sorts.

But a tragic consequence of the model is that since governments will have to provide resources in ever increasing amounts for the support of the model, they will have fewer resources available to sustain welfare and social programs to maintain a large proportion of the population at even a subsistence level. At the same time, they will be experiencing serious difficulties in the balance of payments. All of this is aggravated because foreign capital is most often tax-exempt. The result is chronic insolvency.

As a result, the population as a whole will be increasingly forced into misery or into migration, a situation which is, as we have noted, characteristic of both the Dominican Republic and Puerto Rico. On the other extreme of the income scale, dependent capitalism has created, both in Puerto Rico and the Dominican Republic, a very limited but powerful sector of beneficiaries who act as intermediaries of foreign capital.

Finally, the contradictions mentioned have led and will lead—as a result of the intrinsic logic of the model described—to increased foreign indebtedness and further incorporation into the world capitalist economy in a dependent manner.[4]

The Future of Democracy in Puerto Rico and the Dominican Republic

The fundamental question we are faced with, in light of the contradictions mentioned above, is whether the dependent capitalist model will permit the survival of political democracy in the Dominican Republic and the survival of the electoral system coupled with some respect for civil rights prevalent in Puerto Rico.

Unemployment, unjust distribution of income, and pressures to keep wages low, together with inflation, tax exemption for large enterprises, and regresive taxes for the bulk of the population (all consequences of the dependent capitalist model) can only lead in the long run (unless an alternative model of development is adopted) to the adoption of antidemocratic political structures to keep public discontent in check.

If political conditions have not reached such a level both in Puerto Rico and the Dominican Republic (up to the Balaguer era), it is due to the fact that certain tension-reducers have been injected into both models, none of which can be considered of a permanent nature.

In the case of Puerto Rico, the two principal tension-reducers have been migration—until the early seventies—and massive infusions of transfer payments from the United States. These have been increasing to the point that in 1979 they averaged close to $1,000 per capita, with 73 percent of the families in the island receiving food stamps, a program which by itself accounted for some $900 million in that year. It is only through these payments that a very large proportion of the population subsists and that Puerto Rico can have an enormous deficit in its trade account year after year. These massive flows have also had another consequence. Income and consumption have progressively less to do with the level of production. Consequently, in Puerto Rico there exists a local bourgeoisie with no ties to production activities (and whose economic base is dependent on the level of consumption) and a large proportion of the population which subsists on transfer payments, but is otherwise alienated from the economy.

In part, one can explain the Puerto Rican political movement toward assimilation with the United States as a belief on the part of the local bourgeoisie that statehood is a "guarantee" that those transfer payments will be maintained.

The cost to Puerto Rico of this transfer payment economy is enormous. Puerto Rico is, and will become progressively more so, a stagnant, totally dependent, and mortgaged society subsisting on the dole. The social cost of the situation is evident, and the political cost is the continuation of colonialism, which negates political democracy. Under the so-called Free Associated State, Puerto Ricans will increasingly have as much democracy as a parrot in a cage, for they also will be fed and allowed to speak. Under statehood, Puerto Rico will become a permanent ghetto of the United States; such status would signify the permanence of the dependent capitalist model and, in real political terms, the culmination of colonialism.

For the Dominican Republic, the tension-reduction scenario is somewhat different. Migration has also been an escape valve, but transfer payments have been nonexistent, and foreign aid has been meager compared to needs. Thus the possibilities for a repetition of the Puerto Rican experience are few, and the future is just as bleak as in Puerto Rico with respect to the prospects for a democratic future under dependent capitalism. In the absence of massive migration, and taking into account the historical record of the Dominican military, the ruling groups there will be tempted to adopt a repressive regime in order to control the conflicts which arise from the model's inherent contradictions. This is an option which has been exercised in many Latin American countries already. And it is no coincidence that the expenditure on defense and national security in the Dominican Republic increased from 28 percent of the total budget in 1967 to 37 percent in 1975.[5]

From the very nature of the dependent capitalist model of Puerto Rico and the Dominican Republic, it is obvious that the speed with which both societies move toward nondemocratic structures will depend to a large extent on the policies adopted by the United States.

The recent trends toward tax reduction in the United States do not seem to point in the direction of a continuous and increasing transfer of payments flow to Puerto Rico. In the absence of such payments, massive migration is the only alternative. But with migration having reached the zero point in the past few years due to economic conditions in New York, a wave of repression is a very real possibility.

If the United States is willing to accept a more open migration policy toward the Dominican Republic or an expanded foreign aid program, then tensions there might transitorily be mitigated. The questions, of course, are how long will the United States maintain such a policy in view of the fact that the Latin American community in the United States already constitutes cause for serious concern, and the political obstacles which foreign aid faces in the United States. Most likely, the United States will try to promote a policy for the Dominican Republic which balances the tool of migration and the tool of repression, with foreign assistance playing a minor role. But such a policy is, by its very nature, self-defeating, for the more the dependent capitalist model breaks down, the more migration and repression are needed to keep it from exploding.

In summary, unless an alternate model of development is implemented, Puerto Rico will be able, at best, to choose between the political liberty of a parrot and that of a ghetto dweller with increasing doses of political repression, while the Dominican Republic seems headed toward antidemocratic political structures. To this quest for an alternative model of development both the Dominican Revolutionary Party

(PRD) and the Puerto Rican Independence Party (PIP) have directed their political philosophy and actions.

The socialist democratic development model, which both parties espouse, has three main objectives: an increase in production and employment; economic democracy, which includes, among other factors, a just distribution of wealth and more self-reliant growth; and political democracy.

This is not the occasion to discuss in detail these socialist democratic development models, nor to explain the specific programs contained in both the PRD and PIP platforms directed toward the achievement of such objectives. Nevertheless, it is necessary that we refer to certain basic factors which have to be taken into account if such an alternative model is to become a reality.

Political independence is a necessary condition for achieving an alternative socialist democratic development model based on rational import substitution, redistribution of income and wealth, and the full utilization of our human and natural resources. It is only with independence that Puerto Rico can control the fiscal, monetary, trade, and social policy instruments required to implement such a model.[6] The case of the Dominican Republic up to the end of the Balaguer period demonstrates that political independence is not a sufficient condition, for political and economic powers can exist which are inadequately utilized.

Furthermore, a mobilized and inspired people, willing to make good the words of Máximo Gómez in the face of a foreign debt proposition at the beginning of the century ("What we need is work and savings"), is a prerequisite for the implementation of a democratic socialist model in Puerto Rico and the Dominican Republic. The maintainance of democratic structures in the face of demagogic agitation will present a further challenge.

The establishment of such a model will encounter the opposition of powerful local groups or sectors which benefit from the present model of dependent capitalism. It will also encounter the opposition of the United States multinational corporations and other sectors. These corporations and elites stand to lose their privileges and monopolistic hold upon the economies of both countries. A strategy to deal with this opposition is basic to the agenda of both the PRD and the PIP.

We do not, of course, propose an overnight change. Dependence, which is the consequence of scores of years of subordination, cannot be changed overnight, unless we are willing to risk falling under a repressive regime governing in the name of the people, or under the aegis of a new dependency. Neither do we propose autarchic development. Foreign investments, foreign debt, commerce with the

United States and other developed economies—when rationally controlled, channeled, and limited—constitute an additional tool that can be used within the framework of a democratic socialist model.

What we do propose is that we repudiate the dependent capitalist model as contrary to both economic and political democracy; that we start working in the Caribbean toward the establishment of the democratic socialist model; that we prepare ourselves and firmly realize that, if we are to establish democratic socialist regimes, we will sooner or later have to face powerful enemies; and that we follow such a path toward real democracy, inspired by the high ideals of Caribbean unity. To break dependence from foreign capitalism is to start depending on ourselves.

Notes

1. Figures on the Puerto Rican economy are from the Puerto Rico Planning Board.

2. Banco Central de la República Dominicana, *Estudio Sobre Presupuestos Familiares,* Santo Domingo, 1969.

3. Based on estimates of the Oficina Nacional de Estadística of the Dominican Republic.

4. Evidently, a number of variables and modifications can be introduced into the dependent capitalist model described, and thus the sequence described above as it refers to Puerto Rico and the Dominican Republic need not be followed precisely elsewhere. National conditions will have a significant impact on the form that dependent capitalism takes. Dependent capitalism in Brazil, for example, is a very different process from dependent capitalism in Puerto Rico. In the former, the existence of a large national market has made a difference in many respects, particularly in terms of generating internal linkages between industrial sectors. In the smaller, export platform economies like Puerto Rico and the Dominican Republic, these linkages are virtually nonexistent.

5. The figures are from *Ejecución del Presupuesto* (Dirección del Presupuesto Santo Domingo, 1977).

6. Rubén Berríos, "Independence for Puerto Rico, the Only Solution," *Foreign Affairs,* April 1977.

Index